Modern Comparative Politics Series
edited by
Peter H. Merkl
University of California,
Santa Barbara

ITALY
The politics of
uneven development

ITALY
The politics of uneven development

Raphael Zariski
The University of Nebraska

THE DRYDEN PRESS INC.
Hinsdale, Illinois

Copyright © 1972 by The Dryden Press Inc.

All rights reserved
Library of Congress Catalog Card Number: 78-187769

ISBN: 0-03-079820-5

Printed in the United States of America

2 3 4 5   065   9 8 7 6 5 4 3 2 1

To Birdy, Danny, and Adrienne

FOREWORD TO THE SERIES

This new series in comparative politics was undertaken in response to the special needs of students, teachers, and scholars that have arisen in the last few years, needs that are no longer being satisfied by most of the materials now available. In an age when our students seem to be getting brighter and more politically aware, the teaching of comparative politics should present a greater challenge than ever before. We have seen the field come of age with numerous comparative monographs and case studies breaking new ground, and the Committee on Comparative Politics of the Social Science Research Council can look back proudly on nearly a decade of important spadework. But teaching materials have lagged behind these changing approaches to the field. Most comparative government series are either too little coordinated to make systematic use of any common methodology or too conventional in approach. Others are so restricted in scope and space as to make little more than a programmatic statement about what should be studied, thus suggesting a new scholasticism of systems theory that omits the idiosyncratic richness of the material available and tends to ignore important elements of a system for fear of being regarded too traditional in approach.

In contrast to these two extremes, the Modern Comparative Politics Series attempts to find a happy combination of rigorous, systematic methodology and the rich sources of data available to area and country specialists. The series consists of a core volume, *Modern Comparative Politics* by Peter H. Merkl, country volumes covering one or more nations, and comparative topical volumes.

Rather than narrowing the approach to only one "right" method, the core volume leaves it to the teacher to choose any of several approaches he may prefer. The authors of the country volumes are partly bound by a framework common to these volumes and the core volume, and are partly free to tailor their approaches to the idiosyncrasies of their respective countries. The emphasis in the common framework is on achieving a balance between such elements as theory and application, as well as among developmental perspectives, sociocultural aspects, the group processes, and the decision-making processes of government. It is hoped that the resulting tension between comparative approaches and politicocultural realities will enrich the teaching of comparative politics and provoke discussion at all levels from undergraduate to graduate.

The group of country volumes is supplemented by a group of analytical comparative studies. Each of these comparative volumes takes an important topic and explores it cross-nationally. Some of these topics are covered in a more limited way in the country volumes, but many find their first expanded treatment in the comparative volumes—and all can be expected to break new scholarly ground.

The ideas embodied in the series owe much to the many persons whose names are cited in the footnotes of the core volume. Although they are far too numerous to mention here, a special debt of spiritual paternity is acknowledged to Harry Eckstein, Gabriel A. Almond, Carl J. Friedrich, Sidney Verba, Lucian W. Pye, Erik H. Erikson, Eric C. Bellquist, R. Taylor Cole, Otto Kirchheimer, Seymour M. Lipset, Joseph La Palombara, Samuel P. Huntington, Cyril E. Black, and many others, most of whom are probably quite unaware of their contribution.

Santa Barbara, California   P. H. M.

PREFACE

This book is a comprehensive study of the Italian political system. The major emphasis is on the contrast between such modernizing socioeconomic tendencies as industrialization and urbanization, on the one hand, and a relatively backward political system, on the other. Thus, the central theme is political lag—a transitional phenomenon, which is present to some degree in all democratic political systems, but which poses particularly grave dangers for Italian democracy.

A number of characteristics of this economically booming but politically stagnant society will be explored in this book. Among them will be the inadequacy of political socialization processes, the low level of meaningful political participation, the fragmented character of the political culture, the weakness of grass-roots political institutions at the provincial and local levels, the absence of a united and therefore truly effective opposition, the scanty coordination existing among the various policy-making and policy-implementing structures, and the painfully cumbersome performance of the bureaucracy and the courts. In the course of exploring these topics, we will discuss those works on Italian politics that make particularly significant contributions to the study of comparative political systems.

Somewhat more emphasis will be placed on political socialization and political parties than on formal political institutions. This is a natural response to the present state of the literature in the field of comparative politics, which pays more attention to inputs than to outputs.

The organization of this book is coordinated with that of Peter H. Merkl's core volume in the Modern Comparative Politics Series. This book on Italy also attempts to use frequent comparisons with other political systems, notably France and the United States. Much of the material should be of value to students who are interested, not merely in Italy alone, but also in certain cross-national issues in comparative politics. Because Italy has received so much attention from the Social Science Research Council, much of the writing on Italian politics—by both American and Italian social scientists—reveals an unusually high level of sophistication and rigor, and is especially adaptable for the formulation of hypotheses of a cross-national nature.

I wish to express my appreciation for the cooperation and advice provided by Peter H. Merkl, the editor of the series. I am also grateful to the many Italian colleagues who extended warm hospitality and invaluable advice during my field trip to Italy in the fall of 1966. My colleagues in the Political Science Department of the University of Nebraska have been sources of great moral comfort, and have stoically put up with the anguished lamentations that accompany the creative process. The excellent typing of Mrs. Lawrence Kenney has done a great deal to assuage the irritations that must accompany the process of manuscript preparation. And finally, I must thank my wife and children who have supported me through this arduous task.

Lincoln, Nebraska R. Z.
March 1972

CONTENTS

Foreword to the series   ix

Preface   xi

INTRODUCTION   1

1. **THE LATE ARRIVAL   A brief developmental history**   5

    Geographic Factors **5**/ The Struggle to Build a Nation **9**/ The Problems of Legitimacy and Integration **18**/ Constitutional Development and the Emergence of the Party System **26**/ Italian Industrial Growth **33**/ Agriculture: The Rural Exodus **38**/ Urbanization and Migration: "New York Is in Italy, at Milan" **40**/ Social Stratification and Social Mobility **45**/ Conclusions **48**

2. **ITALIANS IN POLITICS   Political socialization, participation, and recruitment**   52

    Political Socialization: Preparation for Citizenship **52**/ Political Socialization: Family and Peer Group **53**/ Education and Political Socialization **56**/

The Mass Media as Socializing Influences **61**/ Other Influences on Socialization: Workplace, Church, Pressure Groups, and Parties **66**/ Political Events and Political Experiences **71**/ Political Participation: A Contradictory Picture **75**/ Political Recruitment: The Salience of Parties **84**/ Political Recruitment: Some Individual Patterns **85**/ Political Recruitment: The Ruling Class **87**/ Conclusions **90**

3. **A FRAGMENTED POLITY   Themes of political culture**   92

Social Trust: An Ingredient in Short Supply **93**/ Sense of Autonomy: Are Italians Individualistic? **96**/ Sense of National Identity: Is There an Italian People? **97**/ Political Cognition and Political Competence: A Backward Electorate **98**/ Alienation and Violence in Italian Political Culture **100**/ Images of Authority **103**/ A Case of Cultural Lag **104**/ Regional Subcultures: Cultural Dualism or Cultural Pluralism? **107**/ Social and Ideological Fragmentation: Political Subcultures **109**/ Religion in Politics **113**/ Conclusions **115**

4. **A UNITARY SYSTEM WITH A QUASI-FEDERAL GLOSS   Local and national politics**   117

The Communes: The Labors of Sisyphus **118**/ The Commune: Bastion of the Opposition **123**/ The Commune: Styles and Motives of Local Politics **126**/ Links between Local and National Politics **128**/ The Province: Domain of the Prefect **130**/ Local Government: Trends toward Reform **132**/ The Regions: Quasi-Federalism Delayed **134**/ Conclusions **138**

5. **THE GIANTS AND THE PYGMIES   The party system**   140

The Party System: A Multifaceted Phenomenon **140**/ The Party System: An Overview **141**/ Intraparty Politics: The Role of Factions **147**/ Party Organization: A Common Mold **151**/ The Parties and Their Programs **156**/ Membership Composition of the Italian Parties **180**/ Party Leadership: A Middle-Class Preserve **182**/ Party Voting Strength: Bases of Cleavage and Other Variables **185**/ The Electoral System **194**/ Campaign Techniques **196**/ Conclusion: The Role of Parties in the System **197**

6. CLIENTELA AND PARENTELA   Groups, interests, and cleavages   201

The Interest-Group System: Major Characteristics **201**/ Agricultural Interest Groups **206**/ Labor Interest Groups **208**/ Business Interest Groups **212**/ Catholic Interest Groups: The Church and Its Sponsored Organizations **217**/ Conclusions **222**

7. THE UNEASY BALANCE   Policy-making roles and structures   224

The Italian Executive: An Illusory Image of Strength **224**/ The President of the Italian Republic **225**/ The Prime Minister and the Cabinet **232**/ The Italian Parliament **238**/ Legislative-Executive Relations **250**/ Other Policy-Making Structures **252**/ Conclusions **258**

8. THE CLASH OF OUTLOOKS   The policy-making process   260

Ideological Differences as Barriers to Policy Making **260**/ The Process of Policy Making: The Initiation of Proposals **265**/ The Process of Policy Making: Fact Finding and Consultation **270**/ The Process of Policy Making: The Formulation of Alternatives **274**/ Policy Deliberation **276**/ Authoritative Decisions **278**/ Styles in Conflict Resolution and Problem Solving **280**/ Policy Implementation and the Role of the Bureaucracy **283**/ Some Illustrations of Policy Making in Italy **289**/ Conclusions **295**

9. LEGALISM IN CRISIS   Italian courts and judges   298

Prevalent Conceptions of Law **298**/ The Ordinary Law Courts **301**/ The Administrative Courts **304**/ The Constitutional Court **306**/ Judicial Independence in Italy **310**/ Judicial Recruitment and Training **313**/ The Courts in Italian Society **317**/ Conclusions **318**

10. THE LOWERED PROFILE The country's role in world affairs 320

The Italian People and the Outside World **320**/ Goals of Italian Foreign Policy: Past and Present **323**/ Italian Defense Policy **326**/ The Colonial Heritage **327**/ Makers of Italian Foreign Policy **328**/ Conclusions **331**

CONCLUSION The implications of political lag 333

Selected Bibliography 337

Index 349

ITALY
The politics of
uneven development

INTRODUCTION

Among the major industrial nations of Western Europe, Italy occupies a position that is in many ways unique. It has become one of the world's ten leading industrial powers, while at the same time the percentage of its labor force employed in agriculture is higher than in any other nation in the Common Market. However, in this industrial milieu, a very large part of the Italian South is underdeveloped and lagging far behind the rest of the nation in economic progress and per-capita income. In the North, in Milan and Turin, living standards are virtually on a par with those of Northwestern Europe; in the South, in Calabria, Lucania, and the interior of Sicily, the way of life is preindustrial and backward, comparable in many ways to the grim existence eked out by the peasantry in Greece, Portugal, and the more depressed regions of Spain. Between these two extremes, Central Italy and the Northeast represent a kind of intermediate phase of development, with a more prosperous agriculture than the South and with an industrial sector that is beginning to attract more and more investment on the part of entrepreneurs from the congested Northwest Industrial Triangle (the area comprising Northern Piedmont, Northern Lombardy, and Liguria).

In addition to being a land of great contrasts, Italy is, and has been since 1945, undergoing spectacular social and economic change. Nowhere else in Western Europe has there been such a massive migration of population from the rural areas to the cities. Migration between regions (especially from the South to the Northwest) and emigration to other European countries have also been on an imposing scale. These population movements have had a tremendous resulting impact on Italian party politics and on the degree of integration of Italian society—a society that achieved national unification only a little more than a century ago.

Another feature of Italy's postwar transition has been the "economic miracle." The annual rate of economic growth has been one of the highest in Europe and has more than compensated for prewar economic sluggishness and wartime damages. Government-controlled public corporations have helped promote this growth by supplementing the investment efforts of private enterprise, by financing the expansion of certain key industries, and by investing heavily in the development of the South. Even Southern Italy, as a result, has begun to witness the first major stirrings of industrialization, though a wide gap still separates most of the *Mezzogiorno* (the South, including Sicily and Sardinia) from the rest of Italy.

Economic progress has been reflected in a sharp rise in living standards. Commodities such as automobiles, refrigerators, radio and television sets, which used to be regarded as luxuries that only an upper-class or upper-middle-class Italian could aspire to, are now accessible to larger and larger strata of the population. While not yet on a level with Northwestern Europe, Italy is no longer that hopeless land of grinding poverty from which so many emigrants fled in despair. Life is still hard and discouraging for great numbers of Italians. Many have not shared in the rising prosperity, and many more are not progressing as fast as they would like; but there has been tangible improvement and, above all, there is hope for the future.

In the past, some American social scientists and government officials have expressed confidence that economic development in the direction of industrialization and urbanization would tend to reduce political tensions and encourage the emergence and consolidation of modern democratic institutions. More recently, however, observers have come to recognize that economic growth may not only fail to alleviate political tensions significantly, but may actually aggravate them instead. In fact, recent experiences in the United States would seem to indicate that even a mature and prosperous industrial society is by no means immune to destructive political conflict.

Nowhere is the failure of the economic development approach to political problems more evident than in Italy. Twenty-five years after World War II, the Italian Communist party is stronger in electoral terms than it was in 1946. To be sure, it has acquired a more moderate posture and a rather stodgy, almost conservative political style over the years. But it continues to dominate and virtually preempt the camp of the opposition, thus making it almost impossible for the various democratic political parties to present a clear and credible alternative to a Christian Democratic-led government.

In other areas, too, economic and social transition have apparently failed to generate significant political change. According to some observers, Italian political culture is still characterized by widespread attitudes of profound alienation—of distrust of the government and of the politicians who direct it. The politics of patronage, of personal cliques or clienteles dependent upon their benefactor for government jobs or favors, still plays a very important role in the recruitment of legislators and of local councilmen. Such media of political socialization as the family, the schools, and the universities are said to be failing to perform their function of transmitting the values and attitudes of the system to the young people who are entering upon their responsibilities as citizens and voters.

Italian writers, with that rather apocalyptic pessimism which all too often can deceive a foreign observer, are fond of contrasting the modernity of Italian big business with the cumbersome inefficiency of the state structure. But the picture is only partly overdrawn. The Italian bureaucracy still awaits renovation after two decades of economic prosperity, and the labyrinth of bureaucratic procedures makes for delays and bottlenecks that seriously obstruct the decision-making process. The Parliament produces thousands of minor statutes, but is a graveyard of lost hopes for more controversial bills that seek to enact major policy decisions. This often holds true even when the governing cabinet coalition is firmly and publicly committed to the policy in question. Cabinet instability has actually increased over recent years. And finally, local governments and the courts struggle along under the burden of heavy and increasing responsibilities, while lacking the means to fulfill their functions adequately.

This book will explore the relationship between rapid economic and social change, on the one hand, and a political system retaining many of the traditional features of a bygone era and based partly on anachronistic attitudes, on the other. This political lag should, in the natural course of events, be remedied with the passage of time. Meanwhile, however, Italy is undergoing a dangerous transitional phase. The history of the first half of the twentieth century teaches that periods of socioeconomic transition can frequently prove fatal for free institutions. Italy is in the nature of a test case, then; other fledgling democracies may some day have to confront the same perils and dislocations that beset Italian democracy today.

ONE
THE LATE ARRIVAL
A brief developmental history

GEOGRAPHIC FACTORS

In joining the select club of highly industrialized nations, Italy has had to overcome severe handicaps imposed by physical environment and geographic location. The successful negotiation of these obstacles is in itself a tribute to the ingenuity and resourcefulness of the Italian people. Through the years, environmental conditions in Italy have hardly been conducive to economic growth.

Italy covers an area of 116,305 square miles. The estimated population of this nation in 1966 was about 52.9 million. Since population growth ranges from 300,000–400,000 people a year, it seems safe to assume that the 1971 census will reveal a population between 54 and 55 million people.

Italy is about half the size of France in area but has almost 4 million more people than France. It is hardly surprising, then, that social scientists during the 1940s and 1950s spoke of Italy as an overcrowded country with a severe population problem.

However, in the light of recent trends, we can regard the Italian population picture less pessimistically. For Italy is no longer a predominantly agricultural society, and certainly in other industrial nations high population density is by no means incompatible with high living standards. Italy's population density

(455.1 people per square mile in 1966) is impressive by American standards but is actually lower than the population density of such affluent societies as Great Britain, West Germany, and the Netherlands. Moreover, the Italian birth rate is lower than that of the United States, Great Britain, and France, and may be expected to decline further as living standards continue to rise in Southern Italy.[1] In sum, the historic Italian predicament of too many people on too little land seems to be well on its way toward an eventual solution as hundreds of thousands of underemployed peasants leave the overpopulated countryside for the urban centers in Italy's Northwest Industrial Triangle or beyond the Alps altogether.

Northern and Central Italy enjoy an obvious geographic advantage over the South in their greater proximity to the nations of Western Europe. From the tenth to the sixteenth centuries, when the Mediterranean was the principal artery of world trade, Southern and Central Italy were able to benefit considerably from their position in the heart of the Central Mediterranean. But, with the fall of Constantinople to the Turks in 1453, the discovery of the New World in 1492, and the later discovery of the sea route to India and the Spice Islands, followed by an era of overseas colonization and exploitation, the Atlantic replaced the Mediterranean as the principal avenue of maritime commerce. The economic effect on Italy was devastating, and the South—farthest removed from overland trade contacts with Northern Europe—was particularly hard hit. To this day, the proximity of the Northwest Industrial Triangle to Northern Europe by rail is primarily responsible for discouraging businessmen from establishing factories in the *Mezzogiorno*, which is too far from the promising markets beyond the Alps. By the same token, the closeness of Northern Italy to such more developed economies as France, Germany, and Switzerland has been a source of economic and technological stimulation, and has done a great deal to promote industrialization and progress in the North.

Yet, there are signs of a more hopeful future for the geographically remote southern lands. The emergence of North Africa and the Middle East as important sources of oil places a premium on the geographical proximity of Southern Italy to the

---

[1] On the Italian birth rate, see Francesco Compagna, *La questione meridionale* (Milano: Garzanti, 1963), pp. 25–37. See also George H. Hildebrand, *Growth and Structure in the Economy of Modern Italy* (Cambridge, Mass.: Harvard University Press, 1965), pp. 125–128, for an optimistic assessment of Italy's population problem.

southern and eastern shores of the Mediterranean. In addition, the increasingly low cost of transporting raw materials by sea makes it possible to establish profitable industries along the seacoast far from the traditional overland suppliers of coal and iron ore in Northern Europe. Since it is cheaper to transport coal and iron ore by sea to Taranto in Southeastern Italy than to ship them across the Alps by rail to Northern Italian industrial centers, one can readily understand the willingness of the Italian government to establish giant steel and petrochemical plants along the coastline of Southern Italy and Sicily.

Italy's mountainous Alpine frontier has contributed, in one sense, to national integration by providing Italy with clearly defined boundaries. It has prevented that overlapping and intermingling of diverse ethnic and linguistic groups that is so typical of East-Central Europe, where national frontiers rarely correspond to natural boundaries. As a result, Italy has an overwhelmingly Italian-speaking population, with the exception of about 250,000–300,000 German-speaking people in Bolzano province, 100,000 French-speaking people in Val d'Aosta, and a few thousand Slovenians and Croatians around Trieste and Gorizia near the Yugoslav border.

When we observe that there are approximately 75,000 Protestants and some 30,000 Jews in Italy, with the rest of the population at least nominally Catholic, we must conclude that—whatever the other problems—Italy has attained a high degree of ethnic homogeneity and is under the religious dominance of the Catholic church. To be sure, there are cultural differences and regional prejudices among the regions but they no longer call Italian nationality into question, with the exception of the German minority in the South Tyrol. Religious problems are not quite so simple, however. The absence of Protestant competition has aroused a fear of the monopolistic power of the Roman church, and many Catholics have become ardent anticlericals.

However, Italy's mountainous terrain—the towering Alps in the North and the less lofty Apennines extending southward the entire length of the Italian peninsula, from Bologna to the shores of Calabria and Lucania—also has a countervailing disintegrative effect. It does a great deal to maintain that wide gap between the Northern and Southern economies which is still one of Italy's most vexing problems. First of all, while the Po Valley in the North is a continuous expanse of rich farmland stretching all the way from the Western Alps near Turin to the Adriatic Sea, the fertile plains areas of the South and the islands are relatively small and fragmented. Thus, the southern lowlands are isolated from one another by the Apennines chain, which extends virtually to the beaches in many places. Second, while the Po Valley serves as an easily traveled link between the large cities of Northern and North-Central Italy, the Apennines constitute a serious natural barrier to transportation and communication between the major cities of the South. And third, because the Southern Apennines are not as high as the snow-capped Alps, they do not furnish a reliable supply of water from melting snow as do the Alpine peaks. Thus, the South is poorly supplied with hydroelectric energy and with water for irrigation, whereas both tend to be plentiful in the North.

Other geographic and climatic factors also have the effect of widening the North-South gap. For instance, the deforestation of the Central and Southern Apennines and the exodus of subsistence farmers from these unrewarding slopes have complicated the problem of flood control; disastrous flash floods are frequent in the South. Poor quality clayey or loamy soil, which prevails throughout most of the South (apart from the coastal plains), fails to absorb the scanty rainfall and is especially subject to erosion. Also, the rainfall in the South is highly irregular, with long periods of drought in the summer followed by a few months of excessively violent downpours in the winter, thus tending to intensify the water-supply problem.

In conclusion, we will comment upon the natural resources. Here again, nature has not been kind to the Italian people. Only about 10 percent of Italy's coal consumption and 50 percent of her iron-ore consumption are supplied by domestic resources. With regard to these two key minerals, employed in the manufacture of steel, Italy depends largely upon imports, though this competitive disadvantage is partially offset by the low cost of their maritime transportation.

While coal is in short supply, Italy *does* possess a copious reserve of hydroelectric power in the North. Also, moderate deposits of crude oil have been discovered in Southeastern Sicily around Gela and Augusta. Above all, after World War II, a large supply of natural gas was found in the Po Valley and was used to fuel the so-called economic miracle. Po Valley fields are being rapidly depleted, but new deposits of gas have been found in other parts of Italy, notably near Ferrandina in the deep Southern region of Lucania, while intensive exploration is under way in the Adriatic Sea with a view toward utilizing offshore reserves of oil and gas.

But, as is the case with most modern industrial countries, the greatest Italian resource has been the skill, industriousness, and imagination of the Italian people. To a large degree, innovation and improvisation by a host of medium- and small-businessmen has helped to conquer foreign markets for Italian products. The much-maligned business community has displayed flexibility and open-mindedness in approaching problems of production and marketing—qualities that are often sadly lacking when labor relations are involved. And the existence of a large pool of available labor that was willing to accept relatively low wages in exchange for jobs (which were at a premium until the late 1950s) helped keep the prices of Italian products down. Thus, Italy was able to compete effectively in the international marketplace.

THE STRUGGLE TO BUILD A NATION

One of the distinctive features of Italy's political development has been its long delay in attaining national unification. Whereas Great Britain, France, and Spain have been unified nation-states for hundreds of years, Italy did not complete its unification until 1870. Thus, Italy—along with Germany—is a relative newcomer to the European state system. Italy's late arrival on the international scene has made it very difficult for the Italian people to achieve a common sense of national identity. Even the eventual unification of Italy left the identity crisis unresolved, with political consequences that were disastrous to Italian constitutional democracy after World War I.

As Salvadori points out, "Italians are a nation but not a homogeneous race. Culture and tradition, not biological traits, give them unity."[2] The Italian people, in fact, are a complex ethnic mixture, the end-product of a great intermingling among the nations and tribes that have invaded the Italian peninsula over the past 2000 years. The ancient Latins around Rome, the Itali in the Southern interior, the Ligurians in the Northwest, the Etruscans in what is now Tuscany, and the Greeks along the Southern and Sicilian seacoasts were blended with later waves of invaders— the Gauls and the Germans in the North, the Moors and the Normans in the South. This remarkable assortment of tribal and national strains delayed the development of that common culture and tradition to which Salvadori refers. Instead, it helped to produce numerous distinctive dialects that are still spoken in the

[2] Massimo Salvadori, *Italy* (Englewood Cliffs, N.J.: Prentice-Hall, 1965), p. 5.

home and in everyday conversation in the several regions of Italy. While the Italian language and its dialects are based on Latin, the kind of transformation Latin has undergone reflects the ethnic background and composition of each region. Thus, Piedmontese dialect bears some resemblance to French, Lombard dialect has some harsh Germanic sounds, and so forth.

Until a few decades ago, this proliferation of dialects represented a very serious obstacle to the building of an Italian nation. De Mauro estimates that around 1871, outside of Rome and Tuscany (the region whose dialect has evolved into the standard national language), only about 1 percent of the population had learned Italian. And as recently as 1951, one sample survey revealed that 35.4 percent of the population of Italy still used dialect as their sole means of communication and a full 13 percent were actually *unable* to use Italian.[3]

The awkwardness and incongruity of such a communication block was brought home to the author during World War II. While serving with an infantry unit in the Emilian Apennines, he was occasionally asked to act as interpreter. On several occasions, he found himself unable to understand or translate the statements of Emilian peasants who were being asked for information. The reason for this was quite simple: anyone who has been trained to read or speak only standard Italian will find the Emilian dialect, with its chopped-off vowels, to be virtually incomprehensible. And yet, Tuscany—the home region of standard Italian—is just to the south of Emilia. In fact, the best Italian is said to be spoken in the Tuscan city of Siena, which is little more than 50 miles south of the Emilian Apennines.

But ethnic and linguistic heterogeneity do not sufficiently explain Italy's late unification. After all, other European nations—for example, France and Spain—are fully as complex as Italy in their regional and cultural diversity, yet were able to attain nationhood rather early. As we shall see, a number of additional factors appear to share the responsiblity for the unusual delay in the nation-building process in Italy.

Under the Roman Empire, Italy *was* unified, with a single central government, a common language, and a widespread sense of common identity based on Roman citizenship. But even then, Italy was simply regarded as a geographic region of the empire, rather than a potentially sovereign nation. Residents of Italy considered themselves to be Roman citizens or Roman subjects, and

[3] Tullio De Mauro, *Storia linguistica dell' Italia unita* (Bari: Laterza, 1963), pp. 41, 115–116.

did not attach any sense of national allegiance to their identity as Italians. So, while the Italian peninsula was indeed under a single sovereign, its status was merely that of a territorial subdivision of a universal empire and its unity was purely administrative in significance. Yet the common heritage of the Latin language, the Roman legal system, and Roman political and social institutions *did* leave its mark on the popular consciousness, and Italians would never forget that their peninsula had once been the central core of the Roman Empire.

Given this heritage of unity under the Roman Empire, why did Italy fail to attain early national unification? First of all, for several centuries after the fall of the Western Roman Empire, Northern Italy was under Germanic political domination, while Moorish and Byzantine rulers controlled most of the South. Thus, different attitudes and traditions were transmitted by various foreign overlords, and distinctions between the several regions were greatly accentuated as a result.

Then, too, Northern Italy came under the dominion of the Holy Roman Empire in the ninth century. The very existence of this shadow empire was a constant temptation for its Germanic rulers to intervene militarily south of the Alps in an effort to consolidate their control over the North Italian plains. The relatively weak and decentralized Empire squandered German and Italian resources on an impossible dream of a universal state and thus helped to delay the unification process in both Germany and Italy.

On the other hand, the Papal States in Central Italy—the temporal domain of the pope—regarded any effort to unite Italy as a threat to their own sovereignty, and so foiled any attempts by the Holy Roman emperor to gain hegemony over Italy. Violent conflict between the Guelphs (supporters of the pope's interests) and the Ghibellines (adherents of the emperor) eventually resulted in the frustration of the emperor's designs and the continuing balkanization of Italy.

Another reason for tardy unification was the separate pattern of development followed by the South. After an army of Norman adventurers ousted the Moors from Sicily and the Byzantine forces from the Southern mainland in the eleventh century, the Kingdom of the Two Sicilies was established. Thus, at the very time when the cities of Northern and Central Italy were growing in wealth and power and were successfully asserting their autonomy, Italy south of Rome was governed by a centralized but usually inefficient autocracy. This autocracy helped to hasten the degeneration of the Southern economy and stunt the growth of the urban commercial sector. The South began to lag further and further behind the rest of Italy.

Finally, the prosperous and flourishing cities of Northern and Central Italy also played their part in postponing the nation-building process. Enjoying de facto sovereignty, such communes as Milan, Venice, and Florence were virtual city-states, and were regarded as the principal commercial centers of Western Europe. However, the very success of these North Italian communes served to strengthen the centrifugal forces that prevented the formation of a united Italy.[4] While less advanced countries like France and Spain were establishing themselves as unified nation-states in order to reap the benefits of greater physical size, larger population, more intensive exploitation of resources, and broader markets, the Italian city-states pursued their discrete interests and constituted an international state system in miniature, complete with treaties, alliances, and wars between the component communes. As so often happens with successful political systems, the Northern and Central Italian communes failed to adapt to environmental change. As a result, a series of foreign incursions began in 1494, and Italy became a battleground for contending foreign armies. By 1559 Spain emerged victorious and became the paramount power in Italy, ruling directly over a large part of the peninsula, and controlling most of the rest through native puppet regimes. The period of Spanish hegemony lasted until the early eighteenth century, when Austria took over most of Spain's Italian possessions.

Through more than two centuries of foreign rule, Italy's economic and social development fell far behind the more advanced states of Western Europe. The Counter Reformation, enforced by the heavy-handed authority of Spain, stifled intellectual inquiry and produced certain traditions of political servility, of kowtowing to superior authority, which are still discernible in Italian political and social behavior. It was a grim period indeed for a civilization that had once been the envy of Western Europe.

Yet, Italy's subjection to foreign control and the injury inflicted on the pride and self-respect of Italian intellectuals were by no means undiluted evils. In this respect, Italy's experiences resembled those of a number of new African and Asian states: Colonial exploitation turned out to be an excellent device for arousing a dormant sense of national consciousness among the

---

[4] René Albrecht-Carrié, *Italy from Napoleon to Mussolini* (paperback ed.; New York: Columbia University Press, 1960), pp. 7–9.

native intelligentsia. The seeds of Italian national consciousness had already been planted during the Renaissance by such poets as Dante Alighieri (whose *Divine Comedy* established the Tuscan dialect as the literary language of Italy) and Francesco Petrarca, and by such patriotic political writers as Niccolò Machiavelli.

It was the French Revolution and Napoleon's subsequent invasion and occupation of Italy that paved the way for the rise of an Italian nationalist movement. The many sweeping innovations imposed by the French, the frequent reshuffling of state boundaries, and the sense of unlimited horizons that many middle-class Italians suddenly experienced continued to influence Italian attitudes long after the French tide had receded and the Congress of Vienna had restored the traditional authorities to power. By 1815, with the acquisition of a common national consciousness and a common language, and with the increasing dissemination of both through the cultural media, Italy's educated elites were rapidly being converted to the nationalist creed, or were, at any rate, eager for national unification as a means of promoting progress.

But the task for those who would be the architects of a united Italy was not an easy one. The Vienna settlement of 1814–1815 created an Italy divided into eight territorial units, several of which existed before 1796. In the Northwest, the Kingdom of Sardinia controlled Sardinia, Piedmont, Savoy, Nice, and Liguria. In the North and Northeast was the Lombard-Venetian kingdom under direct Austrian rule. In North-Central Italy were several small principalities: the Grand Duchy of Tuscany and the duchies of Parma, Modena, and Lucca. Stretching across Central Italy, like a broad belt cutting the peninsula in two, were the Papal States. And finally, south of Rome lay the Bourbon-ruled Kingdom of the Two Sicilies. In order to achieve national unity, the seven states and principalities previously mentioned, along with the Austrian domain in Lombardy and the Veneto, would all have to be stripped of their separate identities. And in so doing, powerful vested interests would be disturbed and long-standing traditions uprooted.

The events leading up to national unification after 1815 are well documented. We will summarize them here in order to establish a sense of historical sequence regarding that movement of national resurgence referred to as the *Risorgimento*. We are primarily concerned with the political significance of this historical trend.

Between 1817 and 1848, a number of Italian secret societies —such as the *Carbonari* before 1832 and Giuseppe Mazzini's

Giovane Italia ("Young Italy") in the 1830s and 1840s—organized a series of ill-starred conspiracies and even a few actual uprisings. All such rebellions were handily suppressed, with Austrian troops intervening whenever native Italian authorities could not handle the job. Then, in early 1848, a rash of riots, demonstrations, and popular uprisings broke out all over Italy, almost coinciding with the revolutionary upheavals that were beginning to surface throughout Western and Central Europe. A number of Italian states were compelled to grant constitutions to their people. And a popular revolt in Milan forced the Austrian garrison to flee. In that same year, republican governments were temporarily established in Rome and Venice. In response to these events, the Kingdom of Sardinia (Piedmont) declared war on Austria and sent forces into Lombardy, while volunteers from all over Italy flocked to the aid of the Piedmontese Army. But the Austrian armies rallied, defeated the Piedmontese in two successive campaigns, and crushed the Venetian Republic. Meanwhile, a French expeditionary force drove the republican forces out of Rome. This first war of the *Risorgimento* had ended in utter disaster by the summer of 1849.

But the cause of Italian unification had, in reality, received only a temporary setback. In the 1850s, the Kingdom of Sardinia, under a new king, Victor Emmanuel II, and a vigorous, farsighted prime minister, Camillo Benso di Cavour, proceeded to strengthen its economy and its defense capabilities, and to seek allies abroad for a renewal of the struggle against Austria. And in 1856, the Italian National Society was founded by a group of moderate patriots. This organization advocated unification of Italy under the House of Savoy—that is to say, under the Kingdom of Sardinia and its Piedmontese ruling dynasty. Thus, one of Italy's states had become the recognized standard-bearer of the unification drive.

Cavour's policies soon began to reap dividends. In 1859, France joined Sardinia in a new war against Austria. This time, the Austrians were defeated and the peace treaty allowed the Kingdom of Sardinia to annex Lombardy. Following this triumph, revolutions broke out in Tuscany (now including recently annexed Lucca), Modena, Parma, and the Romagna provinces of the Papal States. Since Austria was no longer in a position to intervene, all these states and provinces were annexed by the Kingdom of Sardinia, which yielded Nice and Savoy to France as a means of forestalling French disapproval.

The following year (1860), a leader of republican volunteers, Giuseppe Garibaldi, landed in Sicily leading a thousand men. The arrival of "The Thousand," combined with a popular revolt against the Neapolitan regime in Sicily, resulted in an unexpected victory for the cause of national unification. Garibaldi occupied Sicily, landed on the Italian mainland, and eventually captured Naples, effectively obliterating the Kingdom of the Two Sicilies. At this point, Piedmontese troops were sent southward to take advantage of the unusual opportunity: Most of the territory of the Papal States was occupied and annexed, and Garibaldi's conquests in the South were taken over with his acquiescence. On March 17, 1861, a newly elected Italian Parliament proclaimed the establishment of the Kingdom of Italy under King Victor Emmanuel II, formerly king of Sardinia. Piedmont, a Northwest frontier region with a quasi-French dialect, had managed to unite Italy.

In only two years, the map of Italy had undergone a complete transformation, with all of the former Italian states except a mere remnant of the Papal States now forming part of the new Italian nation-state. The task of Italian unification was all but completed within the next decade. In 1866, Italy joined Prussia in a new war against Austria, and Prussian victories (outweighing Italian defeats) enabled Italy to obtain the Veneto in the final peace treaty. And in 1870, the Franco-Prussian War and the withdrawal of the French garrison from the Eternal City, permitted Italian troops to seize Rome and its surrounding province. Only Trento and Trieste remained in Austrian hands. What had seemed unattainable in 1815, and even in 1849, finally had become a reality.

After this brief survey of the state-building process in Italy, it would be well to stress three major points. First, it should be noted that there was considerable disagreement among the men of the *Risorgimento* as to what kind of united Italy was to be created. The supporters of national unification included: Giuseppe Mazzini, who favored the establishment of a republic based on universal suffrage and on a network of voluntary associations; neo-Guelphs like Vincenzo Gioberti, who wanted a federal union of Italian states, preferably under the presidency of the pope; moderates like Cesare Balbo and Massimo D'Azeglio, who wanted Piedmont to take a cautious lead in expelling the Austrians from Italian soil but who distrusted Mazzini's goals of mass democracy and universal suffrage; federalist republicans like Carlo Cattaneo, who (unlike Mazzini) favored the establishment of a federal system; Giuseppe Garibaldi, who sometimes seemed to advocate combining parliamentary institutions with a Roman-style emergency dictatorship; and finally, Cavour himself, who eventually presided over the creation of the Kingdom of Italy. Cavour might well be classed as one of the moderates, were it not for his willingness to take considerable risks on behalf of Italian unification, and his promotion of a vigorous program of internal reforms designed to augment the power of Piedmont. In short, the *Risorgimento* was by no means a homogeneous movement.

Second, it should be observed that the Piedmontese-dominated Kingdom of Sardinia—with considerable help from France and later from Prussia—bore the main burden and responsibility of the fight for Italian unification. The most articulate and widely recognized political theorist of the *Risorgimento*, Giuseppe Mazzini, failed to exert much influence on the structure and institutions of the new nation. And Giuseppe Garibaldi, despite his picturesque conquest of Sicily and of most of the Southern mainland, had to defer to King Victor Emmanuel II's wishes and allow the Piedmontese Army to reap the fruits of his victory. The end-product of the *Risorgimento* was revolution from above, not at all in the romantic Mazzinian tradition, but rather as the moderates had advocated.

And finally, it should be emphasized that the *Risorgimento* lacked widespread peasant support, and was largely the work of a town-dwelling minority. In the North, the peasantry feared and distrusted the middle-class townspeople from cities like Milan who threatened to deprive the peasants of their traditional feudal privileges while exposing them to the dangers of the free market.[5] Consequently, during the 1848 and 1849 wars, which Piedmont waged against Austria in a futile effort to liberate Lombardy, the Lombard peasantry apparently sympathized with the Austrians. In fact, one historian claims that these peasants actually opened the dikes to release river floodwaters in order to hamper the progress of the invading Piedmontese.[6] And in Southern Italy, when the Piedmontese occupants proceeded to restore law and order, uphold the entrenched rights of landed property, and brutally suppress peasant riots, it became evident that the orientation of the *Risorgimento* was toward the interests of the urban and rural middle classes (which had acquired vast tracts of land formerly belonging to the church). Clearly, the leaders of the *Risorgimento*

[5] On urban-rural hostility, see H. Stuart Hughes, *The United States and Italy* (rev. ed.; Cambridge, Mass.: Harvard University Press, 1965), pp. 37–38; and Franco Catalano, *Storia dei partiti politici italiani* (2nd ed.; Roma: ERI, 1968), pp. 26–27.

[6] Denis Mack Smith, *Italy: A Modern History* (Ann Arbor, Mich.: University of Michigan Press, 1969), p. 39.

were unconcerned about the rights of the common people. The Southern peasant uprising of 1860–1865—the so-called *Brigandage*—was really a primitive and desperate form of protest against the new Piedmontese oppressors. It was eventually quelled, amid frightful atrocities committed by both sides; but it cost more lives than all the wars of the *Risorgimento* put together.[7]

If the peasants were on the sidelines, so to speak, or actually in opposition, who were the principal urban supporters of national unification? The clergy, following the lead of the pope, were generally cool or hostile. The commercial and industrial middle classes apparently did not play as prominent a role as one might expect: The Lombard bourgeoisie was slow to demand reform, and only did so in response to the concerted propaganda of a number of landed proprietors and intellectuals, who used newspapers and pamphlets to spread their message.[8] There was a scattering of artisans in the *Risorgimento* movement, but there were too few industrial workers to provide any movement with a mass base. Even the nobility was split: some sided with the established order; others—especially the less secure, lower-ranking nobles—joined the Italian National Society.[9]

Yet the backbone of the movement, the bulk of the members of the Italian National Society, were young professional men and intellectuals, especially those who had attained relatively modest success in their professions.[10] These men actually had a rather uncertain status in their home communities. They felt insecure about their future prospects yet yearned for social advancement. They resented the power and status of the great feudal landowners yet looked down with suspicion and a certain patronizing contempt on peasants and workers and felt uncomfortable in the company of artisans. As one writer observed, while describing one group of volunteers in the *Risorgimento*:

> In Garibaldi's Thousand, there were no peasants but rather students, independent craftsmen and *litterati*. The backbone of the national revolution was made up of ex-officers such as Cavour and Pisacane, sailors such as Bixio and Garibaldi, doctors such as Bertani and Farini, lawyers like Crispi and Rattazzi, writers and scholars like Amari and De Sanctis. On the other hand few

---

[7] Smith, pp. 40–42, 69–75.
[8] Kent R. Greenfield, *Economics and Liberalism in the Risorgimento* (rev. ed.; Baltimore: The Johns Hopkins Press, 1965), pp. 263–267, 285–287.
[9] Raymond Grew, *A Sterner Plan for Italian Unity* (Princeton, N.J.: Princeton University Press, 1963), pp. 233–234.
[10] Grew, pp. 233–234, 442, 456, 463–464.

men of great possessions were listed in the secret societies, because the *risorgimento*, while anything but popular, was a revolution of the disinherited, of the starry-eyed. The educated unemployed and underemployed were one of its chief driving forces, much the same class of people who later played an important part in the triumph of Mussolini.[11]

THE PROBLEMS OF LEGITIMACY AND INTEGRATION

It has been necessary to dwell at some length on the historical antecedents of Italian national unification in order to focus attention on certain serious shortcomings in the methods that Italian elites employed to build a united Italy and also to enable us to comprehend the persisting problems of legitimacy and national integration confronted by Italy after 1870.

Two American political scientists, La Palombara and Weiner, speak of certain crises that "political systems typically experience as they move from traditional to more developed forms."[12] Three crises that they particularly stressed are legitimacy, integration, and participation. A crisis of legitimacy involves substantial disagreement over the governmental system and over the rules upon which that system is based. A crisis of national integration occurs when a political system has failed to create an "amalgamation of disparate social, economic, religious, ethnic, and group elements into a single nation-state," and when "loyalty, allegiance, and a willingness to place national above local or parochial concerns," are lacking.[13] A crisis of participation exists when strong and persistent demands arise to admit a broader public to involvement in the decision-making process. We shall deal with the problem of participation in Chapter Two, for the most part; we shall devote some attention in a later section of this chapter to one of its facets, the expansion of suffrage.

Analysis of the available evidence shows that the Italian elites had seriously mismanaged the problems of building a nation and of creating a sense of national identity. Thus, the Italian political system became overloaded. It had to face the problem of equitable distribution of the national product in the first decades

[11] Smith, pp. 36–37.
[12] Joseph La Palombara and Myron Weiner, "The Origin and Development of Political Parties," in Joseph La Palombara and Myron Weiner, eds., *Political Parties and Political Development* (Princeton, N.J.: Princeton University Press, 1966), p. 14.
[13] Myron Weiner and Joseph La Palombara, "The Impact of Parties on Political Development," in La Palombara and Weiner, eds., p. 413.

of the twentieth century without really having overcome the crises of legitimacy, national integration, and participation. The key to understanding much of Italy's later problems may be here: An overloaded political system with a backlog of unresolved problems may become unable to cope with new problems, and may thus fail to gain, or retain, the allegiance of its own people. In short, system overload is likely to undermine system effectiveness, and an ineffective system would probably cause widespread alienation.

To illustrate this point let us look at the problem of legitimacy that had not been satisfactorily resolved in 1870. Italy had been unified, not by an orderly process of eliciting the agreement of the several Italian states in convention assembled, but by military conquest. Existing Italian states, some of them with long traditions as legally independent polities, simply were occupied and annexed by the Kingdom of Sardinia. Naturally, "unification from above" was somewhat resented, especially in the South, just as Bavarians and Hanoverians in Germany felt some rancor against the Prussian unifiers.

To be sure, plebiscites were held in each annexed region in order to provide an opportunity for formal popular ratification of the fait accompli. But these plebiscites were blatantly rigged, and annexation invariably won approval by 99 percent of those voting. Giuseppe di Lampedusa's novel, *The Leopard,* tells of the plebiscite conducted in a small Sicilian village: the results were Yes, 512; No, 0. However, the protagonist, Don Fabrizio, learned that there had been at least one negative vote, that of the local accountant, Don Ciccio. That negative vote simply had been counted as an affirmative vote. Presumably there had been other negative votes in the village, for total unanimity was inconceivable. The effect of such a falsified plebiscite on the legitimacy of the new regime can be readily imagined. However, falsification was really unnecessary. As di Lampedusa acutely puts it, "Don Ciccio's negative vote, fifty similar votes at Donnafugata, a hundred thousand 'nos' in the whole Kingdom would have had no effect on the result, would in fact have made it, if anything, more significant; and this maiming of souls would have been avoided." In short, the people of this village became alienated from their government. And di Lampedusa concludes that "a great deal of the slackness and acquiescence for which the people of the South were to be criticized during the next decades was due to the stupid annulment of the first expression of liberty ever offered them."[14]

The formation of the Kingdom of Italy not only involved the

---

[14] Giuseppe di Lampedusa, *The Leopard* (New York: New American Library, 1961), pp. 118, 119.

uprooting of long-established states by thinly veiled military conquest, but was also marked by the absence of any political or institutional concessions to the diverse political traditions of the component regions. A series of decree-laws issued by the Piedmontese government in 1859 made certain modifications in its existing local government institutions and then imposed those institutions on Lombardy and other recently annexed territories. In 1860–1861, after the annexation of the South, there was a short-lived trend toward decentralization: The Ministry of the Interior recommended a form of regional deconcentration of administrative functions, and a consultative committee of members of Parliament and councillors of state went a step further to advocate the establishment of elected regional councils. On November 28, 1860, a new minister of the interior, Marco Minghetti, actually announced the cabinet's support of the proposal for regional councils. But in the ensuing years, 1861–1865, the advocates of centralization had their way and determined the long-range structural character of the Kingdom of Italy. It was not until 1948 that the old regional traditions were finally given legal recognition in the Constitution of the Italian republic.

Why this obstinate refusal to allow some regional experimentation, to follow the example of the Second Reich, which was permitting the various German principalities to retain a good deal of autonomy? Perhaps, as Fried argues, the moderates who controlled the cabinet and dominated Parliament in the 1860s experienced a change of heart between 1860 and 1861, primarily as a result of the annexation of the South. The moderates were already keenly aware of the widespread opposition to unification represented by the ruling classes of the former Italian states, by the clergy, by the peasantry, and by the Mazzinian republicans. They also distrusted the ability of the common people of Italy to govern themselves. Federalism, or excessive decentralization within a unitary state, might enable these centrifugal forces to wreck the newly created Italian state.[15]

> All of these fears and suspicions came to a focus with the annexation of the southern regions. Northerners were dismayed with the great disparities between the North and South in economic conditions, standards of administrative and political conduct, and social structure. . . . Northern politicians and functionaries became convinced that the depressed conditions of

[15] Robert C. Fried, *The Italian Prefects: A Study in Administrative Politics* (New Haven, Conn.: Yale University Press, 1963), pp. 90–92.

the South were due to centuries of misgovernment; that only vigorous action by a strong central government could rehabilitate the South, develop what they mistakenly considered its natural riches, and stamp out traditions of corruption and laxity in government.[16]

Extreme centralization may well have been essential in view of the dangers that the church, the traditionalist elements in the South, and the forces of social revolution posed for the infant Italian state. The fact remains, however, that such disregard for regional feelings *did* provoke unusual indignation and helped to foster a generalized sense of distrust, which has survived to the present day, against the heavy-handed Italian central government. All things considered, the feeling that Italians had little voice in their own local affairs was bound to estrange many citizens from the new order of things.

Finally, the Catholic church and its supporters represented one major piece of unfinished business from the point of view of resolving the crisis of legitimacy. The pope refused to recognize the Kingdom of Italy and remained a self-proclaimed prisoner in the Vatican, rejecting all conciliatory overtures. Devout Catholics, resenting the forcible seizure of Rome and the humiliation of their pontiff, followed the Church hierarchy's advice (the doctrine of *non expedit*, proclaimed in 1874) to abstain from voting in national elections. Shocked by the uncompromising hostility of the clergy and by their successful agitation among the peasantry, the Italian government adopted a number of strong anticlerical measures. Therefore, it was not until 1904 that a few fissures began to appear in the *non expedit* policy. And, then, not until 1913 under the Gentiloni Agreement did Italian Catholics begin to give large-scale electoral support to moderate Liberal party candidates for Parliament. In 1929 a Concordat was finally signed, which brought about a full reconciliation between church and state. By that time, however, the *non expedit* policy had been discarded for about a decade, for, in 1919, a Christian Democratic party—Don Sturzo's Italian Popular party—received the consent of the Holy See, and openly campaigned for the votes of Italian Catholics.

We have covered some of the obstacles to the problem of national integration that had to be overcome—primarily, the cultural gap between the Germanic-Celtic traditions of the North and the Greek-Byzantine-Spanish background of the South; and the Northern heritage of free, self-governing, commercial cities con-

[16] Fried, pp. 92–93.

fronting the long history of feudalism and agrarian backwardness in the South. The men of the *Risorgimento* could not deal with these and other difficulties properly. Their methods tended to aggravate rather than resolve the crisis of national integration.

The most obvious drawback to integration was the elitist character of the *Risorgimento*. To be sure, all political movements are led by an active minority; and even the cadres or activists represent only a small percentage of the potential membership. But in Italy no real effort was made to mobilize the masses. The peasants were virtually left out of the *Risorgimento*, and—especially in Southern Italy—were sometimes treated like conquered colonial subjects rather than fellow-citizens. The failure to give the peasantry a sense of having some stake in the new Italy and the brutal incomprehension with which peasant grievances were ignored certainly retarded the development of a sense of national identity. Apart from the Piedmontese army and a few thousand volunteers, relatively few Italians were active participants in the wars of the *Risorgimento*. There was an utter dearth of that universal sense of active commitment to a great struggle for national liberation which did so much to build up a feeling of nationality among the humbler classes in France during the critical years of 1792–1793.

The elitist character of the *Risorgimento* had a corrupting effect on Italian politics and political leadership. The very fact that the inert masses had been virtually dragooned into a united Italy could not help but breed, among the Italian intelligentsia, an attitude of contempt for the majority and a belief that history is and *should be* made by active minorities. In later years, if the uncomprehending masses insisted on using democratic institutions as a means of blocking the active minority in its ardent pursuit of national greatness, the ruling elite was likely to conclude that parliamentary democracy was an expendable luxury. Such attitudes cropped up frequently in the twentieth century—notably during the conflict over Italy's entry into World War I, when a militant interventionist minority consciously dragged a reluctant nation into a disastrous conflict. The tendency to stress the role of elites in manipulating the masses is very evident in the scholarly writings of theorists like Mosca and Michels.[17] Also, it forms part of the political culture, in that popular attitudes are impregnated with elitist preconceptions. This elitism helps us to understand the initial appeal of fascism to the Italian middle classes. It also helps

---

[17] Gaetano Mosca, *The Ruling Class* (New York: McGraw-Hill, 1939); and Robert Michels, *Political Parties* (New York: Free Press, 1949).

to explain the fact that political discourse in Italy even today is keyed to the level of university and secondary school graduates, and is far too abstract and esoteric for the common people.

We should also cite the key role played by Italian white-collar intellectuals in the *Risorgimento* as another factor retarding national integration. These members of the intelligentsia lacked a secure social status, were idealistic and irrational in their outlook, and were prone to indulge in emotional binges. Tending to view politics in terms of cultural values, many of them professed disillusionment with the compromise and log-rolling that had succeeded the alarums and excursions of the *Risorgimento*. There may have been good reason to suggest that the emotional yearnings of many Italian intellectuals were simply insatiable, and that no conceivable government policies could have met their impossibly high esthetic standards. But the fact remains that the ascendancy of the moderates in the drive toward national unification *did* serve to shatter the idealistic hopes of many Italian intellectuals. Frustrated idealism is a dangerous emotion that can eventually degenerate into political extremism or cynical apathy.

Moreover, the *Risorgimento* had been rather disappointing from a military point of view. Piedmontese troops had fought courageously and well, but it had required French and later Prussian military might to expel the Austrians from Italy. The fortunes of war had not been favorable to the Italian cause. There were, to be sure, some heartening memories of gallant fights against heavy odds: the sieges of Rome and Venice; the stand of the Tuscan volunteers at Curtatone. But generally speaking, the Italian armed forces had been unable to achieve major victories that might have inspired future generations of Italians and provided a unifying national myth.

Also serving to delay national integration was the fact that not all Italian-speaking territories had been redeemed from Austrian control by 1870. The province of Trento, the Adriatic seaport of Trieste, and several Italian enclaves along the eastern shores of the Adriatic Sea were still in Austrian hands. Thus, the irredentists of the early twentieth century had ample grounds for protest, especially since the northeastern frontiers of Italy were not only so drawn as to leave several hundred thousand Italians under foreign rule, but also were very hard to defend from the strategic point of view.

Italian middle-class patriots were not unaware of the abortive character of national integration. The old cliché, "Having created Italy, we must now create the Italians," reflected this awareness. Since the wars of the *Risorgimento* had failed to do the job, it was felt that a policy of imperial expansion, accompanied by at least one major war, might create that national consciousness which allegedly was so sadly lacking. A foreign war might relieve the overpopulation problem in the South by acquiring cheap new land for future settlement. The penetration of East Africa, which culminated in the Italian defeat at Adowa in 1896, the invasion of Libya in 1911-1912, and the steadily rising demands for the liberation of Trento and Trieste, were all manifestations of the strongly felt need to complete the nation-building mission by reviving ancient Roman military virtues, to cement Italian national unity with copious outpourings of Italian blood. This rather strange assumption—that the supposedly sickly condition of Italian national morale, along with the many ills afflicting Italian society, could somehow be cured by a really satisfactory bloodbath—helped to bring about the Italian intervention in World War I.

One major outcome of World War I was the fulfillment of most of the Italian irredentist objectives: Trento, Trieste, Venezia Giulia, and the Istrian peninsula were annexed as a result of the Allied victory. Then, too, the Italian frontiers were pushed forward to the Brenner Pass, thus placing several hundred thousand German-speaking Tyrolese under Italian dominion; while the acquisition of Istria involved control over a large number of Slovenians. But while the war had been suitably bloody, costing about 600,000 Italian lives, Italian national integration had not been consummated. On the contrary, large masses of workers and peasants had served in the war with sullen reluctance. Italy had entered the war without first considering the wishes of the Italian people. The executive branch, backed by the king, had secretly negotiated with the Western Allies, and secretly signed the Treaty of London committing Italy to intervention. Then the executive had brazenly confronted the neutralist parliamentary majority with the accomplished fact, and had relied on interventionist middle-class mobs to overawe the advocates of peace among the parliamentary deputies and their supporters. These procedures hardly soothed the sensibilities of those who had advocated neutrality in the first place.

But while the cleverly engineered Italian intervention served to alienate workers, the ultrapatriotic wing of the middle class, for its part, could hardly restrain its contempt for the "vile plebeians" who had had the effrontery to regard their own miserable lives as being more important than the achievement of great power status for Italy. Thus, class conflict, rendered acute even under normal circumstances by Italy's low standard of living, was further inflamed by the cumulative effect of the war issue. With a divided society too weak to weather the postwar economic and social crisis, Italian constitutional democracy collapsed when the middle classes turned to strong-arm methods to insure their continued hegemony over the Italian state.

From 1922–1943, Italy was under the Fascist dictatorship of Benito Mussolini—a self-advertised totalitarian regime rendered somewhat less oppressive than German Nazism by the venality and inefficiency of the Italian Fascist elites. While Germino does make a strong case for his claim that Fascist Italy was truly totalitarian in ideology and methods,[18] the unpreparedness of the Italian armed forces on the eve of World War II raises serious doubts as to the amount of credence that should be given to fascist ideological rhetoric. The war, in fact, signaled the end of the Fascist adventure: Italy was defeated and invaded by the Allied armies; and large parts of the peninsula, subjected to bombing, shelling, or both, suffered terrible damage.

Yet today, less than three decades after that low point in Italian fortunes, the crises of legitimacy and of national integration seem to have been weathered with a remarkable degree of success. With regard to legitimacy, the present republican form of government was established in 1946 by an institutional referendum. True, the majority on behalf of the republic was not terribly imposing, and the South voted to retain the monarchy. But at least the referendum was conducted in a fair and orderly manner, and the votes were honestly counted. The Constitution was duly adopted in 1948 by a freely elected Constituent Assembly representing all sections of Italy. As a result, even the extreme Left professes to respect the present Constitution. In fact, the Italian Communist party often claims to be the staunch defender of the Constitution against the encroachments of the reactionary forces in Italian life.

With regard to national integration, it seems safe to say that never before in Italian history has there been such a highly developed sense of national identity. To what may we attribute this change? To begin with, there was the epic of the wartime Resistance against the Germans and their Fascist allies. The Resistance was an elite movement, to be sure, but (unlike the *Risorgimento*) an elite broadly representing all classes and political creeds in

[18] Dante Germino, *The Italian Fascist Party in Power: A Study in Totalitarian Rule* (Minneapolis: University of Minnesota Press, 1959), ch. 8.

Northern and Central Italy.[19] Secondly, after the war the Italian "economic miracle" spurred large-scale industrialization and urbanization—trends that generally tend to undermine parochial loyalties. Prosperity and successful competition with other European industrial powers aroused a healthy and pragmatic temper of pride in Italian energy and resourcefulness, free of the morbid and lugubrious power aspirations of the past. And thirdly, as we shall see, massive migration from the South to the Northwest Industrial Triangle has had an integrative, melting-pot effect on Italian society. It is partly because of the satisfactory progress made towards national integration that Italian democratic politicians are now prepared to contemplate that regional self-government from which their ancestors recoiled barely a century ago.

CONSTITUTIONAL DEVELOPMENT AND THE EMERGENCE OF THE PARTY SYSTEM

In contrast with France, constitutional evolution in Italy has been marked by a relatively limited amount of institutional experimentation. During the entire period from 1861 to the advent of the Fascist state in 1922, the Constitution of the Kingdom of Italy was simply the old Piedmontese *Statuto* which King Charles Albert had granted to the people of his Kingdom of Sardinia in 1848. The *Statuto* provided for a parliamentary regime, with a Chamber of Deputies elected by the people and a Senate appointed by the king; but it vested supreme executive power in the monarch himself. To be sure, the fundamental laws of Great Britain also grant formidable powers to the British monarch but only on paper, with the understanding that those powers will really be exercised by a Cabinet responsible to Parliament. In Italy, however, the vagueness of the *Statuto*, combined with the autocratic traditions of the Piedmontese monarchy, permitted the king to assert much more influence than did his counterparts in Northern Europe. The Italian king apparently played a major role in foreign affairs and also in defense policy, and had a fairly free hand in selecting or dismissing a prime minister. In 1915, to cite a case in point, King Victor Emmanuel III openly committed the prestige of the crown to securing an Italian declaration of war against Austria-Hungary, and reappointed the interventionist Antonio Salandra as his prime minister, despite the fact that a parliamentary majority was known to favor neutrality.

[19] Charles F. Delzell, *Mussolini's Enemies: The Italian Anti-Fascist Resistance* (Princeton, N.J.: Princeton University Press, 1961), pp. 295–297, 548.

In 1922, when Mussolini's blackshirt militiamen marched on Rome, the king refused to sign a decree proclaiming a state of siege, issued by Prime Minister Facta. This decree would have authorized the armed forces to take the necessary measures against the Fascist squads. By his refusal, the king in effect compelled Premier Facta to resign and thus ensured a Fascist victory. The king then asked Mussolini to accept the post of prime minister and to form a cabinet. His actions constituted a clear violation of the spirit, if not the letter, of the *Statuto,* and placed upon the House of Savoy a heavy share of the responsibility for Italy's brief but tragic interlude of Fascist dictatorship. This breach of constitutional procedure was one of the main reasons why Italian democrats could not accept the survival of the monarchy after the fall of the Fascist state.

During the Fascist regime (1922–1943), the *Statuto* remained nominally in force; for, since it could be modified by ordinary legislation, there was really no need to discard it. The king remained the ceremonial chief of state, while Mussolini acted as prime minister and *Duce* (leader) of the Fascist party. It was understood that the king was a mere figurehead; but Mussolini's failure to close this legal loophole (as Hitler had done in Germany when he assumed the presidential office of the defunct Marshal von Hindenburg in 1934) was to prove an expensive omission. For in July 1943, with the Allies newly landed in Sicily and the Italian war effort in a state of collapse, the king was finally persuaded to exercise his constitutional prerogative to dismiss Mussolini, and appoint Marshal Badoglio as prime minister.

The king's last-minute conversion to the cause of constitutional democracy was of no avail, however. For the signing of an armistice with the Allies, on September 8, 1943, brought a swift response from the German armed forces on the scene; and both the king and the Badoglio government were forced to flee Rome and take refuge in Brindisi, in the deep South, which was already under Allied occupation. The democratic parties that were emerging in the liberated zones of Italy were all but unanimous in demanding an end to the monarchy and the adoption of a republican constitution. After much discussion and maneuvering, the decision was reached to hold an institutional referendum after the close of hostilities. This action would permit the Italian people to choose between retention of the monarchy and the creation of a republic. In this referendum, on June 2, 1946, about 12 million Italians voted for the Republic of Italy and about 10 million supported the monarchy. After a half-hearted effort to challenge the results, King Humbert II (in whose favor Victor Emmanuel III had abdicated barely a month before the referendum) left the country and took up residence in Portugal.

The Constitution of the Republic of Italy, drawn up and ratified by an elected Constituent Assembly, established a parliamentary republic with a cabinet responsible to both houses of Parliament. Unlike the pre-1922 Parliament, both the Chamber of Deputies and the Senate were elected by popular vote, the appointive Senate of the *Statuto* being discarded as undemocratic. In place of the king, there was now an indirectly elected president, chosen by a convention to be composed of the members of the two houses of Parliament, plus a certain number of delegates from the newly created regions. The president was to be primarily a ceremonial figure, with executive power being exercised mainly by the prime minister and his cabinet. But the precise delineation and extent of the presidential powers was to be a major constitutional issue in the future. The Constitution also provided for judicial review by a Constitutional Court, for the establishment of a High Council of the Judiciary to act as a watchdog for judicial independence, and for the creation of semiautonomous regions to encourage a greater measure of local self-government within the framework of a unitary state. There were some provisions for direct democracy, in the form of the initiative and the referendum. And finally, there was a long recitation of basic rights—civil, procedural, political, economic, and social—in Part I of the new document.

The chief criticisms directed against the Constitution of 1948 have focused in part on the abnormally long list of social and economic rights which the Italian government would inevitably fail to enforce. Statements of principle—such impossible promises as, "Those of capacity and merit, even if without means, have the right to attain the highest grades of study"[20]—could only lead to disillusionment and cynicism among the people. As Calamandrei tartly put it, "in order to compensate the forces of the Left for a revolution which had not been achieved, the forces of the Right did not oppose including in the Constitution a *promised* Revolution."[21] Also decried was the inclusion of the Lateran pacts under Article 7, (that is, the Concordat and the other accords concluded in 1929 between Fascist Italy and the Vatican), as part of the Constitution, subject to modification only by mutual consent of the two signatory parties.

---

[20] Excerpt from Article 34 of the Italian Constitution.
[21] Piero Calamandrei, *Scritti e discorsi politici*, Vol. II (Firenze: La Nuova Italia, 1966), p. 471.

But a more serious flaw in the Constitution has simply resulted from the failure to enact some of its key provisions with dispatch. It took seven years to set up the Constitutional Court and over two decades to move decisively in the direction of establishing the so-called ordinary regions. The referendum and the initiative are still in the process of being introduced. And many provisions of the criminal code of Fascist Italy have never been repealed, despite their dubious constitutionality, although the police often fail to invoke them and the Constitutional Court has, over the years, declared a number of these provisions to be null and void. As the dominant party in Italy, the Christian Democrats (who had an absolute majority in Parliament from 1948 to 1953) are largely to blame for this negligence in the enforcement of explicit provisions of the Constitution, a delay which has given the Italian Communist party the opportunity to pose as guardian of the Constitution.

A basic element of any constitution—even if it is not actually included in the core document—is the electoral law that defines suffrage and delineates the system of representation. For a nation's decision regarding which new groups are to be admitted to the electorate and when, has a great deal of bearing on the question of legitimacy. As Lipset notes, when a political system is unduly slow in granting new strata of the population some access to the decision-making process, that system will find it extremely difficult to retain the loyalty of the groups it frustrates and excludes.[22]

In Italy, the suffrage requirements were extremely restrictive during and after the process of unification; in 1880, out of a population of 28 million, only about 500,000 were eligible to vote. Most Italian adults were barred from the polls by taxpaying and educational qualifications. Small wonder that many Italian peasants and industrial workers felt little sense of identification with a political system so impervious to pressure from the masses.

The first electoral reform, sponsored by Premier Depretis in 1882, gave about 7 percent of the population the right to vote by cutting in half the taxpaying requirement, reducing the educational qualification to mere literacy, and lowering the minimum voting age from twenty-five to twenty-one. The net effect was to enfranchise the lower middle class and the more skilled and educated artisans, thus opening up the possibility that a working-class political party would emerge.

[22] Seymour Martin Lipset, *Political Man: The Social Bases of Politics* (New York: Doubleday, 1960), pp. 78–80.

The next extension of the franchise, promoted by Premier Giolitti in 1912, gave the right to vote to all males who were over age thirty or who had served in the armed forces. This expanded the electorate to 23.2 percent of the population and permitted the entry of the masses into politics.

Finally in 1919, only three years before the March on Rome, universal manhood suffrage was established. In 1946, after the fall of Fascism, women were admitted to the polls for the first time. Within less than a century, and with the sole interruption of a twenty-year dictatorship, a conservative and rather oligarchic constitutional monarchy had become a mass democracy.

It may well be suggested that the long delay in granting the franchise to industrial workers and peasants, followed by the precipitate suffrage reforms of 1912 and 1919, did a great deal to disrupt and weaken democratic institutions. For suddenly and without adequate preparation, great masses of new voters became part of the system. On the one hand, the excessive delay in attacking the problem of participation probably retarded progress in establishing the legitimacy of the regime among Italian workers, and may well have contributed to the rise of extremist tendencies in the ranks of Italian socialism. But on the other hand, as Lipson points out, excessively hasty extension of the suffrage can make it impossible for the established parties to adapt to and absorb the new voters, as did the British parties after the Reform Acts of 1867 and 1884.[23] In Italy, the established parties had virtually no extraparliamentary organization, and the task of absorption proved to be simply insuperable. Thus, the electoral reforms of 1912 and 1919 resulted in the spectacular rise of two massive political movements—Socialism and Christian Democracy—which had hitherto boasted little or no strength in Parliament.

Sartori suggests that the extreme pluralism of the Italian party system—with its numerous parties, its powerful extremist parties nurtured by a strong centrifugal tendency inherent in the system, and the wide distance separating the Right and Left extremes of the political spectrum—may be attributed partly to the fact that proportional representation and universal suffrage were both grafted onto the party system when it was still "atomized" (that is, when the parties were "mostly a facade covering loose and shifting coalitions of notables"[24]). In fact, in the years imme-

---

[23] Leslie Lipson, "The Two-Party System in British Politics," *American Political Science Review*, Vol. 47, No. 2 (June 1953), 337–358.

[24] Giovanni Sartori, "European Political Parties: The Case of Polarized Pluralism," in La Palombara and Weiner, eds., pp. 137–176, especially pp. 167–168.

diately following unification, Italy had a rather peculiar kind of party system. With a very restricted electorate, parties were mere parliamentary factions consisting of "Liberal" local notables, each with his own personal clientele in his home constituency. Some of these Liberal groupings were designated as belonging to the Right (especially those elements connected with landed property), some as belonging to the Left (especially commercial interests and professional men); but the difference between rightist and leftist positions was often more apparent than real.

In 1876, the Left came to power under Prime Minister Agostino Depretis. Depretis was credited by many writers with originating the practice of *trasformismo*, of building a parliamentary majority based on special favors for legislators who agreed to support the government, rigging elections to insure the victory of the government's legislative henchmen, and carefully cultivating local notables and their clienteles. This practice prevented the crystallization of an organized opposition, since many of the ablest potential opposition leaders were simply co-opted into the government coalition.

With the election law of 1882 and the beginnings of industrialization, new parties, characterized by more sharply delineated policy postures and ideological commitments, began to appear. The Radicals (a progressive democratic party appealing to the lower middle class) were formed as early as 1878; the Mazzinian Republicans were willing, by the 1890s, to seek electoral support as an organized political party within the system; and in 1892 the Italian Socialist party was founded. All these groupings operated at a considerable disadvantage because the suffrage was still narrowly restricted.

With the vast extensions of the suffrage in 1912 and 1919, the Socialists became the largest party in Italy. At the same time, devout Catholics who had abstained from participating in national politics throughout the last decades of the nineteenth century began—with tacit papal approval—to play a more active role. After helping proclerical Liberal candidates in 1904 (and, on a much broader scale, in 1913), Catholics formed a full-fledged political party of their own at the close of World War I: the Italian Popular party, led by Don Sturzo. Socialism and political Catholicism thus emerged as the two dominant political forces in the post-World War I prospectus. Meanwhile, the Republicans and the Radicals benefited rather little from the extension of the suffrage and remained virtual splinter parties.

The new Italian mass parties had powerful extraparliamentary party organizations at the national and provincial levels, thus contrasting sharply with the loose coalitions of Liberal notables. But they shared one distinctive characteristic in common with the Liberals: an intense factionalism, which often made it extremely difficult for a party to act as a cohesive unit. The internecine conflict within Italian parties has made almost every party congress a dramatic confrontation of warring tendencies and has constantly posed the threat of schism. It was such a schism in the Italian Socialist party in 1921 that led to the formation of the Italian Communist party (see Chapter Five).

The rise of the Fascist party after World War I represented, to a considerable degree, a middle-class backlash against the long-delayed and suddenly consummated entry of the masses into national politics. Unlike the British Conservatives, who had promptly appealed to the newly enfranchised workers after the passage of the Reform Act of 1867, the Italian Liberals lacked either the time or the inclination to absorb the new voters. Only Prime Minister Giolitti, who had been responsible for the 1912 electoral law and who had attempted to induce the Socialists to enter his cabinet coalition, made some efforts in this direction. Lacking the flexibility of their British counterparts, the Italian middle classes reacted with fear and outrage to the rise of disciplined mass parties like the Socialists, and therefore showed considerable tolerance for the violent repressive methods employed by the Fascist action squads. In just a few years, an armed minority, financed by Liberal industrialists and large landowners and supported by the police, reduced the Socialists to complete impotence and set the stage for Mussolini's march on Rome. During this period, the two mass parties were too torn by internal factional conflict to join forces against the Fascist threat. The tenuous Catholic-Socialist alliance of the early 1960s (the so-called opening to the Left) is in part an effort to avoid a recurrence of the extremist upsurge that overpowered the nation in 1919–1922.

It is interesting to note that, after the fall of the Fascist regime, the pre-1922 parties emerged from their years of exile and resumed their activities as if Fascism had been only a momentary interruption of an established routine. The Liberals reformed their much-diminished ranks (at first representing themselves to the voters as the National Democratic Union), as did the tiny Republican party. The Christian Democratic party inherited the tradition, cadres, and electorate of the old Popular party of 1919–1922. Because of its role in the underground movement and the Resistance, the Communist party loomed as the leading force on the Left wing of the political spectrum, while the Socialist party was soon engaged in its all-too-familiar internal factional conflicts. Even the Fascist party was revived in the guise of the Italian Social Movement. The only major newcomer to the political scene was the Italian Monarchist party, which eventually declined to the status of a splinter movement.

But what exists today is more than a mere reproduction of the pre-1922 party system. For one thing, there has been considerable alteration in the respective strength of the various parties within the system. And secondly, *all* Italian parties today are centralized and disciplined, and maintain cohesive ranks in Parliament. Bitter factional conflict continues, but within certain clearly understood limits: violations of party discipline can, and frequently do, lead to expulsion or to a party split. So the Italian party system has acquired some modern organizational features, has become, in fact, more modern than the French. But at the same time certain traditional political practices of the nineteenth and early twentieth centuries survive, albeit in a somewhat altered form. We shall discuss these practices at a later point in this work.

ITALIAN INDUSTRIAL GROWTH

We have already seen that the long centuries of foreign occupation and political fragmentation had the effect of retarding the development and growth of the Italian economy. As in the case of Germany, the creation of an expanded nationwide market was a prerequisite for large-scale economic progress. Considering the political handicaps compounded by such grave economic shortcomings as the lack of adequate natural resources and the existence of a chronically underdeveloped Southern agriculture, we can readily understand Italian economic backwardness when unification was finally achieved. At a time (1861) when Britain was producing about 3,890,000 tons of pig iron, Italy's output was a mere 26,551 tons.[25]

During the first half-century after the birth of the Kingdom of Italy, progress toward industrialization was often painfully slow. In addition to such obstacles as a lack of adequate public facilities (roads, schools, aqueducts, and so on) and a serious shortage of domestic and foreign capital, there was also the fact that the

[25] Shepard B. Clough, *The Economic History of Modern Italy* (New York: Columbia University Press, 1964), p. 82.

Italian government emphasized defense spending and the pursuit of dubious colonial objectives in Libya and East Africa. These adventurous policies tended to absorb large quantities of savings, which might have been employed to accumulate industrial capital. Clarifying this point further, we might observe how the keenly felt need to create a sense of national identity and resolve the problem of national integration seems to have been a major factor in slowing down economic growth. Finally, the annexation of the South by the Kingdom of Italy, and the forced marriage between the two economies, swept away the tariff barriers that had protected the fragile Southern cottage industries against Northern and foreign competition, and increased the already significant North-South gap.

However, from the late 1890s to the outbreak of World War I, the Italian economy began to develop at an accelerated rate of progress. Rapid economic expansion made Northern Italy one of Europe's major industrial regions, with mushrooming hydroelectric facilities as the prime sources of power to fuel Italian growth. To be sure, the problems of the South persisted. Low Southern living standards held down domestic consumption and restricted the potential market for Italian industrial products. Italy still lagged far behind the established industrial nations of Western and Central Europe—for example, in 1913–1914, Italy produced 900,000 tons of steel as compared to 14 million produced by Germany, 6.5 million turned out by Britain, and 3.5 million issuing from French steel mills.[26]

With the end of World War I, Italy entered upon a period of severe economic crisis that helped to pave the way for the advent of Fascism to power. But the rigorously deflationary policies followed by the Fascist regime made for a rather sluggish, stagnant economy, and eventually the government was compelled to take over the debts and stock holdings of a number of "sick" industries in order to prevent economic collapse. The economic depression of the early 1930s, from which Italy recovered only in part, and the policy of autarky (economic self-sufficiency) introduced by the Fascist dictatorship added to the plight of the hard-pressed Italian consumer.

The ultimate lunacy of Italian entry into World War II resulted in the destruction of about one-third of the national wealth, including 90 percent of Italy's trucks, 34 percent of its steel capacity, and 50 percent of its freight cars. In 1945, industrial output

[26] Rosario Romeo, *Breve storia della grande industria in Italia* (3d ed.; Bologna: Cappelli, 1967), pp. 113–114.

was only one-fourth that of the 1938 levels.[27] Truly, the drive for empire seemed to have led to an irrevocable economic disaster for a nation that had never, even in its most prosperous years, fully attained Western European living standards.

Yet, after an arduous period of postwar reconstruction, Italy has managed to bring about that economic take-off generally described as the economic miracle. During the decade 1951–1960, per-capita income rose more than it had during the entire ninety-year span from 1861–1950.[28] Sometime between 1951 and 1961, industrial workers came to outnumber peasants in the Italian labor force; and, by 1967, 41.1 percent of the Italian labor force was employed in industry, 34.8 percent in "other activities" (the service sector), and only 24.1 percent in agriculture.[29] The rise of the service sector to second place among the main components of the Italian labor force is almost as significant as the great expansion of industry; for an expanding service sector may often be regarded as an index of transition to a mature modern economy.

Fiat has become the leading automobile corporation in Europe, producing about 1.5 million cars in 1969,[30] and has contracted to build a vast auto plant in the Soviet Union. The Italian steel industry now ranks among the ten largest in the world, and had by 1969 reached an annual production rate of 17.5 million tons.[31] And while industrial giants like Fiat, Pirelli (rubber), Montedison (chemicals), Ignis (refrigerators), Finsider (steel), Olivetti (office machines), and ENI (hydrocarburants and petrochemicals) are growing in wealth and power, a number of medium-sized and smaller companies have also been making striking gains. One Italian journalist describes booming industrial towns like Carpi near Modena (Emilia).[32] Carpi was a depressed rural commune at the close of World War II. Its women used to migrate to Vercelli to toil barefooted in the Piedmontese rice fields. Some of those women began to collect scraps of wool and distribute them to their families and friends to be fashioned into sweaters at home. Through industry and ingenuity, these tiny businesses expanded until today many former peasant women are prosperous

---

[27] Clough, pp. 286–288.
[28] Romeo, p. 195.
[29] "The Economic Situation in Figures," *Successo*, Vol. 11, No. 12 (December 1969), international edition, 14.
[30] *La Stampa* (Turin), January 28, 1970.
[31] William Gerber, "Italian Elections, 1968," *Editorial Research Reports*, Vol. 1 (May 8, 1968), 347.
[32] Gigi Ghirotti, *Italia mia benché* (Milano: Comunità, 1963), pp. 125–129.

industrialists. The Italian economic miracle, then, has not been confined to the relatively few big firms that stood out so conspicuously in the early years of the twentieth century.

Perhaps the most striking index of Italian economic progress is the appearance of the kind of novel that expresses the alienation of modern man from industrial society. Luciano Bianciardi, in *La vita agra*, touches on many of the same grievances that used to be expressed, in more vulgarized and clichéd terms, in American popular novels about big-city life and the corporate world. Many of the same familiar characters are found in Bianciardi's work: the prostrate drunk with a fractured skull who is ignored by Milanese passers-by; the ruthless office politician whose weapons are memoranda and behavioral nuances; the Milanese pedestrian who makes the mistake of walking along the street at an excessively slow pace and is jailed for "suspicious actions." And there is that same sense of being on a meaningless treadmill:

> There has been an increase in gross and net national product, in the total and per capita national income, in absolute and relative employment, in the number of cars in circulation and the number of home appliances in operation, in the fees of call girls, in hourly pay, in the price of streetcar tickets and in the total number of streetcar passengers, in the consumption of poultry, in the discount rate, in the average age, the average height, the average infirmity, the average rate of production, and the average hourly speed in the [bicycle] Tour of Italy. . . .
> . . . Whoever does not have a car, will have one; and then we shall provide two cars per family, we shall also give a TV set to each person, two TV sets, two refrigerators, two washing machines, three radio sets, an electric razor, a bathroom scale, a hair dryer, a bidet, and running hot water.
> Everyone will receive these things. As long as everyone works, as long as everybody is ready to tramp about, to kick up a storm, to stamp their feet, to give each other the shaft from morning till night.[33]

We shall discuss the causes of this remarkable economic spurt in Chapter Eight. What should be emphasized here is the danger of allowing oneself to be carried away by the dimensions of the Italian economic miracle. Recent economic progress has narrowed, but certainly not closed, the gap that separates Italy from the rest of Western Europe—for example, in 1901 Italian industrial production was about one-sixth as large as that of Great

---

[33] Luciano Bianciardi, *La vita agra* (Milano: Rizzoli, 1962), p. 176. The actual translation of the word *tafanarsi* is much more explicit than the Nixonian expression employed by this author.

Britain; in 1951–1961, it was about one-third. And in the same period, the relationship of Italian to French industrial production had risen from one-third to two-thirds.[34] Moreover, the Italian industrial economy is still plagued by some grave imbalances: an overconcentration of industry in the Northwest Industrial Triangle (Milan-Turin-Genoa); the continued relative backwardness of the South, whose share of the industrial labor force actually declined from 16 percent to 14 percent in the 1951–1961 period;[35] and the proliferation of myriads of tiny, uneconomic, marginal enterprises in both the industrial and the service sectors of the Italian economy. There appears to be a kind of polarization in the industrial sphere between the big efficient producers, on the one hand, and a host of small and technologically backward entrepreneurs (employing less than fifty workers), on the other.

Perhaps even more alarming are certain persisting social imbalances. Social services have not kept pace with industrial growth. Overcrowded schools, universities, and hospitals; unbridled speculation in urban land development, while Italian cities maintain a ridiculously small acreage of parks and green belts; a severe shortage of low-cost housing, while thousands of luxury apartments remain empty, lacking tenants who are able to afford them; a complex, bewildering and wasteful hodgepodge of overlapping social insurance services—these are only a few of the grievances that contributed to the strike wave of 1969.

Now, with the advent of large-scale industrialization, Italy is faced with a crisis of distribution accompanied by rising expectations. Many Italian workers are all too aware of the fact that the economic miracle was rendered possible partly by low wage rates, and are now demanding a bigger share of the pie.

In fact, to a certain degree advances in living standards have helped to trigger discontent. Granted, there has been a doubling of per-capita income in the past twenty years; but the largest share of the increase in real wages has been absorbed by the expansion of private consumption, while the public services languish. Also, while consumption by private individuals has increased, stimuli to further consumption have multiplied still faster.

> To the worker it almost appears as if whatever is given to him with one hand is taken away by the other. And while for the worker of a certain age bracket the improvement of the tenor of life always appears to be a conquest, for the twenty-year-old

---

[34] Compagna, p. 42.
[35] Calogero Muscarà, *La geografia dello sviluppo* (Milano: Comunità, 1967), p. 101.

workers it tends to be something they have discounted in advance. The car, some household appliances, a couple of Sunday outings, and the wage increase has already evaporated. There remain the longer periods [it takes] to reach the place of employment, the problem of housing, the insufficient social services, etc. And there remains the fact that the relationships of production, and the working conditions, have remained substantially unchanged and heavily affect relationships.[36]

We should exercise due caution in our expectations for the future of Italy's burgeoning industrial society. Prosperity is by no means assured for all time. The boom of the late 1950s and early 1960s was interrupted by the recession of 1963–1965, and the pace of recovery has been somewhat on the slow side. Also, while the exodus from the agricultural sector continues, industry has been expanding its productive capacity, but has not been expanding its labor force to a sufficient degree to absorb the influx from the countryside. As a matter of fact, the drive toward technological excellence in the Northwest includes more and more reliance on labor-saving machinery. As a result, there seems to be emerging a dangerously large pool of unskilled workers in industrial areas like Milan.[37] This development casts considerable doubt on the Lutz thesis that Southern emigration to the North can be counted on to move Italy a long way toward the resolution of the South's problem of surplus labor.[38] Instead, as others have suggested, it might be wiser to bring industries based on local resources to the Southern worker in his native habitat, rather than encourage him to abandon the South in a possibly foredoomed search for a hypothetical job.

AGRICULTURE: THE RURAL EXODUS

As we have already noted, Italy was only recently a predominantly agricultural country. Even today, agriculture plays a bigger role in the economy of Italy than in that of any other Common Market country. In fact, the 1967 figures show Italy topping the European Economic Community members in the percentage of her labor force employed in agriculture (24.1 percent). France,

[36] Gian Lupo Osti, "Sviluppo civile e società industriale," *Il Mulino*, Vol. XVIII, No. 195 (January 1969), 29.
[37] "Milan's Dual Economy," *The Economist*, Vol. 231, No. 6564 (June 14, 1969), 78.
[38] Vera Lutz, *Italy: A Study in Economic Development* (London: Oxford University Press, 1962), pp. 144–152.

the nearest competitor, has only 16.6 percent of her labor force employed in agriculture.[39]

The Italian agricultural picture is far more heterogeneous than that of France. The principal categories of land tenure systems include: the small landowning farmers who inhabit the foothills of the Alps and of the Northern Apennines; the large commercial farmers of the Po Valley, employing sizable numbers of farm laborers (*braccianti*) on a wage basis; the classic sharecropping arrangements (*mezzadria*) in Central Italy—Tuscany, Emilia, and the Marches; and the structurally fragmented agriculture of Southern Italy. In the South, "the peasant is almost always what is called a mixed figure—small proprietor, tenant, sharecropper, wage earner."[40] Many farm laborers in the South are small farmers, who supplement their meager profits by working simultaneously for others. Finally, types of cultivation in the South are more varied than in the other regions: there is the intensive commercial agriculture of the citrus-growing coastal plains; the small marginal subsistence farms of the Southern Apennines; and the extensive form of agriculture of the more barren inland regions. This extensive type of cultivation is referred to by the term *latifondo*. A *latifondo* may be a large estate farmed as a single unit, or may be divided into a number of tiny plots worked by subsistence farmers, tenants, or farm laborers; its common denominator is a rather backward extensive agriculture based primarily on cereal crops.

One of the chief defects of the Italian agricultural system has been the existence of an excessively large labor force in the agricultural sector of the economy, given the shortage of cultivable land and the predominantly hilly and mountainous terrain. Particularly in the South, hunger for land has given vent to the occupation of large estates by peasant squatters. In attacking this and other problems of Italian agriculture, the government has relied on such programs as the land reform, the Fund for the South, and more recently, the Green Plan. These programs will be discussed further in Chapter Eight. Quite briefly, they rely on a combination of various approaches: the expropriation and redistribution of land belonging to large extensively cultivated estates; investments in land improvement, irrigation, and other forms of agricultural pump-priming; and easier credit for Italian farmers.

---

[39] "The Economic Situation in Figures," 14.
[40] Sidney G. Tarrow, *Peasant Communism in Southern Italy* (New Haven, Conn.: Yale University Press, 1967), quote from Vera Lutz on p. 34; see also Tarrow, pp. 30–34, 52–54.

If this problem of too many people on too little land seems somewhat closer to solution today, the real reason has been, not the combination of government programs cited above, but the great exodus from the land that took place after 1954. The same phenomenon occurred in France, although the movement has assumed much more striking dimensions in Italy. While in France about one-fourth of the farm population left the land between 1954 and 1962, about one-half of the Italian peasantry abandoned the countryside between 1954 and 1969.[41] Unfortunately, this movement of population does not entirely serve the long-term interests of Italian agriculture. In far too many instances, farms simply are abandoned instead of being consolidated and rationalized. Also, the departure of young, vigorous workers leaves too many farms in the care of elderly, and therefore less efficient, cultivators.

At present, there are about 4 million peasants left in Italy— 21 percent of the total labor force as compared to 41 percent in 1951.[42] Those who remain on the farms are encountering serious difficulties in finding wives; for the revulsion against the rural way of life has reached a point where women in rural areas are increasingly reluctant to marry peasants (even peasant proprietors) and settle for a life of privation.[43]

There has been some fear that if the exodus continues a labor shortage may develop in agriculture. This prospect leads to the inevitable question: Should something perhaps be done to reverse the flood of migration to already congested urban areas? A terrible economic crisis may be in the offing. Here Italy's problem is different only in degree from that faced by other industrial countries: The perhaps inevitable rural exodus and its possible consequences represent a universal dilemma.

URBANIZATION AND MIGRATION: "NEW YORK IS IN ITALY, AT MILAN"[44]

Along with our consideration of the rural exodus, we must examine the closely related problems of urbanization and migration. Until World War II, Italy was primarily an agricultural nation, as

[41] *La Stampa* (Turin), June 21, 1969. On France, see Lowell G. Noonan, *France: The Politics of Continuity in Change* (New York: Holt, Rinehart and Winston, 1970), p. 45.
[42] *La Stampa* (Turin), June 21, 1969.
[43] Achille Ardigò, *Emancipazione femminile e urbanesimo* (Brescia: Morcelliana, 1964), pp. 19-20.
[44] Quote is taken from Ghirotti, p. 56.

we have seen. Even in those areas which the census designated as urban, the population might well be made up mostly of peasants: the agro-towns of Southern Italy, with populations of up to 25,000, were cases in point. There were a goodly number of sizable cities, to be sure, but the urban-industrial component had not yet come to dominate the Italian economic and demographic scene.

With a sluggishly expanding economy and an excessively heavy population pressure on the land, Italy prior to World War II relied primarily on emigration as a safety valve for internal unrest. Because the industrial cities of the North simply could not absorb the growing population of unemployed and underemployed peasants, large numbers of Italians bade farewell to their homeland and emigrated to other parts of the world. World War I interrupted these migratory currents. Then, a brief postwar migratory revival was soon stopped by restrictive immigration laws adopted by many host countries, and by the opposition of the Fascist regime to any large-scale emigration.

Fascist Italy also took a stand against any exodus from the countryside to the larger towns. In fact, legislation was promulgated in 1931 and 1939 forbidding rural workers to leave the land to settle in provincial capitals or cities "of noteworthy industrial importance," unless they were already assured of a job. This policy represented a major barrier to internal migration, although many peasants managed somehow to move to the cities in clandestine defiance of the law. It was not until February 10, 1961, long after the fall of the Fascist state, that the Italian Parliament, pursuant to an earlier decision of the Constitutional Court, passed legislation repealing these Fascist laws.

The Fascist regime compensated in part for its stand against emigration and internal migration by attempting to promote colonization of the overseas empire. Unfortunately, however, Libya and Ethiopia offered very limited possibilities for Italian settlers. Then, of course, World War II and its aftermath liquidated the Italian colonial empire, resulting in the forced abandonment of the abortive colonization scheme.

With the end of World War II, Italy seemed once again to be face to face with the migration dilemma. Emigration outlets were few and insufficient to meet Italian needs. In the immediate postwar period, the Italian home picture looked terribly dreary: a permanent mass of 2 million unemployed; large numbers of landless underemployed peasants; and abysmally low living standards as compared to Northern Europe.

Two developments permitted a breaking of this impasse. One

was the industrial boom of the 1950s. The second was Italian entry into the Common Market, which permitted large numbers of Italian workers to cross the frontiers legally in search of work. Two complementary migratory flows thus developed: emigration to the Common Market countries and to Great Britain and Switzerland, on the one hand; migration to Rome and to the Northwest Industrial Triangle, on the other. In the 1954–1964 period, net emigration from Italy was 1,343,000. And in the decade 1951–1961, about 2 million people left the South and other depressed areas, either to migrate to other parts of Italy or to emigrate abroad.[45]

The drama of the great emigrations of 1890–1910 repeated itself. Once again the "humble masses" embarked on a journey to opportunity. Every morning in the central railway terminal in Milan, the overnight trains from the South would arrive, their second-class compartments loaded with Sicilians and Apulians making the transition from the nineteenth to the twentieth century in only twenty-four hours. To be sure, an overnight ride in an admittedly uncomfortable train was more palatable than a dreadful journey of weeks in the steerage of a transatlantic ship.

Of course, these migratory currents did have political effects (see Chapter Five). A number of problems arose because of internal migration. First, there was a terrific strain on the public services, schools, and housing facilities of Rome, Milan, Turin, and their satellite towns. When we consider that the population of Turin increased from 700,000 to 1 million in only six years (1958–1964), we get some idea of the frightful congestion that afflicted the Northwest Triangle.[46] Along with this came the inevitable tensions between the native Piedmontese and Lombards, on the one hand, and the Southern newcomers, on the other. Many Southerners had initial difficulties in finding lodgings, especially since many local landlords discouraged or actually rejected Southern tenants. The arrival of so many displaced insecure newcomers led to an increase in crime, with the natural result of further anti-Southern bias.

As time went on, however, these early difficulties were alleviated. As Alberoni and Baglioni show, many of the immigrants had previously rejected their rural way of life and accepted urban values (learned through television) before they ever left their na-

---

[45] Gian Franco Ciaurro, "Movimenti migratori e scelte politiche," in Mattei Dogan and Orazio Maria Petracca, *Partiti politici e scelte sociali in Italia* (Milano: Comunità, 1968), pp. 283–284, 299.

[46] Robert C. Fried, "Urbanization and Italian Politics," *The Journal of Politics*. Vol. 29, No. 3 (August 1967), 519.

tive villages. They had thus undergone a sort of "anticipatory socialization."[47] This interpretation may help to explain the immigrants' eventual willingness to adopt big-city ways, to accept the urban outlook on family and friendship relations, and to intermarry with Northerners after perhaps a generation had elapsed. In the Northwest Triangle, the melting-pot has been relatively successful over the long run.

It is now generally agreed that Southern immigration has been a boon to the Northern economy. But what of the effect on the South itself? Here again we have a certain amount of controversy. Lutz believes that substantial migration from the South should help to spur eventual economic growth there by relieving population pressure.[48] On the other hand, Gallino attacks the unbalanced migratory trend as stripping the South of its labor reserves (a potential asset to the Southern economy) for the benefit of the Northern industrial areas. Gallino is also concerned about the undesirable effects of overdevelopment on the Northwest Triangle: urban sprawl, pollution, traffic congestion, and so on.[49]

The progress of Italian urbanization since World War II has been truly staggering. In 1964, there were 36 Italian cities with a population of over 100,000, and they contained 26.3 percent of the total population of Italy. Four Italian cities—Milan, Turin, Rome, and Naples—had over a million inhabitants apiece; their combined population was 12.3 percent of the Italian total.[50] With the exception of Naples, these metropolitan centers attracted migrants from all parts of Italy. The smaller Italian cities of 100,000–1,000,000 population tended to be the objectives mostly of intraregional migration. Thus, Florence attracted mostly Tuscans, Bologna mostly Emilians, and so on.

Italy is a highly urbanized country by any standards. However, its numerous cities represent a great variety of urban situations, ranging from dynamic expansion to utter decadence. Thus, some thriving industrial centers—Ravenna and Ferrara in the North, Brindisi and Salerno in the South—are experiencing unprecedented growth, whereas such ancient cities as Perugia, bypassed by the rail and road links between Florence and Rome,

[47] Francesco Alberoni and Guido Baglioni, *L'integrazione dell' immigrato nella società industriale* (Bologna: Il Mulino, 1965), pp. 9–12, 104–105, 112–114, 124–132.

[48] Lutz, pp. 144–152.

[49] Luciano Gallino, *Indagini di sociologia economica* (Milano: Comunità, 1962), pp. 363–376.

[50] Francesco Compagna, *La politica della città* (Bari: Laterza, 1967), pp. 38–39.

are decaying. In the South, numerous provincial capitals (Campobasso, for example) are little more than administrative centers, with a rather static economy; and many Southern towns of 15,000–25,000 are only glorified dormitories for the peasants who work in the surrounding countryside.

Even the four metropolitan giants differ widely. Turin is the center of the automobile industry and related enterprises. Milan is a major industrial city and the commercial, financial, and banking heart of the North. Turin and, to an even greater degree, Milan are surrounded by a growing belt of satellite communities and are the hubs of dense networks of commuter railways. They have not yet, however, reached the stage attained by American metropolitan zones: Their suburban areas are still predominantly industrial rather than residential. On the other hand, Rome has relatively little industry (apart from construction), and is primarily an administrative and tourist city. Many migrants come to Rome seeking security in the bureaucracy or fame and fortune in the motion picture industry. All too often, they are disappointed and are forced to fall back on precarious casual employment. Finally, Naples is essentially a decaying city. Only 30 percent of its population is actually employed; as many as 80,000 members of its labor force live a hand-to-mouth existence in such marginal service occupations as errand boy, repairman, peddler, usurer.[51]

Students of French society often decry the massively dominant presence of Paris, which so overshadows and drains the other cities of France. In Italy, too, there is a similar problem, though of a somewhat less acute nature: the problem of the two capitals. To an ever-increasing extent, Rome and Milan overshadow all other Italian cities. Rome, of course, is the political and bureaucratic capital; Milan is the main decision-making center for finance and industry. Of the fifty largest Italian corporations, seventeen have their central office in Milan, eight in Rome, seven in Genoa, six in Turin. Most large Southern industrial enterprises are controlled from Rome; and, for that matter, there seems to be a tendency for some Northern industries to move their headquarters to the capital. Compared with Rome and Milan, Turin ranks a poor third, Genoa is rapidly falling behind, and the Southern cities are not even in the running. Above all, Rome and Milan have far more than their share of research facilities, higher educational centers, museums, theaters, medical centers, and similar modern services that are so attractive to intellectuals and executives.[52]

[51] Alberto Acquarone, *Grandi città e aree metropolitane in Italia* (Bologna: Zanichelli, 1961), pp. 299, 301–302.
[52] Compagna, *La politica . . .* , pp. 217–226.

One last word might be said about urban growth. It has been disorderly, unplanned, chaotic, and has created truly critical situations in the great metropolitan centers. As recently as 1965, the Southern influx into Milan resulted in an urban population with an illiteracy rate of 20 percent—hardly what one would expect in the core city of the Italian miracle.[53] Along with the strains arising from large-scale immigration, the big metropolitan centers have indulged in an orgy of housing speculation, with ugly apartment buildings springing up in their environs. Most real-estate development has focused on luxury apartments, and speculation and corruption have accompanied this heedless search for profits. So, while urbanization has hastened the pace of national integration, there has been a countervailing effect: the creation of massive imbalances that pose a long-range threat to Italian prosperity and social stability.

SOCIAL STRATIFICATION AND SOCIAL MOBILITY

It is practically impossible to summarize the Italian system of social stratification accurately in a few pages. For regional variations do a great deal to complicate the picture. We shall try to qualify our findings, keeping inaccuracies and gross oversimplifications to a minimum.

Ethnic and religious minorities play a minuscule role in Italian society and politics. Protestants and Jews together comprise less than 1 percent of the population. The ethnic minority communities—the Germans in Bolzano Province, the Slovenians along the Yugoslav frontier, and the French in Val d'Aosta—contribute only to the presence in the Italian Parliament of two splinter parties: the Union Valdôtaine and the Südtyroler Volkspartei (SVP). However, among Catholics there *is* a politically relevant cleavage between devout Catholics and anticlericals.

The area of class structure is a more tangled and complex field, rendered rather treacherous by continuing flux. In 1962, there were in Italy almost 8 million Italians employed in industry, about 6.4 million in the tertiary or service sector, and 5.4 million in agriculture.[54] In 1969, the Mansholt Report stated that there were only about 4 million Italians employed in agriculture. We may assume that the industrial and service sectors have expanded

---

[53] Fried, "Urbanization . . . ," 529.
[54] Giuseppe Mammarella, *Italy after Fascism* (rev. ed.; Notre Dame, Ind.: University of Notre Dame Press, 1966), p. 346.

accordingly.[55] Pending more recent census data, it is hazardous to attempt to divide the above groupings into specific occupational and class categories, although Dogan *does* attempt some "conjectural estimates: to be interpreted as a scale of magnitude," apparently including nonworking relatives in each of his categories.[56] He concludes that about one-third of Italian voters were industrial workers and another one-third belonged to the urban middle class in the elections of 1958. His figures for the agricultural electorate are, in all likelihood, out of date because of the rural exodus: his estimate is about 10 million rural voters, approximately one-third of the total.

Like other Southern European countries, Italy is a rigidly stratified society, with serious conflict beween social classes and with a relatively low degree of social mobility (that is, movement from one class to another). Centuries of Spanish rule, the chronic existence during most of Italy's modern history of a large mass of unemployed and underemployed, and the employers' willingness to take advantage of this last condition—these and other factors have deepened the cleavages separating Italy's social classes. The very large number of small firms, many of which are the property of a single small entrepreneur, jealous of his prerogatives and dependent on low wage scales for his profits, tends to accentuate authoritarian relationships between management and labor. The history of Italian class conflict in the late nineteenth and early twentieth centuries is dismal and bloody. The coming to power of the Fascists in 1919–1922 has been widely interpreted as a middle-class counterrevolution against workers and peasants who did not know their place. This class antagonism may have been somewhat alleviated in recent years by economic prosperity and increasing social mobility, but bitter memories are hard to dispel.

What are the means by which social mobility may be achieved? Migration to the Northwest Triangle or to other urban areas has enabled many peasants to acquire the status of industrial workers or service employees; and some, sacrificing living standards for a status symbol, may set themselves up as marginal businessmen by acquiring a pushcart or a tiny shop. Emigration to Northern Europe is another avenue by which upward mobility may be attempted; many Southern migrants leave their families

[55] *La Stampa* (Turin), June 21, 1969.
[56] Mattei Dogan, "Political Cleavage and Social Stratification in France and Italy" in Seymour M. Lipset and Stein Rokkan, eds., *Party Systems and Voter Alignments* (New York: Free Press, 1967), p. 158.

behind and cross the Alps into Germany and Switzerland, taking on the more dirty and dangerous jobs, and saving most of their earnings in order to finance an eventual new start in Italy. And Lopreato tells how emigrants returning from the United States often have saved enough money to buy land and rise to middle-class status.[57]

But education is the surest avenue for the upwardly mobile, although, as elsewhere in Europe, there are serious barriers to upward mobility. When Italy was mainly an agricultural country, the legal requirement was five years of compulsory schooling for all children; but actually many elementary schools had neither the staff nor the equipment to present the legally prescribed five-year program. Growing urbanization and industrialization are alleviating the burden on ill-staffed rural schools, but have created at the same time great strains for the hard-pressed local authorities of Rome and the Northwest Triangle.

Recently, the government has pushed legislation through Parliament to enhance the effectiveness of the school system in encouraging poor but talented individuals. The compulsory span of school attendance has been raised to eight years, so that a youth decides at the age of fourteen, rather than eleven, whether he wishes to go on to higher education. And the so-called general lower secondary school has been set up to provide a common junior high school experience for all children between the ages of eleven and fourteen. Also, upon graduating from the general lower secondary school, one can choose to attend a technical institute instead of a classical high school (*liceo*), without thereby foreclosing his chances of being admitted to a university.

However, opportunities for upward mobility are still rather restricted. For one thing, there are many violations of the revised school attendance laws, especially since students in the public schools are expected to buy their own textbooks and provide for their own transportation. More important, though, is the inadequacy of university facilities. There are simply not enough universities to accommodate the growing student body, while existing universities are fearfully overcrowded, and frequently professors regard their academic career as a sideline to more profitable professional activities outside the university. Then, too, according to one recent estimate, only 6.5 percent of the graduates of the elementary schools manage to enter the universities; and of those who enter, less than 15 percent come from working-class or peas-

[57] Joseph Lopreato, *Peasants No More: Social Class and Social Change in an Underdeveloped Society* (San Francisco: Chandler, 1967), pp. 175–179.

ant homes, whereas slightly over 50 percent are the children of businessmen, professional men, and white-collar workers.[58] Scholarships and other financial aids are deficient both in scope and amount, despite the fact that most universities are located in large cities, so that many students commute from their homes. In short, the problem is not much different from the one other Western European countries confront: higher education is not geared to turn out, in sufficient number, the necessary cadres for an expanding economy and an increasingly modern society. The students, having sensed the archaic, semifeudal, neglected character of the higher educational structure, have reacted with violence and disruption.

CONCLUSIONS

Like France, Italy has been involved in a series of far-reaching changes during the nineteenth and twentieth centuries. In both countries, moreover, there is a heritage of class and religious conflict, which has contributed to the nature of their multiparty systems characterized by the presence of very substantial extremist components. And in both France and Italy, the excesses accompanying revolutionary change (the French Revolution of 1789, the *Risorgimento*) and the late admission of the working class to full political and social citizenship rights contributed to a crisis of legitimacy from which neither the French nor the Italian political system has ever fully recovered. The aftereffects of this crisis are still visible in the extreme pluralism of the Italian party system, in the domination of French and Italian parties over their colonized pressure groups, and in the abstract, ideological nature of political dialogue. In both societies, it should be added, historical memories have tended to divide rather than unite. For instance, the church and the nation-building middle class remained openly "opposed to each other during the crucial phases of educational development and mass mobilization."[59]

But in one respect the French political system has been infinitely more fortunate. Despite its socially divisive nature, the French Revolution *did* create a strong sense of French nationality. However, in Italy, as we have noted, national integration was not achieved until the mid-twentieth century, and the enormous effort

---

[58] "Una scuola da rifiutare," *Note di cultura*, Vol. V (April 1968), 129–131.
[59] Seymour M. Lipset and Stein Rokkan, "Cleavage Structures, Party Systems, and Voter Alignments," in Lipset and Rokkan, eds., p. 49.

needed to create a sense of national identity served to delay any meaningful attack on Italy's many complex social and economic problems.

Thus, political conditions in Italy have been far less favorable for the development and survival of a modern democratic system than has been the case in France. Yet, the Italian pattern of political development has not been notably less successful than the French. We must, of course, concede that Italy fell victim to a Fascist bid for power, whereas a stronger democratic tradition helped the French to repulse attempted ultrarightist seizures of power at the time of the Dreyfus Affair and later during the Algerian War. On the other hand, the republican regime established in Italy by the Constitution of 1948 seems to offer far fewer opportunities for executive abuses than does the "rationalized parliamentarism" of the French Fifth Republic.[60] Remarkably, in view of the greater internal pressures to which they were subjected, Italian parliamentary institutions since 1948 have been more stable than the French. By contrast with the Fifth Republic, Italy is still under her first republican constitution. It might be suggested, then, that the crisis of national integration may well be of secondary importance vis-à-vis the crises of legitimacy, participation, and distribution. Despite her success in achieving early national integration, France is still characterized by social and ideological fragmentation. Even societies like Great Britain, which seemingly settled the integration problem centuries ago, begin once again to encounter disintegrative tendencies (for example, Scottish and Welsh nationalism), when the system fails to afford an adequate sense of participation or a satisfactory distribution of the national product. So national integration may be only a dependent variable.

While some of the more obvious political handicaps faced by the Italian political system have been more or less successfully overcome, continued survival of democratic institutions in Italy depends in large measure on the social and economic health of Italian society. And, in this respect, Italy has always lagged well behind France. The possible implications for the future of Italian democracy are somewhat disquieting. For Italy remains a fragmented society with regard to class conflict. The crisis of distribution, far from being resolved, has actually beeen inflamed by the economic boom, by the flight from the countryside, and by the migration from the South and other underdeveloped regions to the

[60] Noonan, pp. 50–53.

Northwest Triangle and the capital city. Then, too, as living standards rise and expectations escalate, there is a growing demand for more meaningful popular participation in governmental decision making, in the management of industry, and in other centers of policy making in Italian society. Finally, there is unprecedented impatience with the shoddy character of public services, the backward state of the universities, the schools, and the research institutes, and the persisting social and economic imbalances between regions.

It was in response to these new and outspoken attitudes that a political experiment known as the opening to the Left was finally undertaken in 1962. Some significant innovations resulted: the nationalization of the electric-power industry in 1962; the adoption of the first national economic plan—modeled to some degree after the "indicative" noncoercive French system—in 1965; and the first major steps toward the setting up of regional governments. The *Autostrada del Sole*, a high-speed road connection between Rome and the southern tip of Calabria, hopefully will serve to stimulate both industry and tourism throughout the South. Also, public investments in Southern industrial growth by government corporations have finally provoked Fiat, the largest automobile manufacturer in all of Italy, to commit large investment funds to Southern Italy.

Yet, along with these gains there is the infuriatingly slow pace with which university reform and housing speculation are being handled by the political organs. To some degree, entrenched interests (small businessmen of the service sector, suburban landlords) have been responsible for holding up policy output. Certainly, the habit-ridden bureaucracy has seemed to resist changes in its working standards. In some measure, the pork-barrel proclivities of the political parties make for surrender to regional and group demands at the cost of national progress.

However or wherever blame is allocated, one thing seems certain: the system, in the eyes of many Italians, appears to score low on effectiveness. When effectiveness falters, when social change outdistances political adaptation, legitimacy itself may eventually crumble. If this should happen, and if economic horizons should simultaneously darken, Italian democracy might face an unhappy future. The moral to be drawn from Italian political and social vicissitudes over the past few years would appear to be that neither political nor social development need necessarily follow a path of continuing evolutionary progress: development can be arrested, and can even turn into decay. Among the major causes of such decay would appear to be the kinds of imbalances we have described: a dynamic society as against a cumbersome, archaic polity; an advanced industrial sector as against a multitude of marginal industrial and service enterprises; a flourishing Northwest as against a chronically lagging South; national integration as against residual class conflict.

TWO
ITALIANS IN POLITICS
Political socialization, participation, and recruitment

POLITICAL SOCIALIZATION: PREPARATION FOR CITIZENSHIP

Political socialization is a process by which individuals learn to be part of the body politic by being exposed to and indoctrinated in the political culture that prevails in their society. By "political culture" is meant a complex of politically relevant values, attitudes, and beliefs that are accepted by an entire population. In every political system, rulers make a conscious effort to transmit the dominant political culture to the new generations. Political socialization, then, is the business of any and all governments. When employed for these purposes, political socialization performs the function of maintaining existing patterns. However, political socialization can also be used to change or subvert the dominant political culture. This can be done by a government, a political party, an interest group, or even by a family that seeks to train its children to reject the reigning system of values.

Political socialization is a continuing process. It does not cease when a child completes his formal education, but influences that individual throughout his life, with new messages and new lessons. The actual mode of transmission may be either manifest or latent—that is, an individual may have to learn in school (manifestly) that his country's constitution should be revered, or gradually and informally (latently), he may acquire from friends and neighbors a belief that government should confine itself to maintaining law and order, or he may develop a sense of trust in his fellow-citizens. Usually, however, both the manifest and the latent methods of transmission are employed in the political socialization process.

A variety of different agents may help carry out the process: the family; the school; the peer group; friends; neighbors; the job; the voluntary association; the political party; and the traumatic historical event are but a few leading examples. In view of the fact that many societies do not have a dominant, universally recognized political culture, there is no assurance that every agent of political socialization will transmit the same values and attitudes. When the agents of socialization fail to transmit similar messages, the process is called "discontinuous"—in other words, discontinuous socialization is characterized by serious inconsistencies and conflicts among competing values.

Discontinuity is certainly characteristic of the political socialization process in Italy. For in Italy there exists a fragmented political culture—that is, no single political culture dominates the country; instead, Italy is composed of several mutually antagonistic subcultures. Italians do not agree on basic values or attitudes with regard to their political system. Consequently, the individual Italian citizen is subjected to conflicting socializing tendencies. For example, what he hears from his party leaders may be inconsistent with what he has been taught in school. Such cross-pressures create debilitating confusion in the minds of those who find themselves thus exposed to a chorus of discordant voices. Their response may be political apathy, or outright alienation from the political system. In short, this malfunction of the socialization process may seriously threaten the survival of the Italian political system.

POLITICAL SOCIALIZATION: FAMILY AND PEER GROUP

Italy is a democratic republic, which professes the ideal of popular participation in government. Yet, a number of scholars have suggested that the Italian family—the earliest agent of political socialization—is highly authoritarian in character and therefore likely to transmit undemocratic values and attitudes.

However, the evidence available is by no means conclusive. For example, Banfield describes the "nuclear family" (father, mother, and unmarried children) of Montegrano in Lucania as obsessed with its immediate self-interest, thoroughly dominated by the parents, and in a state of cold war with the surrounding community. Yet, Banfield also shows that the nuclear family is far from being a universal Italian phenomenon. In the Po Delta, near Rovigo, so-called extended families, with intricate ties between their various branches, abound.[1] Another study indicates that, in Tuscany, the sharecropping system of land tenure has placed a premium on having large extended families and has also encouraged cooperation among neighbors.[2]

Other negative findings are similarly subject to qualification. Gabriel Almond and Sidney Verba, coauthors of an important study, *The Civic Culture*, point out the lesser degree of participation in family decision making that is accorded Italian children as compared with their American and British contemporaries. But when young people of higher educational background are compared (that is, Italian university graduates with British university graduates), cross-national differences in participation become relatively insignificant.[3] Then again, the American political scientist Joseph La Palombara refers to the severe physical chastisement which normally doting parents may suddenly and arbitrarily inflict on their rebellious children.[4] But is corporal punishment any more destructive of democratic attitudes than the systematic verbal abuse and public mortification meted out to errant French children in Peyrane?[5]

Moreover, the structure and character of the Italian family seem to be changing in the wake of industrialization, urbanization, and migratory currents. The family is becoming smaller in the Northern industrial cities, with elderly people sometimes living in separate neighborhoods, apart from their grown children. In this respect, it is becoming "nuclear," but in the Western European and American sense. It is a small, self-contained family unit like

[1] Edward C. Banfield, *The Moral Basis of a Backward Society* (New York: Free Press, 1967), pp. 83, 104, 110–111, 142–144.

[2] Sydel F. Silverman, "Agricultural Organization, Social Structure, and Values in Italy: Amoral Familism Reconsidered," *American Anthropologist*, Vol. 70, No. 1 (February 1968), 1–20.

[3] Gabriel A. Almond and Sidney Verba, *The Civic Culture: Political Attitudes and Democracy in Five Nations* (Princeton, N.J.: Princeton University Press, 1963), pp. 330–338.

[4] Joseph La Palombara, "Italy: Fragmentation, Isolation, Alienation," in Lucian W. Pye and Sidney Verba, eds., *Political Culture and Political Development* (Princeton, N.J.: Princeton University Press, 1965), pp. 317–320.

[5] Laurence Wylie, *Village in the Vaucluse* (New York: Harper & Row, 1964), pp. 50–52, 66, 78–88, 96, 331–332.

those found in the most advanced industrial societies. More important, however, the authority of the Italian father is being undermined, for an increasing percentage of wives and teenage children have taken jobs outside the home, and contribute to the family income. Thus, wives and children tend to assert themselves in family discussions more than they ever did in the past.

While the Italian family seems to be growing less authoritarian, it continues to function as an organ of political socialization. A recent study of the socialization of party militants, for instance, found that most of the active party members interviewed came from ideologically oriented, politically active families, and had adopted the same political orientation as their respective families.[6] To be sure, party activists are hardly a representative cross-section of the electorate. Moreover, we have no satisfactory data regarding the influence of the family on actual voting behavior. Italian social scientists tend to distrust survey research methods applied to the Italian context on the ground that respondents all too often may lie about their voting behavior for fear of provoking political reprisal. Nevertheless, there are some impressionistic indications that Italian voters are at least as likely as American voters to pattern their voting behavior after that of their fathers: In region after region, the percentages polled by each Italian party fluctuated very little from election to election.

The influence of the peer group on the socialization process cannot be entirely discounted in Italy. The same study of party militants revealed that friendship groups played a key role in socializing and recruiting Italian political party activists.[7] However, once again, party militants do not constitute a cross-section of the electorate, nor do the six medium-sized towns scrutinized in this study necessarily accurately represent the broader Italian society.

One last piece of evidence dramatizes the limitations of both the family and the peer group as agents of political socialization in Italy. Recent surveys disclose that about 66 percent of Italian voters never discuss politics with anyone. In this regard, Italian voters seem to be far more apathetic than German or British voters. Furthermore, the proportion of politically inarticulate citizens remains remarkably high even among university graduates, of whom 43 percent never discuss politics with their families and 33

---

[6] Antonio Tosi's section on the socialization of the activist in Agopik Manoukian and Franco Olivetti, "L'analisi unidimensionale," in Francesco Alberoni, ed., *L'attivista di partito* (Bologna: Il Mulino, 1967), pp. 189–211. A fifth co-author of this book is Vittorio Capecchi.

[7] Tosi, pp. 216–218. For a critique of Alberoni's volume, see Gianni Statera, "Aspetti della partecipazione politica in Italia: Analisi di una ricerca," *La critica sociologica*, No. 6 (1968), 28–43.

percent never discuss politics with their colleagues or workmates.[8] This raises the intriguing question: How in the world can voting behavior patterns be handed down from fathers to sons—as we have suggested may often be the case—in the absence of any political discussion? Perhaps survey research, despite all its limitations, can furnish an answer.

EDUCATION AND POLITICAL SOCIALIZATION

The educational system also falls considerably short of providing a democratic learning experience. Generally, the atmosphere in an Italian classroom is rigidly authoritarian; obedience and knowing one's proper place are stressed. On the wall of a typical classroom in Rome, a visiting American news correspondent observed a picture of the president of Italy, the first line of the Italian Constitution, and a Christian cross. The religious symbol illustrates a very important feature of Italian public schools: Religious education has been compulsory[9] ever since the Concordat of 1929. Certainly, this religious emphasis constitutes an example of manifest political socialization.

To be sure, contemporary history and civics courses are also taught and should presumably foster loyalty to republican institutions, and to some degree they do. One study reveals that a remarkably high proportion of Italian children believe that Italians have a chance to express their opinions about the way their country is run.[10] In this sense of "expressive efficacy," Italian children actually rank higher than American and British children. But expressive efficacy is already high among ten-year-olds (85 percent), who have not yet entered junior high school, and only rises to 91 percent among sixteen-year-olds. Because of the young age at which expressive efficacy is found, it seems possible that manifest socialization procedures in the schools have not been primarily responsible for this phenomenon.

The structure of the educational system has undergone some degree of democratization in recent years by broadening educational opportunities. At the age of six, every Italian child is required by law to enter a five-year elementary school. The law has

[8] Almond and Verba, p. 116; and Pierpaolo Luzzatto-Fegiz, *Il volto sconosciuto dell' Italia 1956–1965* (2nd series; Milano: Giuffré, 1966), p. 508.
[9] Irving R. Levine, *Main Street, Italy* (New York: Doubleday, 1963), pp. 440–441.
[10] Jack Dennis, Leon Lindberg, Donald McCrone, and Rodney Stiefbold, "Political Socialization to Democratic Orientations in Four Western Systems," *Comparative Political Studies*, Vol. 1, No. 1 (April 1968), 82–84.

been widely evaded in the past, but it is estimated that over 90 percent of Italian children from ages six through ten do in fact attend elementary school at the present time.[11] From elementary school, all children are supposed to go on to the recently created *scuola media unica* (general lower secondary school or, in free translation, "unified junior high school"), which is now compulsory, since the school-leaving age has been raised to fourteen. The new, unified junior high school replaces a two-track system of junior high schools, which used to segregate prospective university students from their less academically inclined, or simply less affluent, brethren. After graduation from junior high school, the student must choose between a classical high school, a scientific high school, a technical institute, a vocational training school, or a teacher training school. Only the classical high school (*liceo classico*) provides access to all university faculties; the other types of high schools, with the sole exception of the vocational school, enable their graduates to gain admission to certain specified university faculties only. The vocational high school provides a terminal educational experience.

In the process of broadening educational opportunities, some progress has been made toward social integration. The junior high school is no longer a middle-class preserve, and entry into the classical senior high school is no longer a vital prerequisite for those who later may wish to study the social sciences or humanities at the university. But there is as yet no unified senior high school: social segregation still occurs at this level. Only about 75 percent of Italian children ages eleven to fourteen actually fulfill their legal obligation to attend junior high school.[12] And the university remains an elitist institution, for the most part: Of 100 individuals who enter primary schools, about 6.4 percent reach the university and only 2.2 percent graduate.[13] It should be stressed, however, that Italy does not stand alone in providing an essentially elitist system of higher education: France and Germany suffer from the same bias. At least Italy does not include the additional screening device set up by the French system, *les Grandes Écoles*—that is, the university-level "great schools" for turning out specialized elites in various fields.

At the university level, we have a rather mixed set of findings

---

[11] Edward R. Tannenbaum, "Education in Italy since Unification," unpublished paper presented at the Conference on Modern Italian History, held November 7–8, 1969, at Columbia University, 27.

[12] Tannenbaum, 27.

[13] Guido Martinotti, "The Positive Marginality: Notes on Italian Students in Periods of Political Mobilization," in Seymour M. Lipset and Philip G. Altbach, eds., *Students in Revolt* (Boston: Houghton Mifflin, 1969), p. 187.

as to the quality and effects of political socialization. On the one hand, Almond and Verba point out that higher education makes for a stronger sense of political competence.[14] On the other hand, the Italian university is authoritarian and impersonal, dominated by a few thousand full professors who often devote only a small portion of their working time to university duties. These "barons" of Italian academic life exercise despotic powers over nontenured faculty, unpaid assistants, and students. They teach entirely by the lecture method, are rarely accessible to students (though a U.S. student might plaintively ask, just how accessible is a Harvard or Yale professor?), and administer brief annual oral exams, in which the highest grades seem to go to those students who are most successful in memorizing and regurgitating the professor's lecture notes.

To some degree, the recent student unrest in Italy is a product of these and other deplorable conditions. For Italian universities are more backward than their French and German counterparts, with some Italian universities fearfully overcrowded. Also, as indicated in Chapter One, the middle classes are grossly overrepresented in the universities, and the students of working-class and peasant origins have great difficulty enduring the financial strain of university attendance.

But Italian student unrest cannot be attributed simply to the bias in the social composition of the student body, to the deplorable deficiencies of the universities with regard to physical plant and personnel, and to the financial hardships borne by less affluent students. For if these material factors stood alone, one might expect the poorer students to be in the vanguard of the protest movement. Actually, students from the lower classes generally failed to play a very active part in the protest movement at the University of Rome. These findings emerged from a study of student militancy conducted by Professor Gianni Statera, who concluded that the primary protagonists of the student revolt were upper-class and upper-middle-class students. These affluent students had experienced keen disappointment with regard to the bureaucratized character of the university, the absence of satisfactory interpersonal relations with faculty members and fellow-students, and the lack of romance and excitement in the system.[15]

We must consider that a strong link exists between the Italian

---

[14] Almond and Verba, pp. 349–357.
[15] Gianni Statera, "The Short Spring of the Italian Student Movement," unpublished mimeographed manuscript which was later published in *New Politics*, Vol. 8, No. 1 (1970). See pp. 11, 14–16 of manuscript.

student uprisings and similar manifestations of student unrest in other industrial societies. They appear, in part, to represent symptoms of a growing crisis of participation in the Western world, a protest against the individual's powerlessness in the face of complex institutions. In the glorification of violence as an end in itself, there seems to be an attempt to achieve self-realization *in the present* through a state of artificially induced intellectual excitement.[16] And finally we might note Martinotti's explanation: students, when they become politically involved, are reacting to the marginality of their social position vis-à-vis the adults in society, and they are assuming the guise of protesting outsiders. He sees their present leftist stance as the result of a situation in which class conflict is not strong and in which, consequently, the inconsistency between their political and social positions is not readily apparent.[17] This argument suggests that student activists could readily shift to, say, a radical rightist posture at some future time, should class antagonisms be accentuated.

In reality, during most of the period since World War II, student activism was channeled through organizations associated with the various political parties. On the extreme Right was FUAN (University Front of National Action); Catholic students were represented by FUCI (Italian Catholic University Federation), later known as the Intesa (Entente); CUDI (Italian Democratic University Centers) spoke for the extreme Left; and the UGI (Italian Goliardic Union) was standard-bearer for the centrist groups and for the traditional students' associations. These organizations competed to elect their representatives to the legislative body of the local student union; and each university assembly sent a representative to the national federation of local student unions, UNURI (Italian National University Representative Union). As time went on, however, student interest in this representative system began to decline sharply from its initially moderate level. Campus politics became jargon-ridden and bureaucratic, resulting in student apathy. All in all, the representative student movement *did* perform a significant recruitment function for the various party organizations in spite of the fact that it failed to maintain interest in campus politics.

It is understandable, then, that the second phase of student activism, beginning around 1964–1965, was marked by a demand for direct democracy through student assemblies where all could attend and speak. The subsequent revolts were concentrated

[16] Statera, "The Short Spring . . . ," pp. 11–13.
[17] Martinotti, pp. 198–199.

largely in the faculties of architecture, philosophy and letters, and political science, and garnered some major successes in 1968 when a number of faculties were occupied. Brutal police overreaction at this stage won sympathizers for the movement. But the aimless anarchy of the movement has limited its potential. As things stand currently, the participationist "general assemblies" have developed an elitist structure of their own, the public has reacted with a notable lack of sympathy, and a number of student leaders have deserted the campus to foment unrest in the factories and high schools. Still, the role of students in the strikes of the "hot autumn" of 1969 has apparently been a significant one. But the movement on campus has lost much of its original impetus, and its utter lack of a long-term constructive program is likely to diminish its appeal still further.[18]

The recent proliferation of violence and unrest in the universities indicates fundamental defects in the political socialization process. This seems to be a problem common to all major industrial nations in the free world, not only to Italy. The values embraced by the current generation of student activists—anti-intellectualism, a rejection of human rationality, an impatience with institutions and orderly procedures—are hardly conducive to the strengthening of a democratic system. Students of history—a discipline of which members of the New Left are not overfond—will recall that there is some similarity between the present movement (which regards even the Communist party as a staid member of the establishment) and the anarcho-syndicalism that attracted so many young Italian intellectuals around 1904. Historical perspective shows that twenty years later, by 1924, the starry-eyed disciples of Sorel were still quite active in Italian politics: many of them had become leaders of Fascist militia units or hierarchs in the Fascist party.

Before concluding our discussion of the relationship between education and political socialization, we might refer briefly to two factors which, during the Fascist period, served to convert many young Italian intellectuals to a belief in democratic norms. The first was the influence of Benedetto Croce, the great philosopher and historian, who was left relatively unmolested during the Fascist regime. Many young men who for one reason or another were beginning to nurture doubts about the Fascist regime were apparently led by their study of Croce to reevaluate their attitudes toward individual liberty. The second factor was the erosive effect

[18] Statera, "The Short Spring . . . ," pp. 17–24.

of a set of institutions created by the Fascists themselves. The Fascist University Groups (GUF) sponsored student cultural activities, annual contests, and student newspapers. In order to attract the young to these organizations, the regime allowed considerable leeway for the expression of unorthodox views. As a result of the intellectual questioning that developed within the GUF, a remarkably large group of up-and-coming student leaders (Zangrandi, Grimaldi, and others) became more and more critical of the regime. From these Fascist-sponsored organizations emerged the vanguard of anti-Fascist intellectuals.

THE MASS MEDIA AS SOCIALIZING INFLUENCES

Newspapers, radio, television, and motion pictures transmit values and attitudes to the members of a modern industrial society. By virtue of this function, the mass media act as organs of political socialization. But if current critiques are to be believed, the Italian mass media leave a great deal to be desired in their performance of this particular task.

There are less than 100 daily newspapers in Italy with a combined daily circulation of about 5 million. The largest circulations (approximately 500,000 each) are claimed by *Il Corriere della Sera* (Milan), *La Stampa* (Turin) and *Il Messaggero* (Rome). Every major city of over 500,000 population has at least one newspaper, and even ENI (National Hydrocarburants Corporation, a public corporation) has its own subsidized house organ, *Il Giorno* (Milan), ownership of which is shared by ENI and IRI (the Institute for Industrial Reconstruction, a government holding company). There are about a dozen party newspapers, over fifty independent journals, and a number of Church-sponsored dailies. Finally, an extraordinarily active group of sports journals flourish, to say nothing of several mass-circulation illustrated weekly magazines like *Epoca* and *L'Europeo*.

Recent studies of the Italian press reveal that Italy is not a nation of avid newspaper readers. According to these statistics, only 101 newspaper copies per 1000 population were published in Italy in the early 1960s, as opposed to 506 in Britain, 307 in Germany, and 270 in France. Furthermore, out of every ten Italians in a sample survey, only five reported that they read newspapers at least three times a week; for Germans and Frenchmen, the figures were eight and seven respectively. In television viewing and movie attendance, on the other hand, the Italian public ranked well ahead of both France and Germany.[19]

How does the Italian press compare with its French counterpart? In both countries, there is a significant but declining party press and a much more powerful complex of privately owned "independent" newspapers. In both countries, too, the number of dailies is steadily diminishing, as weaker newspapers go out of business. But the differences seem to outweigh the similarities. For one thing, there is no one outstanding Italian newspaper that compares with *Le Monde* (Paris). Then, too, French independent newspapers try to concentrate on news presentation and keep controversial opinions to a minimum, lest circulation suffer, whereas Italian newspapers are often owned by prominent business families or major corporations and openly reflect the views of their owners.

Moreover, French newspapers generally manage to keep their straight news items segregated from their editorial comments; whereas Italian newspapers usually interweave commentary with news presentation, so that it is very difficult for a reader to separate information from gratuitous editorializing. For the most part, French newspapers are more up-to-date in their format, vocabulary, and selection of features. Italian newspapers, on the other hand, still seem to be aimed at a late nineteenth-century upper-middle-class audience. Their prose is tortured, cumbersome, and full of archaic literary and mythological allusions. In addition, they discuss domestic politics in an indirect and suggestive manner, leaving much to the reader's imagination, and using numerous technical expressions and code words that only a political inside-dopester of long standing could possibly comprehend. Kogan, in fact, estimates on the basis of existing surveys that only 2–10 percent of all Italian newspaper readers actually bother to plow through the political news articles, which are really aimed at a very restricted public composed of some 1500 politicians, businessmen, and trade-union leaders.[20]

It becomes evident that the Italian press is relatively laggard in socializing the Italian masses. Given this situation, then, other mass media such as television must bear more than their share of the responsibility for transmitting values and attitudes. To the

[19] Ignazio Weiss, *Il potere di carta* (Torino: UTET, 1965), pp. 377, 402–403; and Jacques-René Rabier, *L'Information des Européens et l'integration de l'Europe* (Bruxelles: Institut d'Études Européens, Université Libre de Bruxelles, 1965), pp. 24–26, 29–30.

[20] Norman Kogan, *The Politics of Italian Foreign Policy* (New York: Praeger, 1963), pp. 18–19.

degree that the Italian press *does* succeed in affecting public attitudes, it is worthwhile to note that business and church interests dominate the daily press and command the lion's share of newspaper circulation.

Both radio and television broadcasting in Italy have been and are under the monopolistic control of RAI, a government corporation. Despite a number of apparent safeguards, RAI generally has been dominated by the government, and particularly by the leading government party, the Christian Democrats. And just as in France, the leading party in Italian cabinet coalitions has been accused of packing the television and radio networks with its own appointees and of discriminating against, not only the opposition, but also its own centrist allies.[21]

Political bias *did* exist in RAI broadcasting policies, as Mannucci points out so cogently. News programs paid far more attention to government achievements and announcements than to the political parties, the Parliament, and the trade-union movement. From 1953–1961, in fact, only the Christian Democratic party had assured access to RAI facilities during election campaigns. It was only after the successful inauguration of *Tribuna Elettorale* in 1960–1961, when each party competing in the local elections was permitted to hold a 30-minute press conference on television, that the tide began to turn in favor of a more balanced approach to political coverage. The severe factional conflicts in the Christian Democratic party—conflicts that raised the grim specter of an RAI controlled, not merely by one party, but by one faction within that dominant party—apparently led many Christian Democratic leaders to reassess their stand. Since 1961, *Tribuna Politica*, a series of party press conferences and interparty symposia, has become a permanent fixture on Italian television. To be sure, the government enjoys some special advantages: Ministers have the right to appear on television as government, rather than party, representatives, and are not therefore confined by the time allocations connected with *Tribuna Politica*. But all in all, a more equitable situation undoubtedly exists as compared to 1960.

Mannucci takes a very dim view of the socialization functions performed by RAI. Among other charges, he accuses RAI of reinforcing certain archaic and predemocratic values: an exaggerated and unthinking patriotism, a jingoistic worship of the armed forces and of their past military exploits, and an irrational

[21] Cesare Mannucci, *Lo spettatore senza libertà* (Bari: Laterza, 1962), pp. 89–90, 106–119, 248–267.

and extreme subservience to authority. Furthermore, RAI openly stresses the role of Catholicism as the official state religion, has opposed birth control and similar reforms in Italian family life, and seems to direct its message particularly to the provincial petty bourgeoisie. Its programs sometimes exude a heavy middle-class paternalism, and a thinly veiled tone of superiority vis-à-vis industrial workers. The following interview on an RAI program is a case in point:

> INTERVIEWER: What kind of work do you do?
> RESPONDENT: I'm a carpenter. But I'm unemployed. My age, you know.
> INTERVIEWER: Why, how old are you?
> RESPONDENT: Eh, I'm 59. I'm an old man. Nobody wants to hire me any more.
> INTERVIEWER: But do you realize that many gentlemen among our listening audience will feel insulted when they hear it said that a man is old at the age of 59?
> RESPONDENT: Look, at 45 years of age it's better not to apply for work at a factory, because no one will hire you.
> INTERVIEWER: Well, then, instead of applying at a factory, apply for a job somewhere else.

With this piece of gratuitous advice, the interviewer then turned away from the old man and proceeded to tell the audience a long story designed to cast doubts on the old carpenter's credibility.[22]

Since the early 1960s, when Mannucci pinpointed these abuses, there have been some apparent ameliorative trends. A number of non-Christian Democrats have been given managerial posts in RAI. Some superior programs, experimenting with new techniques and approaches, have been instituted on the second channel. But the bulk of television fare remains rather mediocre in character.

One major complaint has political as well as esthetic implications: RAI is terribly selective in its news coverage, tending to accentuate the positive, avoiding strikes, political unrest, and controversial issues that might embarrass the government. For example, during one week when the Italian press was giving detailed front-page coverage to the SIFAR scandal (the alleged planning of a coup d'etat by high-ranking Army officers), television news services completely ignored the issue.[23] Americans, who attribute

[22] Mannucci, pp. 190–191.
[23] Carlo Massa, "La programmazione televisiva in Italia," *Tempi Moderni*, Vol. XI, No. 32 (Winter 1968), 147–148.

their student unrest to the overstimulating effects of their television networks' policy of focusing on spectacular news events and on the antics of disorderly minorities, might take this lesson to heart: In Italy, with a thoroughly domesticated and conformist system of television news reporting, unrest and disorder have been just as widespread as in the United States.

It is probably true that "the mass media serve to reinforce existing orientations rather than to alter old ones or create new ones."[24] This statement certainly seems to fit the role assumed by the mass media in Italy, where the values and attitudes of the early twentieth century are still being espoused, perhaps as a matter of deliberate policy, more likely out of sheer force of habit. In any event, the mass media are doing very little to promote democratic patterns of thought and behavior among the less educated masses. But in the lives of the educated elites, Italy comes much closer to meeting democratic norms. For there is a wide assortment of newspapers and periodicals of divergent political tendencies, and there have been some improvements in the quality of television programs. And if the masses are patronized and ill-served, is this not a problem throughout the Western world? Until the masses have been transformed from passive audience to rational protagonists in the deliberative process, active minorities will continue to control Italy, as they control all other political systems in industrial societies.

The mass media, however, also play a more progressive role. They are "an important mechanism through which traditional societies move toward modernity and political integration."[25] In this respect the Italian mass media—especially television and motion pictures—have exercised a significant influence. They have contributed, for instance, to the "anticipatory socialization" of Southern migrants to Northern industrial centers. As we have already mentioned (see Chapter One), new recruits to Northern urban civilization, prior to their departure from the South, have received a preliminary orientation to the new life from movies and television.[26] In a sense, they have consciously chosen that new life before actually experiencing it.

Television and motion pictures have other positive achievements to their credit. By encouraging nationwide familiarity with

---

[24] Richard E. Dawson and Kenneth Prewitt, *Political Socialization* (Boston: Little, Brown, 1969), p. 198.
[25] Dawson and Prewitt, p. 194.
[26] Francesco Alberoni and Guido Baglioni, *L'integrazione dell' immigrato nella società industriale* (Bologna: Il Mulino, 1965), pp. 104–105, 112–114, 124–132.

standard Italian, they have greatly accelerated the process of national integration. Incidentally, they have actually modified standard Italian somewhat by injecting numerous Roman expressions and intonations into the Tuscan-based national tongue. Finally, they have helped to disseminate those ideals of technological progress and mass consumption which are indispensable in a modern, expanding industrial system. So the role of the mass media is, on the whole, an ambivalent one, with one foot in the tradition-ridden past and one in the uncertain future.

OTHER INFLUENCES ON SOCIALIZATION: WORKPLACE, CHURCH, PRESSURE GROUPS, AND PARTIES

Participation in on-the-job decisions is apparently very closely related to the development of a sense of political competence—far more closely than participation in either family or school decision-making processes.[27] In Italy, the workplace is somewhat more authoritarian with regard to labor-management relations than is the case in the United States, Britain, or even Germany. Italian blue-collar workers are far less likely than their British or German counterparts to be consulted on decisions by their employers or supervisors. Such an authoritarian workplace situation is very likely to undermine an individual's confidence in his ability to influence political events.

Some of the factors that account for this low degree of involvement in decision making on the part of Italian workers may be briefly summarized. For one thing, Italian management often has a paternalistic attitude toward labor, particularly in those many small firms that are owned by a single proprietor (almost 90 percent of all Italian firms). Secondly, there is very little collective bargaining at the plant level. Collective agreements are hammered out between national federations of workers and employers in national-level negotiations. These agreements spell out certain minimum standards, leaving it to the individual employer to decide, unilaterally in most cases, the degree to which he wishes to exceed those minima. As a result of this pattern of bargaining, plant-level union locals do not exist, for the most part. Instead, shop committees are elected, but they reflect the ideological division within the Italian labor movement and can easily be dominated by the employer. These committees rarely do an adequate

[27] Almond and Verba, pp. 341–345, 363–366.

job of policing the agreement reached between management and labor at the national level.

It is true, of course, that Italian unions are beginning to press for plant-level bargaining, and that workers in individual factories are showing an increasing willingness to initiate strike and/or negotiation proceedings on their own, without first clearing the matter with national union headquarters. But this new pattern of behavior is only just starting to emerge, and many difficulties must be overcome before the Italian workplace can evolve into an adequate socializing influence for citizens of a democratic society.

We shall speak at some length about the Catholic church in Chapter Six. For the present, let us simply note the major socializing functions performed by the church and its sponsored organizations. We have already observed that religion is a compulsory subject in the public schools (see Chapter One). Secondly, priests and bishops have not hesitated to admonish the faithful on their duties as voters, and have often taken explicit stands on major public issues (although the 1968 elections proved to be something of an exception to this rule, with the Italian Conference of Bishops issuing a relatively bland statement that was more pastoral than political).[28] Finally, it is significant that there are numerous Catholic organizations that have political leanings—inevitably toward the Christian Democrats. These groups form a sort of recruitment pool for future Christian Democratic party militants, and also contribute to the survival of a separate Catholic subculture.

Frequently, devout Catholics are apt to feel that their commitment to such church-sponsored organizations as Catholic Action outweighs in value and importance their commitment to the Christian Democratic party. With a vast array of Catholic groupings, and with 25,000 parish priests supporting church policies and interests, the church is estimated to have at least *some* influence over 6 million voters. Parish houses are used not only as the headquarters of the parish priest, but also as branch offices for a number of Catholic organizations and charity drives. They often include library and sports facilities and may be used as campaign centers during election periods.

The usefulness of an intricate network of church and church-sponsored organizations for the political fortunes of the Christian Democratic party can readily be imagined. While they do not seem to be terribly successful in making new converts or breaking

---

[28] Alfonso Prandi, *Chiesa e politica* (Bologna: Il Mulino, 1968), pp. 163–173.

into hostile social milieus, these Catholic associations *do* perform a useful function of defense, rather than conquest, by preserving the faith and sense of commitment of those Catholics who are already devoted to the church.[29]

Apart from the church and its sponsored organizations, other voluntary associations also have a great deal of influence on the socializing process. One study shows how the mass movement for the occupation of uncultivated land, undertaken by the peasants in Southern Italy after World War II, brought many normally apathetic Southern peasants to a high state of mobilization. Of course, this movement soon came under Communist party direction.[30] This occurrence brings up a point to which we shall return from time to time: Many Italian pressure groups are intimately connected to political parties.

What kinds of values and attitudes are transmitted by pressure groups to their members? Obviously, the messages vary from group to group. The church and its sponsored associations place a somewhat greater emphasis on the desirability of humility, obedience, and a certain passive attitude toward higher authority. It appears that pressure groups stress one common theme, however: They attempt to inculcate in their members a set of negative attitudes toward other groups and toward the political system. The group is depicted as upholding righteousness and the public interest against an uncomprehending world. Government and its employees are distrusted and regarded as essentially dishonest. Thus, pressure groups in Italy—including the church and its sponsored associations—help to perpetuate a politics of fragmentation and alienation.[31]

Parties also share in the political socialization process, particularly in countries like Italy where the parties are centralized, disciplined, and cohesive, and where they generally profess to be parties of principle and ideology rather than parties of compromise. Kirchheimer has acknowledged the vital function performed by socialist parties in Western Europe around the turn of the century in easing the transition from agrarian to industrial society. The socialist organizations provided many industrial workers with a set of values and goals and a sense of belonging acquired

---

[29] Gianfranco Poggi, *Catholic Action in Italy: The Sociology of a Sponsored Organization* (Stanford, Calif.: Stanford University Press, 1967), pp. 244–246.

[30] Sidney G. Tarrow, *Peasant Communism in Southern Italy* (New Haven, Conn.: Yale University Press, 1967), ch. 11.

[31] La Palombara, pp. 321–322. See also Joseph La Palombara, *Interest Groups in Italian Politics* (Princeton, N.J.: Princeton University Press, 1964), p. 70.

through integration in a class-mass party.³² And to some degree, the Italian Popular party in 1919–1922 also performed this kind of service for Catholic workers. Of course, as political socialization devices, these opposition parties had their limitations. Their actual membership was rather small. The values they transmitted were not in strict congruence with the values being upheld by the Liberal party elites who dominated Italy. And as Di Palma indicates:

> . . . movements that do not achieve their original objectives in a short period of time tend to enforce inequality as an organizational principle . . . and in particular to replace equality and the organization of the disaffected with a selective strategy of political education designed for a limited number of party activists. The irony here—an irony well understood by Roberto Michels—is that the opposition's very success in training a hard core of politically educated and skillful party activists with a stake in the larger politics curtails internal participation in such a way that party followers, especially the socially and psychologically marginal, are ultimately deprived of the opportunity to participate in the larger society.³³

The Fascist regime first imbued the average Italian with the habit of joining a political party as a matter of course. In the early 1940s, 12 percent of the Italian population were members of the Fascist party. And in 1945, as a result of a behavioral predisposition learned during the Fascist era, millions of Italians purchased party membership cards in one of the newly established parties. The chief beneficiaries of this trend were the parties most capable of dispensing patronage in reward for party membership: the Christian Democrats, with their church connections and their well-entrenched positions in the national government; and the Communists, with their local government bastions in North-Central Italy.

Since 1945, political parties have continued to try to transmit their values and attitudes to the members they recruit and to the public at large. In the case of the Communists and the Christian

---

³² Otto Kirchheimer, "The Transformation of the Western European Party Systems," in Joseph La Palombara and Myron Weiner, eds., *Political Parties and Political Development* (Princeton, N.J.: Princeton University Press, 1966), pp. 182–183.
³³ Giuseppe Di Palma, "Disaffection and Participation in Western Democracies: The Role of Political Oppositions," *The Journal of Politics*, Vol. 31, No. 4 (November 1969), 1008.

Democrats, this action has been reinforced by a large number of party-dominated pressure groups. Particularly in the Center and South, these major parties have made enormous membership gains. Naturally, many of the newly recruited members have been merely trying to make social contacts and promote their own material interests. Others, however, have apparently been attracted by the desire for a meaningful commitment to a secular faith.[34]

Yet party membership alone does not necessarily imply exposure to political socialization. Many party members, particularly those who have joined mainly in search of patronage, are rather inactive and are therefore unlikely to expose themselves to the socializing process. More information must be gathered to determine the actual success of party activities and party internal propaganda in promoting the political socialization of members and supporters.

Some of the evidence that is already available is rather surprising. Recent survey research reveals that Communist and Socialist respondents show a higher level of support for democratic attitudes than do Christian Democratic respondents, and are also more tolerant of marriage across party lines.[35] Since there is little or nothing in the internal processes of the Communist party that would tend to transmit democratic attitudes, one is left a bit bewildered about the role of the political party in the socialization process. Perhaps the greater efforts made by the Communist party to elicit a sense of membership participation in party activities and to encourage upward mobility are responsible for the above results. Then again, the fact that the Left is identified with democracy in Italy would lead many men of democratic leanings to join the most leftist party, or at any rate to support it openly. There is, of course, the unwelcome possibility that these surveys may have gauged the respondents' willingness to parrot liberal or democratic slogans, instead of their underlying attitudes. So these results may well be unrelated to any socialization drives sustained by the respective parties.

The socialization function seems to be most effectively performed by political parties when people are undergoing sharp alterations in their life patterns, changing milieus, or experiencing an acute crisis. A case in point is the migration of Southern peas-

---

[34] Belden Paulson and Athos Ricci, *The Searchers* (Chicago: Quadrangle, 1966), pp. 321–323, 326–328.

[35] Timothy M. Hennessey, "Democratic Attitudinal Configurations among Italian Youth," *Midwest Journal of Political Science*, Vol. XIII, No. 2 (May 1969), 167–193; and Almond and Verba, pp. 154–160.

ants to the industrial Northwest. A Southern peasant from Campania might have been accustomed to voting for the Monarchists, who are considered to be virtual outcasts in the Northwestern factories. After an initial period of political uncertainty, the peasant would yield to the active and imaginative proselytizing efforts of the Communist party, the only major party to make a serious attempt to convert the immigrants. In reaching this decision, however, he would be influenced by pressure from more than just Communist organizers: He would also be giving in to the solicitations of his new-found friends, to the leftist atmosphere of his workplace and neighborhood, and to his own desire to ingratiate himself with his trade-union contacts. In short, he would be switching his political allegiance partly in an effort to achieve social integration with his environment.

Some astute observers believe that Italian parties are playing an ever less effective role in the performance of their socialization function. One study points out that the values proposed by the parties are no longer accepted and shared, and are no longer influencing practical behavior.[36] The growing loss of Communist control over the protest movement is a case in point. In the late 1940s and in the 1950s, virtually all protest demonstrations were spearheaded by the Communist party. But neither the student rebellion of 1968 nor the wildcat strikes of the "hot autumn" of 1969 were initiated, organized, or even desired by the Communist party, although the Communists *did* belatedly give some support to these movements in order to avoid being left behind. By the same token, the bonds between the Christian Democrats and their closely linked pressure groups are becoming somewhat frayed.

POLITICAL EVENTS AND POLITICAL EXPERIENCES

Major political events that manifestly affect the life of an individual can have an important part in shaping or reshaping his political values and attitudes. The Fascist experience, the war, and the Resistance were significant events that had a deep impact on young Italians. Some, like Matteo Matteotti (a Socialist leader and son of the Socialist martyr, Giacomo Matteotti) and Giorgio Amendola (a top-ranking Communist and son of a prominent Liberal statesman, Giovanni Amendola) were socialized in the

[36] Fabrizio Onofri, *Potere e strutture sociali nella società industriale di massa* (Milano: ETAS/KOMPASS, 1967), pp. 141–142.

most brutal way imaginable: Matteotti's father was kidnapped and murdered by the Fascists; Amendola's father was so badly beaten by a Fascist gang that he never recovered from his wounds and died several months later. But most of the young men during the Fascist period, with the exception of thousands of exiles and political prisoners, lived fairly normal lives under the regime. They grew up believing in Fascism or, at any rate, opposing only its more vulgar manifestations. Some university students participated in Fascist university symposia (*Littorali*), which were designed to provide students with some outlet for their intellectual vigor and curiosity, and were carried on in an outwardly open and unfettered manner.

Although earlier events had created some misgivings about the Fascist regime, the first major shock to these youths was the entry of Fascist Italy into World War II. One volume containing a series of brief political autobiographies by Italian intellectuals uses frequent references to the wartime experience and to the subsequent Resistance.[37] Michele Abbate, for example, first turned against Fascism after he had observed the careerist, conformist behavior of Fascist party members in his home town of Potenza, and after he had talked to unemployed peasants who "volunteered" to fight for Franco in the Spanish Civil War in order to be able to feed their families. This feeling of animosity on Abbate's part increased in intensity when Italy entered the war and some of his friends died in action. Ugoberto Alfassio Grimaldi was pro-Fascist in his adolescence and early youth, but began to develop a critical consciousness as a result of his participation in the *Littorali*, nurtured still graver doubts after Italy entered the war, and turned against Fascism after the overthrow of Mussolini on July 25, 1943, and the subsequent armistice on September 8, 1943. Francesco Compagna lived a sports-loving, politically apathetic existence as a young man, participated in military operations against Slovenian partisans, but was finally shocked into opposing Fascism by the Italian surrender and its aftermath.

Many of the less illustrious lower-level party activists had similar experiences. In one book dealing with these activists, there is much less emphasis on educational and intellectual experiences, and on the study of Croce. But there is the same tendency to stress the importance of the war and, above all, the Resistance, which often represented the high point in their lives. As one Communist activist put it:

[37] Ettore A. Albertoni, Ezio Antonini, Renato Palmieri, *La generazione degli anni difficili* (Bari: Laterza, 1962).

I lived those days to the full, I felt myself being reborn; for me it is the most wonderful memory of my entire life, those days of liberation. And I would go back and relive it again in order to experience what I experienced in that period, for no other reason [but] only to experience it . . . living in that kind of milieu, in contact with people whose ideals were very rigorous, I joined the Party. . . .[38]

These memories, which account for so much of the moral fervor with which men entered politics after World War II, are playing a far less significant role today. Whereas one-third of a panel of secondary school students interviewed in 1953 cited World War II as their worst memory of the past, by 1963—with a similar panel drawn from the same schools—the figure was down to zero.[39]

Throughout his life, the individual will, from time to time, have some direct experiences with the political system: when he casts his ballot, when he pays his taxes, when he applies for a license, permit, or passport at a government office. Over the years, these experiences will help to shape his attitudes toward the system. In addition to these first-hand contacts, he will also be exposed to accounts from relatives, friends, and acquaintances about experiences they have had or stories they have heard.

What socializing effect do political experiences have in Italy? The Almond-Verba study shows that, as compared with Americans, Britons, and Germans, Italians tend to have rather low expectations of fair and considerate treatment on the part of the bureaucracy and the police, and that this is especially true of less-educated Italians. Numerous Italian respondents offer graphic complaints regarding instances of government corruption, discrimination, or lack of consideration for the general public.[40]

The tax system in Italy helps to create negative attitudes toward the political system. The variety of different income taxes, with their exasperating procedures for assessing income, tends to penalize the honest taxpayer. There is a general income tax, a complementary income tax (or surtax), and a family tax (paid to the municipal government). Also, since the government implicitly assumes that most taxpayers are chronic liars, many tax returns are almost automatically scaled upward by the tax authorities. Anyone who turns in an honest report of his true income (except

[38] Tosi's section in Manoukian and Olivetti, pp. 220–221.
[39] Ugoberto Alfassio Grimaldi and Italo Bertoni, *I giovani degli anni sessanta* (Bari: Laterza, 1964), pp. 108–109, 120–126.
[40] Almond and Verba, pp. 106–114.

for people on wages or salaries for whom this problem does not arise) is apt to have his assessment arbitrarily raised. The final decision concerning the actual tax to be paid may frequently be the result of a lengthy process of negotiation. At the local level, assessment of liability for the family tax provides the party (or parties) in power with an opportunity to reward their friends and punish their enemies: Businessmen who fail to contribute funds to the party or who support minority parties may have to shoulder an unusually heavy tax burden. The result of this unfair, cumbersome, and frequently dishonest system is that there is very little public censure directed against tax evasion; tax evaders are regarded as having outsmarted a basically illegitimate and inequitable internal revenue structure.

There are other sources of alienation in the relationship between the citizen and his government. Many Italians have experienced rudeness or painfully long waiting periods in government offices, or have received arbitrary treatment at the hands of the police. Procedures and equipment in public offices are often sadly antiquated. If the citizen wishes to make out some sort of application in a government office, he must often do so on special paper (*carta di bollo*), which he is required to purchase himself at a government-owned tobacco store. There are many such petty aggravations all of which seem to dramatize the oppressive and parasitic nature of the Italian state.

As a result of these and other experiences, Italians have developed a very low level of trust in the public service. Public-opinion polls indicate that 63 percent of the Italian public believe that one can have anything (including illicit privileges) in Italy as long as he is willing to pay for it. Interestingly enough, however, those who have relatively few contacts with the public service are more apt to accept the rumors (which, on occasion, turn out to be true) of widespread corruption and favoritism in the bureaucracy. Instead, those who have either normal or frequent contacts with the public service are more likely to be unfavorably impressed by the slowness and lack of preparation they observe.[41] This finding suggests that corruption may not be as widespread as the public generally assumes.

At any rate, the experiences Italians have with their own government—whether direct or second-hand—breed alienation rather than transmit certain desired values. Even more responsible

---

[41] Franco Demarchi, "I laureati nella pubblica amministrazione," in Comitato di Studio dei Problemi della Scuola e dell' Università Italiana, *I laureati in Italia* (Bologna: Il Mulino, 1968), pp. 286–287, 289–290.

for this lack of faith are Italy's long experience with foreign oppression and exploitation, and the low level of public participation in the life of the state. Low participation makes for lack of information, a sense of distrust, and a willingness to believe any rumor, however wild and implausible it may be.

POLITICAL PARTICIPATION:
A CONTRADICTORY PICTURE

One of the most intriguing peculiarities of Italian politics is the lack of consistency in patterns of participation. The Italian electorate has been depicted by a number of scholars as being unusually alienated and apathetic—and survey research tends to bear out these assertions. Yet, Italy ranks very high in turnout at general elections and in the number of card-holding members enrolled in the various parties.

Electoral participation in Italy ranks far ahead of most other democracies. Ever since World War II, a remarkably high percentage of eligible voters have actually cast ballots. The figures range from a low of 89.1 percent in 1946 to a high of 93.8 percent in 1953 and 1958, but generally average slightly over 90 percent.[42] In this respect, Italy is well ahead of France, where turnout—considered high by American standards—usually fluctuates between 75 and 80 percent. However, turnout in Italian local and provincial elections is usually considerably lower than the turnout in national elections.

How does one account for such a strikingly high level of participation in Italian elections? One of the main factors is the legal provision, adopted after World War II, that a citizen who failed to vote in a general election, and who had no valid excuse for his absenteeism, would have that fact duly inscribed on his good-conduct certificate—a document he has to present when he seeks employment. While this provision hardly constitutes compulsory voting, it nevertheless exerts some psychological pressure on the voter, especially in a country where people are prone to expect discriminatory treatment at the hands of both their bureaucracy and their private employer.

Other legal provisions tend to facilitate voting and thus contribute to high turnout. The citizen is automatically registered as a

---

[42] Giorgio Galli, ed., *Il comportamento elettorale in Italia* (Bologna: Il Mulino, 1968), pp. 67–72. Coauthors with Galli are V. Capecchi, V. Cioni Polacchini, and G. Sivini.

voter by the local administration of his commune of residence when he turns twenty-one: unlike the American voter, he need take no initiative in the matter. Shortly prior to a general or local election, his communal government sends his election certificate (which contains a notice of the date of the election, the hours during which the polls will be open, and the location of the polling place) directly to his home. Special arrangements are made to enable soldiers, sailors, merchant seamen, hospital patients, and people taking a rest cure away from their home commune to cast their ballots. Emigrants in other European countries are granted reduced railroad rates for their return to Italy and a free round-trip rail passage from the Italian border to their commune of permanent residence. And finally, elections take place 6 A.M.–10 P.M. on Sunday, a day of rest for most Italians. Those who must work on Sunday can vote Monday morning.

These legal pressures and accommodations are supplemented by the canvassing activities of the parties, the church-sponsored Civic Committees, and other pressure groups (most of which serve the interests of a specific party). In addition, citizens are encouraged to vote by the media; the press, the state-owned radio and television network, and the wall posters pasted up by party activists all depict voting as a moral duty which no good citizen can neglect. As a result of these factors, and of the others discussed above, voting turnout in Italy approaches, and sometimes even surpasses, the percentages registered in countries where voting is actually compulsory.

We have already noted that Italian turnout is 10–15 percent higher than turnout rates in France. Since France also has Sunday voting and a registration system that takes the burden of initiative off the citizen's shoulders, we may conclude that the really decisive factors in bringing normally apathetic voters to the polls are the legal pressures, the reduced fares provided for Italians living away from their commune of residence (these Italians may combine the act of voting with a brief, partly subsidized visit to their families and friends), and the strong canvassing organizations and mass memberships of Italian parties.

Another significant characteristic of political participation in Italy is the unusual tendency for Italians to join political parties in far greater numbers than do citizens of most other Western democracies.[43] This tendency, as we have previously observed, is the result of a number of factors: the habit, instilled by the Fascist

[43] Galli, *Il bipartitismo imperfetto* (Bologna: Il Mulino, 1966), pp. 147–158. Galli is an Italian social scientist.

government, of carrying a party card; the socializing influence of Communist-dominated or church-sponsored pressure groups; the desire for political patronage in the form of jobs, contracts, recommendations, and favors, which the Christian Democrats can provide in the underdeveloped South and the Communist local governments can grant in Tuscany and Emilia. Chasseriaud attributes high party membership figures in Italy to the Italian desire for social importance. Membership in a party is a form of distinction, which gives the individual the illusion of playing a meaningful role in society.[44] We should also mention—certainly in the case of Tuscany, Emilia, Umbria, and the Marches—the importance of an historically rooted leftist tradition, which makes party membership a necessary means of achieving social integration in a zone where trade unions, cooperatives, recreational circles, movie clubs, sports associations, and various other kinds of social groups are often dominated by the Communist party.

This last factor, interestingly enough, does not seem to apply to the Christian Democrats. In Northeastern Italy, where Christian Democracy receives its highest voting percentages, and where Catholic associations of various kinds are most firmly entrenched, Christian Democratic membership figures are relatively low. There is not the same positive correlation between party membership and votes cast for the party in general elections as in the case of the Communists.[45] It would appear, then, that while the Communist party acts in some measure as a party of social integration, the Christian Democratic party is mainly a party of patronage, with church-sponsored voluntary associations bearing the primary responsibility for fulfilling the function of social integration.

Thus, two enormous parties dominate Italian politics and enroll as members many people who, in other democratic countries, would be mere sympathizers. The Christian Democratic party in 1967 had about 1.6 million members, while the Communist party had about 1.7 million. The third-ranking party, in terms of membership, was the reunified Socialist party which, in 1967, had about 600,000 members. Only two years later, however, this party had split into two segments: the Italian Socialist party (PSI) and the Unitary Socialist party (PSU). Adding to these leading parties the membership totals of lesser Italian parties, Sernini estimates that 12 percent of all Italian voters have a party card. Only a few Western European parties—the Conservatives and

[44] J. P. Chasseriaud, *Le parti démocrate chrétien en Italie* (Paris: Armand Colin, 1965), p. 204.
[45] Galli, *Il bipartitismo imperfetto*, pp. 153–155.

Labourites in Britain, the Austrian and Swedish Social Democrats —can boast a larger membership.[46]

To be sure, the above membership figures are somewhat deceptive. Local party organizations, especially those of the Christian Democrats, frequently are likely to indulge in the practice of paying membership dues for large numbers of local residents, with the explicit or tacit understanding that the membership cards are to remain in the hands of local party leaders who will act as proxies for these "inactive" members. Sometimes, in fact, membership cards are made out in the names of deceased residents or of people picked at random out of a telephone directory. The reason for this practice is that a local party organization, by buying large quantities of membership cards, can win the right to greater voting strength at a provincial party congress; and an intraparty faction can win control of a local section or provincial federation if its financial resources permit it to purchase enough proxies in this manner. In addition to this fictitious inflation of party membership, we should reiterate the fact that many relatively apathetic people in Italy have joined political parties in order to achieve social integration, receive jobs, obtain the protection of a powerful patron, avoid difficulties with local government officials, and so on. In all such cases, the political commitment of the member to the party is likely to be minimal.

In an effort to avoid the wholesale purchasing of membership cards by party officials, and the resultant unfounded excessive weight carried by the South (where the practice is most widespread) in Christian Democratic congresses, the Christian Democratic party has recently adopted rules designed to curb such abuses. Under these new rules, representation at provincial and national congresses is to be based only in part on the number of members enrolled in a local section or provincial federation, as the case may be. In the future, representation is to be based partly on the relative voting strength evidenced by the party in a given commune or province.[47] Such a provision will be to the advantage of the heavily Catholic Northeast, where there are relatively few Christian Democratic party members as compared with the South, but where the Christian Democrats chalk up close to a majority of the votes, thus far exceeding the results they obtain in Southern Italy.

---

[46] Michele Sernini, *La disputa sui partiti* (Padova: Marsilio Editori, 1968), pp. 59–60.

[47] Ada Sivini Cavazzani, "Partito, iscritti, elettori," in Fabrizio Cicchitto, Gino Rocchi, Bruno Manghi, Luigi Ruggiu, Ada Sivini Cavazzani, *La DC dopo il primo ventennio* (Padova: Marsilio Editori, 1968), pp. 172–173.

Just how active are those party members who are alive and card carrying? The evidence is about what we would expect from our knowledge of other Western countries: only a small minority are active. In his study of the Italian Socialist party in Arezzo province (Tuscany), Barnes found that only 56 percent of the members in his sample had so much as attended a party section meeting during the preceding year—this in a section of Central Italy where political passions run high and are fueled by historical grudges.[48] Most other estimates concur that less than 10 percent of Italian party members are active in their parties. Yet, levels of participation may rise in the weeks just prior to a national party congress, especially a controversial one.

It has become evident by now that actual participation in party decision making is a good deal more limited than membership figures might lead one to believe. Besides, mere attendance at section meetings need not necessarily denote meaningful participation. This is fairly obvious in the case of the Communist party, where bona fide alternatives to the policies outlined by the party leaders are never really submitted to the rank-and-file members at the local level. But even in the democratic parties, factional conflict and freedom of discussion do not necessarily ensure effective grass-roots participation in decision-making. Rather, the rank and file find themselves confronted, at section meetings and provincial congresses, with a set of clear-cut propositions presented by the party executive. Debate over these propositions tends to be monopolized by the official spokesmen for the various factions within the party. Only rarely does an ordinary party member get a chance to speak.

In the Christian Democratic party, there is a considerable area of overlapping membership shared with various church-sponsored organizations, such as Catholic Action, ACLI, and so on. This dual allegiance tends to lessen the sense of commitment to the Christian Democratic party. The party member frequently tends to be committed to his Catholic pressure group, first and foremost, and may view intraparty decision making mainly in the light of his group's interests.

Survey research has also shown that the process of participation is seriously undermined and rendered almost nugatory by the attitudes of the average Italian toward his functions as citizen and voter. Only 10 percent of an Italian sample professed to believe that a citizen should play an active role in community affairs. On this question, Italy trailed far behind the United States, Britain,

---

[48] Samuel H. Barnes, *Party Democracy: Politics in an Italian Socialist Federation* (New Haven, Conn.: Yale University Press, 1967), pp. 76–77.

and even Germany. Italians also rated lower than Americans, Britons, and Germans in regard to their sense of civic competence —that is, in regard to their belief that they could exercise influence over the government. Finally, 66 percent of the Italian respondents claimed that they never discussed politics with anyone, whereas only 29 percent of the German sample gave this rather extreme indication of political apathy.[49]

Students of comparative politics are well aware of the fact that no major Western democracy ranks particularly high in political participation. But our analysis clearly reveals that Italy actually ranks near the bottom with regard to participation and the basic underlying attitudes that condition participation. Despite massive turnout at the polls and despite the impressive membership figures of its political parties, the Italian polity does not really command the active loyalty and involvement of more than a small fraction of its citizens—and this fraction is actually less substantial than in other Western democracies.

For example, the fact that only 35 percent of Italian trade-union members actually pay their dues is indicative of the low level of commitment that characterizes the rank and file of the labor movement.[50] The frequent appearance of anomic interest groups, in the form of violent and spontaneous riots, demonstrations, and wildcat strikes, is another clear indication that organized interest groups and political parties are not adequately performing their function of representing and channeling grievances. The Southern peasants spontaneously occupying landed estates after World War II; the Southern immigrants playing a leading role in the wildcat strikes in Turin during the "hot autumn" of 1969; and the university students venting their anger against a society dominated by entrenched senior citizens and occupying university buildings—these are all symptoms of the failure of parties and interest groups in Italian politics. One last manifestation of Italy's low level of participation is the very poor showing of Italian women, which of course is a reflection of their low status in Italian society. Perhaps this is because such a short time has elapsed since their emancipation. At any rate, the proportion of Italian women who are members of organizations is far lower than in the United States, Britain, and Germany, and this low participation holds true even among more educated women.[51]

[49] Almond and Verba, pp. 116, 169, 186.
[50] Joseph A. Raffaele, *Labor Leadership in Italy and Denmark* (Madison, Wis.: University of Wisconsin Press, 1962), p. 81.
[51] Almond and Verba, pp. 251–253.

How can this climate of apathy-cum-rebellion be explained? To some extent, the answers are not uniquely Italian. Not only in Italy do men feel crushed and overawed by the pressures and complexities of modern industrial society. Michels' iron law of oligarchy, with its effect of discouraging rank-and-file participation, is applicable to the United States as well as to Italy. Yet, certain special problems are present in the Italian situation, for how else can relative Italian backwardness with regard to political participation be explained?

We may cite several factors that will warrant further exploration by students of comparative government. We have already discussed the inadequacy of most of the Italian agents of political socialization. The family, the school, and the workplace fail to train the individual in the attitudes and methods of democratic participation. The mass media are either geared to middle-class tastes or devoted to pure entertainment for the edification of the masses. The bureaucracy is painfully slow moving, and a highly centralized unitary system of government stifles local initiative. All these conditions tend to reduce political participation in Italy.

Then, too, Italian society is highly stratified. Because of rigid class distinctions, even working-class parties have a remarkably high proportion of people of middle-class origin among their leaders. And in these cases, middle-class leaders are more likely than working-class leaders to attain high-ranking executive positions.

As we shall see during the discussion of Italian political culture in Chapter Three, Italian society is not distinguished by a high degree of mutual trust. Men are suspicious of each other's intentions and motives. Individuals will often be afraid to take part in political activity for fear of reprisal measures that might be taken against them by employers, bureaucrats, and others.

And finally, industrialization and urbanization may be undermining participation to a large extent. Urbanization takes a peasant out of his traditional rural environment where there is likely to be a dominant party whose rule rests on long-hallowed voting habits. In this rural setting, almost all of the agents of socialization push the voter in the same direction. As Barnes puts it, discussing Arezzo, "it is very easy in this commune to be a PSI (Italian Socialist party) member for traditional and social reasons."[52] On moving to the big city, the former peasant usually finds that no one party is dominant and that cross-pressures abound in the social milieu.

[52] Barnes, p. 155.

In a very real sense, moreover, participation falters because of a failure of leadership. Italian political parties, still led by those who assumed the helm after World War II, have failed to revamp their ideas to fit a changing society. Their specialized jargon does not seem to be addressed to modern problems and simply does not get through to the average citizen. The gerontocracy that dominates Italian society is present also in parties and pressure groups. It may take many long and frustrating years of apprenticeship before a young man can enter the ruling circle of a local party organization. Thus, many young Italians have not been content to work through the youth organizations or through the young people's branches of the political parties. As a matter of fact, the proportion of young people enrolled in the political parties has been sharply diminishing over the years.[53]

It is evident, then, that Italy, like other major industrial powers, is confronting a serious crisis of participation. The drive to set up self-governing regions, enjoying a quasi-federal relationship with the central government in Rome, is one attempt to react to this crisis. A decentralized structure may make local participation more relevant by bringing some major functions of government closer to the people. However, as citizens of federal states like the United States and Canada can testify, there are no easy answers to this crisis. Local elites are perhaps more active and self-assertive in the United States than they are in Italy; but even in America the ideal of a public-spirited, intensely involved citizenry seems far short of attainment.

Barnes cites one mitigating argument to be considered in assessing the Italian pattern of participation. It is true that Italian working-class parties tend to mobilize their rank-and-file members, rather than provide them with a genuine opportunity to participate in decision making. Yet, by mobilizing the politically incompetent, by giving them a channel for peaceful protest, and by providing them with a plausible alternative for which they may vote without sacrificing their preconceived emotional commitments, the Communist and the Socialist parties may actually be contributing to the survival of Italian democratic institutions.[54] In Italy, unlike the United States, those who reject the existing system find an effective means of protest in the ballot box.

Do some classes or occupational groups have a greater tendency to participate in politics than others? The evidence is not

---

[53] Antonio Carbonaro, "Modelli interpretativi dei comportamenti dei giovani," in *Lo stato democratico e i giovani* (Milano: Comunità, 1968), pp. 132–137.
[54] Barnes, pp. 244–251.

terribly startling. As we would expect, working-class members of Italian political parties are more active than peasant members, and members of middle-class origin rank well ahead of industrial workers. Also, we are not surprised to discover that education stimulates participation: intellectuals are overrepresented in leadership posts.

A more intriguing dispute concerning differential rates of participation centers around the question of whether there is a higher rate of participation in Northern Italy than in Southern Italy. On the one hand, voting turnout since World War II has been slightly higher in the North—an average of about 94 percent as compared to 90 percent in the South.[55] On the other hand, statistics show that the South has far more than its proportional share of Christian Democratic party members. But Southern membership figures are swollen by exaggeration and, to the extent that they are accurate, often reflect a passive desire for patronage rather than an active dedication to party goals.

In perhaps one respect, political participation is unquestionably higher in the South: Southerners are more likely to make use of their legal privilege of writing in four preference votes on the ballot in general elections.[56] Italy uses a list system of proportional representation for elections to the Chamber of Deputies. So each voter chooses one of several competing party lists. However, he may also, if he wishes, supplement his list vote by writing in the names of four preferred candidates chosen from the list for which he has voted. Preference votes determine which of the candidates on the party's list will be entitled to occupy the parliamentary seats assigned to the party on the basis of proportional representation. Given this preferential voting system, the order in which a party's candidates will be eligible to enter Parliament will not necessarily coincide with the order in which the names originally appeared on the party's list. Since illiterates may simply write down the order numbers, rather than the names, of the candidates they prefer (the first man listed is number 1, and so on), and since the number 3 is easier for an illiterate to write than the number 2, candidates usually prefer to occupy the first and third places on their party's list and try desperately to avoid being assigned to the ill-starred second slot.

In this peculiar form of participation, which is somewhat analogous to the role of the primary voter in the United States, the

[55] Tarrow, pp. 165–166.
[56] Luigi D'Amato, *Il voto di preferenza in Italia* (Milano: Giuffré, 1964), pp. 13, 43–45, 107–114, 189–192.

Southern Italian voter is far more likely than the Northern or Central Italian voter to make use of his option to choose four personal preferences from among the names on his party list (two-thirds to three-fourths of Southern voters use this privilege as against a bare majority of Northern voters). Essentially, this difference seems to be a reflection of the personalism of Southern politics, in which the voter is often supporting a local boss rather than a party.

POLITICAL RECRUITMENT: THE SALIENCE OF PARTIES

Political parties play a very prominent part in the recruitment of individuals to the legislative and executive branches of government, and to the bureaucracy as well. This is most evident in the process of nominating candidates for the Senate and the Chamber of Deputies. Candidates are nominated by provincial party committees and winnowed out by circumscription or regional party committees. The central party organization in Rome retains the veto power and also the power to propose one candidate of its own for each electoral circumscription of two to four provinces. There is, then, nothing corresponding to the American direct primary. A local notable may seek to bypass this process by placing himself at the head of an independent local list; but given the nature of Italian voting habits, his chances of being elected without the support of one of the national parties are virtually nil. The nominating function is dominated by Italy's highly centralized, cohesive, and disciplined parties.

However, the parties do not stand entirely alone. In elections for the Chamber of Deputies, as we have mentioned, the voter may indicate his preference for up to four candidates on his party's list. These lists originate in the appropriate provincial party committee, are then combined and pruned by circumscription and regional party committees, and then scrutinized sharply by central headquarters in Rome. Clearly, the requests of intraparty factions and of ancillary or friendly pressure groups must be given a respectful hearing at the early stages, thus spreading the nominating function over many diverse groups.

Political friendships also exert a good deal of influence on this process of drawing up nomination slates. Many a politician started his career as the youthful protégé of a veteran patron. Andreotti began his career under De Gasperi's protective wing.

When several protégés are molded and led by the same old master, we have the beginning of a faction. For example, when they had achieved prominence, Andreotti and Scelba both began forming personal followings of their own, doing for others what De Gasperi had done for them.[57]

In sharp contrast is the recruitment process in France, where parties are weaker in membership and in organizational strength. In French elections, local notables frequently run for office as independents without benefit of a national party label; they even have a fair chance of being elected by their constituencies in preference to the candidates of the national parties. It would be interesting to explore further the causes underlying this contrast. Possibly the French electoral law (single-member districts with run-off as compared to Italy's multimember districts with proportional representation) is responsible. Then again, the smaller population of French constituencies as compared with Italy's multimember, interprovincial circumscriptions might be considered. Lastly, we might refer to La Palombara's suggestion that the greater threat from the extreme Left in Italy makes for more party cohesion on the Right and Center of the political spectrum.[58]

POLITICAL RECRUITMENT: SOME INDIVIDUAL PATTERNS

Analytical biographies of contemporary or recent Italian political leaders are few and far between, though there are numerous thinly disguised campaign tracts. However, some works on current political leaders have risen above the level of mere lionization. For instance, there is a journalistic but penetrating study of Amintore Fanfani who, in the course of his political career, has held several cabinet posts, spent several years as general secretary of the Christian Democratic party, and served three separate times as prime minister of Italy.[59] There are also several good biographies of the late Alcide De Gasperi, former leader of the Christian Democratic party.[60]

[57] Marco Cesarini Sforza, *L'uomo politico* (Firenze: Vallecchi, 1963), pp. 94–96.
[58] Joseph La Palombara, "Political Party Systems and Crisis Governments: French and Italian Contrasts," *Midwest Journal of Political Science*, Vol. II, No. 2 (May 1958), 131–135.
[59] Piero Ottone, *Fanfani* (Milano: Longanesi, 1966).
[60] See, for instance, Elisa A. Carrillo, *De Gasperi: The Long Apprenticeship* (Notre Dame, Ind.: University of Notre Dame Press, 1965); and Maria Romana Catti De Gasperi, *De Gasperi, uomo solo* (Milano: Mondadori, 1964).

An examination of the life histories of Fanfani, of De Gasperi, and of another prominent Christian Democratic political leader, Giovanni Gronchi, does not permit us to reach any major or unexpected general conclusions about Italian patterns of political recruitment. For one thing, in the absence of a larger sample of political biographies, we must hesitate to generalize from the particular. As long as political biography remains a neglected aspect of our discipline in Italy, biographical data will have only an illustrative and mildly suggestive function to perform.

Are there any common strands at all, any tentative points, that emerge from the study of a few life histories of prominent Christian Democratic politicians? Some common denominators *can* be isolated. For one thing, it is noteworthy that Fanfani, De Gasperi, and Gronchi all came from middle-class, but not really prosperous, backgrounds. Fanfani's father was a lawyer and notary public in a small town in the Province of Arezzo (Tuscany); Gronchi's father was a bookkeeper in a bakery in Pontedera, Province of Pisa (Tuscany), and later served as agent for a delicatessen firm; and De Gasperi was the son of a local chief of police in a small town in Trento province, which was under Austrian rule until 1918. These biographical data tend to confirm what we have already said about the predominantly middle-class character of Italy's political elites.

There are also certain similarities in the socialization processes of the three men. Gronchi, Fanfani, and De Gasperi were all active members of Catholic lay organizations long before they entered the university. Fanfani attended the Catholic University of Milan; Gronchi, the Pisa Normal School; De Gasperi, the University of Vienna. It would appear, then, that a university background is almost essential for a top-ranking political leader in Italy.

Top-level Italian politicians are more frequently intellectuals (particularly professors and journalists) than is the case in the United States. Fanfani was a professor of economics from 1930 until his internment in 1943; Gronchi was a high-school teacher from 1909–1915; and De Gasperi was editor of a provincial Catholic newspaper in Trento from 1905–1911. Italy appears to resemble France in this category of recruitment, where pedagogue-politicians and journalist-politicians abound.[61]

These three cases would appear to indicate that the process of political recruitment is completed fairly early in life. Fanfani joined a Christian Democratic discussion group in 1941, at the

[61] Henry W. Ehrmann, *Politics in France* (Boston: Little, Brown, 1968), pp. 127–129.

age of thirty-three, and was summoned to Rome to work for the Christian Democratic party in 1945, shortly after the Liberation. He was elected a deputy to the Constituent Assembly in 1946, and named to the cabinet as minister of labor in 1947. (All this before his fortieth birthday!) Gronchi was only thirty-two when he was first elected to the Chamber of Deputies in 1919, shortly after his demobilization from the army. De Gasperi was elected to the Austrian Parliament in 1911, only six years after receiving his degree from the University of Vienna. Apparently, then, the familiar American phenomenon of the successful businessman or country gentleman who, in late middle age, decides to embark on a political career is relatively unknown in Italy.

One is struck by the speed with which Gronchi, Fanfani, and De Gasperi attained positions of great prominence in their parties (the Popular party in the case of Gronchi and De Gasperi, the Christian Democratic party in the case of Fanfani). But these were newly founded parties in periods of rapid social and economic change, and they had plenty of room at the top. Presumably, the parties of today, with their patronage plums and entrenched vested interests, would not permit such accelerated political mobility.

POLITICAL RECRUITMENT: THE RULING CLASS

There are a number of ways to analyze political elites. One possible approach is to examine in depth the lives of prominent politicians hoping to uncover the relationship between their careers or leadership styles and the total political picture. This method of political biography is relatively untried in contemporary Italy. A second possibility is to study a sample of the ruling class or, more commonly, some segment thereof—party activists or members of Parliament. Some segmental views of particular elites will be touched upon in later chapters. And finally, one can view the political elite as a ruling class, and then attempt to isolate the people who play a significant role in the political process and those who have an important share in the making of political decisions.

The broadest approach to the Italian elite is taken by the sociologist Cesare Mannucci, who focuses on the 2.5–3 million Italians who have graduated from secondary school.[62] He is con-

---

[62] Cesare Mannucci, "Gli italiani tra passato e futuro," *Comunità*, Vol. XX, No. 137 (May–July 1966), 1–17.

vinced that this large stratum has received an archaic and formalistic education, and that its members are therefore ill-equipped to grasp recent major advances in the social sciences. As a result, they lack the ability to approach political problems empirically or scientifically. These failings in the educational system may help account for the deficiencies of legislators, administrators, and judges who are drawn from the broader universe of educated Italians

Other definitions of the elite are considerably narrower: The Shell Italiana Corporation issued a study defining the Italian ruling class as comprising some 300,000 professional and managerial personnel. Another report claims that only 4000–5000 persons are really in a position to exercise a notable influence on Italian society—and this group is defined as a single, rather cohesive, ruling class, and not merely a set of competing ruling elites.[63] One Italian journalist, Marco Cesarini Sforza, numbers among the elite members of Parliament, members of the regional councils, and some 20,000–21,000 party officials and 10,000-odd members of politicians' staffs. Cesarini Sforza then finds the members of this elite to be intellectually and culturally backward compared with other strata of the ruling class, such as industrialists or archbishops.[64]

Cesarini Sforza's model of the typical Christian Democratic leader is of considerable interest. This prototypical individual was born in a small provincial town, a member of a numerous family of modest means. While still a teenager, he joined Catholic Action and sang in his church choir. Between the ages of twenty and twenty-two, he joined the Italian Catholic University Federation (FUCI) and entered the teaching profession. His activity in FUCI led him into politics. After a short period of activism, he became the secretary of a local section of the Christian Democratic party. Between the ages of twenty-five and thirty, he was elected delegate to the national congress of his party. At about the age of thirty-five, he ran for Parliament, was defeated in his first bid, but elected on his next attempt. In Parliament, his career depends partly on his oratorical ability and partly on his factional affiliation. He may become an under-secretary of state after three or four years in Parliament. Later, if all goes well, he may become a minister or the head of a public enterprise.[65]

[63] Jean Meynaud, *Rapporto sulla classe dirigente italiana* (Milano: Giuffré, 1966), pp. 338–341, 361–363, 369–371.
[64] Cesarini Sforza, pp. 28–32, 34–37, 168–169, 175–178.
[65] Cesarini Sforza, p. 224.

Galli's analysis of what he calls "the political class" focuses on some 2000 professional politicians at the national level—members of Parliament and members of national party executive organs.[66] First of all, he is struck by the unusually high proportion of middle-class people and unusually low proportion of workers in the Italian "political class" as compared with Northern European countries (even in the top echelons of the Communist party, the proportion of university graduates has been steadily rising at the expense of bona fide proletarians). Second, he denies Cesarini Sforza's charge that the "political class" is culturally inferior to business and professional elites, is composed of men who could not make the grade in their professions, or is made up of power-oriented incompetents. Instead, Galli suggests that the chief cause of the failures of the Italian "political class" is its restricted numerical strength.

Being relatively few in number, top-level Italian politicians are compelled to take on a great number of extra public functions. Every single Christian Democratic Senator and Deputy has at least one full-time public post (minister, mayor, provincial president, and so on) in addition to his parliamentary duties, and is also likely to occupy a burdensome executive position in the national or provincial party organization. In addition to all this, many members of Parliament seek to carry on professional activities outside of Parliament. Having so many full-time jobs to perform, the Italian political leader is apt to botch them all.

Galli's explanation for the underlying cause of this condition is intriguing, if somewhat conspiratorial: Sensing public discontent against an overly static system, the "political class" seeks to block any effective expression of this malaise and any consequent circulation of elites by occupying all the key posts in the political system, even if this means a crippling slowdown in the operation of the system, particularly with regard to policy output. Thus, the cumulation of offices creates a situation in which Italian political leaders at the national level "by virtue of wanting to decide everything, decide nothing."[67]

(In the preceding discussion, the reader may have observed with some dismay that terms like "elite," "ruling class," "political class," and "governing class" seem to mean different things to different authors. This impression is, unfortunately, correct. For a discipline that has loudly proclaimed scientific pretensions, political science has yet to develop an agreed-upon terminology. To a

[66] Galli, *Il bipartitismo imperfetto*, ch. 10.
[67] Galli, *Il bipartitismo imperfetto*, pp. 356–357.

deplorable degree, every political scientist acts as his own Noah Webster.)

Italian recruitment patterns seem to result in bringing an abnormally high proportion of professional men and intellectuals into the upper echelons of the policy-making structures. This imbalance perhaps helps to account for the impenetrable jargon that dominates Italian political discourse. More businessmen and trade unionists (*of working-class origin*) in politics might offset this condition. But political participation is even lower in Italy than in other Western European countries. Thus our discussion comes full circle as we observe that inadequate socialization and participation patterns have a deleterious impact on political recruitment. For only where democratic values have been poorly transmitted is politics likely to repel those individuals who do not make their living by manipulating symbols.

CONCLUSIONS

Our examination of political socialization, participation, and recruitment in Italy has revealed the intricate relationships that have been established among these three processes. Discontinuous or otherwise inadequate socialization patterns are apt to discourage political participation and arbitrarily delimit the reservoir of alert manpower from which elites can be recruited. In its turn, curtailed political participation will make the transmission of the system's values to the politically underprivileged a well-nigh hopeless task, will in fact provoke the emergence of new values challenging the very existence of the system. And, of course, a nonparticipating body politic will provide inhospitable soil for the recruitment of new leaders and will hardly be likely to promote rotation in office. Finally, it is evident that patterns of recruitment that result in gross overrepresentation of a given class or category can isolate the political elite from the masses, thereby alienating large segments of the public from the values and styles of the political system.

In studying these processes, we have inevitably left some major questions unanswered, some promising avenues unexplored —for example, the entrancing field of intranation comparison. We have spoken of the Italian family, the Italian workplace, the Italian peer group. However, this has been a rather deceptive form of conceptual short-hand; for in Italy, as in most countries, there are many social and cultural differences among regions, and between urban and rural areas.

The question of the relative importance of each of the agents of socialization will naturally engage the attention of future researchers in the field of comparative politics. For obvious reasons, it has not been possible to devote much time or space to such a complex problem in this volume. But one or two tentative impressions might be ventured on the basis of our findings. It would appear that, in Italy, later socialization experiences frequently outweigh in importance the impressions and values received by the child early in life. As a recent study points out, Italian youths in the ten-to-sixteen age bracket are not strongly alienated from the political system. As a matter of fact, they seem to have great confidence in their right to express their opinions freely—a high sense of expressive efficacy, in other words.[68] Only after some direct adult experience with the actual working of the system, it would appear, do Italians begin to lose faith.

The differences between the findings of the study just cited and the bleak portrait of Italian political culture traced by Almond and Verba raise a basic question regarding the value of cross-national comparisons at a given moment in history. As Burrowes recently proposed, it might make more sense to examine the development of attitudes and belief systems within a given society, or within a small set of similar societies, over an extended period of years.[69] The Italy of *The Civic Culture* may be quite different from the Italy of the 1970s; in fact, we have already seen some evidence of changes in basic attitudes. The case for what Burrowes refers to as "longitudinal analysis" seems powerful indeed. Certainly the long-term relevance of the Almond-Verba findings appears rigorously limited by the time factor.

[68] Dennis, Lindberg, McCrone, Stiefbold, 81–84, 96–97.
[69] Robert Burrowes, "Multiple Time-Series Analysis of Nation-Level Data," *Comparative Political Studies*, Vol. 2, No. 4 (January 1970), 465–480.

THREE
A FRAGMENTED POLITY
Themes of political culture

Political culture can be defined as a complex of politically relevant values, attitudes, and beliefs that are accepted by an entire population. There are certain common cultural features characterizing the Italian people with regard to such attitudes as social trust, individualism, alienation, and sense of civic competence. But regional and social differences in a heterogeneous nation like Italy are often so profound as to condition political attitudes and produce subcultures. As we shall see, some authors suggest that there is a North-South division in Italian political culture. But we might be justified in raising much finer distinctions. For example, there is a great difference between Socialist-Communist Emilia and the Catholic Veneto; yet both regions are part of Northern Italy, a section that is often referred to as a unit, as if it were marked by ideological and social homogeneity. And how can one really speak of a Southern political subculture when even the island of Sicily is divided between a backward, Mafia-infested West and a relatively progressive East?

SOCIAL TRUST:
AN INGREDIENT IN SHORT SUPPLY

Among the more important dimensions of political culture is social trust, or the ability of people in a given society to feel confidence in the motives and actions of their fellow-citizens. Obviously, some measure of mutual trust is essential in a democratic politics of compromise. Men are not likely to cooperate voluntarily if they distrust each other. On the dimension of social trust, we must observe that Italy ranks very low indeed.

In his best-selling book, Barzini writes:

> An Italian learns from childhood that he must keep his mouth shut and think twice before doing anything at all. Everything he touches may be a booby-trap, the next step he takes may lead him over a mine-field; every word he pronounces or writes may be used against him some day. He must pay attention to the unknown people who may be photographed in a group with him at some ceremony or on an outing; at a later date the picture may turn out to be the damaging proof of complicity with scoundrels or of compromising political allegiance, and may eventually destroy him.[1]

The Barzini thesis that a constant struggle for survival foments mutual distrust in Italy is bolstered by a good deal of evidence. Banfield gives a grim description of amoral familism in the Southern town of Montegrano, where the reigning tenet appears to be: "Maximize the short-run advantage of the nuclear family; assume that all others will do likewise."[2] Lopreato reaches similar conclusions regarding the lack of social trust in the South, and underlines them using a pungent quotation from his conversation with a Calabrian peasant: "Italy is a stinking place. We are all like cats and dogs, constantly at each other's throats. I don't know why, but one can't trust even the Lord God himself."[3] Survey research reveals that Italians are often unwilling to discuss politics or reveal their past voting behavior. But, as noted in Chapter Two, a far different pattern of interpersonal relations exists in a Central region (Tuscany) where economic conditions are less harsh than in the South and where land-tenure arrangements encourage co-operation among sharecroppers.

---

[1] Luigi Barzini, *The Italians* (New York: Bantam, 1964), pp. 113–114.

[2] Edward C. Banfield, *The Moral Basis of a Backward Society* (New York: Free Press, 1958), p. 83.

[3] Joseph Lopreato, *Peasants No More: Social Class and Social Change in an Underdeveloped Society* (San Francisco: Chandler, 1967), p. 66.

To some degree, the lack of mutual confidence is explainable in terms of Italy's experience with totalitarian rule. During the Fascist regime, any friend or neighbor might turn out to be a police informer, and looseness of tongue was inadvisable. But distrust is also a natural response to the ruthless competition that must perforce develop in a small, crowded peninsula, where 50 million people are vying for a limited supply of wealth and power.

Lack of faith in one's fellow-citizens almost invariably leads to lack of trust in the integrity of government institutions. We have already referred to the widespread belief in the venality of the bureaucracy. There is a similar lack of confidence in the legislature, the political parties, and the courts. One author ruefully recalls the question posed to him by some of his friends shortly after he entered Parliament, "But whatever possessed you, a respectable person, to involve yourself in that garbage?"[4] Another writer traces the unpopularity of parties and politicians back to the victory of the so-called Left in 1876, a development that brought a new class of professional politicians to power. This new ruling group lacked the prestige conferred by the *Risorgimento* upon the founding fathers of Italian national unification. The excessive promises made by the proponents of unification (such as the members of the Italian National Society) had led the Italian middle classes to expect that the formation of the Kingdom of Italy would automatically usher in an era of progress and good feeling. As a result, the Italian voting public was emotionally unprepared for the influence-peddling and logrolling that accompanied the first stages of parliamentary democracy in a developing nation. Ever since that time, party politics has had a bad image, not only among the apathetic, but also among the active participants in the political process. Politicians are widely regarded as being lazy, undisciplined, unprincipled, and dishonest.[5] The judicial branch also receives its share of disapproval. As Barzini cynically suggests, many Italians are reluctant to go to court unless they are clearly in the wrong; for in that event, they often can rely on cumbersome trial proceedings to postpone judgment indefinitely.[6]

At this point, however, we must bring up some contradictory

---

[4] Piero Calamandrei, *Scritti e discorsi politici*, Vol. I, (Firenze: La Nuova Italia, 1966), p. 323.

[5] Marco Cesarini Sforza, *L'uomo politico* (Firenze: Vallecchi, 1963), pp. 5–25.

[6] Barzini, pp. 109–110.

and rather perplexing evidence. If social distrust leads to distrust of political institutions, and if the South is characterized by a greater degree of social distrust than the North, we would expect Southerners to distrust the government more than Northerners do. Yet, this does not turn out to be the case. Even in Banfield's study of Montegrano, the peasants do not seem to be suspicious of the state; rather, many seem to view the government as a friend and a source of assistance.[7] A more recent study, based on raw data accumulated by Almond and Verba and made available by the Inter-University Consortium for Political Research, furnishes further confirmation. According to this survey, Southerners are more aware than Northerners regarding the local impact of national government policies and are also more likely than Northerners to view such policies in a favorable light. Moreover, Southerners seem to have somewhat higher expectations of fair treatment and serious consideration at the hands of government agencies, civil servants, and the police.[8] Thus, any effort to draw a line of progression from a substandard and precarious way of life, to pervasive social distrust, to distrust of governmental institutions themselves is not, as yet, fully justified by available research. This finding again raises the broader question of what the real differences are between Northern and Southern political cultures.

Another puzzling discrepancy should be noted. One result of social distrust presumably should be to discourage the formation of associational ties, to undermine cooperative ventures of any kind. Banfield certainly brings out the reluctance of the amoral familists of Montegrano to organize themselves for the purpose of obtaining civic improvements.[9] Yet, other authors caution us that Southern Italians *do* form a multitude of groups (usually clienteles revolving around a powerful patron) for a variety of purposes; and a number of recent case studies reveal rather different patterns from Montegrano in *other* Southern towns.[10] Perhaps, then, Montegrano is not at all typical of large sections of Southern Italy, to say nothing of the North and Center.

In spite of the obvious gist of these reports, we must not leave the impression that Italy is a kind of twentieth-century jun-

---

[7] Banfield, pp. 39–41.

[8] Kenneth A. Bode and Timothy M. Hennessey, "Region as a Political Variable: Within-Nation Differences and Political Culture in Italy," paper delivered at the 1967 Annual Meeting of the Midwest Political Science Association, West Lafayette, Indiana, April 27–29, 1967, pp. 21–24.

[9] Banfield, pp. 18–20, 31.

[10] Sidney G. Tarrow, *Peasant Communism in Southern Italy* (New Haven, Conn.: Yale University Press, 1967), p. 56.

gle where every man's hand is raised against his neighbor. In a highly civilized society, with a long and illustrious history, there are certain mitigating features that make the competitive and discordant characteristics of Italian life more tolerable. For example, there is less violence in Italy than in America, and it is relatively safe to walk the streets of Italian cities at night. Close family ties may be partly responsible for this: The rootlessness and lack of proper parental guidance, which characterizes such large segments of American youth, are not nearly as common in Italy. Also, there is a tradition of compassion and understanding for human frailties that helps to soften the blows which are all too frequently suffered by the weak and maladroit. Even when Italians behave like the ruthless, unprincipled opportunists Barzini describes, they lack the cold, self-righteous cruelty of people who are blindly convinced of their own virtue. There was no equivalent of Auschwitz south of the Brenner Pass.

SENSE OF AUTONOMY:
ARE ITALIANS INDIVIDUALISTIC?

Certain features of Italian politics and Italian society suggest that a sense of individual autonomy is not a dominant element in Italian political culture. To be sure, there are certain manifestations of extreme individualism in Italian public and private life: the reckless driving habits so common on Italian highways; the tendency of otherwise respectable middle-class Italians to shove their way to the head of the queue; the penchant for tax evasion. But beneath the anarchic folkways and surface gaiety that so impress visiting tourists, there are rigorous norms that must be followed, social codes that must be obeyed, a public opinion that must be paid due reverence. The obsessive desire to "make a good impression" (*fare una bella figura*)[11] is certainly a conformist syndrome, which helps to account for the unusually elegant and yet conservative garb worn by so many poverty-stricken lower-middle-class Italians. Barzini cites the need, felt by every ambitious young Italian, to join a clique or faction, to acquire a powerful protector, and to curry favor with that protector at all costs.[12] Relationships in these informal groupings are usually hierarchical; individuals do not have equal standing. So, while

[11] Norman Kogan, *The Politics of Italian Foreign Policy* (New York: Praeger, 1963), p. 4.
[12] Barzini, pp. 236–243.

anarchic individualism *does* exist in Italian political culture, it seems to be generally restricted by overriding group expectations, and usually manifests itself as a kind of cathartic release of tension, a sporadic violent reaction against an unusually conventional social order.

SENSE OF NATIONAL IDENTITY: IS THERE AN ITALIAN PEOPLE?

As we have already seen, late unification imposed serious delays on the process of national integration, and the overcentralization and militarism imposed by the North Italian ruling class did little to improve matters. Regional and local dialects have survived to the present day, and have given way only slowly and grudgingly to the standard national tongue. Moreover, the sluggish rate of Italian urbanization, industrialization, and economic growth did much to keep parochial loyalties alive.

According to La Palombara, provincialism is still a very powerful force in Italy today, and the process of "making Italians" out of Piedmontese, Lombards, Tuscans, Sicilians, and so forth, is far from complete. He cites in support of his thesis the fact that Italian respondents in Almond and Verba's *The Civic Culture* show relatively little admiration for their political and governmental institutions as compared with American and British respondents. Yet, La Palombara is compelled to admit that separatism has been but a negligible force in Italian politics over the past twenty-five years.[13] A more sanguine view is stated by Bode and Hennessey, who assert (also on the basis of data in *The Civic Culture*) that:

> . . . it is clear that Italy lags behind the other nations in the development of a widespread and active sense of national consciousness. There is, however, a large reservoir of latent citizenship in that country as in all the others; the feeling that man, as a citizen, has some obligation to his country is widespread. In much the same way that political party identification is a socio-religious phenomenon for many Italians, citizenship also implies passive and essentially apolitical obligations. Identity with nation, then, appears to be a complaisant and acquiescent phenomenon

---

[13] Joseph La Palombara, "Italy: Fragmentation, Isolation, Alienation," in Lucian W. Pye and Sidney Verba, eds., *Political Culture and Political Development* (Princeton, N.J.: Princeton University Press, 1965), pp. 282, 286–289, 298–300.

which combines a diffuse pride in being "Italian" with a politically passive sense of citizenship. The notion prevails that a man serves his country well enough by being a good, moral, upright person, paying taxes and obeying the law.[14]

As we have already indicated, the Resistance experience (which, however, was shared only by Northern Italians and somewhat estranged the South), the economic miracle, and the migration of peasants to the cities of the Northwest Triangle have all contributed to national integration. And, of course, television, radio, and the motion-picture industry have helped to propagate an Italian national image. In fact, even when the movies or other mass media deal with regional characters or regional dialects, the effect is to strengthen national unity by giving the audience the proud sense of belonging to a richly variegated, and hence more interesting, national society. The creative technique is a familiar one to Americans who remember the World War II films with their galleries of stereotypes: the tall, slow-spoken Texan; the tough-talking but basically decent kid from Brooklyn; the cleancut Midwesterner. In like manner, Italian films may feature a laconic Piedmontese, a businesslike Lombard, a hearty devil-may-care Roman, and so on.

Quite apart from such rather transparent devices, the experiences of the last half-century have forged certain indissoluble bonds among the people of the Italian peninsula. For all effects and purposes, the battle for national (as opposed to social) integration has been won. In fact, there is a good deal of untested evidence which suggests that Italians today may have a clearer sense of their national identity than do Americans.

POLITICAL COGNITION AND POLITICAL COMPETENCE: A BACKWARD ELECTORATE

Political cognition may be defined as awareness of and knowledge about the political system in its governmental and political aspects. Cognition is an important prerequisite to understanding political culture. People who are found to rank low in political cognition literally do not know what is going on in the world around them, and have no basis for reaching rational political judgments.

[14] Bode and Hennessey, p. 14.

Various surveys of Italian opinion indicate a pattern of lack of exposure to and information about political events. One early study revealed that 62 percent of the Italian respondents (as compared with only 32 percent of a British panel and 25 percent of a German panel) claimed that they *never* followed accounts of political and governmental affairs.[15] A more recent set of polls, conducted in 1962 and 1964, contained some startling revelations. Only 50 percent of a national sample of Italians had heard or read about the opening to the Left (the outstanding political issue in 1962 and for several preceding years), and 55 percent did not even know what the term meant. In 1964, 37 percent of the voters could not name the prime minister and 46 percent could not name *a single one* of the parties represented in the Moro cabinet.[16] In short, parochial orientations to the political process—orientations characterized by almost complete lack of awareness—are particularly numerous in Italy.

Political competence is the ability to influence the formation of public policy, and administrative competence is the ability to obtain one's rights from law-enforcement agencies and other branches of the bureaucracy. A citizen who lacks these capacities is apt to feel helpless and perhaps even frustrated in his dealings with governmental authority. As a result, he may view the political system with bovine passivity, or disenchanted apathy, or even angry and active antagonism. On the other hand, an individual's low objective competence may be offset by his high subjective competence; that is, he may have relatively little ability to influence public policy or obtain his rights under the law, but may have a sense of great confidence in his ability to do these things—confidence that lacks any objective justification. Subjective competence may stave off the apathy or alienation to which we have just alluded.

Applying these criteria of political competence, we once again find Italy ranking well below the United States, Britain, and Germany. Only about one in three Italian respondents seems to expect serious consideration to be accorded his viewpoints in a government office or police station. And an unusually high proportion of Italian respondents seem to have no clear idea how to go about changing an unjust law or regulation.[17] However, a more

[15] Gabriel A. Almond and Sidney Verba, *The Civic Culture: Political Attitudes and Democracy in Five Nations* (Princeton, N.J.: Princeton University Press, 1963), p. 89.

[16] Pierpaolo Luzzatto-Fegiz, *Il volto sconosciuto dell' Italia* (2nd series; Milano: Giuffré, 1956–1965, 1966), pp. 488–489, 680–681, 696–697.

[17] Almond and Verba, pp. 109–110, 180–186.

recent study of Italian, German, British, and American adolescents indicates a far higher rating for Italy with regard to subjective competence (equated by the authors of the article with "sense of political efficacy"). On most of the questions posed in this new survey, Italian adolescents seem to grow more confident about their competence as they grow older.[18] But apparently subjective competence does not long survive the entry into adult responsibilities. We can interpret from this finding a sad commentary on the Italian political system: With experience, comes the end of youthful illusions.

ALIENATION AND VIOLENCE IN ITALIAN POLITICAL CULTURE

Alienation is widely regarded as a major characteristic of Italian political culture. We define it as a thoroughly negative attitude toward the political system and toward the institutions established by the system. The view expressed by one peasant in Ignazio Silone's novel, *Fontamara*, is not at all atypical: " 'All governments are made up of thieves,' he said. 'Naturally, it's better for the peasants if the government is made up of just one thief, rather than five hundred, because a big thief, no matter how big he is, always eats less than five hundred little ones.' "[19] Men who hold such views are hardly likely to take great risks on behalf of democratic institutions.

Numerous observers find alienation in the very meager measure of pride expressed by Italian voters with regard to their political institutions, the general tendency to regard the government as an enemy, and the belief that corruption is everywhere. This set of attitudes represents a state of mind known as *qualunquismo*—a term derived from the *Uomo Qualunque* (Average Man) party, an extreme rightist movement of the 1946–1948 period. *Qualunquismo* glorifies the "average" middle-class voter who pays his taxes and minds his own business, relentlessly attacks the weaknesses—real and imaginary—of the democratic political process, reviles both politics and politicians, and expresses a nostalgic yearning for some form of authoritarian solution.

In recent years, some scholars have objected to the view that

---

[18] Jack Dennis, Leon Lindberg, Donald McCrone, and Rodney Stiefbold, "Political Socialization to Democratic Orientations in Four Western Systems," *Comparative Political Studies*, Vol. 1, No. 1 (April 1968), 79–82 .
[19] Ignazio Silone, *Fontamara* (rev. ed.; New York: Dell, 1961), pp. 108–109.

Italy has an alienated political culture. They point out that party activists (both Communist and Christian Democratic) have assumed a posture of commitment to the evolutionary improvement of the system and of intense participation in social and political life.[20] Also, they suggest that the mere fact that one-fourth of the Italian electorate votes for the Communist party cannot by itself be regarded as prima facie evidence of an alienated political culture. For the Communist party has been preaching reformism and seeking votes through the normal political processes for the past twenty-five years, and young Communists show a remarkably high level of support for the present multiparty system.[21] Finally, some scholars have discovered that Italian adolescents have a strong sense of *expressive* efficacy; in other words, they feel great confidence in their right to vent opinions and complaints.[22] Even in the absence of a strong sense of political competence, expressive efficacy provides an outlet for grievances and can help head off alienation. Of course, as we have previously suggested, alienation may come with the worries and frustrations of adulthood.

One symptom of alienation in Italian politics is the frequent outbreak of anomic political behavior in the form of riots and violent demonstrations. This kind of thing can quite easily lead to bloodshed, especially since Italian policemen are somewhat prone to use firearms indiscriminately when the going gets tough. But it must also be recognized that Italian police are subjected to greater and more frequent provocation than are police in most Northern European countries. An impromptu street demonstration, accompanied by chanted slogans and an eventual confrontation with the police, is a standard and almost expected reaction to any public grievance. Not only do the downtrodden and disinherited use such methods: During the "radiant days" of May 1915, well-dressed middle-class mobs agitated violently for Italian entry into World War I.

It may be said, then, that violence forms an accepted part of Italian political style. It tends, therefore, to have an almost ritualized quality about it. There is a definite scenario to most demonstrations and a set of limits that are usually not transgressed by

---

[20] A. Manoukian, "Conclusione," in Francesco Alberoni, ed., *L'attivista di partito* (Bologna: Il Mulino, 1967), pp. 520–525. Coauthors include V. Capecchi, A. Manoukian, F. Olivetti, A. Tosi.

[21] Timothy M. Hennessey, "Democratic Attitudinal Configurations among Italian Youth," *Midwest Journal of Political Science*, Vol. XIII, No. 2 (May 1969), 189–193; and Sidney G. Tarrow, "Political Dualism and Italian Communism," *American Political Science Review*, Vol. 61, No. 1 (March 1967), 40–41.

[22] Dennis, *et al.*, 82–84.

either the police or the demonstrators. These limits are quite broad, however; the infliction of a few score casualties, including (as a climax to the proceedings) a handful of dead, is by no means ruled out.

Why are Italians so inclined to resort to anomic political behavior? One reason has to do with the agonizing slowness and inefficiency of Italian decision-making processes. Violence has to be employed as an attention-getting device, to dramatize a need. If the need is acute enough and continues to be ignored, then violent protest will escape outside manipulation and take on a momentum of its own, the rules of the game will be set aside, the casualty lists will mount uncontrollably. Thus it was with the peasant riots in Southern Italy in 1948–1949, which compelled the De Gasperi government to rush through emergency land-reform legislation. Similarly, the riots in the summer of 1960 were an elemental protest against a prime minister who was suspected of repudiating the values of the Resistance and of conspiring to set up a rightist dictatorship.

Political violence is also a product of the lack of mutual trust in Italian society. You do not reason or compromise with people you cannot trust; force is the only language they understand, or so the thinking goes. You do not go through legal channels, if political institutions are shot through with corruption. And if you are the leader of a group that has a grievance, you must occasionally display your militance in order to prove that you are not selling out to the ruling powers. These statements are examples of the irrationality that accompanies a lack of mutual trust.

Lastly, political violence has a cathartic function: It releases some of the tensions and frustrations that are always lurking beneath the surface in Italy. Thus, riots can occur when one least expects them and for the most unpredictable reasons: a rash of unemployment at Battipaglia; the shutting down of certain central government field offices at Sulmona; the home team's loss of a crucial soccer match at Caserta. Nevertheless, let it be reemphasized that this is a controlled catharsis with a dual effect: It expresses the alienation felt by so many Italians, but it also checks and domesticates this alienation by giving people a chance to act out their protest. Just as Italian interpersonal relations are not as spontaneous and amicable as they may appear to the foreign observer, seemingly anarchic and/or anomic behavior in Italy is not nearly as aimless and destructive as would be the case if true anarchy or anomie prevailed.

The limited and ritualistic nature of Italian political violence is better understood if we bear in mind the fact that Italy is not an especially violent society. Apart from the activities of the Mafia in Western Sicily and the banditry in Sardinia, there are far fewer violent crimes in Italy, in proportion to the total population, than in the United States. And even the activities of the Mafia and of the Sardinian bandits could be regarded as apolitical modes of dissent in especially underprivileged and exploited sections of Italy. The Mafioso and the bandit chief may be romanticized by the local populace as Robin Hood figures defying the authority of an illegitimate state.

IMAGES OF AUTHORITY

In Chapter Two on political socialization, and in the early part of this chapter as well, a number of themes relating to images of authority in Italy appeared. The traditional image seems to be a precarious mixture of obedience, reverence, resentment, and distrust. In the home, at school, on the job, in church, authority must be obeyed without cavil. How willingly it is obeyed, is another matter. Obedience has not been practiced uniformly in all parts of Italy—witness the long-standing opposition to the church in Emilia.

As for the government, it is viewed with mixed feelings. The traditional image of authority certainly contains a great deal of distrust and animosity directed against the government, the political parties, the professional politicians, and the bureaucrats. But there is evidence of powerful countervailing attitudes. Thus, there is testimony that Italian public opinion distrusts the government and tends to condone tax evasion, while at the same time, Banfield reports that the peasants of Montegrano have a neutral or positive orientation toward the government. We note the widespread view that the bureaucracy is corrupt, inefficient, and low in prestige; but we can also cite a study which indicates that the Southern lower middle class has great respect for the state and its institutions as bearers of high civil values, and that the members of this class often enter the bureaucracy in the hope of obtaining moral satisfactions and high social status.[23] The attitude toward the state that we find in the traditional image of authority would have to be described, then, as ambivalent.

In one respect, however, there is no ambivalence. If the government is despised and distrusted, it is not in the name of indi-

---

[23] Franco Demarchi, "I laureati nella pubblica amministrazione," in Comitato di Studio dei Problemi della Scuola e dell' Università Italiana, *I laureati in Italia* (Bologna: Il Mulino, 1968), pp. 248–249.

vidual freedom. When Italians take a dim view of the legitimacy of the central government's actions, they are usually defending the entrenched rights of the family, the employer, the church, or the Mafia—all hierarchical organizations in which obedience has been required as a matter of course. Thus, when the Mafia chieftain, Calogero Vizzini, was told he was breaking the law, he replied, "Let the Romans keep the laws they make. In this part of the world we have our own way of doing things."[24] Vizzini was hardly speaking as a staunch defender of individual freedom. In short, the individual is defended against governmental authority, but only that he may serve some other master. There is no major Italian tradition of exaltation of the lone individual; there is no significant Italian laissez-faire counterpart of the French Radical tradition; there is no Italian Alain.

The traditional concept of authority is being seriously challenged at the present time, as evidenced by increasing pressures for individual rights in the family, growing demands for democratization in the schools and universities, a rash of wildcat strikes aimed against both the autocratic employer and the established trade-union hierarchy, and a rising tide of rebelliousness in certain Catholic organizations. What we have previously referred to as the crisis of participation is really a vast movement to restructure authority in Italy. Unfortunately, the newer images of authority are rather blurred, and it sometimes appears that no new structures have really been planned to replace the old. In fact, Matteucci warns that Italy is experiencing a crisis of "populist insurgency," characterized by a passionate and uncritical rejection of rationality and expertise and an authoritarian impatience with modern constitutional procedures. This type of populist movement is not unprecedented: Matteucci cites the interventionism of 1915 and the Left-wing Fascist factions of 1919–1922.[25] The historical parallel is rather frightening, to say the least.

A CASE OF CULTURAL LAG

In Italy, as in any other nation, there is a continuing conflict between traditional and modern motives. We shall deal briefly in the next section of this chapter with one of the most widely discussed features of this conflict—the difference between Northern

---

[24] Norman Lewis, *The Honored Society* (New York: Putnam, 1964), p. 103.
[25] Nicola Matteucci, "La cultura politica italiana fra l'insurgenza populistica e l'età delle riforme," *Il Mulino*, Vol. XIX, No. 207 (January–February, 1970), 5–8.

and Southern Italy. Some scholars feel that North-South differences have been overemphasized and that the primary conflict of cultural themes exists between urban-industrial areas and predominantly agricultural areas. For example, in tradition-bound rural areas, people are apt to ascribe more importance to primary groups such as the family; in modern urban-industrial areas, secondary associations such as trade unions are likely to command a greater share of an individual's allegiance. In urban-industrial areas, people are more likely to vote for a party, without being overly concerned about the identity of the candidates; in rural areas there is more likely to be a politics of personality reminiscent of feudalism.

The conflict between the traditional and the modern also manifests itself in male-female differences and generational differences. Survey research has revealed that Italian women are more traditional than Italian men in their attitudes; they are more conservative, more apathetic, and less informed than men. In fact, Italian women rank below American, British, and German women on all these dimensions. Likewise, generational differences in Italy mirror the conflict between the traditional and the modern, just as they do throughout the Western world. Italian youth has shown increasing impatience with entrenched customs and has pressed for more participation in decision making in the schools, and in the family as well.

The same dichotomy between modernity and tradition exists in other areas of Italian life. For example, there is the paradox of an archaic educational system, riddled with semifeudal abuses, which is supposed to recruit individuals to serve a modern industrial economy and a democratic polity. There are some forces in the society (big business, the banking community, the trade union confederations, and the public corporations with their ruling elites of technocrats) that are committed to modernity, to economic and social progress. Other forces (the farm organizations, the civil service) tend to resist change. There are political parties, like the Christian Democrats and the Communists, that have been somewhat more aware of the modern need to increase popular participation in decision making. The Socialists, on the other hand, labored for many years under the traditionalist illusion that the problems of popular discontent would be resolved on the day when Socialist ministers entered the Cabinet. And within each party, there are elements that cling to outdated ideological habits, while more modern and pragmatic elements are concerned primarily with winning elections.

Contemporary observers of Italian parties speak of a trend

toward greater pragmatism, away from ideological shibboleths. The party activist as missionary, propagating a faith, is giving way to the party activist as political professional, always prepared for dialogue and compromise.[26] For some observers, this process is not proceeding rapidly enough. Public opinion is increasingly indifferent to the outdated values sustained by the political parties and is ever more vulnerable to the appeal of values emanating from power centers that the Italian state cannot effectively control: large corporations, both domestic and international, and major foreign powers. This trend is leading to a major fracture between civil society and political society.[27] On the other hand, Matteucci believes that the shift toward pragmatism has taken place too rapidly and without sufficient concern for underlying goals. Because the Italian political class during the last decade has lacked firm values and a clear model of the society it wished to construct, the opening to the Left has degenerated into logrolling opportunism, thus paving the way for the irrational and destructive insurgency of the populist Left.[28]

Matteucci's thesis is convincing but it does not really affect the validity of the widely held view that there is a severe cultural lag in Italian politics and society. While the "material culture" (economic techniques, procedures, and organizational methods) has been modernizing, the "nonmaterial culture" (cognitions, beliefs, customs, and rules prevailing in the society) has retained a rather archaic quality. In fact, an old-fashioned political style typical of the more backward areas, with an emphasis on patronage and personal cliques, continues to restrict political progress at the cabinet level. Personal rivalries, such as the conflicting presidential ambitions of Fanfani and Moro, help to bring about cabinet crises that are virtually inexplicable in policy terms. Also, the language used by leading politicians to address the public continues to reflect the ideological political style of a bygone era.

Mannucci believes that the cultural background of the political and bureaucratic elites may be largely to blame for this phenomenon of cultural lag.[29] In schools and universities, Italians are never really taught to relate abstract ideas to empirical data: the normative and the empirical are kept in watertight compartments. One learns about abstract legal principles but not how to

[26] Manoukian, p. 520.
[27] Fabrizio Onofri, *L'uomo e la rivoluzione* (Bologna: Il Mulino, 1968), pp. 17–26.
[28] Matteucci, 14–23.
[29] Cesare Mannucci, "Gli italiani tra passato e futuro," *Comunità*, Vol. XX, No. 137 (May–June 1966), 1–17.

apply those principles to concrete cases. One digests a great deal of historical information, but is not pressed to develop general hypotheses from that information. Newer approaches in political science, administrative science, sociology, and psychology are just beginning to penetrate the universities, against the staunch resistance of the academic establishment. The problem-oriented approach employed in American universities has yet to gain widespread acceptance in Italy. It is only natural that a political class emerging from such an educational system would mirror the defects and lacunae of the system.

Of course, in accepting Mannucci's thesis, we may be guilty of failing to avoid the pitfall of moralism: for it is an uncontrovertible fact that the American political class, exposed to the empirical, problem-oriented, scientifically up-to-date system of American higher education, has also committed serious blunders from time to time.

REGIONAL SUBCULTURES: CULTURAL DUALISM OR CULTURAL PLURALISM?

Many authors and observers speak of an Italian dual culture: the European North and the Mediterranean South. In the industrially advanced North, men are appointed and promoted on the basis of their achievements, universal rules are followed in judging the rights of individuals before government agencies, time-honored customs and traditions are fairly easily set aside. In agriculturally backward Southern Italy, family and friendship ties often have a major impact on an individual's career prospects; a prominent local patron often can obtain special privileges for a member of his clientele. In other words, universalistic achievement criteria prevail in the North; particularistic ascriptive criteria dominate the South. One subculture is predominantly legal-rational, the other predominantly traditional.

Additional traits of the Southern subculture are cited by La Palombara and Tarrow.[30] They include a fierce and emotional loyalty to the family, an archaic concept of feminine honor and fidelity (which makes it possible to refer to the murder of an unfaithful Southern wife as "Divorce, Italian Style"), a tendency to seek security and status rather than money, a relative absence of entrepreneurial initiative, and a prevalent cynicism (which is

---

[30] La Palombara, pp. 303–309, 314–315; and Tarrow, *Peasant Communism . . .* , pp. 55–59, 226–228, 230, 233–238, 245–246.

really a product of the resentment felt toward modern organizations and institutions imported from the North). Southerners are also depicted as less informed about political events and less likely to join interest groups, although Southerners can and do form groups for purposes that fit in with their urgent needs or to resist outside interference. Even Southern Communist provincial leaders reflect the paternalism of the Southern subculture by treating their rank-and-file members of peasant origin with a certain air of condescension and superiority and by showing less concern for ideology than do Northern Communist provincial leaders. Moreover, the South did not experience the Resistance and does not revere that particular tradition.

But the cultural dualism approach has been challenged with increasing intensity. While obviously the contrasts between the South and the rest of Italy with regard to living standards, educational facilities, public health, and so forth, cannot be denied, Bode and Hennessey have uncovered some striking similarities between Southern and Northern political attitudes. For instance, there seem to be no major differences between Northerners and Southerners with regard to interest in national election campaigns, possession of politically relevant and accurate information, and perception of the impact of government policy on their daily lives. Southerners are more favorably inclined than Northerners toward the local and provincial activities of the national government; in their sense of efficacy and political competence, they either equal or surpass the North. They are also more administratively competent: They have more confidence in their ability to receive equal treatment and consideration from the bureaucracy and the police. The heavy influx of radio and television into the South and the feedback from returning emigrants have both had their effect in the growing integration and nationalization of the South. Bode and Hennessey admit that there *is* "a qualitative difference between political life north and south of Rome,"[31] but these differences do not include cognition and feelings of political competence.

A more telling critique is delivered by Kogan, whose main objection to the concept of cultural dualism is that Italian society is too complex to be subjected to such an oversimplified form of classification. First of all, clienteles and cynicism are not confined to the South, but also exist in large areas of the North, especially the rural regions. Also, he questions the value of speaking of "the North" or "the South." As he shows, there are several Norths and

---

[31] Bode and Hennessey, p. 33.

many Souths.[32] There are at least three political regions in the area North of Rome: the Northwest Triangle, the Veneto, and North-Central Italy. And certainly Sicily differs from both Sardinia and the Southern mainland. What is important here is that we must recognize the need to make necessary intranation and intraregion distinctions.

SOCIAL AND IDEOLOGICAL FRAGMENTATION: POLITICAL SUBCULTURES

Ideological differences, reinforced by class differences, divide a society into separate subcultures. Chapter One described how the sharp cleavages among classes in Italy and the heritage of bitter class conflict offer a plausible explanation for the counterrevolutionary violence that accompanied the advent of Fascism in 1920–1922. In order to understand contemporary Italian politics, it is essential to bear in mind the rigidly stratified character of Italian society, and to inquire into the question of what social changes are taking place now.

Italy has come a long way from those cruel times when the Fascist action squads burned down trade-union headquarters and lynched labor leaders, and when it was possible for a Fascist university student to write a scornful and menacing open letter to a newspaper, condemning the local peasant girls for wearing silk dresses on Sunday as if they belonged to the middle class.[33] Today, a middle-class Italian would not dare to use the familiar form in addressing a servant or laborer or shop assistant, as was frequently done before World War II. Social distinctions are still more noticeable than in the United States, especially in the South and other less developed areas of Italy. Where in Anglo-Saxon countries "Mister" is the accepted form of address, Italians prefer an exaggerated use of titles: Italian professional men are addressed as Engineer Rossi, Accountant Verdi, Attorney Spini, Land Surveyor Bianchi; any university graduate—whether lawyer, shopkeeper, or police captain—is referred to in the press as "Doctor." For that matter, any man with a briefcase entering a Roman or Southern restaurant automatically merits the title of "doctor," as this author discovered when he visited Italy as a mere graduate student.

---

[32] Norman Kogan, "Review of Sidney G. Tarrow, 'Peasant Communism in Southern Italy,'" *American Political Science Review*, Vol. 62, No. 4 (December 1968), 1282–1283.

[33] Angelo Tasca (pseudonym, Angelo Rossi), *The Rise of Italian Fascism 1918–1922* (London: Methuen, 1938), p. 122.

To be sure, class distinctions are much less noticeable in the Northern industrial cities. Some industrial workers, particularly the ones employed by ultramodern firms like Fiat or Olivetti, are able to maintain middle-class living standards. As the proportion of white-collar workers rises, the boundaries of class conflict become blurred. And a new technological elite, based on skills rather than family ties, is emerging. All over Italy, ready-made clothes make class differences less obvious than they were in the past, and the ubiquitousness of television makes it possible for even illiterates to learn to speak Italian. But public opinion surveys reveal that, even in the mid-1960s, there were still basic differences between the living standards of industrial workers and white-collar workers with regard to such indices as possession of a television set, a refrigerator, or hot running water.[34] Also, the ethos of the self-made man, which usually develops in a highly mobile social situation, is not fully accepted in Italy: Middle-class people of working-class origin seem to have much difficulty gaining social recognition from the established members of their "new" social class. It is, perhaps, for this reason that middle-class Italians of working-class origin are apt to be more leftist than the other members of the middle class, while their counterparts in the United States are apt to be ultraconservative.[35]

Given this continuing division in Italian society, which has not yet fully recovered from the fratricidal bitterness of the past, it is hardly surprising that Italy has developed middle-class and lower-class subcultures. No single political party has acquired monopolistic control over either of these subcultures. For instance, not all members of the lower class support the Communists; many support the Socialists and even the Christian Democrats. Also, the middle class divides its support among *all* the parties, not just the Christian Democrats and Liberals. So, although the Communists, the Social Democrats, the Christian Democrats, and even the Neo-Fascists each have a series of closely affiliated or allied interest groups, it would be a trifle misleading to identify each party as constituting a separate subculture. For, as Barnes recognizes:

> . . . there is no evidence of great differences in outlook between one businessman who supports the PLI [Italian Liberal Party] because of its economic conservatism and his colleague who votes

[34] Luzzatto-Fegiz, pp. 1543–1546.
[35] Joseph Lopreato, "Upward Social Mobility and Political Orientation," *American Sociological Review*, Vol. 32, No. 4 (August 1967), 586–592.

Christian Democratic for business reasons and out of fear of communism, nor of differing basic attitudes between a landowning farmer who votes Christian Democratic to protect his farm and the sharecropper who votes Communist because he does not own land. The differences lie in perceptions of interests and how best to further them—not in *Weltanschauungen*. This is not to deny the existence of a specifically Catholic subculture in Italy which would prefer an integral Catholicism, but it is far from being coterminous with Christian Democracy.[36]

It would, therefore, be too superficial and somewhat misleading to refer to each political party as the outgrowth and expression of a distinct class and/or ideological subculture. Most Italian writers tend to cite three major subcultures, based on the three main currents of opinion among Italian intellectuals: a liberal subculture, a Christian-social or Catholic subculture, and a Marxist subculture.[37] The liberal subculture is sometimes referred to as bourgeois or laic (that is, nonclerical). It rests on the teachings of Benedetto Croce and on the traditions of men like Camillo Benso di Cavour who led the *Risorgimento*. It includes free-enterprise advocates like Luigi Einaudi and supporters of a kind of New Deal welfare capitalism like Ugo La Malfa and the *Il Ponte, Il Mulino,* and *Comunità* groups. The liberal subculture embraces the numerically weak but extremely influential republican tradition of Giuseppe Mazzini, and includes members of the Liberal and Republican parties and a number of moderate Socialists. With no real agreement on social or economic policy, however, the only bases for political consensus are a certain attitude of suspicion vis-à-vis the Catholic church and an affirmation of the virtues of the capitalist system (in its laissez-faire or Keynesian version, as the case may be). The Liberal party section of the subculture opposes the Left-Center coalition cabinet, while the Republican party section supports it. But both the Liberals and the Republicans backed the divorce law. Finally, one should point out that many middle-class people who vote Christian Democratic may really be laissez-faire liberals at heart.

The Christian-social or Catholic subculture is concerned with preserving Catholic ideals of family and social life, replacing class conflict by class collaboration, and using the wealth and power of

---

[36] Samuel H. Barnes, "Italy: Opposition on Left, Right, and Center," in Robert A. Dahl, ed., *Political Oppositions in Western Democracies* (New Haven, Conn.: Yale University Press, 1966), p. 321.

[37] Ferdinando Di Fenizio, *La programmazione economica* (Torino: UTET, 1965), pp. 57–59.

the state to attack poverty and resolve urgent social problems. It professes reverence for the ideas of Giuseppe Toniolo, Romolo Murri, Don Luigi Sturzo, and the more progressive papal encyclicals. But it also includes a more conservative business-oriented group, the so-called liberal Catholics (in Italy the term "liberal" has a conservative connotation). These conservative Catholics occasionally are apt to defect to the Liberals or even to the Monarchists or Neo-Fascists if they find the policy of the Christian Democratic party too progressive. The subculture is supported almost exclusively by Christian Democrats; but in reality many Christian Democratic voters identify with the liberal subculture for reasons of economic interest.

Like the other two subcultures, the Marxist tradition contains many component strands: communists in the tradition of Antonio Gramsci and Palmiro Togliatti, intransigent socialists who differ from the communists mainly in their unwillingness to accept the leadership of a foreign communist party and in their greater attachment to democratic methods, and several shadings of reformist socialists in the tradition of Filippo Turati. There are fully four parties whose members are more or less committed to this subculture: the Communist party, the Italian Socialist Party of Proletarian Unity (hostile to the Left-Center coalition), the Italian Socialist party or PSI (favorable to the Left-Center) and the Unitary Socialist party or PSU (also favorable to the Left-Center but somewhat more cautious and much more anti-Communist than the PSI).

One could hardly regard the decimated Monarchist and Neo-Fascist parties as forming the nucleus of an ultraconservative subculture. But before Fascism thoroughly discredited Italian conservatism, there was a militant conservative movement that preached ultranationalism and imperialism, and actually rejected the democratic gains of the *Risorgimento* and the Giolitti period. Its thirst for war and conquest would have repelled the current generation of young Italians.

There are certain similarities between French and Italian political subcultures. In both France and Italy, the Marxist subculture is split into orthodox and reformist currents. In both countries, too, progressive and conservative tendencies have vied for supremacy among devout Catholics, with the progressives gradually gaining. And in both countries, the so-called liberal tradition is divided internally between laissez-faire and welfare-state proponents.

But, there are also some significant contrasts between French and Italian subcultures. For one thing, there is no "Gaullist family" in Italian politics. Perhaps partly for this reason, the Italian Catholic subculture is much more powerful and pervasive than the French: In Italy, unlike France, the public schools are Catholic strongholds. Secondly, since Italy has no strong tradition of a democratic revolution, the progressive (radical or republican) component of the liberal subculture is much weaker than in France, and consequently the Italian liberal tradition is much more firmly oriented toward big business.

In modern Italy, it appears that the boundaries between subcultures are beginning to crumble. Liberalism and Catholicism have been collaborating ever since World War II, and the opening to the Left in the early 1960s brought the non-Communist component of the Marxist subculture into the government coalition. Communist-dominated, Socialist-dominated, and Catholic-dominated trade-union confederations have been cooperating closely in recent strikes and have shown increasing independence vis-à-vis their respective sponsoring parties. Some church-sponsored organizations have expressed a certain unwillingness to accept directives from the more conservative segments of the church hierarchy. Furthermore, a certain number of prominent Christian Democrats seem to be making veiled overtures to the Communists. The possibility of a Catholic-Communist alliance can no longer be entirely excluded. This denouement would follow logically, in fact, from the pragmatic characteristics that seem to be replacing the ideological propensities of the main Italian parties.

RELIGION IN POLITICS

Earlier in this book, we traced the evolution of the politics of the Catholic church from the *non expedit* policy before 1904, to occasional support for sympathetic candidates in 1904–1913, to large scale electoral support for Catholic and allied candidates in 1913, to the backing given the Popular party in 1919–1925. We have mentioned the Concordat of 1929 and some of the major gains it entailed for the church—for example, the teaching of religion in the public schools, and Catholic penetration of the teaching profession (neither has yet occurred in France). And we have pointed out that the church and its sponsored organizations have shown a marked preference for the Christian Democratic party, and have not hesitated to advise voters accordingly.

The differences between Italian and French Catholicism

might be touched upon briefly. In France, only about one-fourth of the population is made up of *practicing* Catholics; in Italy, the proportion is closer to one-half.[38] The French party representing political Catholicism (the MRP) was unable to compete successfully with the Gaullists and was gradually squeezed out of existence; in Italy, on the contrary, the Christian Democrats have been the dominant party ever since 1945. The French Catholic Church has been generally on the defensive, and has rarely dared to interfere in matters of culture or personal taste. The Italian Catholic Church has not hesitated, not only to intervene in politics, but also to warn the faithful against certain books and motion pictures and to condemn certain radio and television programs.[39]

Church intervention in Italian politics has gone far beyond the thinly disguised campaign speeches delivered by priests and bishops. There have been repeated attempts to meddle in the internal politics of the Christian Democratic party. For example, in the so-called Sturzo operation of 1952, the Vatican tried to pressure Prime Minister De Gasperi to accept an alliance with the Monarchists and Neo-Fascists in the forthcoming Roman municipal elections. Beginning as early as 1956, numerous Catholic bishops took a firm stand against the opening to the Left; and in May of 1958 this opposition was endorsed by the Conference of Bishops. It was only the change to a more moderate line adopted by Pope John XXIII (whose predecessor, Pius XII, had frequently issued controversial interventionist statements himself, thus setting the tone for the bishops) that gradually induced the Italian bishops to take a more prudent approach. For by the early 1960s, the clergy were becoming conscious of the impossibility of compelling the Christian Democratic party to follow clerical directives, and also were beginning to perceive that further attempts along these lines might shatter Catholic unity.[40] Yet, a few bishops continued to speak out.

Church-state conflict in Italy varies in intensity from region to region. Like the West of France, the Italian Veneto is a very heavily Catholic region, where the peasantry is intensely religious and devoted to the church. On the other hand, the Romagna provinces of Emilia, which used to rebel frequently against papal

---

[38] Luzzatto-Fegiz, pp. 1286–1288, and Lowell G. Noonan, *France: The Politics of Continuity in Change* (New York: Holt, Rinehart and Winston, 1970), pp. 129–130.
[39] Cesare Mannucci, *Lo spettatore senza libertà* (Bari: Laterza, 1962), pp. 273–284.
[40] Alfonso Prandi, *Chiesa e politica* (Bologna: Il Mulino, 1968), pp. 100–113.

rule in the days when the papal states existed as a sovereign entity, are anticlerical to this day; and the residual resentment against past abuses by the church has done a great deal to strengthen the local Communist parties in that region.

Not only has the church, and its sponsored organizations, like Catholic Action and the Civic Committees, played an active role in election campaigns, but there has also been a great deal of fairly successful lobbying and participation in the distribution of patronage. For instance, La Palombara reports that:

> . . . within each diocese it is widely believed that nothing can happen politically that does not have the bishop's sanction; the extent of the Vatican's involvement in social welfare activities and in the vital economic and financial activities of the country is generally considered to be vast; overt attempts by the clergy to orient the political attitudes of the masses—even to dictate legislative, administrative, and judicial decisions—often reach alarming and widely publicized proportions.[41]

Since 1962, the church has lowered its profile and taken a much less intransigent line. The opening to the Left is now accepted as possibly a permanent part of the Italian scene: A Catholic-Socialist alliance is no longer seen as a threat to Christian values. Pope Paul has apparently advised the clergy not to intervene in domestic politics except when basic moral issues are at stake.[42] In this regard, the overwhelming vote against church intervention in politics registered in a 1961 DOXA poll may have helped shape Vatican thinking.[43] The very fact that a divorce law was finally passed in 1971 indicates how far Italy has come from the days of papal and church supremacy in the late 1940s.

CONCLUSIONS

In attempting to describe the political culture of Italy, we are impressed by the conflicting evidence that seems to emerge from the various fields of investigation. On the one hand, we have drawn a bleak picture of a society torn by mutual distrust, of men who must conform to the demands of their group or clique and

---

[41] La Palombara, p. 301.
[42] Alberto Cavallari, *Il Vaticano che cambia* (Milano: Mondadori, 1966), pp. 50–51.
[43] Luzzatto-Fegiz, pp. 1292–1298.

who lack political initiative. The low level of information and the inadequate sense of political competence in Italy is truly depressing. Finally, there is evidence of deep-rooted alienation.

Yet, other studies provide a somewhat less forbidding profile of the Italian body politic. For example, social distrust is not universal: True, the towns that seem to attract foreign researchers are apt to be picturesque and usually backward from an economic and social point of view, and are likely—as a consequence—to be characterized by a lack of mutual trust. But we must ask: To what degree is finding social distrust attributable to sampling error (in the Almond-Verba study) or to distortion in the process of selecting research sites?

Some bits of evidence seemed to point in a more positive direction. The problem of national identity no longer seems to be the threat to Italy's future that it was before World War II. Italian adolescents seem to be unusually optimistic about their political competence, considering the fact that they had presumably been exposed to such negative agents of socialization as the autocratic family and the teacher-dominated archaic school. Also, data on alienation are rather ambivalent: certain categories of Italians are definitely *not* alienated, and those who are do not necessarily represent a real threat to the political system. In fact, the whole concept of alienation needs clarification: must it imply negative affect (active dislike of the system), or do ignorance and indifference qualify?

Finally, the concept of political culture seems useful enough as a guideline to stimulate research, but it is rather deceptive if applied to a national society. Is there ever an Italian or French or Ruritanian political culture? It is rather disquieting to see the results of cross-national studies in which the different historical experiences of component regions are perforce ignored. From what we have seen of the variety of subcultures that can be postulated within a given "political culture," it would appear that intranation comparison promises a bigger payoff than the kind of cross-national survey so much in vogue. Elegant research design cannot alter the fact that a national sample often blurs and confuses the regional distinctions that must be made if a nation's political system is not to be presented in a rather misleading and oversimplified fashion.

FOUR
A UNITARY SYSTEM WITH A QUASI-FEDERAL GLOSS
Local and national politics

Like France, Italy has a unitary system of government—a system in which supreme power is vested in the central government, and in which regional and local units of government possess only such powers as the national government chooses to allow them. To be sure, the present Constitution of the Italian republic vests certain powers in twenty self-governing regions; but only the five "special" regions (Sicily, Sardinia, Val d'Aosta, Trentino-Alto Adige, and Friuli-Venezia Giulia) wield any exclusive powers at all. The other fifteen "ordinary" regions are granted only concurrent powers: Laws passed by their regional assemblies must not be in conflict with the interests of the nation or of other regions.

The three main tiers of governmental authority below the national level correspond to three types of geographic subdivisions. In descending order of importance, they are the region, the province, and the commune. There are twenty regions in all, ranging from tiny French-speaking Val d'Aosta, with less than 100,000 inhabitants, to mighty Lombardy, with a population of almost 7 million. These regions might be compared with the ancient provinces of France (Burgundy, Normandy, and so on) in that they have, for the most part, long historical traditions, and that their people share a sense of cultural and ethnic identity

118　ITALY

which differentiates them, however slightly, from the inhabitants of other regions.

Contained within the twenty regions are ninety-three provinces (similar to the French departments). Each of these provinces (with two or three special exceptions) has a prefect appointed by the central government. There are about 8000 communes (similar in function to the French *communes*). The population of the French and Italian commune can vary from a small rural hamlet to a vast urban agglomeration such as Rome, Milan, or Paris. Most communes, however, in both France and Italy, are located in rural areas and consist of small urban centers or villages and the surrounding countryside. Legally, there is no basic distinction between urban and rural communes, and no real effort to differentiate urban from rural local governments.

It has been pointed out that French communes (there are 38,000 in all, in a nation of about 50 million people) tend to be unusually small, with an average population of 1300. Italy, with more than 50 million people and only 8000 communes, has an average of 6000 inhabitants per commune.[1] In fact, the population of the average Italian commune is high when compared with Switzerland and Germany as well. There is, however, a good deal of unevenness in the Italian communal set-up. Some parts of Italy have hundreds of excessively small communes of the kind so endemic to France: They are especially numerous in the Alps and in some parts of the Central and Southern Apennines. On the other hand, Ostia and Mestre, each with about 100,000 people, have not even attained communal status as yet, but are still considered to be outlying "fractions" of Rome and Venice, respectively. And the commune of Rome contains not only the sprawling metropolis and its suburbs but also large tracts of sparsely settled pasture land surrounding the city.

THE COMMUNES:
THE LABORS OF SISYPHUS

The rule-making and administrative structures of the commune include the communal council, the communal junta, the mayor, and the local bureaucracy. The communal council is elected by

[1] Franco Demarchi, "Considerazioni sociologiche sull' ordinamento territoriale: disfunzioni attuali e indirizzi di riforma," in Giuseppe Maranini, ed., *La Regione e il governo locale* (Milano: Comunità, 1965), Vol. II, pp. 93–94. See also Lowell G. Noonan, *France: The Politics of Continuity in Change* (New York: Holt, Rinehart and Winston, 1970), pp. 154–155.

A UNITARY SYSTEM WITH A QUASI-FEDERAL GLOSS

popular vote, with proportional representation being employed to elect councilmen in communes with a population above 5000 and a majority-list system being used in smaller communes. The size of the council varies from a low of fifteen to a high of eighty, depending on the population of the commune. From its own ranks, the council elects a communal junta (executive council) consisting of from two to fourteen assessors, depending again on the size of the commune. The council also elects the mayor, who not only heads the local government but also, in performing certain official acts, functions as an executive agent of the national government. The permanent staff of the commune is headed by the communal secretary, a career civil servant who is appointed by the prefect of the province but works under the supervision of the mayor, who may demand his transfer. Communal officials appoint the rest of the permanent staff, following general guidelines laid down by national law.

Over the years, Italian lawmakers have seen fit to entrust a wide variety of functions to the communes, including: the building of local roads; the licensing of new housing construction; the performance of minor and strictly local police duties; the provision of public health and sanitation; the issuance of zoning regulations; the operation of certain commercial activities like public transportation, bakeries, and municipal restaurants; and so on. Some of these functions are obligatory (prescribed by national law); others are nonobligatory—especially social-welfare activities, such as school lunches, assistance to the poor, and veterinarian facilities. The long delay in setting up the regions after 1945 would seem to indicate a strong government bias against decentralization; but the sour effect of delay was sweetened somewhat by turning a broad range of tasks over to the communes.

This compensatory movement toward decentralization has been accompanied by an enormous increase in the magnitude of the job facing the communes, especially in the booming Northwest. The influx of immigrants into the great industrial cities created a crying need for new low-cost housing, new schools, and expanded administrative services. Pollution, chronic traffic jams, and mushrooming construction along the great interprovincial roads added to the problems facing the mayor and his junta. All this made for a sharp rise in communal spending; during the 1950s, communal indebtedness actually tripled over a five-year period. Many of the added expenses were simply dumped into the laps of the struggling communes by a series of legislative and executive acts that failed, in many cases, to provide the necessary fiscal resources to defray the newly created costs. There was no special compensation for poorer communes and no real effort by the national government to single out and penalize the more badly organized and financially negligent communes.

Moreover, as needs skyrocketed, local financial resources proved to be increasingly skimpy. As a matter of fact, the communes were getting an ever smaller share of the taxpayer's *lira*: before 1914, 27 percent of total tax revenues went to the local governments; today, the figure is about 20 percent.[2] The five main local taxes raised by the communes were a property tax, a tax on consumption, a tax on animals, a family income tax, and a license tax on business and professional activities. Over and above these locally levied taxes, the communes received specified proportions of the proceeds from a number of national taxes. But these assorted sources of income still did not measure up to the growing demands on the communal exchequer.

Furthermore, the communes did not have fiscal freedom of action. With taxes yielding an insufficient revenue, and with an inadequate share of the national government's revenues earmarked for the coffers of local government, the communes lacked the legal authority to raise new taxes—to develop their own tax mix, in other words. They were also unable or unwilling to apply the fiscal techniques necessary for coping with the enormous rise in land values that resulted from real estate speculation: The owners of new housing developments demanded the installation of expensive utility services from the communes, while managing to shelter their profits from equitable taxation.[3] To an ever-worsening degree, then, the communes found themselves facing bankruptcy. The resulting widespread practice of issuing municipal bonds to cover their deficits led to a very high level of indebtedness and to ever more burdensome interest payments. By March of 1970, 4000 of Italy's 8000 communes were registering budgetary deficits. The worst was yet to come: January 1, 1972, was set as the date for a new tax reform to go into effect, abolishing the local income tax on families and the local tax on consumption, thus further undermining the solvency of Italian local governments.[4]

Not the least of the communes' problems is the very strict

---

[2] Vincenzo Ciangaretti, "Finanza locale, finanza nazionale ed europea," in Maranini, ed., Vol. III, pp. 75–76.

[3] Alberto Acquarone, *Grandi città e aree metropolitane in Italia* (Bologna: Zanichelli, 1961), pp. 113–116.

[4] *La Stampa* (Turin), March 6, 1970.

supervision under which they are compelled to operate. The prefect, who is the centrally appointed administrative chief of the province, has the power to overrule decisions of the communal council on the ground of illegality. He may also disallow municipal contracts on their merits if they exceed 3 million *lire* (about $5000) and strike him as inexpedient. Moreover, the provincial administrative junta (consisting of six state officials, including the prefect, and of four additional members chosen by the elective provincial council) has the power to disapprove most communal council decisions of a financial nature on the ground of inexpediency or lack of merit. It can thus, for example, reject municipal budgets, refuse requests to float loans, veto new or increased taxes, and turn down a communal bid to place a local public utility under communal ownership and operation.

In addition to these local controls on policy making by the communes, there are restraints exercised at the national level. For instance, communal regulations concerning rates, taxes, public buildings, and local police must be sent to the minister of the interior in Rome who, after consulting the Council of State, may declare them void on the ground of illegality. An unbalanced communal budget is subject to disapproval by the Central Committee for Local Finance in Rome. In short, the communal authorities operate on a rather tight leash.

The prefect has an arsenal of formidable weapons to use against recalcitrant communes. If communal authorities fail to carry out their legal obligations, the prefect may appoint a special commissioner to do it for them. If various communes wish to form a consortium for the performance of some mutually desirable task, approval by the prefect must first be obtained. If the mayor of a commune violates his legal obligations, or if other reasons involving a grave threat to public order so dictate, the prefect may suspend the mayor from performance of his functions, or suspend him from office altogether, and replace him temporarily with a prefectoral commissioner. Communal juntas may be suspended in the same manner, and so may communal councils. These powers of suspension may be invoked, not only by the prefect, but also by the president of Italy on the advice of the prime minister. Finally, a deadlocked communal council, which cannot agree on a mayor and junta, may be dissolved by the prefect.

As Fried points out, these powers can be and have been abused.[5] In fact, they have frequently been employed to harass

[5] Robert C. Fried, *The Italian Prefects: A Study in Administrative Politics* (New Haven, Conn.: Yale University Press, 1963), pp. 255–256.

Left-wing mayors and juntas. Public order may be interpreted in a very broad sense. For instance, the mayor of Lentella was suspended because, when the archbishop of Chieti passed his podium during a religious procession, he ostentatiously turned his back. Or, to cite another case, the mayor of Pescara was suspended for having given several hours off from work to some female municipal employees, in order that they might attend the International Women's Festival.[6] Even the device of the prefectoral commissioner has lent itself to some stretching of the law. For, once a special commissioner has been appointed by the prefect, the law states that elections for a new communal council should be held within three or, in special cases, six months. This law, however, has been systematically flouted; some prefectoral commissioners have remained in office for years on end.

Although scores of abuses have occurred, we must not assume that the prefect has absolute power over Left-wing mayors and communal juntas. As Fried indicates, vetoing of communal welfare schemes by the prefect or by the provincial administrative junta can cause a backlash of protest in favor of the Left-wing parties that control a local government. For that reason, a Left-wing communal council may deliberately seek to provoke such a veto. Prefectoral decisions that do *not* involve the suspension of local officials may be appealed to the Council of State, in many instances, and not infrequently those appeals are successful. Also, the very rigorous supervision to which Left-wing local governments have been subjected has helped to keep them honest, thus enhancing the reputation for integrity enjoyed by the extreme Left-wing parties, in contrast to the free-wheeling Christian Democrats.[7] And finally, it is possible that the arbitrary removal of a mayor may provoke popular resentment and make a martyr of the abused victim. Thus, such actions, if repeated too frequently, can be politically counterproductive.

Another serious handicap suffered by the communes is their lack of control over two of the most basic functions of government: education and law enforcement. The schools are under the direction of the Ministry of Public Instruction in Rome. The provincial representative of the ministry, the purveyor of studies, is responsible neither to the elected organs of local government nor to the prefect. He does, of course, consult the prefect frequently, but these are dialogues between hierarchical peers. As for the police, the commune commands only the *vigili urbani* ("city

[6] Acquarone, pp. 91–92.
[7] Fried, pp. 256–257.

watchmen"), who regulate traffic and enforce local ordinances. The major burden of law enforcement falls upon the shoulders of the national police. Crimes of violence and the repression of riots and violent demonstrations are the responsibility of the public security guards of the Ministry of the Interior and the *Carabinieri* of the Ministry of Defense. It is the prefect, rather than the mayor, who can send these forces into action in the event of an emergency. In this respect, Italy resembles France: The schools and the police are run from the nation's capital. The fact that so many communes in France and Italy are governed by the Communist party may help to explain the survival of this pattern.

Some mention should be made of another communal shortcoming, perhaps an inescapable one—namely, the failure of the communes to recruit high-quality executive career personnel. In view of the competition from private enterprise and from the national civil service, it has been very difficult for the communes to attract the better university graduates. Also damaging to the image of the commune as employer have been the lack of an adequate in-service orientation and training program, the very slow system for promotions, and the absence of meaningful major distinctions among civil-service grades. Recent studies have shown that local government employees are more critical of current recruitment and training practices than are national government employees.[8] Moreover, local government employees appear to be far more worried than are their national colleagues about the interference of politicians in the day-to-day operations of the bureaucracy.[9] The offices of local government would seem to be much more vulnerable to the intrusion of party politics than is the national bureaucracy.

THE COMMUNE: BASTION OF THE OPPOSITION

In addition to its function as an organ of local government, the commune provides an opportunity for opposition parties to exercise power below the national level. During the quarter-century since 1945, several thousand Italian communes—some sporadi-

---

[8] Federica Garzonio Dell' Orto "I funzionari e la carriera," in Istituto per la Scienza dell' Amministrazione Pubblica, *Il burocrate di fronte alla burocrazia* (Milano: Giuffré, 1969), pp. 127, 179.

[9] Luciano Visentini, "La burocrazia locale nel Mezzogiorno come gruppo sociale," *Tempi Moderni*, Vol. X, No. 30 (Summer 1967), 20–23. See also Dell' Orto, pp. 119–120.

cally, some continuously—have been under the rule of parties of the extreme Left or extreme Right. Some fairly important communes (for example, Bologna, Modena, Siena) have been under Communist party domination ever since the Liberation. This situation may have actually strengthened Italian democracy by making Communist leaders and activists less intransigent, more willing to bargain and compromise within the system. As Weiner and La Palombara state:

> The fact is that Italian Communists have not had to face with frustration and despair the prospect of never sharing in the exercise of political power. Below the national level thousands of Communist leaders hold elective and appointive office. While this has not served to make the P.C.I. a willing participant in national conflict resolution it has dulled the cutting edge of the party's anti-systemic drive.[10]

What kind of experience have opposition-dominated communes undergone? For one thing, as we have seen, they frequently have been subjected to discriminatory treatment by the central government and its agents. But as Evans indicates, by keeping its budget balanced, the Communist administration of Bologna was able to avoid excessive dependence on the national government. Apart from one case—where the provincial administrative junta revoked all old-age pensions paid by the city of Bologna to former employees—Evans concludes that interventions by the prefect and the junta have generally been reasonable.[11] Discrimination is apt to occur more frequently in the South, where a long tradition of political favoritism lessens the risks incurred by such behavior. As a matter of fact, discrimination by the prefects in Southern Italy may also be directed against non-Communist laic parties of the Center or moderate Left, parties that are usually allied with the Christian Democrats at the national level. For instance, a cold war was waged by the provincial administrative junta of Potenza province and the Potenza provincial office of the Ministry of Labor against the Republican-dominated commune of Guardia Perticara.[12]

Yet, despite the unfriendly scrutiny of the prefect and of the

[10] Myron Weiner and Joseph La Palombara, "The Impact of Parties on Political Development," in Joseph La Palombara and Myron Weiner, eds., *Political Parties and Political Development* (Princeton, N.J.: Princeton University Press, 1966), p. 419.
[11] Robert H. Evans, *Coexistence: Communism and Its Practice in Bologna, 1945–1965* (Notre Dame, Ind.: University of Notre Dame Press, 1967), pp. 36–38.
[12] Leonardo Sacco, *Sindaci e ministri* (Milano: Comunità, 1965), pp. 159–166.

field offices of the national government, Communist local administrations have not only been able to survive such biased treatment, but have also been able to indulge their own prejudices, often with impunity. Paulson and Ricci recount how the Communist mayor and council of Castelfuoco used the allocation of relief money, the rigging of local tax assessments, the distribution of public jobs, and the award of government contracts as means of rewarding friends and punishing enemies.[13] Degli Esposti alludes to the discharge of hundreds of non-Communist local government employees in Bologna—employees who were gradually forced out to make room for party members.[14]

When in power at the local level, the Communists have frequently been quite conservative, even stodgy, in their administrative style. Their administrations have been relatively free from scandal, but have shown marked favoritism toward party members in the allocation of positions in the local bureaucracy (this is hardly a significant deviation from Italian political mores!) and have been fairly slow to push for needed municipal reforms. Quoting Degli Esposti, Galli cites the fact that the Communist municipal authorities at Bologna took ten years to draw up and approve a municipal plan and that Bologna was the last major city in Italy to license supermarkets.[15] The reason underlying this sluggishness in policy output is that the Communist party in Bologna has been trying very hard to obtain the support of the lower middle class—the small shopkeepers and artisans who feel they can survive economically only by fighting against the twentieth century.

It appears, then, that whenever the Italian Communist party is able to gain control of a local government, it ceases to be a party of protest but rather tries to reflect an orderly and moderate image of a realistic party with limited goals. It seeks to establish closer ties with the business community and with non-Communist intellectuals. In short, it appears in the guise of a middle-of-the-road movement. After twenty-five years of performing this role in Bologna and other cities, it is not surprising that the Communist image has begun to correspond to the Communist reality.

But a word of caution is needed. It may be dangerously misleading to assume that Bologna's pattern of Communist party behavior is nationwide. As Degli Esposti notes, the nearby

[13] Belden Paulson and Athos Ricci, *The Searchers* (Chicago: Quadrangle, 1966), pp. 159, 209.
[14] Gianluigi Degli Esposti, *Bologna PCI* (Bologna: Il Mulino, 1966), pp. 34–36.
[15] Giorgio Galli, *Il bipartitismo imperfetto* (Bologna: Il Mulino, 1966), pp. 295–296.

Emilian cities of Modena and Ferrara also have had Communist mayors for many years, and yet economic progress and industrial expansion proceeded at a much faster clip in those cities.[16] Once again, we see that excessive reliance on a prototype case study could produce incomplete and rather deceptive results.

THE COMMUNE: STYLES AND MOTIVES OF LOCAL POLITICS

One important feature of Italian local politics is the important role of patron-client relations (referred to by Italians as *clientela* relationships), particularly in the South. One study describes this kind of relationship at work in Sicily.[17] In a society where only members of one's own family can be trusted, where all others are potential enemies, and where members of the upper classes receive preferential treatment, many a lower-class Sicilian must try to find a strategically placed protector from the upper or upper-middle class. The patron can recommend him for a job, intercede on his behalf with the bureaucracy, or induce creditors to give him more time to pay his debts. In exchange, the client will provide his patron with information, political support, occasional errands, and small services. In extreme cases he may even be willing to commit physical violence on his patron's behalf. In effect, the patronage system permits a relatively humble person to establish personal communication with high officials through a powerful intermediary. The influence of the Mafia in Sicilian life must be understood in terms of this technique for bypassing legal channels through a system of mutual obligation. A Mafioso literally goes through life doing "favors" for his "friends" and expecting favors in return. (The code name for the Mafia in Sicily is "the friends of the friends.")

Actually, patronage is a way of life throughout the South. The power of local authorities to assess local taxes, assign communal lands, and appoint local employees is used to reward the faithful and chastise the reprobate. It is no accident, then, that so many Southerners join political parties. The local party secretary is merely a modern version of the old-style patron. Southern deputies have built distinguished careers on providing personal favors

---

[16] Degli Esposti, pp. 71–73.
[17] Jeremy Boissevain, "Patronage in Sicily," *Man*, Vol. I, No. 1 (March 1966), 18–33.

for their constituents: Deputy Maxia of Sardinia specialized in expediting pension claims, and Deputy Pitzalis of Sardinia was mainly concerned with the appointment and transfer of schoolteachers.[18] Also, central government agencies such as the *Cassa per il Mezzogiorno* (Fund for the South) have apparently engaged in politically inspired favoritism.

But there is a good deal of evidence to suggest that patronage relationships are not confined to Southern Italy. For example, one scholar recounts, in a study of a small Umbrian village, the important role played by large landowners on behalf of their sharecroppers during the late nineteenth and early twentieth centuries.[19] Since the sharecroppers usually could not vote before 1913 or 1919, they could hardly expect to command the same respect from government officials as a full-fledged voting citizen. They needed, therefore, to have some prominent local elector, preferably their landlord, mediate between them and the outside world and, if necessary, take up the cudgels on their behalf.

This function, once performed by the local landed gentry, has now been taken over by other agents, as the laws of inheritance and the political and economic upheavals of the past half century have gradually whittled down the large estates. Today, the party secretary and the village priest are the most important sources of information, help, and recommendations. But there are many more mediators between the local and the national systems than was the case in the past. As Silverman points out:

> The clerk whom one sees about collecting government insurance benefits is not the same person as the official agent to whom one sells surplus wheat. Moreover, if the clerk's response is unsatisfactory, one can go to an official of the union of *mezzadri* [sharecroppers] or to the ACLI [Christian Association of Italian Workers] center in the Church. The number and diversity of indirect links to the larger society and particularly the existence of alternative possibilities preclude the presence of mediators.[20]

Moreover, not only are the intermediaries more numerous, but they are also drawn from all strata of society, not just the upper classes.

---

[18] Raphael Zariski, "Intra-Party Conflict in a Dominant Party: The Experience of Italian Christian Democracy," *The Journal of Politics*, Vol. 27, No. 1 (February 1965), 26.
[19] Sydel Silverman, "Patronage and Community-Nation Relationships in Central Italy," *Ethnology*, Vol. 4, No. 2 (April 1965), 172–189.
[20] Silverman, 187.

A recent study indicates that a politics of personality seems to play a very important role in intraparty politics in Tuscany, and that in a prosperous environment, patronage can take the form of allocating positions that satisfy party members' *status* aspirations.[21] In the Northwest Industrial Triangle, on the other hand, there is little evidence that the political parties (with the sole exception of the Communists) have done much to establish bonds with the incoming immigrants. Certainly, we need more case studies, particularly from the less static areas of Italy, before we can reach satisfactory conclusions about the role of patronage.

Another aspect of local political style is the unwillingness or inability of Italians to cooperate for the solution of local problems. Banfield stresses this theme to the utmost in his study of Montegrano.[22] The Almond-Verba study shows that only 9 percent of the Italian respondents (as compared to 59 percent of the Americans, 36 percent of the British, and 21 percent of the Germans) would try to influence their local government by enlisting the aid of others, while about 43 percent said they would act alone either by directly contacting a political leader or by voting against him in the next elections.[23] This lack of cooperativeness in local political behavior, this lack of perception regarding the potential influence of voluntary associations, is a basic feature of Italian political culture. On this count, education seems to make little difference: Education may make an Italian feel more politically competent but it will not necessarily increase his propensity to play an active role in voluntary associations. "Political competence thus grows with higher education or occupational status, but cooperative competence seems to be rooted in specific national political cultures."[24]

LINKS BETWEEN LOCAL AND NATIONAL POLITICS

The Italian political parties, highly centralized, cohesive, and disciplined as they are, tend to constitute a very effective (perhaps overly effective) link between local and national politics. When

[21] Gianfranco Bettin, "Partito e comunità locale. II. Partito o federazione di correnti," *Rassegna Italiana di Sociologia*, Vol. X, No. 4 (October–December 1969), 651–652, 657–658, 663–665, 667, 671–677.

[22] Edward C. Banfield, *The Moral Basis of a Backward Society* (New York: Free Press, 1958), pp. 85–104.

[23] Gabriel A. Almond and Sidney Verba, *The Civic Culture: Political Attitudes and Democracy in Five Nations* (Princeton, N.J.: Princeton University Press, 1963), pp. 189–213.

[24] Almond and Verba, p. 213.

local elections are held (and normally, thousands of communal and provincial councils come up for re-election on the same day), they are treated by the national parties as test runs for the national parliamentary elections that will take place some months or years later. The national parties mobilize their activists and put forth very strenuous efforts, for any gains or losses are regarded as being of national significance. Also, while local themes are not absent from the campaign, national and international issues tend to be stressed. As in national elections, people are strongly encouraged to vote, and turnout is therefore remarkably high, usually 85–90 percent, although it does fall a bit short of national peaks.

Partly as a result of the more centralized and cohesive character of Italian parties, with their large memberships, partly as a result of the great emphasis on the national significance of local elections in Italy, there are much closer ties between local and national politics in Italy than in France. But also, the reliance on national issues in local elections naturally tends to downgrade local politics somewhat and can hardly be said to contribute to greater concern for local issues and problems on the part of Italian citizens.

The mass media contribute to grass-roots awareness of national politics, although both the newspapers and the government-owned radio and television network have been guilty of some seriously biased treatment of news events: ubiquitous editorializing even in so-called news stories (in the case of the press) or an outright rejection of bad news (in the case of the radio and television network). The media really fall abysmally short in their coverage of local issues and problems. There is an almost universal failure to give adequate in-depth attention to local politics. Even though the second page of every newspaper is devoted to local news, and the activities of the communal council and the local parties are given some attention, there is relatively little effort to explain, to interpret, to go beyond bare news and human interest stories. An editorial almost never deals with a local issue. Some newspapers, like *Il Messaggero* (Rome) and *La Stampa* (Turin) are trying to remedy this policy of neglect somewhat, but there is still a long way to go. As for television, Mannucci comments acidly on the quality of its regional news coverage, which rarely deals with political or administrative matters with any degree of sophistication and penetration.[25]

It is important to know the relative circulation of the partisan

[25] Cesare Mannucci, *Lo spettatore senza libertà* (Bari: Laterza, 1962), pp. 167–169.

and the independent press in order to be able to assess whether, in a given society, communication systems are isolated one from the other.[26] Using this yardstick, we note that the party press in Italy consists of some 11 daily newspapers with about 15 percent of the national circulation of roughly 5 million, church-dominated or Catholic-sponsored organs comprise another 10 percent, and the so-called independent press constitutes 60 percent of the total national circulation.[27] But most of the "independent" newspapers back the Right or the Right-Center of the political spectrum. About half of the circulation of the party press is accounted for by the Communist daily *Unità*. The press would appear to function to some degree, then, as an instrument for cultural fragmentation, at least in the case of Catholics and Communists. But more research is needed on this score; Barnes points out that Socialist party members who read their party newspaper (*Avanti!*) regularly are usually likely to read also the Florentine conservative daily *La Nazione*.[28]

THE PROVINCE: DOMAIN OF THE PREFECT

The principal structures of the province concerned with rule making and administration are the provincial council, the provincial junta and its president, the provincial bureaucracy, and, of course, the prefect, whose powers over the communes we have already discussed. The provincial council is elected for a five-year term on the basis of a rather complicated formula combining single-member districts and proportional representation. (The formula is not dissimilar from the one employed to elect members of the Italian Senate.) It has from a minimum of twenty-four to a maximum of forty-five members, depending on the population of the province. It elects, from its own membership, a provincial junta of from four to eight members to carry on executive functions, and also elects the president of the provincial junta. As in the case of the commune, the province has its own bureaucracy, headed by a provincial secretary. The status of the provincial bureaucracy is similar to that of the communal bureaucracy: inadequate recruitment, training, and promotion policies, plus political interference, make

---

[26] Peter H. Merkl, *Modern Comparative Politics* (New York: Holt, Rinehart and Winston, 1970), p. 256.

[27] Ignazio Weiss, *Il potere di carta* (Torino: UTET, 1965), pp. 414–421.

[28] Samuel Barnes, *Party Democracy: Politics in an Italian Socialist Federation* (New Haven, Conn.: Yale University Press, 1967), pp. 211–212.

A UNITARY SYSTEM WITH A QUASI-FEDERAL GLOSS 131

for low morale and serious recruitment and retention problems. The functions of the province are narrower in scope than those of the commune: they include the provision and maintenance of provincial roads, the care of mental patients, assistance to abandoned illegitimate children, assistance to the blind and deaf-mute, the provision of certain facilities for secondary schools, and so on.

The top-ranking official in the province is the prefect, who holds the same supervisory powers over provincial councils and juntas as he does in regard to the communes. He has far-reaching powers to maintain law and order and protect the public safety in the event of strikes, riots, disasters, and natural calamities. In the event of social conflict, he will offer his services as a mediator between the contending sides. Should mediation fail and violence threaten, he can order the police into action and call upon an extensive arsenal of police powers, many of them dating back to the days of the Fascist regime.

In several respects, however, the Italian prefect is not as powerful and imposing as his French counterpart. For one thing, he is not the coordinator and supervisor of the field agencies of the central government as is the French prefect; such agencies are not housed in the prefectures in Italy, as they are in France. His influence over central government field agencies is not carefully spelled out by law, as is the case in France, but is dependent on whatever informal pressures he can exert. In France, central government ministries communicate with their field services via the prefect; in Italy, the prefect is not in a legal position to intercept and clear communications from a ministry to its field services. In France, control over local government is centered in the prefect; in Italy, he must share his power of control with a number of ministries and their field representatives. In short, as Fried notes, France has an integrated prefectoral system, while Italy's is unintegrated.[29]

Fried offers a number of reasons why Italy, in the 1860s, did not adopt a prefectoral system modeled exactly on the French. Among the principal reasons given is the fact that the liberal ruling groups in Italy feared an all-powerful prefect would pave the way for the kind of authoritarianism which then existed in the France of the Second Empire. Also, in the Italian system of cabinet government operating in the 1860s, ministers were able to resist losing control over their field services; when the Napoleonic

[29] This discussion of the Italian and French prefectoral systems is drawn from Fried, pp. 116–118, 249–295, 303–308.

prefectoral system was first established in France, ministers were not in a position to defend their autonomy. There was also a fear that vesting too much power in the prefect would enable him to function as a rallying point for separatist tendencies—an odd apprehension, given the French experience. There were other reasons of an organizational or administrative nature. But primarily the historical circumstances under which a prefectoral system is adopted (Napoleonic autocracy or constitutional liberalism) will have much to do with its eventual pattern of development.

Given these misgivings about the possibility of a Bonapartist tendency, why did Italy adopt a prefectoral system at all? Here again, Fried explains it in terms of the potential for fragmentation and dissension in Italian society in the 1860s. The fear of centrifugal tendencies, the need to secure acceptance of the regime by the preindustrial political elites, and the usefulness of a strong agent of the central government in promoting and safeguarding the nation-building process at the local level—all these factors contributed to the adoption of prefectoral institutions, however modified. The prefectoral system was a device for achieving centralization and preventing the break-up of the newly established Kingdom of Italy.

LOCAL GOVERNMENT: TRENDS TOWARD REFORM

A number of tendencies toward the reform of local government institutions have already manifested themselves in Italy, and other reforms have been proposed. To begin with, there is the problem of excessively small communes. It is not as chronic and widespread as it is in France. But it *does* arise in some parts of Italy, particularly in the more mountainous regions. One response has been the formation of so-called Mountain Communities or Valley Communities, either by the voluntary initiative of groups of communes or by prefectoral decree. About fifty or sixty such communities—each comprising several communes—have been formed for planning purposes.

Demarchi suggests that an intermediate agency of local government be set up between the communal and provincial levels.[30] This agency would correspond to the French *arrondissement* with

[30] Demarchi, pp. 97–101, 108–114.

A UNITARY SYSTEM WITH A QUASI-FEDERAL GLOSS

its subprefect. Such intermediate units of local government are apparently already in existence in France, Germany, Austria, and Switzerland, and help bring the government closer to the people.

What of the commune itself, however? If it is fairly large and does not require a merger with other communes, what reforms would improve its efficiency and responsiveness? One type of reform measure employed to an increasing extent in Italy aims at making communal government more accessible to the public by a policy of deconcentrating its functions, by setting up neighborhood branches of city hall, and by trying to arouse participation at the neighborhood level. Bologna, for instance, has been divided into fourteen *quartieri* (quarters, or wards), each with a council chosen by the communal council and each presided over by a delegate from the mayor's office. Under this arrangement, each neighborhood is able to communicate more effectively with the communal government regarding its needs, and citizens are able to obtain local government services more expeditiously without having to make the pilgrimage to city hall. Other cities have already taken steps toward a similar deconcentration of civic functions. The results thus far have been rather mixed: the communal authorities are kept better aware of neighborhood problems; but many people prefer to utilize city hall services instead of going to their neighborhood center, and local participation continues to be at a rather low ebb.

A more pressing issue is the problem of how to govern metropolitan areas, as dozens of satellite communes receive the overspill of population and industry from the central cities, and send thousands of commuters into the central cities every day to use their services and add to their problems. The activity of real-estate speculators in the metropolitan areas also creates a disorderly and destructive pattern of growth. One method of coping with these critical trends is for a commune to adopt a city plan for regulating urban growth. However, this is a very lengthy procedure, and a plan that has been approved by the communal council may be vetoed or modified by the provincial administrative junta or the minister of public works, or may be gutted by interest-group pressure. Another device tried in recent years is the formation of intercommunal plans drawn up by consortia of several participating communes. This, too, is a rather cumbersome device, and lends itself to economic sabotage and noncooperation by communes that disagree with majority decisions. Rather than rely on such voluntary or compulsory compacts or consortia, Acquarone would like to see the provinces revitalized and used to originate plans for the metropolitan areas of the country.[31] This scheme, however, must deal with the problem of metropolitan areas that do not fit neatly within the boundaries of any one province. In addition, any regulatory scheme must come up against powerful group pressures.

THE REGIONS: QUASI-FEDERALISM DELAYED

In the 1860s, the Kingdom of Italy deliberately rejected regionalism and embarked upon a course of national centralization, for fear of sacrificing the precarious national unity so recently acquired. After 1870, there were occasional sporadic outbursts of regional feeling, but it was not until World War II and the Liberation of 1945 that the cause of regionalism once again came to the forefront. The revulsion against Fascist overcentralization, the long months of 1944–1945 when thousands of Italian partisans governed sizable areas of Central and Northern Italy without outside help or interference, and the sense of regional self-sufficiency engendered by the war—all these factors had some part in stimulating regionalist sentiment. Thus, for example, when the Allied troops entered Florence in the summer of 1944, they found the city already in the hands of the Tuscan Committee for National Liberation (CLN), which claimed jurisdiction over the entire region and which had already filled all local administrative posts with its own appointees.

It was only natural that this pent-up sense of regional pride, combined with the demand for greater participation in self-government at the grass roots, should have the effect of generating pressure for regional self-government at the Constituent Assembly in 1946. Two relatively small parties—the Republican party and the Action party—came out for the creation of autonomous regions. The party of the moderate Right (the Liberal party) was generally opposed, though all parties were internally divided on this issue. The Communists and Socialists were rather cool to the idea of regional autonomy, whereas the Christian Democratic party—following in the footsteps of the Popular party of 1919–1926—tended to be largely favorable. It is interesting to note that, after the smashing victory of the Christian Democratic party in

[31] Acquarone, pp. 156–179.

1948, the roles were reversed: The Communists and Left-wing Socialists began to clamor for regional autonomy, whereas the Christian Democrats, securely ensconced in the seat of power, dragged their feet.[32]

The Constitution of 1948, as finally adopted, provided for five special regions and fifteen ordinary regions. The special regions, each with a unicameral legislative body and an executive junta, were to be created immediately (except Friuli-Venezia Giulia, whose boundary was being disputed with Yugoslavia); the ordinary regions were to be set up within a year of the day the Constitution went into effect. It should be noted that the special regions, which received broader powers than the ordinary regions, were all zones with particularly acute problems. Val d'Aosta was French-speaking, Trentino-Alto Adige had a large German-speaking minority, and Friuli-Venezia Giulia contained sizable numbers of Slovenians. Sicily and Sardinia were both islands, separated from the mainland by a body of water and by cultural mores and customary folkways as well. In fact, Sicily had even spawned a small separatist movement in 1945.

The special regions are endowed with certain limited exclusive powers, which must however be exercised in accordance with the Constitution and with respect for international obligations and national interests, and must not be in conflict with national reform laws. In the event that a region, in exercising its exclusive powers, transgresses any or all of these limits, the national government can appeal the regional law to the Constitutional Court (on the ground of unconstitutionality) or to the Parliament (on the ground that the national interest is at stake). Both the special and the ordinary regions have concurrent powers to legislate within the principles established by national law in certain fields, and can also adapt the details of national laws to local needs. But the concurrent powers of the ordinary regions are far more restricted than the concurrent powers of the special regions.[33]

A central government commissioner is stationed in the capital of each region. He has a suspensive veto over acts of the regional council. In the event the regional council reenacts a law which he has vetoed, he can refer the issue to the Constitutional Court or to Parliament, depending on whether the issue is constitu-

---

[32] Leonard Weinberg, "Ideology and Pragmatism in Italian Politics: The Case of the Regions," *Rocky Mountain Social Science Journal*, Vol. 6, No. 1 (April 1969), 117–126.

[33] George Woodcock, "Regional Government: The Italian Example," *Public Administration*, Vol. 45, No. 4 (Winter 1967), 405–406.

tional or simply involves the national interest. He also has the power to dissolve the regional council and call for new elections. In short, the region is under stringent surveillance and certainly cannot be compared with a regional unit of government in a federal system, especially since the central government has full power to revise a Regional Statute (the fundamental law of the region) without the consent of the region involved. This can be done either by act of Parliament or by a constitutional amendment, depending on the regional law under consideration.

After 1948, the Christian Democrats lost interest in creating the ordinary regions. They feared that several regions would come under Communist control, that the regions would place an additional burden on national resources, and that perhaps national unity might be mildly endangered. Their go-slow policy worked. It was not until 1962–1963 that the Socialist party was able to obtain a commitment from the Christian Democrats to set up the fifteen ordinary regions, as one of the planks of the joint program accepted by the parties that were taking part in the opening to the Left. And it was not until 1970 that a financial law for the regions was passed and regional elections were held. Moreover, once the regional councils for the ordinary regions were elected, it was supposed to take two more years at least, until the summer of 1972, before the basic regional statutes could be drawn up by the regional councils and approved by Parliament, before framework laws could be passed by Parliament defining the powers of the ordinary regions, and before the necessary funds and state personnel could be turned over to the governments of the ordinary regions.[34]

During the past decade and a half, the Constitutional Court has taken a rather restrictive view of the powers attributed to the regions, extending the reserved powers of the central government while nibbling away at the exclusive and concurrent powers of the regions. A series of adverse court decisions, directed against the special regions, seem to portend a rather curtailed and straitened future for the fledgling ordinary regions.

Why have the ordinary regions been so long delayed? As we have already noted, the Christian Democrats were in no hurry to set them up, because they did not want to weaken their virtual monopoly of power at the national level, and also because they feared that the Communist party would be able to gain control of the three regions of Emilia, Tuscany, and Umbria in North-Cen-

[34] *La Stampa* (Turin), January 29, 1970.

tral Italy, thus establishing a so-called Red belt across the peninsula and cutting Italy in two. Also, several of the special regions (especially Sicily) had been guilty of gross extravagance, of refusing to decentralize functions to the provinces and communes, of padding the public payroll, and of perpetuating needless feuds with the central government. The assertive demands made by the special regions and the tendency of their party branches to resist national control (a tendency which, in Sicily, led Milazzo and his cohorts to secede from the Christian Democratic party) did not endear regionalism to national politicians. In short, resistance to the establishment of the ordinary regions was based on the short-run self-interest of those in national seats of power.

Given this powerful opposition, how can we explain the eventual decision to create the ordinary regions? First of all, the Constitution provided for them, and failure to enforce its provisions detracted from the legitimacy of the regime. Not only the Communist party opposition, but also the moderate Left and Center were extremely persistent in stressing the anomaly represented by a democratic constitution that was, in part, ignored by a government that had sworn to defend it. Secondly, by the early 1960s, the Christian Democrats needed Socialist party help in order to maintain a stable cabinet, and the price set by the Socialists for their collaboration included the establishment of the ordinary regions. Finally, the obvious inadequacy of local and provincial economic planning, the growing awareness of the need for a more ample territorial foundation for grass-roots economic planning, and the tendency of the Italian ministries in Rome to use the regions named in the Constitution when making their statistical calculations and projections—all these factors pointed toward the desirability of going ahead with the regions. Thus, regionalism tended to dovetail with another reform movement, economic planning, and the two tended to complement each other.[35]

In 1964, regional economic planning committees—including provincial and communal council representatives, presidents of chambers of commerce, spokesmen for industry and labor, and field directors of several ministries—were set up by the minister of labor. The regional plans they were to formulate would have to conform to the directives laid down by the budget minister. Palazzoli astutely points out that there was a movement under way to shift the terms of reference of Italian regionalism. In place of the political and administrative goals postulated by the founding fa-

[35] Robert C. Fried, "Administrative Pluralism and Italian Regional Planning," *Public Administration*, Vol. 46, No. 4 (Winter 1968), 375–384.

thers of 1946–1948—goals such as greater decentralization—the objectives visualized for the regions were now predominantly economic. In short, the region had become "instrumentalized" into a convenient tool for preparing and executing the national economic plan at the grass roots. Italian regionalism was beginning to resemble the emerging regionalism of France, with no federal or quasi-federal pretensions.[36]

Will the ordinary regions foster more popular participation in decision making and more decentralization? Or will they become mere geographic subdivisions created for the purpose of ratifying a national plan? Only time will tell, though past precedent seems to favor the second alternative. La Palombara points to some of the risks involved in this experiment. For example, the rich regions might be able, by virtue of their superior brainpower and resources, to widen the gap that separates them from the poorer regions of the South. But his reaction to such objections is that risks must be taken if *democratic* (hence adequately informed) planning is to be safeguarded.[37]

CONCLUSIONS

Developments in Italian local and regional government have considerable bearing on the problems of national integration and political participation. The setting up of regional units of government is a rather strong indication that Italian ruling elites are confident in the ability of the Italian polity to resist separatist tendencies. There could be no clearer vote of confidence in the existence and prospects for survival of an Italian nation than this erection of political subdivisions that are bound, by their very nature, to revive memories of the political distinctions that existed in Italy during the Renaissance. To be sure, this regional arrangement is not federalism; the regions do not begin to have the power or prestige of the American states or German *Länder*. But there is definitely a departure from the rigid centralization of the past, when local initiative was discouraged and stifled and when all political roads led to Rome.

In many ways, Italy seems to be adopting a modified version

---

[36] Claude Palazzoli, *Les Régions Italiennes: Contribution à l'étude de la decentralisation politique* (Paris: Librairie Générale de Droit et de Jurisprudence, 1966), pp. 549–551.

[37] Joseph La Palombara, *Italy: The Politics of Planning* (Syracuse, N.Y.: Syracuse University Press, 1966), pp. 117–119.

A UNITARY SYSTEM WITH A QUASI-FEDERAL GLOSS

of the French pattern of regional planning. Power remains concentrated at the center (though somewhat less so than in France, where the regions are confined entirely to assisting in economic planning), but there is to be a systematic effort to consult the periphery, to bring it into the planning process. Whereas before 1922 the Italian government relied very heavily on reports from the prefects in the field for information on developments throughout Italy, there will now be representative regional organs to express grievances and give advice. The net result is likely to be an improvement in the flow of communication between the provinces and Rome, both in a quantitative and in a qualitative sense. With more plentiful and reliable information available, economic planning is likely to be more successful in achieving its goals and correcting its errors.

Progress toward a solution of the problem of political participation is still uncertain. The responsibilities given the regions will undoubtedly encourage local elites to take a more active role in public affairs, and there may be a revival of that intense civic pride which made possible the great flourishing of Italian communal life during the Renaissance. There may also be more experimentation and initiative at the local, provincial, and regional levels. But given the highly technical functions assigned to the regions (functions which may have little meaning for the average citizen) and given the fact that such vital functions as education and policing remain with the central government and its provincial agents, one wonders whether the Italian masses will really be brought into the political process by the establishment of the regions. In other words, the problem of meaningful mass participation remains unresolved in Italy, as it really does in most of the Western world. And some of the reforms projected or under way —such as the creation of metropolitan districts—may actually aggravate that sense of impotence, of remoteness from the seat of power, which afflicts so many Italians of the lower and lower-middle classes.

FIVE
THE GIANTS AND THE PYGMIES
The party system

THE PARTY SYSTEM: A MULTIFACETED PHENOMENON

The Italian party system, like the party system of any Western democracy, lends itself to a variety of approaches. One can focus on the very significant role played by the extraparliamentary party organizations in making and unmaking governments, dragooning deputies and senators, and influencing the recruitment of civil servants. One can view the Italian party system as one of "extreme pluralism," to use Sartori's term, characterized (1) by at least five relevant parties; (2) by a Left, Right, and Center pole; (3) by a high degree of polarization (that is, a great distance separating the Right and Left extremes); and (4) by a strong centrifugal tendency (the parties at the extremes gain strength at the expense of the party or parties at the Center).[1] Or one can accept Galli's analysis of the Italian party system as an "imperfect two party system," with two giant parties appropriating the lion's share of the votes and most of the patronage plums, while a

---

[1] Giovanni Sartori, "European Political Parties: The Case of Polarized Pluralism," in Joseph La Palombara and Myron Weiner, eds., *Political Parties and Political Development* (Princeton, N.J.: Princeton University Press, 1966), ch. 5.

number of smaller parties compete for the remainder and struggle for the privilege of junior partnership in a cabinet coalition.[2]

These views are only a few of a potentially large number of perspectives from which Italian parties may be observed. Parties may be studied in terms of their organization and power structure. They may be examined with a view to distinguishing their policy goals—an arduous and thankless task where some Italian parties are concerned. They may be of interest because of the character of their membership and ruling elites: To what degree are these representative of the larger society? What groups are overrepresented? And finally, their electoral base may be studied in order to formulate certain theses about voting behavior.

THE PARTY SYSTEM: AN OVERVIEW

Italy has a multiparty system, which is to say that more than two major parties exist. On the extreme Left is the Italian Communist party (PCI), which received 26.9 percent of the votes cast in the elections for the Chamber of Deputies in 1968. Allied with the Communist party is a small, militant party of Left-wing Socialists, the Italian Socialist Party of Proletarian Unity (PSIUP), which received 4.4 percent of the votes in 1968. Closer to the center of the Italian political spectrum are two democratic Socialist parties, the Italian Socialist party (PSI) and the Unitary Socialist party (PSU). Their respective shares of the total vote in the regional elections of 1970 (the two parties were formed in 1969) were 10.4 percent and 7 percent. The tiny Republican party (PRI), with only 2 percent of the vote in 1968, nonetheless manages to play a significant balancing role in the system. On the moderate Right, acting as a democratic opposition party and representing the views of a substantial segment of the business community, there is the Italian Liberal party (PLI), which received 5.8 percent of the votes in 1968. Further to the Right are the Monarchists (Italian Democratic Party of Monarchical Unity, or PDIUM) and the Neo-Fascists (Italian Social Movement, or MSI). Their voting totals in 1968 were unimpressive at 1.3 percent and 4.5 percent, respectively. Finally, ranging across a large portion of the Italian political spectrum from the moderate Left to the moderate Right, is the Italian Christian Democratic party

[2] Giorgio Galli, *Il bipartitismo imperfetto* (Bologna: Il Mulino, 1966).

(DC), the dominant party in the Italian system, with 39.1 percent of the votes cast for the members of the Chamber of Deputies in 1968.

No one party normally obtains a majority of the seats in the lower house of the legislature. Thus, cabinets must either be coalition cabinets or must command the parliamentary support of more than one party.

The reasons for the development of a multiparty system in Italy may be restated briefly. First of all, the electoral system, employing a form of proportional representation, encourages the survival of such splinter parties as the Republicans and the Monarchists. Secondly, the rapid extension of the suffrage in 1912 and 1919, after an overly long delay, made it almost impossible for the existing Liberal groupings to absorb the new recruits to the electorate in time to prevent the rise of mass parties that claimed the right to speak for these newly-enfranchised lower-income voters. Thirdly, the presence of large agrarian and artisan sectors of the economy make it possible for certain historically rooted minor parties, such as the Republicans, to retain their traditional bases of support in some of the more static areas of Central Italy. Fourthly, the existence of fundamental and partly overlapping cleavages between the working class and the middle class, and between the devout Catholics and the nonpracticing Catholics, makes it very difficult for voters to coalesce into two, and only two, major parties. For how can there be one predominantly working-class party, or one predominantly middle-class party, when there are both strongly Catholic and firmly anticlerical workers, and when businessmen and professional men—normally a class which serves as a bulwark of conservatism—cannot agree among themselves on the church-state controversy? Also, considering the profundity of those cleavages, how can a majority of Italian workers support a moderate Socialist party if their memory of past oppressions by the employers and by the Fascists so embitters many members of the working class as to alienate them from the system?

A final factor accounting for the Italian multiparty system is the cumulation of problems that has tended to overload the Italian polity.[3] The problem of national integration was resolved only after World War II. But the issue of the role of religion in Italian society and the question of admitting the working class to full citizenship with regard to both voting and collective bargaining (a

---

[3] See Myron Weiner and Joseph La Palombara, "The Impact of Parties on Political Development," in La Palombara and Weiner, eds., pp. 414, 428–429.

major aspect of the problem of participation) have never been fully settled and continue to haunt the Italian political scene today. These questions, combined with the conflict over the distribution of the national product, have created the cleavages referred to above; continued failure to settle these issues has made the cleavages deeper and harder to bridge.

As Sartori points out, the Italian party system is characterized by "extreme pluralism."[4] It has an extreme Left pole (the Communist party), an extreme Right pole (the Neo-Fascist Italian Social Movement), and a dominant Center pole (the Christian Democrats). Also, there has been a marked centrifugal tendency, with the Christian Democrats losing some ground over the past twenty years, while the extreme Right remains stabilized and the Communists steadily gain strength. To be sure, this tendency seems to have been arrested in the 1968 general elections, when the Christian Democrats gained slightly, and in the 1970 regional elections, when the Communist percentages dropped almost imperceptibly. But at any rate, this picture presents a major contrast with France, where the fortunes of the French Communist party have been marked by sporadic and unpredictable fluctuations rather than steady upward progression.

In Italy's pluralist party system, the dominant Christian Democratic party—the Center pole of the system—can never be fully ousted from office. With almost 40 percent of the seats in the Chamber of Deputies, its support is indispensable for the survival of any cabinet coalition. A setback for the Christian Democratic party in a general election will, at the most, induce it to change allies. Sartori refers to this process as "peripheral turnover."[5] The junior partners of the Christian Democrats can hope for only minor cabinet responsibilities: This expectation induces them to make irresponsible promises, seeking to outbid the Christian Democrats, since they know they will never be called upon to take primary responsibility for governing the country and delivering on their promises. As for the Communists, who are permanently barred from even a demeaning junior-partner role, their promises tend to be both frantic and extravagant. Thus, faced with no credible challenge to their rule, the Christian Democrats can safely put off vital decisions that might hurt their party's interclass image. In the light of Sartori's analysis, the immobilism in the Italian political system becomes infinitely more understandable.

The presence of a dominant party is itself a distinguishing

[4] Sartori, pp. 153–156.
[5] Sartori, pp. 157–158.

hallmark of the Italian multiparty system. The hegemony of the Christian Democrats (DC) is the result of a number of factors: (1) the moral bankruptcy of the traditional Liberal ruling elites as a result of their failure to prevent the rise of Fascism; (2) the charismatic leadership of the Christian Democratic leader Alcide De Gasperi in the years immediately following World War II; (3) the availability of former leaders and cadres of the Popular party (a powerful Catholic party which flourished from 1919–1925); and (4) the absence in most of Italy of that virulent anticlericalism which has rendered life so difficult for the Catholic church in France. These factors, combined with the great fear of an imminent Communist party takeover that infected so many Italians after 1945, resulted in the transformation of the Christian Democratic party into a "catch-all 'people's party,'" appealing to all segments of the population and interested primarily in immediate electoral success.[6] No longer a party of ideas, the DC begins to bear some resemblance to American parties, except that it is much more tightly organized. Like the Democratic and Republican parties in the United States, it formulates programs that are deliberately vague, and are designed to build a consensus among the voters rather than give the voters a clear lead.

Other striking characteristics of the Italian party system may be briefly noted. As in France, the Communist party (PCI) in Italy is the second largest party in the system. And this situation obviously raises serious questions about the survival of Italian democracy; for numerous observers believe that the PCI is an "antisystem opposition," committed to the eventual destruction of Italian democratic institutions. There is, however, no real consensus on this score. The fact that the Italian Communists continue to adopt an independent stance vis-à-vis the Soviet Union, profess their loyalty to democratic values, and cooperate with the majority party in the parliamentary standing committees, leads some scholars to suggest that Communist protestations of loyalty to democratic traditions should perhaps be taken at face value.[7]

We should also observe the chronic divisions in the ranks of Italian socialism, where three socialist parties vie for supremacy. This remarkable divisiveness may be in part a reaction against the highly centralized and cohesive character of Italian parties: A

---

[6] Otto Kirchheimer, "The Transformation of the Western European Party Systems," in La Palombara and Weiner, eds., pp. 184–200. To be sure, the DC's attachment to Catholicism *does* repel the strongly anticlerical voter.

[7] Michele Sernini, *La disputa sui partiti* (Padova: Marsilio Editori, 1968), pp. 67–69, 122–124.

defeated minority faction may simply choose to secede from the party rather than face disciplinary sanctions. And of course, the electoral system based on proportional representation may be regarded as a kind of insurance policy protecting a secessionist splinter group from political extinction or against exile from Parliament. In France, where a system of single-member districts with run-off elections prevails, the Left-wing Socialists (the PSU, or Unitary Socialist party) received 3.9 percent of the votes on the first ballot in 1968 but were unable to elect a single candidate to the National Assembly. In Italy, where multimember districts and proportional representation are employed, the Left-wing Socialists of the Socialist Party of Proletarian Unity (PSIUP) were only a trifle stronger, polling 4.5 percent of the total vote. Yet, twenty-three PSIUP deputies entered the Italian Chamber of Deputies after the 1968 elections. Thus, Duverger's theory regarding the allegedly decisive impact of the electoral law on the nature of the party system—a theory that has been widely criticized for placing insufficient stress on such environmental factors as social structure and historical tradition—may be partly vindicated by our overview of the Italian party system.[8] As Sartori has perceived, the importance of the electoral law has been too readily discounted.[9]

Studying the Italian party system is, in one important respect, a far less bewildering task than that of threading one's way through the labyrinths of French party politics. For Italian parties do not, as a rule, assume one label when running for office and a different label when forming a parliamentary group. This pernicious practice has long been the bane of both students and teachers of French politics. Indeed, one is hard put to explain why a man should run for office as a Radical and then identify himself in Parliament as a member of the Democratic Center. Possibly, the more flexible rules for forming parliamentary groups in Italy may help to explain why even tiny parties like the Monarchists and the Republicans retain their titles in the Italian Chamber of Deputies. A French party must have thirty deputies in order to form a parliamentary group in the French National Assembly. Instead, in the Italian Chamber of Deputies, a nationwide party need not even have ten deputies in order to form such a group.[10] There is no need, then, for such small parties as the Liberals and the

---

[8] Maurice Duverger, *Political Parties* (London: Methuen, 1954), *passim*.
[9] Sartori, pp. 166–169.
[10] Aristide Savignano, *I gruppi parlamentari* (Napoli: Morano Editore, 1965), pp. 43–48, 216. Until recently a minimum of ten deputies was required to form a parliamentary group in the Italian Chamber of Deputies.

Monarchists to form a joint parliamentary group with some mysterious label. Thus, there may be a logical reason why the French practice has not been adopted in Italy.

Finally, we should point to the disproportionate weight exerted by *two* of the parties in Italy's multiparty system.[11] Ever since 1948, the Communists and the Christian Democrats have together polled over 60 percent of the total number of votes cast in elections for the Chamber of Deputies: 79.5 percent in 1948, 62.6 percent in 1953, 65.1 percent in 1958, 63.6 percent in 1963, and 66 percent in 1968. They have been able to do this because of their numerous array of members and activists, their financial strength, and their possession of a capillary network of mass organizations and party-dominated pressure groups. The other parties simply have not been in a position to compete effectively against such massive resources. The Socialists and Social Democrats have been far too wrapped up in their internecine feuds, while the middle-class Liberals have been understandably diffident (in view of the aura of distrust that has surrounded the Italian bourgeoisie as a result of its collaboration with Fascism) about establishing contact with the masses at the grass roots.

Facing such ineffectual competition, the Christian Democratic Party has not only inherited the Catholic electorate, which voted for the Italian Popular party before 1922, but has also won the support of a very large proportion of those moderate middle-class voters who backed one or another of the various Liberal party groupings in the days before the Fascist regime. On the other hand, the Communist party has, since 1946, emerged as the leading party on the Left and has steadily gained ground, but mostly at the expense of the Socialists and of its other leftist neighbors. Thus, the Christian Democrats have become the leading "moderate" party, but have also become faction-ridden and immobile as a result of their great heterogeneity. The Communists, for their part, have become the leading "radical" party, but have also come to represent an insurmountable obstacle to the formation of a united and effective Left opposition.

Each of these two dominant parties must protect and strengthen its frontiers against its neighbors. That is to say, the Communists try to gain votes at the expense of the Socialists and Social Democrats, and the Christian Democrats try to avoid losing votes to the Liberals and to the other rightist parties. These gains and losses mostly occur *within* the Left segment (Communists,

---

[11] The following analysis is drawn from Galli chs. 4 and 5.

Socialists, Social Democrats, Republicans) and *within* the Right-Center segment (Christian Democrats, Liberals, Monarchists, Neo-Fascists) of the political spectrum. Rarely do significant numbers of voters shift their allegiance from the Right-Center to the Left or vice versa. And these spatially delimited gains and losses are usually fairly marginal: only 3–6 percent of the Italian electorate shifts its position from one election to another. Moreover, the strength of the extreme Left has not really risen, despite Communist gains. Now that the Socialists and the Social Democrats have both expressed their willingness to collaborate with the Christian Democrats, only the Left-wing PSIUP is still allied with the Communists at the national level. And the combined strength of the Communist party and the PSIUP in 1968 was 31.4 percent of the total votes—not even half a percentage point higher than the 31 percent polled by the extreme Left in the 1948 debacle!

The message conveyed by the above data, and by Galli's masterful analysis, is clear. Behind a facade of free-wheeling, pluralistic multiparty politics, Italy is really operating under an "imperfect two-party system" in which there is no clear alternation in office between government and opposition and in which elections have a minimal effect.

INTRAPARTY POLITICS: THE ROLE OF FACTIONS

In addition to the hegemony of two dominant parties, the existence of extreme pluralism and of a high degree of polarization, and the development of "catch-all" parties, the Italian party system also happens to be infested with factionalism. In every Italian democratic party, there are one or more ruling factions and several opposition factions. Factionalism, to be sure, is not a uniquely Italian phenomenon, but the Italian variety is characterized by a very superior stage of organization and cohesion. In a number of Italian parties, factions have their own newspapers or journals, their own parliamentary subgroups, their own sources of income, and their own share of party patronage. Also, they have their own factional leader, who is empowered to negotiate with other factional leaders within his party, in order that a settlement of outstanding disputes may be reached. The relationship between contending factions has much in common with the fierce competition that is carried on by the parties in an extremely polarized multiparty system.

Factionalism plays a key role in the process of nominating parliamentary candidates and party officials, for nomination contests are essentially factional fights. Hence a would-be deputy or a would-be provincial secretary of a party organization is well advised to associate closely with an organized faction that can call on support from its own national headquarters. For purely local grass-roots revolts by isolated provincial party leaders against the national party leadership are almost bound to fail.

Factionalism in Italian parties has greatly complicated the character of Italy's multiparty system. For what may appear to be a coalition cabinet composed of parties commanding a firm majority in Parliament may turn out to be a slender reed when one or more of the component parties contains a powerful faction that views the cabinet formula with hostility. Many times Christian Democratic-led cabinets have had to resign because of the opposition, not of one of the parties allied with the Christian Democrats, but of a faction within the Christian Democratic party itself. True, the parties are centralized and disciplined, and the parties in Parliament generally vote as cohesive blocs. But the threat of a party split resulting from factional disaffection can cause the leadership of a party to abandon or postpone a sensitive policy decision. It is thus not too difficult to understand the immobilism of Italian government policy: intraparty politics, even more than interparty politics, represents a major barrier to innovation.

Neo-Fascist party congresses have also been marked by factional conflict. Even the Communist party, which regards factionalism as a cardinal sin, is not completely immune to it. Factions in the Communist party cannot organize openly and seek adherents at the grass roots; but the existence of factions in the top echelons of the party has become more and more evident as a result of debate at party congresses and disputatious articles in the party press. For example, some Communist "sectarians" openly yearn for a return to the autocratic methods of the Stalin era; Amendola and his supporters have spoken of a possible new leftist party, incorporating both Socialist and Communist elements and synthesizing the more positive features of each; Ingrao advocates a dialogue with the Catholics as a possible prelude to a Communist-Catholic rapprochement. And of course there are both revisionist and Leninist tendencies in the Communist party. Between these contending elements, Secretary Luigi Longo and Vice-Secretary Mario Berlinguer try to steer a middle course.

But of course, it is the democratic parties—particularly the two largest democratic parties (the Christian Democrats and the Socialists)—that are torn by the most violent and public factional conflicts. In these parties, the competition for preference votes in the general elections seems to be a more dramatic and crucial process than the effort to increase the party's total strength in Parliament.

The bases of factional division in Italian democratic parties tend to vary. In the Socialist and Social Democratic parties, the chief sources of controversy have been the issue of Socialist participation in a coalition cabinet in which non-Socialist parties were bound to play a dominant role, and the question of what political allies, if any, the Socialists should cultivate. The question of alliances has also been paramount for the Christian Democrats, with the more conservative elements opting for cooperation with the Liberals or even with the Monarchists, while the Rank-and-File Left faction advocated an alliance with the Socialists long before such an alliance came to be regarded as a feasible alternative. However, strategic motifs may sometimes be mere rationalizations for the careerist ambitions of individual factional leaders and their clienteles. Firmly held ideological views may also, on occasion, serve to orient the actions of some political activists, although a variety of personal motivations are probably more significant in accounting for factional alignments.

American and Italian scholars have attempted to study factional conflict in Italian parties with a view to formulating some general hypotheses. One study of factions in the Christian Democratic party concludes that Christian Democracy's status as a dominant party makes for an intraparty politics based increasingly on clashes between leading personalities rather than on principles and/or grand strategy. It also results in the blurring of distinctions between the various factions, and in considerable ideological volatility among leading politicians of the dominant party.[12] To some extent, the leftward migration of such formerly centrist or conservative Christian Democratic leaders as Taviani, Piccoli, and Moro, and the more conservative stance assumed by such erstwhile leftist leaders as Sullo and Fanfani, would seem to bear out this hypothesis. But a particularly telling illustration of this point is provided by the case of Giulio Andreotti. In the 1950s and early 1960s, Andreotti led the Primavera faction, which pressed for an alliance with the rightist parties; in the summer of 1970, Andreotti's efforts to form a cabinet failed, partly because the Social Democrats feared he was overly leftist in his sympathies.

Another study suggests that moderate, depolarizing factions

---

[12] Raphael Zariski, "Intra-Party Conflict in a Dominant Party: The Experience of Italian Christian Democracy," *The Journal of Politics*, Vol. 27, No. 1 (February 1965), 19–34.

(factions that seek their allies at the Left-Center rather than on the extreme Left) will generally prevail in a Socialist party in provinces where the party is particularly strong in terms of votes, or where a high degree of industrialization exists, or where there is a highly competitive electoral situation between Left-wing and Right-wing parties.[13] Some doubt is cast on these conclusions by a more recent investigation. Using aggregate data analysis, Sidney Tarrow emerges with some negative findings: There is no positive statistical correlation between the strength of moderate Socialist or Christian Democratic factions in a provincial party organization and the existence of a high level of economic development in that province.[14] But Tarrow's failure to segregate the Catholic-dominated Northeast from the politically competitive Northwest in analyzing his data at the regional level raises some questions as to the validity of his findings. The query as to whether or not economic growth will necessarily lead to political depolarization remains substantially open for further investigation.

Factional conflict may also be studied in view of the factors which tend to encourage intraparty democracy in the form of factional competition. In a study of the Italian Socialist party in the Tuscan Province of Arezzo, Samuel Barnes points to the following phenomena as contributing to its internal democracy.[15] First of all, most Socialist leaders and activists show a preference for internal democratic norms and are willing to tolerate opposition factions within the party. Second, since the multi-party system permits dissidents to react against undemocratic party practices by simply seceding from the party and joining an adjacent party on the political spectrum, internal democracy is helpful in preventing such an exodus from taking place. And last, the Socialist party leaders do not dominate all the communications channels reaching their rank-and-file supporters. For example, many Socialist party members in Arezzo read an independent conservative and a Communist newspaper as well as their own Socialist daily; and the Socialists' Left opposition faction receives encouragement and some patronage jobs from local Communist leaders and from the Communist-dominated trade unions.

[13] Raphael Zariski, "The Italian Socialist Party: A Case Study in Factional Conflict," *American Political Science Review*, Vol. LVI, No. 2 (June 1962), 381–390.

[14] Sidney G. Tarrow, "Economic Development and the Transformation of the Italian Party System," *Comparative Politics*, Vol. 1, No. 2 (January 1969), 163–169.

[15] Samuel H. Barnes, *Party Democracy: Politics in an Italian Socialist Federation* (New Haven, Conn.: Yale University Press, 1967), pp. 62–64, 87–89, 212–213, 224–233.

PARTY ORGANIZATION: A COMMON MOLD

Chapter Two referred to the rather tight control exercised by Italian parties over the recruitment of candidates. This point is related to the high degree of party centralization, cohesion, and discipline common to all Italian parties. The central party organization has a qualified veto power over parliamentary nominees, whose candidacies are submitted by provincial and circumscriptional (that is, interprovincial) party organs. Cohesion is evident when members of the party in Parliament generally vote together as a solid bloc. And in all Italian parties, breaches of party discipline are often—but not always—punished by suspension or expulsion from the party.

How does one account for these qualities of cohesion, discipline, and centralization, which are so often conspicuous by their absence in French parties? The fact that French deputies are elected from single-member districts, while Italian deputies are elected from large multimember constituencies, is a partial but not entirely satisfactory explanation. For sometimes an entire Italian provincial or regional party organization may be controlled by an opposition faction, in rebellion against the central party leadership. Such a faction will propose a slate of parliamentary candidates dominated by its supporters; and in such an event, the central party leadership may have to abstain from the wholesale use of its veto power, for fear of weakening the party.[16] In other words, since the multimember lists in Italy are drawn up initially by grass-roots party organs, they need not necessarily make for more central control.

Cohesion and discipline prevail, not only in classic branch-type parties like the Socialists and the Christian Democrats, but also in a predominantly middle-class party like the Italian Liberal party. Although Duverger seems to imply that middle-class parties do not respond well to cohesion and discipline,[17] this implication does not seem to be borne out by the Italian party system. Instead, in France, it is precisely the middle-class parties like the Radical-Socialists and the Independents that show an inability to preserve their internal unity on parliamentary roll-calls.

Certain culture-bound explanations for the lack of party discipline can be deflated by using the comparative approach as La

[16] Zariski, "Intra-Party Conflict . . . ," 22.
[17] Duverger, pp. 20–21, 25–27.

Palombara has done.[18] For instance, some observers attribute the undisciplined character of certain French parties to their heterogeneity—to the great variety of classes and groups they represent. Yet, in Italy, such parties as the Christian Democrats are far more heterogeneous in their voting strength and membership composition than any single French party, with the possible exception of the Gaullists; this variegated character does not prevent the Italian Christian Democrats from constituting a solid bloc of usually reliable votes in the Italian Parliament.

Nor can one blame the intellectualism and the ideological style of party leaders and activists for a low level of party cohesion, as some students of French politics have done. For again, Italy has a rather similar type of intellectual party elite, with a political style long on philosophical speculation and short on problem-oriented discourse. Yet, the Italian intelligentsia shows a capacity for submerging its ethical and philosophical predilections and backing its party leadership to the hilt.

Why does this happen in Italy and not in France—or, at any rate, not to the same degree? The most convincing explanation is La Palombara's stress on the greater and more imminent danger represented by the extreme Left in Italy, as compared to the French Communists and their allies. After all, before 1956, the Italian Socialist party was allied with the Communist party and was therefore considered to be part of the extreme Left. The combined vote of the extreme Left in Italy was about 40 percent of the total number of votes cast in parliamentary elections, whereas the French Communists and their allies polled about 25 percent of the total vote. With a relatively slim anti-Communist majority in the Parliament and in the country, Italian deputies of centrist and rightist persuasion may have viewed any breach of party discipline as a possible weakening of the anti-Communist front at a time when a Communist takeover was not beyond the realm of possibility.[19]

But perhaps we are mistaken in taking Italian party cohesion at its face value. For, while party lines generally hold firm, there *are* occasional successful intraparty revolts, departures from party cohesion by significant factional groupings. Above all, the threat of such revolts may frequently have the result of stifling policy innovations introduced by the ruling elites of the governing parties (especially the Christian Democrats). Opposition of this sort will

---

[18] Joseph La Palombara, "Political Party Systems and Crisis Governments: French and Italian Contrasts," *Midwest Journal of Political Science*, Vol. II, No. 2 (May 1958), 117–142.

[19] La Palombara, "Political Party Systems . . . ," 131–135.

develop behind the scenes, rather than out in the open. Threats of secession and expressions of strong and basic disagreement with the line pursued by the party leadership will alert the leaders to the potential costs of proceeding with their proposed policy. As a result, many a new initiative will be abandoned, usually by being unaccountably bogged down in committee; while the party, by avoiding controversial stands, manages to maintain a facade of unity in the eyes of the world. Thus, cohesion may serve as a camouflage for immobilism.

The relatively large memberships enrolled in Italian parties is one characteristic that tends to differentiate them clearly from French parties. Another key feature of Italian party organization is the decisive role played by the extraparliamentary party organs in guiding the policy decisions adopted by the parties in Parliament. In cabinet crises, the directorates (executive committees) of the various parties will not hesitate to issue public statements to instruct their representatives in Parliament. These statements will indicate the course of action to follow, or consent to a party's entry into, or support of, a given cabinet coalition. Also, party secretaries and vice-secretaries are often consulted during the exploratory talks that occur during a cabinet crisis. Prolonged negotiations between extraparliamentary party leaders are not uncommon during such talks. Above all, it has been pointed out by Maranini and others that almost all cabinet crises in Italy have been extraparliamentary in origin: A decision taken at a meeting of the party directorate, a resolution passed at a party congress, or even a hostile statement issued by a party secretary may cause the collapse of a cabinet coalition and the fall of a cabinet.[20] It is because of this tendency in Italian politics that Maranini speaks of the degradation of parliamentary institutions by an irresponsible "partitocracy."

However, it is dangerous to exaggerate or oversimplify the relationship between the extraparliamentary party leadership and the party parliamentary group. It is true, of course, that the basic statutes of almost all of the Italian parties recognize the power of the extraparliamentary party organs to designate the policies the parliamentary groups must follow.[21] But it should also be borne in mind that the party secretaries are themselves usually members of Parliament, and that deputies and senators usually make up

[20] Giuseppe Maranini, *Storia del potere in Italia: 1848–1967* (Firenze: Vallecchi, 1967), pp. 409–410.

[21] Mario Bassani, *Partiti e parlamento* (Milano-Varese: Istituto Editoriale Cisalpino, 1965), pp. 22–29, 46–47, 56–59. For the party statutes of the various parties, see C. E. Traverso, V. Italia, M. Bassani, *I partiti politici: leggi e statuti* (Milano-Varese: Istituto Editoriale Cisalpino, 1966), Part III.

over 50 percent of the membership of the major extraparliamentary party organs.[22] There is, then, so much intermeshing between the party directorate and the party parliamentary group that it is misleading to give the impression that two distinct and separate entities are involved. Yet, there is a strong element of validity in Maranini's complaint: Regardless of who is making the decisions, the *locale* of decision making in an Italian cabinet crisis gives the public the partly erroneous sensation that its political destinies are being decided by faceless party bureaucrats.

One last qualification needs to be stated. While the extraparliamentary party organization may issue a general statement of policy or a platform, the choice of priorities in the application of the policy will frequently be left to the parliamentary leadership of the party. For instance, in the spring of 1967, the secretariats of the parties participating in the Left-Center coalition government stated that the cabinet had the right to determine which of the reform measures agreed upon by the coalition parties were to be adopted at any given time.[23] So, while the scales are generally weighted on the side of the extraparliamentary party, the relationship is not as one-sided as it might appear. As a matter of fact, there have been occasions when parliamentary groups have successfully defied the party apparatus.[24]

Thus, Italian parties share certain similar organizational features: a high degree of cohesion and discipline, a relatively large membership, and a major role for the extraparliamentary party organization in the decision-making process. We might add an additional similarity with regard to the organizational structure. Generally speaking, all Italian parties are organized by communes (the communal section), provinces (the provincial federation) and regions (the regional committee or federation), with power centered at the national and—to a lesser degree—at the provincial level. Each party has a system of representative assemblies—usually referred to as the sectional assembly, the provincial congress, and the national congress—which meet periodically to elect the permanent party organs at each level. These permanent organs usually include, at the national level, a quasi-legislative body (known as the national council in the Christian Democratic party and the Liberal party, while the Communists, Socialists, and Social Democrats have a central committee); an executive organ

---

[22] Giuseppe Reale, "I partiti del centro sinistra e la crisi di governo del giugno 1963," *Partiti e democrazia: Atti del III Convegno di San Pellegrino* (Roma: Edizioni Cinque Lune, 1964), p. 906.

[23] Sernini, p. 12.

[24] Vittorio De Caprariis, *Le garanzie della libertà* (Milano: Il Saggiatore, 1966), pp. 216–217.

(referred to, in most parties, as the directorate); and an administrative organ (the secretariat); while the leader of the extraparliamentary party is known as the party secretary. Similar organs exist at the provincial level (the federal committee, the directive committee, and the secretariat) and, in more rudimentary form, at the local level.

There are some structural differences that should be cited, however. For one thing, the Communists, Socialists, and Social Democrats have all attempted to supplement their local sections with a system of workplace organizations, the Communist "cells" and the Socialist and Social Democratic "shop nuclei." This does not appear to have been a particularly successful organizational device; the territorial sections tend to overshadow the workplace units. Secondly, the Communist party bans open factional activity and manages to prevent factions from competing for votes at party congresses. By the same token, centralization and the control of higher over lower party organs are far more rigidly enforced in the Communist party than in other Italian parties. And finally, the actual structure of the smaller parties (the Social Democrats, the Liberals, and the Republicans) is far more skeletal than that of the Christian Democrats and the Communists. The smaller parties lack the funds and membership to justify the hiring of a large corps of full-time employees, and are far less successful than the Communists and Christian Democrats in recruiting volunteer activists. In most cases, their local organizations come to life only around election time.

One additional important organizational aspect of Italian parties should be mentioned. Tarrow points to the fact that the Communist party has developed a separate organizational strategy for Southern Italy.[25] Unable to rely on a highly developed infrastructure of trade unions, peasant leagues, cooperatives, and other party-dominated mass organizations, as it can do in Northern and Central Italy, the Communist party in the South has tended to encourage the formation of broad, vaguely delineated "people's" movements. Each such movement claims to represent a wide range of social classes and groups. Examples include the Committees for the Land, in which land-owning peasants and even small absentee landlords rub shoulders with sharecroppers and farm laborers. Class differences in the countryside are often blurred by the variety of economic roles acted out by the average peasant (the same individual may own and work one small plot of

---

[25] Sidney G. Tarrow, *Peasant Communism in Southern Italy* (New Haven, Conn.: Yale University Press, 1967), pp. 34, 210–225, 237–246, 268–271, 279–291, 354–367.

land, cultivate another plot on a tenancy contract basis, and toil on yet another plot as a farm laborer paid by the day). Therefore the Communists have chosen to adopt a form of organization that deemphasizes class differences, and seems to degenerate eventually into a politics of personality, dominated by local clienteles. Thus, the Communist party in the South has taken on many of the characteristic features of the society it set out to transform.

THE PARTIES AND THEIR PROGRAMS

Following is a lengthy analysis of the influential political parties in Italy. As a reference, it may be helpful to study Tables 5.1 and 5.2, both of which provide general pictures of the Italian party strengths.

Table 5.1 Percentages of the total vote polled by Italian parties in elections for the Constituent Assembly in 1946 and for the Chamber of Deputies from 1948 through 1968[a]

	1946	1948	1953	1958	1963	1968
Communists (PCI)	19	31[e]	22.6	22.7	25.3	26.9
Social Proletarians (PSIUP)	—		—	—	—	4.5
Socialists (PSI)	20.7[b]		12.7	14.2	13.8	14.5[g]
Social Democrats (PSU)	—	7.1	4.5	4.5	6.1	
Christian Democrats (DC)	35.2	48.5	40	42.4	38.3	39.1
Republicans (PRI)	4.4	2.5	1.6	1.4	1.4	2
Liberals (PLI)	6.8[c]	3.8	3	3.5	7	5.8
Qualunquists (extreme Right)	5.3	—	—	—	—	—
Monarchists (PDIUM)	2.8	2.8	6.8	2.2+ 2.6[f]	1.7	1.3
Neo-Fascists (MSI)	—	2	5.9	4.8	5.1	4.5
Others	5.8[d]	2.3	2.9	1.7	1.3	1.4

[a] Data for this table are drawn from sources cited in footnote 34, this chapter.
[b] In 1946, Socialists and Social Democrats were united in a single party. The party split in 1947.
[c] The Liberal list in 1946 was known as the National Democratic Union.
[d] The "others" category in 1946 included the short-lived Action party, many of whose members joined the Socialists and Republicans.
[e] In 1948, the Communists and Socialists formed a single electoral bloc: the People's Democratic Front. The experiment was not repeated.
[f] There were two Monarchist parties in 1958.
[g] In 1968, the Socialists and Social Democrats ran together as a united party: the Unified Socialist party. In 1969 this party was destroyed by another scission.

Table 5.2 Seats won by the various parties in the Italian Constituent Assembly in 1946 and in the Italian Chamber of Deputies from 1948 through 1968[a]

	1946	1948	1953	1958	1963	1968
Communists (PCI)	104		143	140	166	171
Social Proletarians (PSIUP)	—	183[e]	—	—	—	23
Socialists (PSI)	115[b]		75	84	87	91[g]
Social Democrats (PSU)	—	33	19	22	33	
Christian Democrats (DC)	207	305	262	273	260	265
Republicans (PRI)	23	9	5	6	6	9
Liberals (PLI)	41[c]	19	14	17	39	31
Qualunquists (extreme Right)	30	—	—	—	—	—
Monarchists (PDIUM)	—	14	40	11+ 14[f]	8	6
Neo-Fascists (MSI)	—	6	29	15	27	24
Others	35[d]	5	3	5	4	10

[a] Data for this table are drawn from sources cited in footnote 34, this chapter.
[b] In 1946, Socialists and Social Democrats were united in a single party. The party split in 1947.
[c] The Liberal list in 1946 was known as the National Democratic Union.
[d] The "others" category in 1946 included the short-lived Action party, many of whose members joined the Socialists and Republicans.
[e] In 1948, the Communists and Socialists formed a single electoral bloc: the People's Democratic Front. The experiment was not repeated. Most of the Deputies elected on this ticket were Communists.
[f] There were two Monarchists parties in 1958.
[g] In 1968, the Socialists and Social Democrats ran together as a united party: the Unified Socialist party. In 1969, this party was destroyed by another scission.

The Communist party (PCI)

The Italian Communist party (PCI) was founded in 1921 at Leghorn by a group of secessionists from the Italian Socialist party. The refusal of the Italian Socialist party to expel its reformist elements in accordance with the peremptory demands of the Third International provided the pretext for Antonio Gramsci and Amedeo Bordiga to lead their followers out of the Socialist party and to found the PCI shortly thereafter. Within the next few years, Gramsci emerged as the leader of the PCI, while Bordiga's faction was eliminated. But Gramsci's victory was an empty one; for in 1922 Mussolini and his Fascist movement came to power. After 1926, the PCI (as well as all other non-Fascist parties) was outlawed. Gramsci himself was arrested in 1927 and died in prison ten years later. During the period between 1926 and 1943, the PCI had to operate as a clandestine organization on Italian soil—an exacting role, but one that the PCI was better fitted to perform than was the case with other anti-Fascist parties. During this period, the leadership of the PCI outside of Italy was exercised by Palmiro Togliatti, who was living in the Soviet Union. It was Togliatti who, on his return to Italy in March 1944, took over the leadership of the PCI and transformed it into the largest party in Italy in terms of members and second largest in terms of votes.

The underground struggle against the Fascist regime, and later against the Nazi occupation of 1943–1945, reaped copious returns for the PCI. It was during this period that the Unity of Action Pact, signed in Paris in 1934, initiated that Communist-Socialist alliance which was to last for over a decade after the Liberation. The fact that the PCI in Italy was operating underground minimized the impact of the Nazi-Soviet Nonaggression Pact of 1939 on Italian public opinion.[26] While the French Communists, operating in the glaring publicity of a democratic society, felt compelled to execute a loud and self-righteous about-face on the subject of defense against German aggression, the PCI was under no real obligation to undertake a vigorous defense of the pact and consequently did not share in the political odium that was incurred by other Communist parties in Western Europe. Thus, when the Fascist regime collapsed in 1943 and the Germans overran Northern Italy, the PCI was better prepared than other parties to play a leading role in the Resistance movement. It was the brilliant and heroic performance of the Communists in the Resistance that enabled them to sink deep roots among the masses and to attract many idealistic intellectuals to their cause.

After the war, the Communists emerged as one of the leading parties in Italy. True, they still ranked behind the Socialists in the June 1946 elections to the Constituent Assembly: the PCI polled 19 percent of the total vote, while the Socialist party garnered 20.7 percent. But the great scission that split the Socialist party in January 1947 gave the Communists their opportunity to forge ahead at the expense of their ravaged ally. Ever since 1947, the PCI has been the leading party on the Left wing of the Italian political spectrum. Moreover, the Communist electorate has risen slowly but steadily, from 22.6 percent of the total votes cast in 1953 to 26.9 percent in 1968.

The PCI's program has usually been the ambiguous product

[26] Tarrow, *Peasant Communism* . . . , p. 105.

of a nimble balancing act performed by the party leadership, with a view to reconciling the ideas of various tendencies within the party and also maintaining some equilibrium between the demands of the international Communist movement and the requirements of the Italian domestic political situation. But in Togliatti's concept of the *Via Italiana al Socialismo* ("Italian road to socialism"), it is made fairly clear that the PCI proposes to come to power legally, preserve the multiparty system, and respect constitutional guarantees. Also Togliatti has explicitly declared the usefulness of parliamentary institutions for the socialist society of the future and has indicated that the proletariat must seek to cement alliances, not only with the peasants, but with white-collar workers and small businessmen as well. So, the PCI *appears* to be firmly committed to democratic methods and democratic alliances—and indeed, no other Italian party has been more vociferous in demanding that the provisions of the Italian Constitution be enforced with despatch. Yet, as Galli points out, the PCI has had to continue to defend Leninist principles, which are virtually impossible to reconcile with democratic norms.[27] For this and other closely related reasons, supporters of Italian democracy tend to be rather skeptical about Communist intentions.

Other incongruities may be discerned in the programs and policies of the PCI. For instance, in local elections—in Bologna and other communes—the PCI has not hesitated to cater to anticlerical sentiment whenever such tactics seemed likely to pay off in terms of votes.[28] Yet, it was the PCI which, in the Constituent Assembly in 1946-1947, voted with the Christian Democrats to incorporate the provisions of the Concordat of 1929 into the Italian Constitution. And, as we have noted, an important tendency in the PCI seeks an alliance with the Catholics, possibly accompanied by the entry of the PCI into the cabinet and the formation of a "conciliar republic."[29]

In the area of foreign affairs, the PCI has criticized the intransigence of the Chinese Communist party (CCP), but has insisted on the right of the CCP to enjoy autonomy within the world Communist movement and has resisted the efforts of the Communist party of the Soviet Union to arrange for an international Communist conference at which the Chinese could be properly

[27] Galli, pp. 83–87.
[28] Gianluigi Degli Esposti, *Bologna PCI* (Bologna: Il Mulino, 1966), pp. 122–128.
[29] The term "conciliar republic" refers to the recent Vatican Council and to the late Pope John XXIII's alleged policy of seeking reconciliation with the Communist world.

pilloried. The PCI has sharply criticized the Soviet Union for its invasion of Czechoslovakia, but has continued to demand that Italy withdraw from NATO, despite the aggressive Soviet propensities which the Czech coup revealed so clearly.

In the domestic sphere, the record is equally contradictory. On some matters (the nationalization of the sugar, drug, and cement industries), PCI proposals have been clear and explicit; on others (the form that planning was to take, the reform of the bureaucracy), the PCI has had little to offer but vague, ambivalent phrases.[30] Generally, the PCI tries to project the image of a solid, mature opposition party, imbued with a sober sense of responsibility, but it must also attempt to appear in the eyes of the voters as a party of protest. It purports to seek the fundamental reform of Italian society, but merely presents the voters with an unevaluated, undifferentiated shopping list of proposals, while making no real effort to work out an order of priorities. And many of its proposals, directed at defending the established privileges of small shopkeepers and small farmers, have seemed to run directly counter to its self-professed mission as a forward-looking reform movement. It is hardly surprising, under the circumstances, that observers like Galli have concluded that the leaders of the PCI have neither the hope nor the intention of ever coming to power and are primarily concerned with defending their existing privileges and entrenched positions within the system. As Galli puts it, "The PCI is neither a conspiracy nor a peril: it is only an enormous waste. It is a party committed to the justification of its own existence . . ."[31]

Yet, we must devote a great deal of attention to the PCI for two reasons. First, it is the second largest party in Italy in electoral strength, and second, it seems to be becoming the pivot of the Italian political system, as more and more speculation arises concerning the possibility of the eventual admission of the PCI to the ranks of the dominant cabinet coalition. Although this possibility appears to be highly unlikely, the very fact it is being so widely discussed is in itself significant.

Also, the PCI is of considerable interest because, with all its rigidities and weaknesses, it is much more dynamic and successful than the French Communist party. The Italian Communist party

---

[30] For a discussion of the programs of the various Italian parties, including the Communist party, see Orazio Maria Petracca, "Tattica e strategia nei programmi elettorali," in Mattei Dogan and Orazio Maria Petracca, *Partiti politici e strutture sociali in Italia* (Milano: Comunità, 1968), pp. 51–120.

[31] Galli, p. 99.

has consistently displayed more spirit of initiative and independence. Also, the PCI has attracted a higher proportion of younger voters, has been less diluted by the presence in its ranks of the middle classes, has lost a smaller proportion of its members over the years, maintains control over a larger proportion of local governments, and has a stronger labor movement under its domination (this last advantage may be disappearing, as we shall see). Greene attributes at least some of these indexes of superiority to the more competent and flexible leadership of men like Gramsci and Togliatti, to the more respected role assigned to intellectuals in the PCI as contrasted to the French Communist party, and to the more vigorous competition the PCI has had to encounter from Socialism and progressive Catholicism.[32] So, on a comparative basis at least, the PCI may not entirely deserve the scornful treatment it has received from Galli. Nevertheless, when all is said and done, it *does* represent a massive force for ambiguity, an obstacle to clarification, as it maintains an "ambivalent posture of half-accepting, half-rejecting the system of which it is a part."[33] Whether its future course will lead to absorption into the system, segregation as a permanent "untouchable" minority within the system, or erosion at the hands of competing democratic leftist parties, remains to be seen.

The Italian Socialist party of Proletarian Unity (PSIUP)

The PSIUP was founded in 1964, shortly after the Italian Socialist party ushered in what appeared to be a new era in Italian politics by entering the Christian Democratic-dominated cabinet of Aldo Moro in the latter part of 1963. The leftist factions in the Socialist party had long been dissatisfied with the moderate policies being pursued under the leadership of Peitro Nenni, but the alliance with the Christian Democrats was the last straw. And so, secession resulted and the PSIUP was formed under the leadership of Lelio Basso and Tullio Vecchietti. Its attitude has been one of outright rejection of the Left-Center coalition formula (a Christian Democratic-Socialist-Social Democratic-Republican alliance, excluding the Communists on the Left and the Liberals on the Right) as a

---

[32] Thomas H. Greene, "The Communist Parties of Italy and France: A Study in Comparative Communism," *World Politics*, Vol. XXI, No. 1 (October 1968), 1–38.

[33] Donald L. M. Blackmer, *Unity in Diversity: Italian Communism and the Communist World* (Cambridge, Mass.: The M.I.T. Press, 1968), p. 412.

solution to Italy's problems. In fact, it takes the position that the Left-Center coalition only provides a convenient shield for the forces of neocapitalism, which are trying to entangle the leftist parties into merely administering the day-to-day operations of the system.

The PSIUP expresses a deep distrust of Social Democracy, while favoring a dialogue with the more progressive segments of the Catholic movement. It also gives voice to grave doubts as to the feasibility of effective democratic planning in a capitalist system. With regard to domestic political alliances, it accepts a close entente with the Communists, but leaders like Basso really aspire to the eventual formation of a broader leftist grouping in which Socialists (but not Social Democrats) would play the leading role. In the international sphere, the PSIUP identifies with the neutralist countries of the "Third World" and looks askance at imperialism of both the American and the Soviet varieties. Despite its alliance with the Communist party, it does not hesitate to assume a posture of criticism vis-à-vis its gigantic partner, and also to adopt a more intransigent stand against the Left-Center formula and against neocapitalist tendencies than do the Communists.

The Italian Socialist party (PSI) and the Italian Social Democrats (PSU)

Italian socialism has always been a sorely divided movement ever since the Italian Socialist party was founded at the Congress of Genoa in 1892. On the one hand, the so-called Maximalists, or orthodox Marxists, have insisted that the Socialist party refuse to take part in coalition cabinets dominated by bourgeois forces and have also demanded that the party either remain in glorious isolation or cement alliances with forces farther to the Left (since 1921, with the Communists). On the other hand, the Reformist elements have sought to establish ties with other democratic parties, have spurned collaboration with the Communists, and have advocated that Italian socialism bear its share of responsibility for governing the country, even at the price of collaboration with bourgeois democratic parties.

As a result of these internal tensions, the Italian Socialist party has been subject to a series of major splits: On a number of occasions, the outnumbered Reformists have left the party and have formed a Social Democratic party under a variety of different labels. Such a secession took place shortly after World War I, and it took a Fascist victory in Italy and long years of exile to heal the breach. A more spectacular party split occurred in 1947, when Giuseppe Saragat, fearing imminent fusion between the Socialist party and the Communist party, led his followers out of the Socialist party and founded the Social Democratic party. After 1947, the Socialists collaborated closely with the Communists, while the Social Democrats formed part of De Gasperi's Center coalition.

Under the leadership of Pietro Nenni, the Socialist party gradually drifted away from its intimate alliance with the Communists at the national level. This process was slow and gradual, and did not get under way until 1956 when the relaxation of international tension, the advent of new leadership in the Soviet Union, and the unsavory revelations about past Stalinist crimes emboldened Nenni to embark on a new course. After many vicissitudes, the long-discussed opening to the Left was finally consummated in 1962: The Christian Democrats formed a coalition cabinet with the Republicans and Social Democrats—a cabinet which received the external support of the Italian Socialist party. In 1963, the Socialists finally entered the Christian Democratic-led cabinet of Aldo Moro. In only seven years, Nenni had renounced the Unity of Action Pact with the Communists, had partly overcome the deep distrust that divided Socialists from Catholics, and had prevailed against the counterattacks of leftist opposition factions within his own party. The reunification between the Socialists and Social Democrats, which was finally achieved in 1966, seemed to mark a fitting culmination of Nenni's efforts: The Unified Socialist party, it was hoped, would soon establish itself as the leading leftist force in the country.

However, as is so often the case, the widespread expectations of a political renaissance proved to be rather premature. The entry of the Socialists into the Moro cabinet led to the secession of the leftist factions and the formation of the Italian Socialist Party of Proletarian Unity (PSIUP) in 1964. The recession of 1963–1965 and the chronic slowness of the Christian Democrats in enacting such previously agreed-upon reform measures as the establishment of the regions led to considerable Socialist dissatisfaction with the Left-Center formula. And even after the formation of the Unified Socialist party in 1966, Socialists and Social Democrats continued to be divided by animosities and mutual suspicions of twenty years' standing.

The parliamentary elections of 1968 seemed to confirm the doubts of those who had been skeptical about both the Left-Center cabinet formula and socialist reunification. The Communists and Christian Democrats both gained ground. The secessionist

PSIUP obtained 4.5 percent of the votes cast. And while the combined vote of the Socialists and Social Democrats in 1963 had been 19.9 percent (13.8 percent for the Socialists, 6.1 percent for the Social Democrats), the Unified Socialist party obtained only 14.5 percent of the votes in 1968. While this loss of ground could be attributed mostly to the votes polled by the PSIUP, the 1968 outcome still represented a bitter pill for Socialists and Social Democrats to swallow. Where were all the disillusioned and discouraged leftist voters who—according to the prevalent mythology—were waiting for socialist reunification to impel them to return to the socialist fold?

Given these bitter disappointments, the Unified Socialist party was bound to encounter once again the internecine conflicts that have always been the bane of Italian socialism. More leftist elements in the party began to speak of the need to bring the Communists into the majority coalition in order to force through the overdue reforms that had been promised but not delivered by the Christian Democratic senior partners. Such a course of action was regarded as utterly unacceptable by the Social Democratic elements. When, in the summer of 1969, a leftist "new majority" gained control of the national executive organs of the party, the former Social Democrats, led by Mario Tanassi, and some of the more moderate Socialists, led by Mauro Ferri, seceded and formed the Unitary Socialist party (PSU). The "new majority" in charge of the rump Socialist party readopted the old label of Italian Socialist party (PSI). There are now three parties claiming to speak for Italian socialism. Ranging from Left to Right, they are the PSIUP, the Socialists (PSI), and the Social Democrats (PSU).

The relative strength of these three parties was reflected, to a considerable extent, by the 1970 regional election, in which the PSI, the PSU, and the PSIUP polled 10.4 percent, 7 percent, and 3.2 percent of the votes, respectively.[34] The three socialist parties had obtained a combined total of 20.6 percent of the votes, enough to put them almost on an equal plane with the Communists, who chalked up 27.9 percent. But Italian socialism is di-

---

[34] For figures on the 1970 regional elections, see *La Stampa* (Turin), June 11, 1970. For figures on the various general elections, see "The Italian General Election," *Italian Affairs*, Vol. II, No. 3 (June 1953), 10, covering the elections of 1946, 1948, and 1953; "The General Elections," *Italian Affairs*, Vol. VII, No. 5 (September–October 1958), 38; "The General Election: Italy's Fourth Republican Parliament," *Italian Affairs: Documents and Notes*, Vol. XII, No. 3 (1963), 67; and "General Elections 1968: Official Results," *Italy: Documents and Notes*, Vol. XVII, No. 3 (May–June 1968), 200.

vided into three parts. And this chronic splintering syndrome weakens the credibility of a potentially viable leftist alternative to the Communist party.

Both the Socialists and the Social Democrats support the Left-Center coalition formula. The Socialists are somewhat more concerned about the need for the coalition to act vigorously to carry out its prior commitments, whereas the Social Democratic leaders regard the coalition per se as so important to the survival of Italian democracy that they are willing to tolerate those interminable delays in policy output for which the Christian Democratic Party has become so notorious. At the same time, the Social Democrats have accused several of the Socialist leaders (especially Riccardo Lombardi) of making excessive and unreasonable demands on the Christian Democrats.

Some Socialist leaders, we have already noted, have suggested that it might become essential to bring the Communists into the governing coalition as the only way to put some impetus behind the push for social reform. But the Social Democrats of the PSU are adamantly opposed to any prospect of bringing the Communist party into the cabinet coalition. In fact, it was the suspicion that De Martino and other Socialist leaders might be laying the groundwork for precisely such an addition to the Left-Center formula which led to the break-up of the Unified Socialist party in 1969.

Regarding specific policy issues, both the Socialists and the Social Democrats, unlike the PSIUP, support the North Atlantic alliance. But the Socialist party insists that the North Atlantic Treaty must be interpreted in a purely defensive sense, while the leaders of the Social Democratic party have been much more unequivocal in their pro-Atlantic orientations. Both the Socialists and the Social Democrats support the entry of Great Britain into the European Economic Community (EEC). But the leaders of the Socialist party have advocated extensive reciprocal trade agreements between the EEC and various other nations of the world, especially the Third World, whereas the leaders of the Social Democratic party have shown some hostility toward the Socialist party's Third-World orientation.

While the Communists and the PSIUP express open distrust regarding the possible enactment of European economic plans by the EEC, Socialist leaders have accepted the desirability of supranational planning, but with the proviso that this must not entail interference with the formulation of *national* economic plans. The Social Democratic leaders, on the other hand, are so firmly attached to the ideal of a united Europe that they have simply failed to echo the Socialist party's expressed concern for the future of national planning.

Both the Socialists and the Social Democrats are committed to national planning, but their understanding of the concept appears to differ. The Socialist party sees national planning as a key to those "structural reforms" to which Socialist politicians are constantly, and somewhat ambiguously, referring. Apart from the possible nationalization of the cement and pharmaceutical industries, nationalization is to be employed only when essential as a means of removing structural obstacles to the economic plan.

By contrast with the Socialist approach, Social Democratic leaders have taken great pains to reassure private entrepreneurs that planning would not involve any sacrifice of freedom of choice. In fact, instead of discussing "structural reforms," Social Democratic chieftains like Giuseppe Saragat have advocated a so-called Swedish-style socialism, in which the central government would confine itself to building roads, schools, and hospitals, while keeping direct physical regulation of private enterprise to a minimum and relying primarily on fiscal tools to affect the movement of the economy.[35] There is evident here a certain reaction against nationalization as a means of attaining reformist goals. On this score, it should be remembered that the Social Democrats did not go along with the Socialist proposal that the industries in which the state owned stock should be reorganized and placed under direct government management.

On certain issues, the parties of the Left (the Communists, the PSIUP, the Socialists, and the Social Democrats) are basically in agreement. They all oppose government aid to parochial schools; they all have advocated the passage of legislation setting up the ordinary regions; and they have all supported the passage of divorce legislation, against the strenuous opposition of the Christian Democrats.

But apart from these and other limited areas of agreement, the Social Democrats are separated from the Communists by a wall of mutual distrust; and this estrangement exists, with somewhat less intensity, also in the relations between the Social Democrats and the Socialists. Almost two decades of separation and of acrimonious exchanges of recriminations have taken their toll; and the Social Democratic leaders suspect the present leadership of the Socialist party of seeking to bring the Communists into a coalition

[35] Giorgio Galli, "La polemica sulla socialdemocrazia," *Il Mulino*, Vol. XIII, No. 10 (October 1964), 1033–1035.

cabinet. When the Socialist party refuses to cut its ties with the Communists in the trade unions and in local governments, Social Democratic leaders are outraged and think they discern ulterior motives. The Socialist assertion that local alliances with a Communist municipal or provincial junta will be continued only where the sole alternative would be the appointment of a prefectoral commissioner to govern the local unit, is not accepted by the Social Democrats. And the recent Socialist decision to enter Communist-led regional juntas in Central Italy has also disturbed Italian Social Democrats. Given the lack of faith that Socialists and Social Democrats have in each other's intentions, it is hardly surprising that socialist unification lasted only three years.

From the above discussion, it would appear that the Social Democrats have been rather centrist and standpattish, while the Socialist party has taken a bold and progressive approach to Italian problems. But the Socialist party's performance in office has drawn a good deal of criticism from its more zealous friends and potential allies. It is alleged, for example, that Socialist leaders have concentrated exclusively on the economic aspects of planning, and on the problem of attaining key positions in the power structure, while failing to address themselves to the problem of local participation in the planning process.[36] Generally speaking, Christian Democratic leaders have seemed more aware than Socialist leaders of the need to democratize the planning process. Other observers accuse the Socialist party of having entered the cabinet without a broad strategy, of standing for little more than a vague humanitarian concept of the welfare state, of being preoccupied mainly with patronage considerations.[37] Actually, it appears that Nenni and Lombardi have failed to give a clear picture of the ultimate goals of Italian socialism: Nenni, in fact, has seemed to indicate that the main reason why the Socialist party should take part in the cabinet coalition is to prevent a repetition of the Fascist take-over of 1922, which a Catholic-Socialist alliance might have prevented. Instead of taking a clear stand regarding the future of Italian socialism, Socialist leaders have spoken of "structural reforms" without always clarifying their meaning.

In view of the fragmented character of the Italian Socialist movement, it is doubtful whether even massive infusions of funds and activists would suffice to restore its lagging fortunes. More likely, the answer may lie with the continuing progress of Italy

[36] Franco Rizzo, *Partiti Piano e Stato* (Roma: Edizioni Montecitorio, 1966), pp. 160–171.
[37] Sernini, pp. 137–138.

toward a mature industrial economy, the growth in the percentage of skilled workers in the industrial labor force, and the eventual development of a more autonomous and pragmatic trade-union movement. But whatever promise the future may hold, the present looks rather bleak.

The Italian Christian Democratic party (DC)

The Christian Democratic party (DC) is a relative newcomer on the Italian political scene. It was founded in September 1943, on the heels of the armistice with the Western Allies. However, the DC is not the first political party to have represented the Catholic outlook before the Italian electorate: The Popular party of Don Luigi Sturzo was founded in 1919 and dissolved under Fascist pressure in 1926. And long before the establishment of the Popular party, political Catholicism had manifested itself through the widespread activities of a multiplicity of Catholic organizations. Since the Holy See had issued its admonition (the *non expedit*) to the Catholic masses in 1874 against either running for national office or voting in national elections, Catholic activism had to seek an outlet through the formation of interest groups, such as rural savings banks, workingmen's associations, peasant leagues, and parochial and diocesan committees.

The Catholic organizations largely tended to support the Liberals at the polls in the early twentieth century as the papacy began to indicate that it no longer insisted on Catholic nonintervention. This policy represented the triumph of clerico-moderates like Filippo Meda, who believed in cooperating with the Liberal state in order to resist the advance of socialism. Instead, Christian Democratic elements, led by disciples of Romolo Murri, stressed the need for social reforms and demanded independence from church control. When the Popular party was finally founded in 1919, Don Sturzo combined Murri's sense of the need for a progressive posture on social problems with Meda's recognition of the permanence of liberal institutions. Under his leadership, the Popular party became one of the more innovative forces in the turbulent politics of the 1919–1922 period. Advocating the decentralization of government functions, the strengthening of local authorities, the popular election of the then appointive upper chamber of Parliament, the enfranchisement of women, the adoption of proportional representation in Italian elections, the strengthening of Italian voluntary associations through some form of functional representation, and the promulgation of an extensive land-reform scheme, the Popular party appealed to a broad spectrum of Italian opinion. It managed to poll slightly over 20 percent of the votes cast in the general elections of 1919 and 1921.

The Popular party, however, was soon beset by the same maladies that afflict the DC today—that is, internal factional discord and an ambiguous relationship with the Catholic church. The party contained clerico-moderate elements, who sought closer ties with the business-oriented Liberals and were skeptical about social reform; conservative Catholics, who felt an alliance with the ultranationalists, or even with the Fascists, might be in the best interests of the church; and trade unionists and progressive Catholics, who demanded a more daring program of reforms and who sought some kind of accommodation with the Socialists. Sturzo's efforts to steer a middle course among these widely divergent outlooks and aspirations were to no avail. When he and other party leaders seemed to be considering the possibility of an alliance with the Socialists in 1922, the Vatican clearly signaled its displeasure, and began to exert discreet but firm pressure on Don Sturzo to resign as party leader. Suspicion of the Socialists, fear that Fascist violence might be directed against various church-sponsored organizations, and hope that Mussolini might move toward a resolution of the church-state controversy—all these factors were present in the church's decision to encourage cooperation with the new Fascist regime.

However, the disappearance of the Popular party in 1926 did not mean the end of political Catholicism for the duration of the Fascist era. Catholic Action, a church-sponsored organization of Catholic laymen, was permitted to survive under the terms of the Concordat of 1929, and served as an excellent recruiting ground for a whole new generation of Catholic leaders—men like Fanfani and Moro, who would eventually replace the old guard of ex-Popular party veterans a decade after the Liberation. When the Fascist government finally collapsed in 1943, Italian Catholics were ready to take part in a democratic struggle for power.

The Christian Democratic party was formed in 1943 at a time when the Italian Liberals, and the business community as well, were under suspicion because of their earlier collaboration with Fascism. With the Liberal party largely discredited, with business and landed interests very much on the defensive, and with the forces of the Left seemingly on the verge of seizing power, the Christian Democrats seemed to be the last hope for Italian conservatives. Given this situation, and given the inspiring leadership of De Gasperi, the DC was able to attain unprecedented electoral strength: 35.2 percent of the votes in 1946, 48.5 percent in 1948, 40 percent in 1953, 42.4 percent in 1958, 38.3 percent in 1963, and 39.1 percent in 1968. In no election since World War II did the Christian Democrats fail to receive a plurality of the votes. And in no postwar election did the DC totals dip below 35 percent. This performance, spectacular by Italian standards, was based partly on the traditional Catholic strongholds of Northern and Northeastern Italy. But it was also based, in large measure, on the penetration of virgin territory where the Popular party had been weak. Southern Italy, for example, became a DC stronghold as its vaguely Liberal clienteles drifted toward the party with the bigger battalions.

In the twenty-five years since the Liberation, the DC has played a leading role in every Italian cabinet. In fact, ever since the resignation of the Parri cabinet late in 1945, every Italian prime minister has been a Christian Democrat. But the dominant party has never, except in 1948–1953, had an absolute majority in either house of the Italian Parliament. Allies have proved indispensable, then, either within or outside the cabinet. This has raised the obvious questions, the sources of the endless factionalism troubling the affairs of Italian Christian Democracy: which allies? what cabinet formula?

Under De Gasperi's leadership, the DC at first pursued—from 1947 to 1953—a centrist coalition policy, based on an alliance with the three minor Center parties: the Social Democrats, the Republicans, and the Liberals. From 1954 to 1962, this formula was rendered impracticable by the growing antagonism between the Social Democrats and Republicans on the one hand, and the business-oriented Liberals on the other. During this period, then, the DC oscillated between Left-Center and Right-Center coalitions, with the occasional use of an all-DC "monocolor" minority cabinet as a device to gain time. The Right-Center solution—a DC-Liberal coalition with Monarchist and Neo-Fascist support—was unacceptable, not only to the Social Democrats and Republicans, but also to many members of Left-wing factions in the DC itself. A limited Left-Center solution—a DC-Social Democratic-Republican coalition, excluding the Socialists—was opposed, not only by the Communists and Socialists, but also by the moderate and extreme Right, and simply lacked enough parliamentary support to insure a stable cabinet. Over the long run, democratic stability could only be safeguarded by bringing the Socialist party into the democratic coalition; and in 1962, this giant step forward (the opening to the Left) was finally completed. Since 1962, a new and expanded Left-Center solution, with the Socialists taking part in DC-dominated coalition cabinets, has come to be the standard norm in the Italian political system. Occasional breakdowns in the Left-Center alliance between the DC, the Socialists, the Social Democrats, and the Republicans, are patched over during prolonged cooling-off periods, characterized by noncontroversial all-DC minority cabinets that are confined to routine administrative tasks.

During these years of chronic uncertainty, the DC's main problems have been internal. For within the ranks of Christian Democracy are to be found proponents of virtually every conceivable type of cabinet solution and descendants of each and every traditional variety of political Catholicism. Murri's integralism, his desire to erect a state based on Catholic concepts of social justice, has had its disciples in the present-day DC—certainly Dossetti, possibly Fanfani. Meda's clerico-moderates, with their drive for an entente with the bourgeoisie, are with us today in the form of Scelba's Popular Centrism faction. And just as Miglioli and other Popular party leaders of the Left supported the idea of an alliance with the Socialists, there are Left-wing Christian Democrats today who at least hint at the possibility of an eventual working relationship with the Communist party. Whoever is secretary of the DC must emulate Don Sturzo and maintain a balance among the contending factions.

The factional picture is further complicated by the fluidity of factional alignments, by the tendency of factions to be based largely on conflicts between leading personalities, many of whom show a disconcerting ideological flexibility. In 1962, for instance, Moro was secretary of the DC, had the support of the more moderate centrist elements, and was regarded as well to the Right of Fanfani, who was then the main spokesman for the Left opposition. Today, Fanfani is allied with Party Secretary Forlani, and the standard-bearer of the leftist opposition factions is none other than Moro himself.[38] Small wonder that Moro could give vent to his notorious Freudian slip during a television interview. When asked by a reporter whether the DC placed too much emphasis on the need for prudence, Moro replied, "The DC emphasizes everything."[39] No other Italian party has succeeded so well in being all things to all men. But the mercurial ambiguity of a catch-all party carries an exorbitant price tag: It tends to foment a widespread

[38] *La Stampa* (Turin), July 26, 1970.
[39] "Centro sinistra e politica locale," *Il Mulino*, Vol. XII, No. 3 (March 1963), 240.

feeling of alienation from the political process, a low sense of political efficacy, a superficial and perfunctory style of participation on the part of the citizenry.

Our investigation of factionalism in the DC would appear to go a long way toward justifying Sernini's rather harsh interpretation of the DC's programmatic goals: The DC, he claims, is interested only in retaining power at all costs.[40] Actually, however, to make such a statement is to attribute a uniformly pragmatic political style to a party that contains an assorted mix of individuals and factions, many of whom have very strong ideological commitments. It is precisely because of the difficulty involved in molding together so many different aspirations into a single party that the DC has been compelled to avoid the adoption of excessively concrete policy stands.

In the area of domestic affairs, the more welfare-oriented elements in the DC have gradually gained the upper hand. Thus, the DC has been able to enact programs for land reform and low-cost housing, adopt tax-reform measures, nationalize the electric-power industry (after yielding to pressure from the Socialists), strengthen the public sector of the economy, and establish a system of national economic planning similar in some respects to the French model. But somehow, these programs have been ambiguous victories. For the Christian Democrats have not really been able to achieve effective regulation of Italian economic life in such sensitive areas as urban real-estate development, industrial monopoly, and the taxation of corporate securities. One reason for this failure has been the great economic power of the Italian business community: Without its confidence and support, recession can wreck the future of the Italian economy. Another cause of the DC's lack of drive in certain areas of public policy has been the existence of powerful conservative factions within the DC itself. And finally, as Galli suggests, the DC may have failed to take the measures necessary for the construction of a truly modern capitalist system simply by virtue of the fact that its leaders—progressive and conservative alike—basically distrust both capitalism and the business community. According to Galli, the DC Left's approach to economic policy and social welfare is essentially charitable and distributive—for example, divide the estates among the peasantry, even if productivity should suffer in the process—and often seems oblivious to the realities and needs of a modern industrial system.[41]

[40] Sernini, p. 141.
[41] Galli, *Il bipartitismo imperfetto*, pp. 75–79.

Whatever one may think of the plausibility of Galli's thesis, the impact of factionalism on the decision-making process in the DC can hardly be questioned. As a result of this factionalism, the DC platforms have tended to list a long series of Italian economic and social problems and to indicate rather cryptically that the DC would somehow resolve those problems. The dominant element in the DC has had concrete solutions to propose but has often had to water them down or abandon them in order to ward off internal party disunity. Thus, for example, the DC's approach to planning is designed to avoid any major restraints on the power of organized business. Or, to cite another case in point, the DC has never openly opposed the creation of the regions, but has spoken of establishing them "at the right time" and has supported restrictions on the powers of the regional organs. And finally, when real-estate interests agitated against an urban planning bill introduced by Minister of Public Works Fiorentino Sullo, the DC leadership deserted and disavowed their own minister and declared that the DC was *not* committed to the Sullo bill.[42] Thus, in its ambivalence and indecisiveness, the DC reflects contradictory tendencies of Italian society, influenced both by demands for social reform and by the standpat predilections of large segments of the Italian business community. It is not surprising, under the circumstances, that when concrete reform measures *have* been adopted (for example, land reform, the nationalization of electric power), this has usually been made possible only by unrelenting pressure from the DC's actual or prospective allies.

There is one area of domestic policy on which the DC speaks with a decisive voice. Whenever the interests of the church are involved, Christian Democracy takes a clear and unequivocal stand. Thus, for instance, Christian Democratic spokesmen are always ready to defend government aid to parochial schools, the holding of religious classes in the public schools, the maintenance of the ban on divorce, and other privileges that the church enjoys. After more than twenty-five years of showing virtually no interest in enacting legislation to enforce the constitutional provision providing for referenda, the DC in 1970 sought to get such legislation adopted, as a means of having an impending divorce law submitted to the court of public opinion. When religious considerations are at stake, the DC ceases to be a catch-all party and becomes a party of principle.

In the field of foreign affairs, the DC has generally taken a

---

[42] On these DC policies, see Petracca, pp. 79–80, 86–88, 103–104, 110–111.

"European" position, favoring Italy's cooperation in NATO and in the Common Market, advocating British entry into the EEC, and supporting a close Italian alignment with United States foreign policy leadership. There is also here, however, some element of discord. Some DC leaders, like Fanfani and Gronchi, have advocated a more independent Italian foreign policy, have attempted to assert an Italian presence in the Eastern Mediterranean as a bridge between the West and the Arab world, and have taken a more neutral attitude toward world problems. Since Gronchi has served seven years as President of Italy, and Fanfani has been both prime minister and minister of foreign affairs, these minority elements within the DC have not been without their influence on Italian foreign policy.

The Italian Republican party (PRI)

The Italian Republican party (PRI) is heir to a glorious tradition —the tradition of Mazzini and Garibaldi—but has never commanded the kind of mass support enjoyed by the Socialists, the Communists, and the Christian Democrats. Even in the late nineteenth century, the PRI lagged well behind the major parties in electoral strength. Too progressive and reformist for the Italian bourgeoisie, too anticlerical and iconoclastic for the peasantry, insufficiently committed to the class struggle in the eyes of the proletariat, the PRI has tended to be a chronic loser. Apart from its traditional strongholds in a few Central provinces, the PRI has tended to be a party of elites, of forward-looking intellectuals, rather than a mass party.

Since World War II, the Republican party has continued to be a virtual splinter party, despite its illustrious anti-Fascist record. In 1946, it polled 4.4 percent of the votes cast—its best performance in the entire quarter-century since the Liberation. But this rather modest success was followed by a steady decline that reached its nadir in 1958 and 1963, when the PRI only received 1.4 percent of the votes. A slight recovery in 1968 brought the PRI to the 2 percent mark, which was hardly grounds for much optimism regarding the future. Only in the delicately balanced Italian multiparty system could an extremely small party like the PRI carry much weight.

As a matter of fact, the PRI's handful of votes in Parliament have frequently been crucial to the survival of a cabinet. Since 1945, the PRI has been in the cabinet more often than not. It participated in the centrist coalition cabinets presided over by De

Gasperi between 1947 and 1953. After the electoral debacle of 1953, the PRI became increasingly critical of the centrist formula; and from 1956 on, the leaders of the Republican party openly affirmed the necessity of enlisting Socialist support for a democratic coalition. So the Italian Republican party was campaigning for the opening to the Left long before either the Christian Democrats or the Socialists were ready to commit themselves. Under the leadership of Oronzo Reale and Ugo La Malfa, the PRI has done more than its share to achieve this major breakthrough in Italian politics.

The Republican program is leftist but non-Marxist. First of all, it involves a rather anticlerical posture, including a concern for the rights of religious minorities and an attitude of hostility toward the privileged position enjoyed by the church under the terms of the Concordat. Secondly, the PRI is firmly attached to democratic institutions and has tended to oppose any collaboration with the Communist party. In the realm of socioeconomic policy, the PRI has strongly favored land reform, the strengthening of the cooperative movement, greater state intervention in the regulation of economic life, and instituting a system of national economic planning. An apostle of autonomy and decentralization, the PRI has pushed for the creation of the regions. Finally, in the field of foreign affairs, the PRI has staunchly supported NATO and the cause of European integration. In short, Italian Republicanism bears considerable resemblance to the American New Deal, but lacks the mass appeal—and utter pragmatism—of the latter movement.

The Italian Liberal Party (PLI)

In approaching Italian Liberalism, it is well to keep a number of historical facts firmly in mind. First, before the achievement of virtually universal manhood suffrage in Italy in 1919, Liberalism played a dominant role in Italian politics. Even in the elections of 1919 and 1921, the Liberals were well ahead of the Popular party and the Socialists: the so-called constitutional lists polled 46.3 percent of the votes in 1919 and 47.1 percent in 1921. The great bulk of this massive Liberal electorate flowed into the ranks of Christian Democracy after 1945.[43]

There was, properly speaking, no Italian Liberal party (PLI) before 1922. Rather, there was a bewildering assortment of fac-

---

[43] Galli, *Il bipartitismo imperfetto*, pp. 108–112.

tions, tendencies, and cliques revolving around a number of leading personalities. The very limited suffrage of the late nineteenth and early twentieth centuries, and the single-member district system that prevailed before 1919, encouraged the survival of the kind of politics of personality to which Duverger refers in discussing caucus-type parties.[44] There *were* some broad distinctions between various Liberal groupings, such as the contrast between the neutralist, Left-oriented Giolitti, who sought to bring the Socialists into the system, and the interventionist, Right-oriented Salandra, who pushed for an alliance with the Fascists. But a nationwide party organization outside of Parliament, party cohesion, party discipline—these hallmarks of a modern party in a parliamentary system—were totally lacking.

And finally, it is well to understand that the Fascist experience did much to discredit Italian Liberals. Liberals had dominated the power structure in the years before 1922 and they had utterly failed to check the onslaught of Fascism. Their close alignment with property-owning interests was regarded with much suspicion, in view of the invaluable support Italian Fascism had received in 1920–1922 from the Italian industrial and agricultural bourgeoisie. Their relatively modest role in the Resistance made it difficult for them to appeal to the imagination of the younger generation. It is not hard to understand, then, why after World War II the Christian Democrats were able to mobilize most of those middle-class voters who had backed Liberal groupings in pre-Fascist days. For the DC was a party of order, which appealed to all social classes and had a much more honorable and defensible record vis-à-vis the Fascist experience.

In the years since World War II, the electoral fortunes of the Liberal party have been rather scanty. In 1946, the National Democratic Union (a Liberal list) obtained 6.8 percent of the votes. Only two years later, the Italian Liberal party polled a mere 3.8 percent; and further declines were registered in subsequent years. Only in 1963 did there appear to be a sharp upswing in Liberal popularity among the middle classes, a result of resentment against the opening to the Left; even then the Liberal vote only rose to 7 percent. More recent general elections represent a significant retreat from 1963: In 1968, the PLI received only 5.8 percent of the votes.

The weakness of the Liberals may be attributed in part to the success of the Christian Democrats—with the backing of the

---

[44] Duverger, pp. 17–23, 46–47.

church and of an imposing array of church-sponsored organizations, and with the masterful postwar leadership of De Gasperi—in winning the support of Italy's middle-class electorate. But the Liberals also suffer from a chronic weakness which the Christian Democrats have been able to avoid: They are an excessively class-oriented party, with an electoral base limited almost exclusively to the urban and rural upper-middle classes. This rightist bias became especially pronounced after Giovanni Malagodi was elected party secretary in 1954—an event soon followed by the secession of the Left-wing factions of the PLI.[45]

The PLI collaborated with De Gasperi's centrist coalitions from 1946-1953, and also participated in several centrist cabinets in subsequent years. But by 1957, it had become impossible for the Liberals to serve in the same cabinet with the Republicans and Social Democrats. From that time on, the Liberals have pressed for a centrist or Right-Center coalition (the latter possibly including the Monarchists). Yet their conservative economic policies have so repelled the Republicans and Social Democrats as to render both a centrist alliance and a Right-Center coalition intolerable in the eyes of these parties. For that matter, the Left-wing factions of the Christian Democratic party would also reject such a solution. On the other hand, the Liberal party's attachment to democratic institutions renders an alliance with the Monarchists and Neo-Fascists unpalatable for most of the party's leaders. With so many alternative possibilities foreclosed, the Liberal party has become increasingly isolated.

In the field of domestic affairs, the Liberal program is almost diametrically opposed to that of the Republicans, with one or two notable exceptions. The opening to the Left is regarded with skepticism and hostility. The land-reform programs of the 1950s were opposed; extensions of the public sector of the economy and further government regulation of the private sector have been strongly resisted; and national economic planning is accepted only to the extent that business is allowed to remain master in its own house and play a decisive role in the formulation of the plan. As a matter of fact, the Liberals seem to use the term "planning" to denote a policy of retrenchment and consolidation of the state's holdings in the economic sphere, and also a general overhaul of the swollen bureaucracy. The commitment to a free market economy is very intensive indeed: It is felt that the government would do well to confine its domestic expenditures to necessary public

[45] Arnaldo Ciani, *Il Partito Liberale Italiano da Croce a Malagodi* (Napoli: Edizioni Scientifiche Italiane, 1968), pp. 104–118.

works (schools, hospitals, roads, and so forth) and to improving the social security system. Finally, the Liberal party is strongly opposed to the creation of the ordinary regions and would prefer to achieve a limited degree of decentralization by strengthening the existing provincial governments.

Where the Liberals and Republicans tend to agree is in the spheres of church-state relations and foreign policy. Like the Republicans, the Liberals favor a secular state, the elimination of special privileges for the Catholic church, and a ban on discrimination against religious minorities. They have also aligned themselves with the Republicans (as well as with the Socialists and Communists, in this instance) behind the passage of the divorce bill of 1970. And in foreign affairs, they have shared the Republicans' views in backing European integration and Italian cooperation with the United States line in NATO. If anything, their uncritical willingness to take part in Western defense arrangements has marked them as more "Atlantic" than other democratic parties. One unsympathetic view depicts the PLI as "more American than the Americans."[46] Thus, in foreign affairs as in domestic socioeconomic affairs, the Liberals are a party of the moderate Right. But unlike the French Independents, they tend to be leftist on church-state issues, albeit less ardently so than the Republicans.

The Monarchists (PDIUM)

The present title of the Italian Monarchist party is the Italian Democratic Party of Monarchical Unity (PDIUM). Unlike the other parties discussed thus far, the PDIUM has a very brief historical background. Before World War II, the monarchy seemed relatively secure, hence there was no felt need for a Monarchist party. After 1945, however, promonarchist forces had to organize in a vain effort to resist the threat to the crown, and a Monarchist party was eventually formed. This party was especially successful in capitalizing on Southern resentment of what had been an essentially Northern drive to establish a republic. The Monarchists reached their peak of strength in 1953, when they polled 6.8 percent of the votes, with a particularly good showing in the South. Since that time, there has been an increasingly rapid decline, accompanied by a series of scissions and reunifications resulting from factional squabbles between Lauro and Covelli, the two most prominent Monarchist leaders. By 1963, the reunified Monarchist party was little more than a splinter movement, receiv-

[46] Ciani, p. 254.

ing only 1.7 percent of the votes cast. By 1968, the figures were even lower: Only 1.3 percent of all Italian voters expressed a preference for the PDIUM. It seems safe to say, under the circumstances, that an early restoration of the monarchy does not appear to be likely.

Apart from their increasingly muted pleas for the return of the House of Savoy, the Monarchists have generally taken a stance on behalf of the status quo and could today almost be regarded as a party of the moderate Right. The PDIUM favors a Right-Center coalition cabinet, based primarily on Christian Democratic support, but relying also on the help of the Liberals and Neo-Fascists. On other aspects of policy, they agree, more often than not, with the Liberals. Like the Liberals, they oppose the opening to the Left, oppose further expansion of the publicly owned sector of the economy, oppose the establishment of the ordinary regions, oppose government regulation of business and agriculture, and defend propertied interests. Also they echo the Liberals' advocacy of an active and loyal Italian role in NATO, though they tend to be rather noncommittal on the subjects of European integration and the EEC. On the church-state issue, however, the Monarchists part company with the Liberals, and support a proclerical line.

The Neo-Fascists (MSI)

The Neo-Fascists of the Italian Social Movement (MSI) are, like the Monarchists, a postwar party of nostalgia. Just as the Monarchists long for the traditions of the House of Savoy, the Neo-Fascists mourn the vanished glories of Mussolini's Fascist empire, with a special sigh of regret for the notorious Italian Social Republic of 1943–1945, a puppet regime propped up by German bayonets in Northern and Central Italy. Like the Monarchist party, the MSI reached its zenith in 1953, when it polled 5.9 percent of the total vote. And, like the Monarchists, it has declined in strength since 1953. This decline, however, has been neither sharp nor continuous: The lowest point was reached in 1968, after many ups and downs, with 4.5 percent of the total votes cast. While the MSI has not known the scissions and reconciliations that have agitated the ranks of Italian Monarchism, it has nevertheless not been immune to the virus of factionalism. There has, in fact, been a fairly clear division between the "liberal," parliamentary pro-business fascism of men like Michelini and the antidemocratic corporative fascism of men like Almirante.

It is interesting to note that the Neo-Fascists, like the Communists, deny any intention of setting up a totalitarian state and piously proclaim their allegiance to democratic methods. But they *do* favor a national and corporate state based on functional representation, and these goals—along with their symbolism and political style—conjure up disturbing memories of the pre-1945 past. On most policy issues, the MSI line does not seem to differ significantly from that of the Monarchists. They, too, tend to favor a Right-Center coalition, seek to prevent the establishment of the ordinary regions, and want planning to be confined to a purely "indicative" function. In foreign affairs, they go a step beyond the Monarchists in the enthusiasm of their Atlantic commitment. After all, a Western anti-Bolshevik crusade would be much to their liking. Also, they want to expand NATO to include Spain and Portugal. Although it supported British entry into the Common Market, the MSI has stood virtually alone among Italian parties in showing some sympathy for the Gaullist obsession with national interests. Yet, after reviewing the conventional rightist program advocated by the MSI, we must realize that this party is more than just another party of the Right. For many of its younger members have revealed a distressingly familiar tendency to rely on direct and violent physical action against their political opponents.

MEMBERSHIP COMPOSITION OF THE ITALIAN PARTIES

We know that a remarkably high number of Italians join political parties, either on their own initiative or through the purchase of a party card on their behalf by some party official (see Chapter Two). About 4 million Italians are party members, with about 90 percent belonging to the Communist (1.7 million), Christian Democratic (1.6 million), and socialist parties (about 750,000 in the three socialist parties: the PSI, the PSU, and the PSIUP).[47] In view of the relatively skeletal nature of the smaller parties—the pygmies of Italian politics—most attention has focused on the membership composition of the giants, particularly the Communists and the Christian Democrats.

In its membership composition, the Communist party is more of a working-class party than either the Socialist or the Christian Democratic parties. Over 40 percent of its members were indus-

[47] Sernini, p. 59; and Jean Meynaud, *Les partis politiques en Italie* (Paris: Presses Universitaires de France, 1965), pp. 55–60.

trial workers in the early 1960s, as compared to about 30 percent of the Socialist party membership and around 21 percent of the Christian Democrats.[48] In the South, where industrialization is relatively laggard, the working-class component of the Communist party's membership drops to around 30 percent. Here, the agricultural share of its membership rises to about 40 percent, as compared to approximately 27 percent for Italy as a whole. As Tarrow rather ruefully puts it, "the Communist Party [in the South] has as its largest membership bloc the group with the very poorest organizational potential—the poor peasants and agricultural semiproletariat."[49] Since the farm laborer (*bracciante*) in the South is only semiemployed and rarely works on large commercial farms (unlike his counterpart in the Po Valley), he is very hard to organize and poorly disciplined. The rural makeup of the Communist party in the South seems to have a self-perpetuating effect; it leads the party to place particular stress on the land issue, and this emphasis in turn tends to repel the working-class cadres the Communist party so sorely needs.

Taking Italy as a whole, the Communists seem to have a larger proportion of peasants among their members (about 27 percent) than do the Christian Democrats (about 20 percent). But most of the peasant Communists are sharecroppers and farm laborers, whereas most of the Christian Democratic peasant members are small landowning farmers. As might be expected in view of the exodus from the countryside, the proportion of peasant members is declining in both parties.

Population groups that are more heavily represented in the Christian Democratic party than in the Communist party—in addition to small farmers—are housewives, artisans or shopkeepers, and white-collar workers. Housewives (25.5 percent of DC membership in the early 1960s as compared to 13.4 percent of PCI membership) are the largest single occupational group in the ranks of Christian Democracy. Two social groups showing the largest percentage increases in their proportion of Christian Democratic membership are the civil servants (13.5 percent of the total) and the pensioners (7.8 percent of the total).[50] The expan-

[48] Except where otherwise indicated, Communist and Christian Democratic membership figures are drawn from Giorgio Galli and Alfonso Prandi, *Patterns of Political Participation in Italy* (New Haven, Conn.: Yale University Press, 1970), p. 123. For figures on the Socialists, see Meynaud, p. 59.
[49] Tarrow, *Peasant Communism* . . . , p. 207.
[50] Ada Sivini Cavazzani, "Partito, iscritti, elettori," in Fabrizio Cicchitto, Gino Rocchi, Bruno Manghi, Luigi Ruggiu, Ada Sivini Cavazzani, *La DC dopo il primo ventennio* (Padova: Marsilio Editori, 1968), pp. 174–177.

sion of these two categories would appear to reflect the Christian Democratic party's increasingly weighty role as a dispenser of patronage.

About half the membership of the Communist party is concentrated in the area of greatest Communist voting strength, North Central Italy, including Emilia, Tuscany, Umbria and the Marches.[51] In this area, the Communist party has many public jobs and perquisites to distribute, as well as nonmaterial rewards. The Christian Democrats, on the other hand, have relatively weak membership totals in the Veneto, the traditional Northeastern electoral bulwark of political Catholicism. This is so despite, or perhaps because of, the fact that Catholic laymen's organizations are particularly strong in the "white" Northeast. But the Christian Democrats are remarkably successful in recruiting new members in the underdeveloped South, where a DC party card is believed to be a passport to priority consideration in the allocation of government jobs and favors from government agencies.[52]

In addition to relying on the attractions of patronage and perquisites in underdeveloped areas like the South, the Christian Democrats also appeal to conservatively oriented middle-class people in highly industrialized regions. Galli can thus aptly describe the DC as a kind of hybrid: a Catholic party, an urban middle-class party, and a peasant party, all in one.[53] In short, while the Communist party is mainly a working-class party in its membership composition, its Christian Democratic rival is an interclass party.

PARTY LEADERSHIP:
A MIDDLE-CLASS PRESERVE

The leadership strata of the various Italian parties have a middle-class character. Moving from the level of executive committees of the local party sections, to the provincial executive committees, to the national central committees, middle-class leadership predominates, even at the lowest levels, and tends to increase in magnitude in the higher echelons of the party hierarchy.[54] Only in the Communist party are a sizable proportion (40 percent) of the members of sectional executive committees composed of men and

[51] Galli, *Il bipartitismo imperfetto*, pp. 153–154.
[52] Galli, *Il bipartitismo imperfetto*, pp. 154–157.
[53] Galli, *Il bipartitismo imperfetto*, pp. 157–162.
[54] Unless otherwise indicated, data on party leadership are drawn from Galli, *Il bipartitismo imperfetto*, pp. 166–169, 174–181.

women of proletarian origin. This proportion diminishes steadily in the provincial and national headquarters. Moreover, even within a self-styled ultraprogressive party like the Communist party, the percentage of leaders who are of working-class origin dips sharply South of Rome. For the traditional, rigidly stratified character of Southern society, and its deferential mores, make it more difficult for workers and/or peasants to rise to positions of power and status. Apart from its Southern wing, however, we may indeed describe the Communist party as an avenue of upward mobility for certain selected elements of the lower social strata. The Christian Democrats, by contrast, tend to recruit leaders who are overwhelmingly bourgeois or petty bourgeois in origin. The lower middle class, then,—schoolteachers, white-collar workers, and the like—uses the Christian Democratic apparatus as a means of self-advancement.

Supposedly, leaders are chosen according to the party statutes. The local executive committee of an Italian party is elected at the local section meeting open to all party members in the commune or in the subdivision of a large commune, as the case may be. By the same token, the provincial congress is supposed to elect the members of the provincial executive organs, and the same process is specified for the national level. But the reality is, of course, different from the model of intraparty democracy constructed by the party statutes. Local section meetings are normally dominated by the local executive committee, and the executive committee is in turn controlled by a small group of activists who handle the affairs of the local section year after year. Thus, elections to local party posts normally involve a process of co-optation: The local leadership group handpicks its nominees, who are more or less automatically approved by the rather passive rank and file.[55] At the provincial and national levels, the politicians already serving in executive organs at those levels are primarily instrumental in nominating new members from the levels below.

To the extent that contests *do* take place, they are channeled and managed from above by highly organized factions. And once leaders are entrenched in power, especially at the national level, they are singularly hard to displace. Such names as Togliatti (the late Communist leader), Nenni (former leader of the Socialist party), Saragat (Social Democratic leader, then President of

[55] Antonio Landolfi, *Il Partito Socialista: oggi e domani* (Milano: Edizioni Azione Comune, 1963), pp. 49–50. Landolfi was speaking of the relatively democratic Italian Socialist party, but his analysis is applicable to other mass parties as well.

Italy), Fanfani (a leading Christian Democrat), and Malagodi (Liberal leader since 1955) have dominated Italian politics for decades. Usually, only death or senility removes Italian political leaders from their offices.

Recent studies have provided some valuable insights into the attitudes of party leaders and into ongoing changes in the composition of party leadership strata. For instance, the local and provincial leaders of the Italian Socialist party (PSI) are more strongly committed to internal democracy within the party than are the rank-and-file members. This leadership support for democratic norms—an attitude that is pretty much in line with what we know about elite attitudes in the United States and elsewhere—combines with a state of lively and continuous factional competition to produce a large proportion of broker-type leaders in the PSI.[56]

As for changes in the composition of party leadership strata, one major trend is becoming increasingly evident. The top echelons of the party leadership, especially in the mass parties like the Communists and Christian Democrats, are being colonized increasingly by men who have risen through the ranks of the party bureaucracy. The "great notables" of the immediate postwar years —the illustrious lawyers and other professional men who had acquired a strong personal following—are vanishing, as more and more political professionals come to the fore. This trend is nothing new for the Communist party, which has always encouraged the development of career politicians. But it does represent something of a fresh departure for the Christian Democrats, a party that lacked an adequate bureaucracy before 1954.[57] The rise of the party bureaucrat has been particularly accentuated in the South, where the Christian Democratic party bureaucracy became the focus of a new clientele system, centering around an organization rather than around "great notables." This clientele system makes use of the vast patronage possibilities opened up by Christian Democratic control over the various government and semipublic agencies with field offices operating in the South. With jobs and favors to dispense, Christian Democracy has entrenched itself very firmly in its new Southern bastion.

While not necessarily part of the *official* leadership stratum at the local and provincial levels, party activists *do* play an unofficial

---

[56] Barnes, pp. 215–230.
[57] Tarrow, *Peasant Communism* . . . , pp. 322–332; and J. P. Chasseriaud, *Le parti démocrate chrétien en Italie* (Paris: Armand Colin, 1965), pp. 325–326 and 340–343.

subaltern leadership role; and, of course, many activists *are* members of local or provincial executive committees. It is estimated that there are only about 10,000 Socialist activists as against 90,000 Communists and 70,000 Christian Democrats. The number of activists in other Italian parties is rather negligible. Also, there is a similar imbalance in the number of full-time salaried officials employed by the various parties: a decade ago, the Communists employed about 10,000, the Socialists about 500, the Christian Democrats between 6000 and 7000, and the Social Democrats around 200.[58] These figures may have changed somewhat in the past ten years but there is little reason to believe that the relative proportions employed by the various parties have undergone significant alterations. One useful function served by these statistics is to show the inferior status of the Italian Socialist party, which lacks the resources to hire large numbers of professional political careerists.

PARTY VOTING STRENGTH: BASES OF CLEAVAGE AND OTHER VARIABLES

To what degree are social, economic, and regional cleavages in Italian society reflected in election returns? One politically relevant cleavage divides devout Catholics from anticlericals. In regions such as the Veneto, where the church is strong and popular, traditional attachment to the Catholic church has been translated into a steadfast allegiance to the Christian Democratic party. This deep-rooted Catholic tradition may itself be the product of historical experiences during the nineteenth century. When Lombardy and the Veneto were under direct Austrian rule (until 1859–1860 in the case of Lombardy, until 1866 in the case of the Veneto), the Catholic church was the principal Italian center of authority. Loyalty to the church became intertwined with loyalty to the Italian language and culture, and there developed that same strong attachment to the church and its interests that we find (in a much more accentuated form) among Irish and Polish Catholics. Also the church had very extensive landholdings in the Veneto.[59]

In other areas, especially in North-Central Italy, anticlericalism may help to produce large voting percentages for the Commu-

[58] Marco Cesarini Sforza, *L'uomo politico* (Firenze: Vallecchi, 1963), pp. 29–30.
[59] Chasseriaud, p. 128.

nists, the Socialists, and even the Republicans. Here again, tradition may be partly involved. Umbria, the Marches, and part of Emilia were, until 1861, under the sovereignty of the Papal States, and frequently rebelled against papal rule. Tuscany has an antipapacy tradition dating back to the Renaissance, except for the now-Christian Democratic province of Lucca, which used to be a separate independent duchy on friendly terms with the Papal States. As a result, there is a heritage of anticlericalism in these areas. Anticlericalism helped to lead to the questioning of other forms of traditional authority; and both Emilia and Tuscany were hotbeds of political unrest in the late nineteenth and early twentieth centuries. Both were Socialist and—to a much lesser degree—Republican strongholds, and later drifted to the extreme Left.[60]

But certain social cleavages should also be emphasized in accounting for the strength of the various parties. For example, Communist and Socialist successes in North-Central Italy may also be related to the fact that this is the principal sharecropping zone of Italy—and the frustrated status aspirations of the Central Italian sharecroppers render them very vulnerable to extremist appeals.[61] Also, there are large masses of farm laborers in parts of Emilia, as well as elsewhere in the Po Valley. And the grievances of these two social groups (sharecroppers and farm laborers) have been nourished and reinforced by historical events. For when Fascist reaction came to the fore in 1919–1922, it took on its most virulent, vindictive form in North Central Italy. It was in Tuscany and Emilia that the most brutal "punitive expeditions" were launched by the Fascist combat squads against the trade unions and the Socialist local administrations. For in these areas, Fascism assumed the guise of a veritable class war, designed to put the sharecroppers, farm laborers, and industrial workers in their place once and for all.

Here, incidentally, the contrast with France is intriguing. French tenant farmers, located largely in traditionalist Brittany, tend to vote for conservative parties; and French farm laborers, employed mostly on medium-sized farms (a far cry from the large commercial farms of the Po Valley), are thus socially integrated into the families of their employers and shielded from Communist

---

[60] Mattei Dogan, "Political Cleavage and Social Stratification in France and Italy," in Seymour M. Lipset and Stein Rokkan, eds., *Party Systems and Voter Alignments* (New York: Free Press, 1967), p. 184.

[61] Dogan, pp. 146–148. See also Giorgio Braga, *Sociologia elettorale della Toscana* (Roma: Edizioni Cinque Lune, 1963), pp. 12, 110.

party influence. It would appear, then, that the leftist or traditionalist character of the agricultural milieu, the historical background of the region in question, and the nature of the social relationship between the landless peasant and his employer or landlord (impersonal or paternalistic, as the case may be) will have a great deal to do with the way sharecroppers and farm laborers vote.[62]

As for other agricultural voters, the large landowners tend to support the parties of the Right (the Liberals, the Monarchists, and the Neo-Fascists). The medium and small landowners, on the other hand, are overwhelmingly Christian Democratic, in contrast to the French small farmers of the Massif Central, who frequently vote Communist, especially in the departments with an anticlerical tradition. The allegiance of even marginal small farmers to Italian Christian Democracy is in all likelihood related to the small farmers' dependence on the semipublic Federation of Agricultural Consortiums (*Federconsorzi*) for credit, low-cost seed, and other assistance. The *Federconsorzi* is, in turn, thoroughly controlled by the Christian Democratic-dominated small farmers' organization, the National Confederation of Direct Cultivators.[63]

Among industrial workers, the Communists are estimated to receive about 40 percent of the working-class vote, with almost 30 percent going to the Socialists and Social Democrats, and about 25 percent to the Christian Democrats. There seems to be some evidence that the Communists are more successful among unskilled and/or illiterate workers, while the Socialists and Social Democrats are strongest among skilled workers in the large industrial communes, and in zones where illiteracy rates are particularly low.[64] Some Italian scholars have therefore concluded that the electorate of the non-Communist Left "better reflects industrial society in the course of development"[65]—more so than the Communist electorate, in fact.

The urban middle class constitutes about one-third of the electorate. And here it would appear that the parties of the Left are most successful in seeking the votes of white-collar workers and lower-level civil servants, about 40 percent of whom vote for

---

[62] For an assessment of these and other social cleavages affecting voting behavior, see Dogan, pp. 129–195.

[63] Joseph La Palombara, *Interest Groups in Italian Politics* (Princeton, N.J.: Princeton University Press, 1964), pp. 235–246.

[64] Giorgio Galli, ed., *Il comportamento elettorale in Italia* (Bologna: Il Mulino, 1968), pp. 205–211, 242–245, 274, 304–306. Coauthors include V. Capecchi, V. Cioni Polacchini, and G. Sivini.

[65] Galli, ed., *Il comportamento elettorale* . . . , p. 243.

the Communists, Socialists, or Social Democrats. On the other hand, shopkeepers and artisans—the *self-employed* lower middle class—give about half their votes to the Christian Democrats and 25 percent to the Monarchists and Neo-Fascists. Between these two extremes, the so-called middle bourgeoisie (army officers, high-school teachers, engineers, medium-sized shopkeepers, priests) and the upper bourgeoisie (bankers, industrialists, and so on) tend to support the Liberals and the Christian Democrats (the moderate Right and Right-Center), rather than the extreme Right-wing movements that are so much more militant in their defense of entrenched privileges. There are, of course, some local situations that complicate the picture—the strength of the Monarchists in Naples and of the Neo-Fascists in Rome, for instance. Within the ranks of the Left, the Socialists and especially the Social Democrats are far more successful than the Communists in obtaining white-collar votes.

There is, then, a certain rightist leaning in the voting behavior of the Italian middle classes; but the bourgeoisie does not show that doctrinaire resistance to all forms of progress which Marxist dogma might lead us to expect. Actually, the only segment of the bourgeoisie that gives a sizable percentage of its national vote to the extreme Right is the self-employed petty bourgeoisie, which might have the most to gain from an alliance with the working class and the landless peasantry, but which is obsessed with its inability to compete effectively in a modern capitalist society.

As we have already suggested, the electoral fortunes of the various parties fluctuate from region to region. Thus, in the Northeast (especially the Veneto), the Christian Democrats normally receive about 50 percent of the votes and far overshadow the other political forces, whereas in North-Central Italy the Communists and Socialists are dominant, and the Christian Democrats poll only about 25 percent of the votes. In the Northwest Industrial Triangle, where skilled workers and urban white-collar employees are particularly numerous, the Christian Democrats command about one-third of the votes, the Communists and Socialists together usually receive about another one-third, and the minor Center parties (Social Democrats, Republicans, and Liberals) are far stronger than elsewhere in Italy and thus hold the balance of power. And finally, in the South, the Christian Democratic voting totals range from 30–50 percent of the votes cast. Here the Monarchists and the Neo-Fascists are a third force (rapidly dwindling in the case of the Monarchists).

Some additional demographic variables might be mentioned

in passing. For instance, it appears that the Christian Democrats do particularly well in attracting the support of senior citizens, whereas the reverse is true of the Communists.[66] Also, the remarkable success of the Christian Democrats in obtaining women's votes should be stressed: About two-thirds of those who cast ballots for the Christian Democratic Party are women, and 64 percent of Italian women vote for the Christian Democrats.[67]

We thus emerge with some crude composite profiles of the various party electorates. The Communist party appeals particularly to unskilled industrial workers, farm laborers, sharecroppers, young bachelors, and illiterates. Its main regional bastions are North-Central Italy and, to a lesser degree, the South. The Socialists receive their major support from skilled workers, sharecroppers, farm laborers, and white-collar workers. The Social Democrats have a narrower electoral base: skilled workers and white-collar workers. Both the Socialists and Social Democrats are particularly successful in the Northwest Triangle and in the Veneto, but of course fail to dominate any region. The Christian Democrats find their main areas of strength among women, small property-owning farmers, the middle-classes generally, and senior citizens, with some support from a sizeable minority of industrial workers. They control the Veneto and are moving steadily toward a position of hegemony in the South. The Liberals are strongest in the Northwest Triangle among members of the urban middle classes.

But these demographic variables may give too pat and superficial a picture. For instance, in the Red Belt of North-Central Italy, a variety of voters support the Communist party because it is, and long has been, the party in power at the local level. These supporters even include shopkeepers and other businessmen who want to stay on good terms with the incumbent party and who are pleased by the reassuring conservatism of such Communist local governments as the one in Bologna.[68] It is, of course, true that the Communist vote reflects, to a very considerable degree, the frustrated economic and status aspirations of the would-be upwardly mobile in a transitional society. But a party that possesses

---

[66] Vincenzo Tomeo, *Mutamento sociale e scelta politica: il comportamento elettorale nella provincia di Milano dal 1946 al 1963* (Milano: Giuffré, 1967), pp. 246–247, 263.

[67] Cavazzani, p. 178; and Chasseriaud, pp. 184–185.

[68] Achille Ardigò, "Il volto elettorale di Bologna," in Alberto Spreafico and Joseph La Palombara, eds., *Elezioni e comportamento politico in Italia* (Milano: Comunità, 1963), pp. 825, 839–840. This tendency is apparently more likely to manifest itself in local elections than in national elections.

a number of entrenched positions in local government is also apt to develop a network of vested interests, of voters who support an incumbent administration in order not to rock the boat.

The direct relationship that exists between the number of radio and television sets in use and the electoral strength of the Communist party comes as something of a surprise given Mannucci's blistering indictment of the government's domination over the radio and television networks, and of the discriminatory programs and news coverage reflecting that domination. Actually, Galli explains this seeming inconsistency. Many PCI members listen to Radio Prague rather than to Italian broadcasts. Moreover, Italian radio and television programs are thoroughly analyzed and criticized by the Communist press and by Communist opinion leaders in party section headquarters, and in workingmen's bars and meeting rooms, where public television is often available for an entire evening for the price of one drink.[69] Galli reproduces an account of a broadcast of *"Tribuna Politica"* in one such bar:

> When "Tribuna Politica" is on, the room is filled with shouts, with invective, with wisecracks, and also with whistles [Italian boos]. If Michelini [a leader of the Neo-Fascist Party] speaks, someone yells, "Clown! Blackshirt!"; if a Minister speaks, you can hear Zizua cry, "Rulers are all alike!"; but if Togliatti speaks, the audience becomes attentive and quiet, you can hear only a few voices expressing encouragement or approval, like "Good man! That's telling 'em!"[70]

It is evident that, after this kind of filtering process, government broadcasts are bound to lose much of their propagandistic effectiveness. Thus, control over a large number of formal and informal party-sponsored channels of communication enables the PCI to offset and actually turn to its own advantage the Christian Democrats' dominance over radio and television programming.

In analyzing the electoral fortunes of the various parties, we must also bear in mind the importance of certain organizational factors. Only the two giant parties (the PCI and the DC) have such an extensive clientele of organized interest groups under their control or influence, and such a well-developed party press, as to be able to maintain continuous contact with the grass roots and, above all, to have access to voters who cannot see their way clear to joining a party.

[69] Galli, *Il bipartitismo imperfetto*, pp. 270–282.
[70] Galli, *Il bipartitismo imperfetto*, p. 272.

In the case of the Communist party, the groups it controls include the Italian General Confederation of Labor (the CGIL, the largest trade-union confederation in Italy), the National League of Cooperatives and Mutual Aid Societies, the National Association of Italian Partisans, the Union of Italian Women, the National Peasants' Alliance, the Italian Union of Popular Sports, and a number of others.[71] In addition to these and other Communist-dominated organizations, there are, of course, pro-Communist factions in various other interest groups which Communist elements do not actually control. These organizations function as sources of funds and volunteer assistance for the Communist party and help to exploit moods of protest among the masses. But on the other hand, they have failed to acquire much strength in the South or in other virgin territories; and an abnormally high proportion of their membership is located in North-Central Italy. Also, they tend to drain the energies of the Communist party somewhat, by compelling Communist activists to take on additional organizational burdens.

The Christian Democrats, for their part, have an even more imposing array of affiliated and allied groups. There are, first of all, the organizations directly sponsored by the Catholic church—Catholic Action, with its various subdivisions: the Union of Men, the Union of Women, Italian Catholic Action Youth, the Italian Catholic University Federation, the Teachers Movement, and so on. In addition to the Catholic Action complex, which is directly dependent on the church hierarchy, there are a number of specialized Catholic lay organizations, which are not formally dependent on the church, although they may, and often do, accept church guidance. These include the National Confederation of Direct Cultivators (small farmers), the Italian Association of Catholic Teachers, the Christian Association of Italian Workers, and the Civic Committees. Then, the Christian Democrats control a trade-union confederation—the Italian Confederation of Workers' Unions (CISL)—and the Confederation of Italian Cooperatives. In Northeast Italy, where the Christian Democratic party has a relatively small membership, it is evidently the Catholic associations that get out the massive Christian Democratic vote.[72]

These various groups have performed an excellent vote-getting job for the Christian Democratic party. But, by virtue of their

---

[71] These groups and groups associated with the Christian Democratic party are discussed in Agopik Manoukian, ed., *La presenza sociale del PCI e della DC* (Bologna: Il Mulino, 1968). Coauthors include L. Brunelli, U. Canullo, G. Degli Esposti, G. Galli, A. Lena, L. Pepa, A. Picchi, A. Prandi, A. M. Rossi, B. Scatassa, A. Sivini Cavazzani, L. Turco.

[72] Galli, *Il bipartitismo imperfetto*, pp. 189–190.

very number and heterogeneity, they have tended to create internal cleavages within the selfsame grouping. Rather than dominate and aggregate the activities of its allied interest groups, Italian Christian Democracy has simply reflected the divergent interests of the far-flung segments of the Italian Catholic world. Almost any policy would inconvenience and therefore alienate one of the groups listed above. The natural reaction of the Italian Christian Democratic party has been to postpone controversial issues, thus relying on immobilism as a requisite for survival.

Additional channels of communication with the masses are provided by the party press.[73] The Italian Communist press, headed by its daily newspaper *L'Unità*, represents about 10 percent of the national newspaper circulation. But the Christian Democrats and the Catholic church and lay organizations have a much more extensive and penetrating array of published media. True, the Christian Democratic daily, *Il Popolo*, has a relatively small circulation; but there are also a number of regional newspapers, such as *Il Gazzettino* of Venice, which receive financial assistance from the Christian Democrats and from state agencies. *Il Quotidiano* (Rome) reflects the views of Catholic Action. *Il Giorno* (Milan) is controlled by the National Hydrocarburants Corporation (ENI, a public corporation which is headed by a Christian Democrat). If one adds to these the various diocesan dailies, which serve as the organs of the more important bishops, and the numerous Catholic magazines, the Catholic press has a circulation about double that of the Communist party and its allies and sympathizers. But the Catholic press seems to have less influence than the Communist press on voting behavior. The former labors under the disadvantage of speaking with multiple discordant tongues, resulting from the same kind of open factional conflict that rages within the ranks of Christian Democracy.

There is very little to be said for the other parties with regard to their ability to communicate with the masses. The Socialists have a minority position in the Italian General Confederation of Labor (CGIL) and in the Communist-dominated cooperatives. The Social Democrats have a marginal minority position in CISL, the Catholic-dominated labor confederation. The Socialists, Social Democrats, and Republicans dominate the Italian Union of Labor (UIL), which is, however, only the third largest labor confederation in Italy. The Neo-Fascists have a feeble labor confederation of their own, CISNAL. The Liberals *do* have fairly strong ties

[73] Manoukian, pp. 655–666.

with the manufacturing and landed interests represented by the Italian General Confederation of Industry (*Confindustria*) and the Italian General Confederation of Agriculture. Their strong influence in the world of big business assures them of a more-than-sympathetic hearing from much of Italy's "independent" press, which is owned largely by a number of giant corporations. In this regard, the Liberal party has a significant advantage over the Socialists, Social Democrats, and Republicans, whose press organs are either defunct (*La Giustizia*, Social Democrat) or anemic (*Avanti!*, Socialist; *La Voce Repubblicana*, Republican). But the "independent" press is hardly designed to sway a mass audience.

Are any major changes taking place in Italian voting behavior as the result of the numerous social changes of the past two decades, such as migration, rising living standards, and so on? Some Italian scholars have suggested that Southern immigrants are converted into supporters of the Communist party after they have arrived in Milan and Turin. But Stefano Passigli explains Communist gains in the Northern cities as a general leftist trend among Southern voters, who repudiated the traditional culture and were attracted to communism before they ever moved North.[74] As for the effect of the "economic miracle" in reducing leftist votes, some caution is in order. In a region like Tuscany, a worker or peasant may indeed be better off than he was ten years ago. But because of the mass media, he is now also much more aware of the higher living standards *others* enjoy; obviously, the sight of thousands of tourists amusing themselves does little to alleviate his resentment.[75] So, while social change has taken place, the worker's perception of social change may be considerably retarded. Voting patterns do not respond as quickly as economic determinants might lead us to expect.

Dogan speaks of the movement of the Communist electorate in terms of "social ataxia" (pathological noncoordination):

> While the migratory movement pushed northward, Communism slipped southward; while the country became more and more urban, Communism became more and more *rural*; while Italy became increasingly industrialized, Communism became increasingly *agrarian*. Thus Communism goes against the stream. Society goes in one direction; Communism in the other.[76]

[74] Stefano Passigli, *Emigrazione e comportamento politico* (Bologna: Il Mulino, 1969), pp. 87–128.
[75] Braga, p. 110.
[76] Dogan, p. 192.

But the 1968 election results introduced a discordant note into this interesting analysis: The biggest Communist gains were in the Northwest Triangle and in North-Central Italy; in the South, the Communists lost ground in several regions and made marginal gains in the rest.[77]

Thus, developing trends in the electoral strength of the various Italian parties are still hard to pin down. One thing seems definite: Change is taking place at a very slow rate indeed. Fluctuations in the strength of different Italian parties are often to be counted in fractions of a percentage point. Voting shifts are usually localized: A party gains at the expense of its neighbor on the political spectrum, not at the expense of a party diametrically opposed to its views. Moreover, while votes may be exchanged between the Communists and the various socialist parties, or between the Christian Democrats and their neighbors on the Right, the strength of the Left-of-Center bloc and the Right-of-Center bloc (the latter including the Christian Democrats) remains fairly stable. Small wonder, then, that the Italian Chamber of Deputies has never been dissolved before its term expired. After all, what would be the use of dissolution and new elections if the new Chamber should simply be a reproduction of the old?

THE ELECTORAL SYSTEM

In electing members of the lower house of Parliament, the Chamber of Deputies, Italy relies on a list system of proportional representation. (Immediately prior to 1919, a single-member-district system with second ballot was employed.)[78] The country is divided into thirty-two electoral circumscriptions. One (the Val d'Aosta) is a single-member constituency by virtue of its small population; the rest are multimember districts consisting, in almost all cases, of two or more provinces. In each circumscription, the parties present lists of candidates. Each party list is the product of a long process of interfactional consultation and bargaining at the provincial, circumscription, and national levels. The voter indicates the party list of his choice by making an "×" next to the appropriate party symbol and then proceeds, if he so desires, to write the names of his three or four most highly preferred candi-

---

[77] *La Stampa* (Turin), May 22, 1968.
[78] For an excellent discussion of the Italian electoral system, see John Clarke Adams and Paolo Barile, *The Government of Republican Italy* (2nd ed.; Boston: Houghton Mifflin, 1966), ch. 11.

dates from among the names on that party list. After the votes have been counted, the seats to be filled from that circumscription are distributed among the various party lists on the basis of proportional representation: An electoral quotient is obtained by dividing the seats to be assigned, plus a small incremental number, into the total number of votes cast in the circumscription, and the quotient is then divided into the number of votes cast for each party. Remainders and unassigned seats are allotted to a special National College in Rome and distributed among competing party lists there. As a result of this procedure, each party obtains a number of parliamentary seats roughly proportionate to its share of the total vote. The *preference* votes are then used to determine *who* shall represent a party in the Chamber. If a list in the First Circumscription is entitled to five deputies, the five candidates on that list who have polled the highest number of preference votes will go to Rome.

The system employed in electing senators is more complex. Each of the nineteen regions is divided into single-member districts. After the votes are cast, those candidates who have received over 65 percent of the votes (very few candidates achieve this kind of majority) are automatically elected to the Senate. The rest have to pool their votes with all the other votes cast for their party in their region. On the basis of these regionally pooled votes, the remaining seats are distributed among the parties in each region in accordance with the D'Hondt (highest average) system of proportional representation. After it has been thus determined that a party in a given region shall be entitled to, say, three senators, those three candidates who have polled the highest percentages of the total vote in their respective single-member districts will be elected. Thus, in a given region, Socialist candidate X with 25,000 votes (50 percent of the votes cast in his district) will go to Parliament rather than Socialist candidate Y with 35,000 votes (only 45 percent of the votes cast in *his* district).

The effect of these electoral systems may be briefly summarized. They help to keep splinter parties alive: The Republicans and the Monarchists might be now defunct were it not for proportional representation. The system of nomination of lists by party organs, a system in which the voters have no voice, certainly encourages control by the extraparliamentary party organization over individual deputies and senators. On the other hand, the system of preference votes employed in the election of members of the Chamber of Deputies has the effect of undermining the party organization somewhat. Contending factions compete desperately with each other in an effort to corner the available supply of preference votes. Powerful pressure groups, affiliated or allied with the party, are able to get their men elected on the party list by instructing rank-and-file members to concentrate their preference votes where they will do the most good. Even individual citizens can strike a blow against unpopular incumbents by giving their preference votes to some relatively unknown candidate on the party's list. Factionalism, pressure group interference in party affairs, and the creation of impregnable personal fiefs by deputies who are particularly adept in nursing their constituency are some of the costs of straying from the strict principle of the list system. To be sure, the system gives the voter more of a voice, and this may offset some of the drawbacks we have just cited.

CAMPAIGN TECHNIQUES

Some basic changes have taken place in Italian political campaigns since the heady days immediately following World War II. Whereas in 1946 and 1947 the party leaders used to address mammoth Sunday rallies in the principal squares of Italian cities, such rallies in the 1960s and early 1970s are much more sparsely attended. Whereas the electoral struggle used to be depicted as a conflict between the forces of good and evil, the parties now rely on milder, less alarmist themes, such as the Christian Democratic slogan of 1958: "progress without adventures." Whereas entire cities used to be bedecked with streamers and plastered with wall posters, the parties now employ more modern and sophisticated methods of communicating with the public. They have begun to resort to campaign banquets, the use of sound-trucks and moviemobiles, and the insertion of paid political advertisements in the "independent" newspapers. And they have recruited a few "nonpolitical" candidates to run on their party slates in order to confer some aura of universality. Moreover, since the television show, *Tribuna Politica,* was inaugurated several years ago, the parties have had access to television time for the purpose of presenting their respective cases to the general public.

Also, the parties are placing much more emphasis on what they call their "capillary penetration" of the Italian electorate. They send letters and pamphlets through the mail to members of specific categories of citizens—migrants, steel workers, shopkeepers—instead of treating all voters as if they were members of one undifferentiated mass. Thousands of party activists and volunteers from organizations that are allied or affiliated to a party try to carry the party message to the grass roots through word-of-mouth communication. Needless to add, the Communists and the Christian Democrats are best equipped to promote their candidates in this manner.

How effective are the various campaign methods in actually influencing voting behavior? The evidence is inconclusive at best, but there are reasons to suspect that—apart from enabling the parties to hold on to their habitual supporters—campaign techniques do little to influence voting behavior. Cesare Mannucci concludes that there is little evidence that television has had any major impact in affecting voting trends.[79] In fact, as we have mentioned, there seems to be a positive relationship between the number of television sets in operation and the Communist vote, despite the fact that state-owned television has been pretty much under the domination of the Christian Democrats. The relative immobility of the Italian electorate is another piece of negative evidence: But perhaps if campaign resources were not so unevenly allocated, the Communists and Christian Democrats would not be able to prevent an erosion of their electorate, and Italian elections would reveal greater fluctuations in voting behavior. Finally, party identification is abnormally strong in Italy—over three-fourths of Italian voters in a 1958 study had made up their minds long before the election.[80] There is little indication, then, that Italian political campaigns have a major impact on election results.

CONCLUSION:
THE ROLE OF PARTIES
IN THE SYSTEM

The foregoing discussion has largely confirmed the various theories regarding the character of the Italian party system. Sartori's thesis that the system is centrifugal, polarized, and multipolar, as well as rendered immobile and unresponsive to peripheral turnover; Galli's view that Italy has an imperfect two-party system in which both the overweening strength of the giants and the feebleness of the pygmies are self-perpetuating; and Kirchheimer's concept of the catch-all party—these theories appear to be borne out,

---

[79] Cesare Mannucci, "La propaganda politica dalla piazza alla casa: video e voto in Italia," *Comunità*, Vol. XXII, No. 150 (January–February 1968), 58–60.
[80] Alberto Spreafico, "Orientamento politico e identificazione partitica," in Spreafico and La Palombara, eds., pp. 690–691, 721–722.

with some qualifications, by the data at our disposal. What remains to be investigated is the general question of the role of parties in the Italian political system.

One major criticism directed against Italian parties has been based on the allegation that they have usurped the functions of the rule-making structures of government. It is pointed out that extraparliamentary party organs make decisions that are regarded as binding on the party's parliamentary group, that cabinet crises are often both originated and settled by the parties outside of Parliament, that the government agencies and public corporations are thoroughly colonized by patronage appointees. Also, it is held that rigid party discipline deprives the Italian member of Parliament of his right to vote his conscience on major issues. This iron-clad discipline, it is claimed, is the result of the electoral system based on proportional representation. For these reasons, Italian democracy is viewed as a "partitocracy," a regime ruled by party bureaucracies rather than by the people's representatives.[81]

Defenders of Italian parties have been numerous and articulate. They have pointed out that, before 1919, in the days of the single-member district, the party system was plagued by chronic instability, rampant indiscipline, and continuous pressure directed by powerful interest groups against individual members of Parliament. They suggest that, in the absence of strong parties, pressure groups would be sure to fill the void. They warn that, given the presence of a strong Communist party, a system of single-member districts might lead to a Right-Left polarization that might endanger Italian democracy. And finally, they call attention to the fact that the extraparliamentary party organs are usually dominated, not by faceless party bureaucrats, but by members of Parliament.[82]

But if the charge that the parties represent an illicit departure from an idyllic past is easily refuted, there are more serious indictments, to the effect that the parties are failing to come to grips with the problems and exigencies of the late twentieth century. They still resort to an archaic and obscure jargon for initiates in their statements about public affairs, thus contributing to the puzzlement and indifference of a bemused public. Their ideologies are outworn and irrelevant and cry out for renovation. Their internal processes are semioligarchic (although this seems to be the result of a universal trend in Western democracies, rather than a specifi-

[81] Maranini, pp. 387–393, 403–438, 471–472, 483–515.
[82] Silvio Gava, "Partiti e parlamento," in *La Democrazia Cristiana di fronte al comunismo* (Roma: Cinque Lune, 1964), pp. 23–24, 31–41.

cally Italian failing). Their internal bureaucracies have a tendency to resist innovations of any kind, for fear of damaging their own security of tenure. And finally, there is the charge, made by both La Palombara and Sernini, that parties fail to aggregate demands, fail to filter and arrange interest-group demands into some sort of credible and balanced package; instead they simply act as spokesmen for interest groups or—in the case of a "catch-all" party like the Christian Democrats—as a passive arena for interminable and inconclusive group conflict.[83] On this last score, chastened American scholars might ask themselves how well *any* democratic political party, including their own, *really* performs the function of interest aggregation.

Perhaps the most serious defects of the Italian party system however, are to be found in the structure of the party system itself rather than in the structure and behavior of individual parties. Since there is no united opposition party to serve as an alternative, the multiplicity of parties and the presence of a dominant party that must be included in every cabinet creates a situation in which voters never have the comforting sensation of "turning the rascals out." Election follows election and the same men remain at the helm, with only a few new faces, and an occasional reshuffling of assignments, to mark a half-hearted departure from monotonous continuity. It is not so much a question of the absence of meaningful turnover. Far more important is the absence of any *appearance* of turnover. The alternations in power that take place in Anglo-American systems usually mean far less in terms of concrete policy outcomes than they *appear* to mean. But the legitimacy of democratic institutions may well depend on deceptive symbolism of this nature. The policy output of the Italian political system is sadly deficient. And the multiparty system, plus the intraparty factionalism that characterizes Italian party politics, have much to do with this failure. But the real weakness of the system is its inadequate symbolic output, its failure to give men the sense, however illusory, that the government and the parties have the situation well in hand.

Finally, we should point out that this limited turnover, combined with the constant and almost ritualistic squabbling between and within parties, tends to discourage interest and participation. Voters and rank-and-file party members lose interest in a politics dominated by seemingly irremovable elites. The use of formulas that seem to have little or no relation to current issues makes the

[83] Sernini, pp. 68–69, 103; and La Palombara, *Interest Groups* . . . , pp. 84–99.

parties seem somehow irrelevant. Consequently, there is developing a certain atmosphere of distrust and contempt toward the major parties, an impatience with the endless formalities of the democratic political process. The student riots and the wildcat strikes are straws in the wind, indicative of a widespread alienation from established structures and procedures. As long as the economy continues to expand and living standards continue to rise, the failure to resolve the problem of participation will not represent a major threat to system survival. But the problem will remain as a formidable piece of unfinished business, which Italy—and other democracies including the United States—will ignore at their peril.

SIX
CLIENTELA
AND PARENTELA
Groups, interests, and cleavages

THE INTEREST-GROUP SYSTEM: MAJOR CHARACTERISTICS

As befits a society in transition, the Italian interest-group system still retains some of the hallmarks of the tradition-bound past. For one thing, anomic interest groups in the form of rampaging mobs still make frequent appearances on the Italian scene. The 1970–1971 riots in the city of Reggio Calabria, where an indignant populace erected barricades to protest the Italian government's decision to designate the city of Catanzaro as capital of the Region of Calabria, are by no means isolated episodes. Also, we can discern in Italy a somewhat more pronounced tendency for institutions to act as pressure groups than we are accustomed to find in advanced Western societies. Some of the public agencies and corporations—especially the National Hydrocarburants Corporation (ENI)—have acted very openly as powerful lobbies, attempting not only to influence government decision makers, but also to appeal directly to the public, to say nothing of trying to gain control of the Christian Democratic party. Finally, the nonassociational interest group—the group that articulates its demands on an occasional, ad hoc basis, without bothering to set up a clearly defined organizational structure—is still common in Italy. A case in point would be the conferences called by such journals as *Il Mondo* and *Il Mulino* to discuss some issues of vital importance and to exercise pressure on the government with a view to achieving some major reforms. By attracting prestigious people of various shades of opinion from all over Italy, these conferences generate considerable political persuasion behind their demands.[1]

But since Italy has recently achieved a high degree of industrial progress and since large parts of Italy are now as modern as the rest of Western Europe, a system of associational interest groups has developed and multiplied. To an ever-increasing extent, associational interest groups—groups that have been created specifically for the purpose of interest articulation and that operate on a continuous basis with the aid of professional staffs—have begun to dominate the interest-group system. It has become all too clear that violence is usually a counterproductive technique that advertises a group's political impotence; that a public agency which acts too blatantly in promoting its own interests and demands is undermining its public status and its future role; and that a widely advertised assemblage of petitioning notables is no substitute for a permanent public relations office, feeding a steady flow of sorely needed information to governmental policy makers. So, while past prejudices and cleavages are indeed dying hard, there seems to be a visible trend under way toward modernization of the Italian interest-group system, as goals become less diffuse and as methods become more moderate and sophisticated.

Given this trend, it becomes possible to compare Italian interest groups to those of more prosperous European countries, for underlying similarities now make such a comparison meaningful. The European country whose pattern of interest groups most resembles that of Italy is, of course, France. Both countries have their interest-group systems fragmented by ideological cleavages, particularly in the sphere of organized labor. In both Italy and France, to be more specific, there is a Communist-dominated labor confederation, a Social Democratic-dominated labor confederation, and a Catholic-dominated labor confederation. In both countries, anomic group behavior has been somewhat more common, and less repugnant in the eyes of public opinion, than elsewhere in Western Europe. Finally, in both France and Italy, big business suffers from a rather poor public image, resulting from a

---

[1] On the major forms of interest articulation in Italy, see Joseph La Palombara, *Interest Groups in Italian Politics* (Princeton, N.J.: Princeton University Press, 1964), pp. 79–84. Much of the material in this chapter is drawn from La Palombara.

heritage of pre-1945 collaboration with extreme rightist regimes—the Vichy government and the Italian Fascist dictatorship, respectively.

But there are also some basic contrasts between the two pressure-group systems. Some of these contrasts result from differences between the two economies and between the two societies, and will be discussed in the sections identifying the principal categories of pressure groups. This class of differences includes the somewhat greater political aggressiveness of Italian big business as compared with French, the presence in Italy of a confederation of *small* farmers, and the somewhat lower bargaining power of Italian labor.[2] The activities of the public sector of the Italian economy, and of the Roman Catholic church and its sponsored organizations, deserve special attention. And the relations between interest groups and parties in Italy have been far more intimate than is the case in France. In fact, a number of major Italian interest groups play a vital role in intraparty factional conflict.

Other differences may be traced to the marked dissimilarity between the political structures of the two systems. The Italian Parliament still has considerable influence on the decision-making process, unlike its emasculated French counterpart. Consequently, interest groups are tempted to intervene there, to seek to obtain access to the legislative arena. The Italian standing committee system, in particular, with its offbeat procedures for enacting a bill into law *in committee* without bringing the bill to the floor for final reading, certainly provides an ideal locale for pressure groups to apply behind-the-scenes influence. In short, in the France of the Fifth Republic access to the bureaucracy is at a premium, whereas access to Parliament is a prize of dubious value. In Italy, on the other hand, it pays to cultivate senators and deputies, who, even though bound by party discipline, can always plead a pressure group's case in caucus sessions. Several pressure groups go beyond mere lobbying in the Italian Parliament: They try to get their high-ranking officials elected directly to Parliament on some party's list. To be sure, this form of direct representation of interest groups in Parliament is a mixed blessing from the groups' point of view. Pressure-group officials acting as deputies may have to side with their party leadership against the interests of the group they represent or face disciplinary sanctions. Therefore, group representa-

---

[2] Jean Meynaud and Claudio Risé, *Gruppi di pressione in Italia e in Francia* (Napoli: Edizioni Scientifiche Italiane, 1963), for a comparison between French and Italian pressure groups. Most of the comparative material in this chapter is drawn from their work.

tion in Parliament may serve to undermine pressure-group autonomy.

In fact, the relationship between pressure groups and parties lends a rather esoteric quality to the Italian political system. Americans are familiar enough, from their own experience, with the kind of relationship that La Palombara refers to as *clientela*, a situation in which a given government agency comes to regard a given pressure group as a representative spokesman for a given sector of the economy, and then proceeds to rely primarily on that pressure group for advice and support. This kind of rapport exists between the Italian General Confederation of Industry (*Confindustria*) and the Ministry of Industry and Commerce. But what is foreign to the American milieu is the relationship known as *parentela,* in which close and intimate bonds develop between a number of pressure groups and the dominant party in the system.[3] Catholic Action, for instance, serves as a recruiting ground for men and women who will eventually join the Christian Democrats, helps the Christian Democrats in election campaigns by sponsoring the Civic Committees, and is regularly consulted by the Christian Democratic party on parliamentary nominations. The Italian Confederation of Direct Cultivators has its own bloc of "friendly" deputies and senators in the Christian Democratic parliamentary group. And finally, the Christian Association of Italian Workers (ACLI) and the Italian Confederation of Workers' Unions (CISL) have actually formed an organized and relatively cohesive faction within the Christian Democratic parliamentary group.

Chapter Five identified some of the pressure groups that have very close ties with the Communist party: the Italian General Confederation of Labor (CGIL), which is, however, evolving toward a greater measure of autonomy; the National Association of Italian Partisans (ANPI); the Italian Movement of Peace Partisans; the Union of Italian Women (UDI); the National Peasants' Alliance (ANC); the Italian Union of Popular Sports (UISP); the Italian Recreational and Cultural Association (ARCI); and the Italian Confederation of Cooperatives and Mutual Savings Funds. But these groups are essentially created and sponsored by the party—with the sole exception of the CGIL and the cooperatives—and are therefore largely incapable of playing any kind of autonomous role. They *do* provide the party with volunteer activists and campaign funds, particularly in the case of the cooperatives and unions, and help to establish some contact with sympa-

---

[3] On *clientela* and *parentela,* see La Palombara, chs. 8 and 9.

thizers ("fellow-travelers") who cannot quite see their way clear to joining the party.[4]

The *parentela* groups connected with the Christian Democratic party are, of course, another affair. First of all, they have been neither created nor sponsored by the party. Most have been founded by persons affiliated with Catholic Action and have received the encouragement or benevolent neutrality of the Catholic church. They are not, therefore, mere servants of Italian Christian Democracy. To the extent that they *are* subject to outside pressures—and some, like the Christian Association of Italian Workers (ACLI) and the Italian Confederation of Workers' Unions (CISL), steer a pretty independent course—those pressures come from the Vatican, not from Christian Democratic national headquarters. Rather, the groups that relate to the Christian Democratic party on a *parentela* basis are constantly competing for influence over the party and its policies, backing one or another of the party's many feuding factions, or sometimes forming a faction themselves. In national elections, the *parentela* groups demand that their representatives (who are, of course, also Christian Democrats) be included on the Christian Democratic election slates. Having accomplished this goal in most multimember districts, they then proceed to campaign very actively for the preference votes of Christian Democratic voters. Command of both campaign workers and campaign funds often enables the *parentela* pressure groups to bring about the election of candidates they endorse, and thus to create a number of outstanding political debts among the members of the Christian Democratic parliamentary group. Over the course of time, observers have come to take more of an interest in this intraparty competition for preference votes than in the sluggish and relatively insignificant fluctuations that take place in the electoral strength of the various parties.

Parentela groups have also been of considerable financial assistance to the Christian Democrats, but this assistance is freely given and may be freely withdrawn. Unlike the Communist party, the Christian Democratic party is not so dominant over its closely affiliated or allied pressure groups as to be able to dictate terms of financial aid. Thus, we see the *Confindustria* actually acting as a *parentela* pressure group between 1946 and 1954, then withdraw-

[4] On DC and PCI *parentela* groups, see Agopik Manoukian, ed., *La presenza sociale del PCI e della DC* (Bologna: Il Mulino, 1968). Coauthors include L. Brunelli, U. Canullo, G. Degli Esposti, G. Galli, A. Lena, L. Pepa, A. Picchi, A. Prandi, A. M. Rossi, B. Scatassa, A. Sivini Cavazzani, L. Turco.

ing its support from Christian Democracy in favor of a more exclusive concern for the election of rightist candidates belonging to various parties. After Fanfani became party secretary in 1954, the Christian Democrats relied more heavily on help provided by the Direct Cultivators and by a number of Catholic organizations. But above all, Fanfani solicited help from the Christian Democratic-controlled public sector of the economy—especially from firms dominated by the publicly owned Institute for Industrial Reconstruction (IRI) and from the National Hydrocarburants Corporation (ENI), directed until 1962 by Enrico Mattei. Thus, as we can see, even institutional groups have developed a *parentela* relationship with the Christian Democratic party. Financial subsidies from *parentela* groups have been a weapon in the intraparty factional struggle. For example, Mattei's ENI is said to have helped the Left wing of the Christian Democratic party, whereas the Direct Cultivators, after an initial flirtation with Fanfani and his Left-wing supporters, shifted their aid to the moderate and rightist currents of the party.

AGRICULTURAL INTEREST GROUPS

As we have already noted, Italy is still more of an agricultural nation than France or Germany; but a vast rural exodus has been under way for over a decade. Because of the more restricted amount of arable land at the disposal of Italian peasants, Italian family farms are generally much smaller than their counterparts across the Alps. In fact, many of them barely approach the subsistence level. For this reason, the Italian farm organization that speaks for medium and large landowners—the Italian General Confederation of Agriculture (*Confagricoltura*)—represents only a minority of Italian agricultural proprietors: about 1.5 million farm families in all, a number of which are also enrolled in the National Confederation of Direct Cultivators.[5] *Confagricoltura*'s close ties with the General Confederation of Italian Industry (*Confindustria*), to whose influence it tends to defer, have weakened its claim to act as the principal spokesman for Italian agriculture with regard to the basic issue of agricultural survival in an industrializing society. It was in protest against the steady process of industrial encroachment on the agricultural sphere—a process marked by the large-scale acquisition of farm lands on the part of industrial entrepreneurs and industrial firms—that extreme rightist ele-

[5] J. P. Chasseriaud, *Le parti démocrate chrétien en Italie* (Paris: Armand Colin, 1965), p. 262.

ments broke away from *Confagricoltura* to found the Centers of Agricultural Action.[6]

A much more powerful farm organization is the National Confederation of Direct Cultivators, representing about 1,750,000 farm families, who mostly live on small plots. It is estimated that the Direct Cultivators represent about 80 percent of Italian small landowning farmers, while their Communist-backed rival, the National Peasants' Alliance, commands only about 10 percent of the small landowners.[7] Because of its control over the Federation of Agricultural Consortiums (*Federconsorzi*), a quasi-public federation that performs a great variety of services (credit, subsidies, storage, and so forth) for Italian farmers, the Confederation of Direct Cultivators has been able to become the most influential farm pressure group in Italy and a major faction within the ranks of Italian Christian Democracy. Its leader for the past two decades, Paolo Bonomi, has done a great deal to promote the aggrandizement and reinforcement of this association, so much so that the press frequently refers to it as "the Bonomiana."

Under Bonomi's command, the Direct Cultivators have become one of the most redoubtable power blocs on the Italian political scene. For example, the withdrawal of Bonomi's support in 1959 helped Fanfani's enemies to defeat him at the Florence congress of the Christian Democratic party. Bonomi has been much criticized for pursuing an allegedly reactionary line in agricultural policy, for supporting the stockpiling of wheat as a means of bolstering wheat prices, and for trying to conserve the subsistence farm as the backbone of Italian agriculture. Also, he has been accused of supporting reactionary elements in the Christian Democratic party. Finally there have been numerous denunciations of his use of public funds, disbursed by *Federconsorzi*, to increase the political influence of his own pressure group. For many years, these criticisms could be blithely ignored, as Bonomi's Confederation of Direct Cultivators continued to bestride the Italian political scene like a colossus. But more recently, the Direct Cultivators appear to have suffered a sharp decline in self-assertiveness and influence. The reasons are not hard to discern: Bonomi's efforts to stem the tide of agricultural transformation have evidently failed; and the rural exodus is rapidly eating away his base of support.[8]

---

[6] Jean Meynaud, *Rapporto sulla classe dirigente italiana* (Milano: Giuffré, 1966), pp. 82–83.
[7] Meynaud, pp. 84–85.
[8] Mario Pendinelli, "Il declino di Bonomi," *Nord e Sud*, Vol. XV, No. 107 (168) (November 1968), 27–36; and Mario Pendinelli, "Bonomi, il PCI e i coriandoli di terra," *Nord e Sud*, Vol. XVII, No. 125 (186) (May 1970), 32–35.

The rest of the Italian agricultural interest-group array may be dealt with briefly. There are three federations of farm laborers: one associated with the Communist-dominated CGIL, one with the Catholic-dominated CISL, and one with the Social Democratic-Republican UIL. Also, there are three complexes of agricultural co-ops: the Italian Cooperative Confederation (controlled by Catholic Action), the National Association of Cooperatives (in which Catholics play a major role), and the Communist-run National Association of Agricultural Cooperatives. We may observe at this point that, apart from *Confagricoltura*, most of the major farm organizations in Italy are under either Communist or Christian Democratic leadership. We may also note the far greater numerical importance of the small subsistence farmers in Italy, as opposed to France, and the success of the Christian Democrats in capturing the votes of these small farmers. But this victory may prove to be short-lived; for this stratum is gradually being eroded by the rural exodus, and this erosion is also undermining the electoral base of Italian Christian Democracy. By the same token, to be sure, Communist and Socialist sharecroppers and farm laborers are also being drained out of the rural areas. The two conflicting trends conceivably may be balancing each other, to the point where election returns from rural districts fail to reflect the massive changes that are shaking the Italian countryside.

LABOR INTEREST GROUPS

Looking at the forces of organized labor, we see once again some striking similarities between the Italian and French pressure-group systems. In Italy as in France, organized labor is weakened by politically inspired divisions in its ranks. The largest trade-union confederation in both countries—the Italian General Confederation of Labor (CGIL) and the French CGT—is Communist-dominated; the second-largest labor confederation—the Italian Confederation of Workers' Unions (CISL) and the French CFDT—is led and largely manned by Catholic trade unionists; and the Social Democratic-led labor confederation—the Italian Union of Labor (UIL) and the French CGT-FO—runs a poor third. In both France and Italy, the unions are numerically rather weak, have chronic difficulties in collecting dues from their members, are unable to achieve cooperative relations with most employers, are viewed with incomprehension and suspicion by the general public, and have usually lacked the means to embark on prolonged strikes in pursuit of their economic objectives. Plant-level bargaining is the exception rather than the rule: Contracts with management are hammered out at the national level on an industry-wide basis. The unions simply do not possess the local leadership and resources to enable them to police the local enforcement of a national contract, or to negotiate special local agreements within its general framework. Thus the hypercentralization of the two political systems appears to be reflected in collective-bargaining arrangements.

But Italian labor suffers from certain additional disabilities of its own. The severe unemployment and underemployment that afflicted the Italian economy during most of the post-World War II era did a great deal to dilute labor's bargaining power. The long years of Fascist rule, during which unions and strikes were outlawed, heightened the antilabor bias of the Italian middle classes, and may have contributed to the more violent style adopted by the Italian police when dealing with labor unrest. Where the French policeman confronted by violent protest will make liberal use of his truncheon, his Italian counterpart is much more likely to resort to gunfire at the moment of climax. The organizing efforts of Italian unions have been seriously hampered by regional differences, especially by the existence of tradition-bound, underdeveloped Southern Italy. The existence of a large mass of farm laborers—a virtual rural proletariat—has done much to radicalize the Italian labor movement and thus alienate potential allies. And finally, the ties between unions and political parties have been much closer than in France, with the result that, for many years, the parties exploited the labor unions for their own purposes. Italian unions have been somewhat slow, therefore, to assume an autonomous self-serving role.

For a few years after World War II, Italian labor was united in a single vast labor confederation: the Italian General Confederation of Labor (CGIL). But the CGIL was dominated by Communist elements that proceeded to use organized labor as a political tool to disrupt the economy, protest government policy in both the domestic and international spheres, and seize control of the streets. The riots and quasi-insurrections that followed the attempted assassination of Palmiro Togliatti (leader of the Communist party) in July 1948 resulted in the first of a series of secessions by Catholic, Socialist, and Republican elements in the CGIL. By 1950, the new alignment was clearly delineated. The CGIL now contained only a Communist majority and a Socialist minority. The Catholic trade unionists and some Social Democrats had formed the Italian Confederation of Workers' Unions (CISL); and a group of Social Democratic and Republican labor leaders had formed the Italian Union of Labor (UIL). At present, the CGIL claims about 3.5 million members, the CISL about 2.3 million, and the UIL from 500,000 to 700,000.[9] There is also a Neo-Fascist labor confederation (CISNAL) with about 100,000 supporters. All these figures must not be taken at face value, however, for exaggeration of membership figures is a form of political gamesmanship among Italian labor leaders.

In addition to its success in retaining control over Italy's largest labor confederation, the Italian Communist party has also obtained a firm hold on the National League of Cooperatives, which has over 2 million members. The Catholics dominate the Italian Confederation of Cooperatives, which also has a membership of over 2 million. But these fairly recent figures actually represent a sharp loss for the Communist-dominated cooperative movement and corresponding gains for the Catholic confederation. The pattern is not dissimilar from what we observed in the trade-union field, where the CISL gained heavily at the expense of the CGIL. And the similarity may be carried a step further: In both cases, Communist losses and Catholic gains tended to take place before 1960 and were followed by a kind of stabilized equilibrium. The lesson to be derived from these strikingly similar trends may be briefly summarized: When the Communist party gains control of an interest group, it cuts short that group's potential for future expansion. The party itself may reap dividends by exploiting the sympathies of some of the group's members, but many other members will leave the group, not to return until the Communist presence has been eliminated.[10]

An organization that is not, strictly speaking, a labor union, but that caters primarily to industrial workers and peasants is the Christian Association of Italian Workers (ACLI). The ACLI was formed for the purpose of giving political, religious, and social training to Italian workers. Among the functions it performs are the management of cooperatives, vocational training, the provision of low-cost housing to its members, and the management of various medical and social services. It has about 1 million members, many of whom are also members of the Catholic trade-union confederation, the CISL. Ironically enough, workers and peasants

---

[9] These estimates are drawn from Manoukian, ed., pp. 41, 109, and from Joseph A. Raffaele, *Labor Leadership in Italy and Denmark* (Madison, Wis.: University of Wisconsin Press, 1962), pp. 79–81.

[10] On this point, see Manoukian, ed., pp. 81–108, especially 105–108.

seem to be more heavily represented in the ACLI than they are in the CISL, which tends to recruit most of its membership from the ranks of office employees. But the two organizations have been on rather cordial terms; in fact, CISL and ACLI deputies have formed a single faction within the Christian Democratic parliamentary group.

In the last few years, some new trends appear to have taken shape in the Italian labor movement. First of all, there is a growing tendency to steer an independent course, free from the restraints of party supervision and control. There have been numerous examples of this pressure for trade-union autonomy. In the mid-1950s, the CISL deputies abstained on the vote regarding the "just cause" (for eviction of sharecroppers) provision in the tenancy contracts bill. This action was a clear breach of party discipline, for the rest of the Christian Democratic deputies voted in favor of the "just cause" provision. Along the same lines, Communist and Socialist deputies belonging to the CGIL abstained from voting on the Five-year Plan; yet the Communist party voted nay.[11] A more dramatic manifestation of autonomy took place in 1969, when the Communist-dominated CGIL and the Catholic-dominated CISL both declared that a member of Parliament could not simultaneously hold a trade-union office.[12] In that same year, a convention of the ACLI proclaimed an end to the "collateral relationship" of unconditional support for the Christian Democratic party.[13] All this does not yet add up to an autonomous labor movement. Party pressures continue to have a telling effect, and the ACLI, for example, has had to retreat into ambiguity. But the trend seems to be unmistakably clear.

In the second place, the "democratic" labor confederations —the CISL and the UIL, but especially the CISL—have become much more militant in pressing their claims. Whereas, in the 1950s, the Catholic-dominated CISL was continually trying to adopt a more conciliatory stance than the Communist-dominated CGIL, it has since become much more intransigent in the demands it makes on employers.[14] At the same time, the CISL has

[11] Giovanni Bechelloni, "Sindacati ed elezioni politiche," in Mattei Dogan and Orazio Maria Petracca, *Partiti politici e strutture sociali in Italia* (Milano: Comunità, 1968), p. 248.
[12] *La Stampa* (Turin), January 17, 1970.
[13] *La Stampa* (Turin), May 20, 1969.
[14] Bruno Manghi, "La dinamica della CISL: dal moderatismo ad una nuova coscienza politica," in Fabrizio Cicchitto, Gino Rocchi, Bruno Manghi, Luigi Ruggiu, Ada Sivini Cavazzani, *La DC dopo il primo ventennio* (Padova: Marsilio Editori, 1968), pp. 112–113, 121–123.

broadened its objectives beyond the limited sphere of collective bargaining to include such goals as more generous government pensions and better low-cost housing programs.[15] With the near-achievement of full employment in the early 1960s and with the influx of great masses of forward-looking young workers into the factories, the unions have had to adjust their strategies to the rising expectations and newly acquired bargaining power of their rank and file. For the pressure from the splinter sects of the new Left and from the student movement have been designed to exploit any union weaknesses that might be discerned and to foment wildcat strikes wherever union leadership falters.

The greater autonomy and militance displayed by organized labor, culminating in the strike-ridden "hot autumn" of 1969, have had an over-all unifying effect. To an ever-increasing extent, the three great labor confederations, once mortal enemies, have been coming to rely on each other for mutual support in their conflicts with the employers. There has been a growing awareness of the advantages of labor unity, and consequently one hears occasional calls for the formation of one big union to marshal the united efforts of all Italian workers. The day of labor reunification is, in all likelihood, a long way off. But voluntary cooperation across ideological boundaries has begun to bridge the wide gaps formed in the ranks of organized labor as a result of Italy's cultural fragmentation. And so employers are being compelled to view the labor movement with new respect.

BUSINESS INTEREST GROUPS

The French and Italian business communities have a number of points in common. Both have suffered severe damage to their respective images as a result of their having had cordial relations with fascist or authoritarian regimes. Both are, as a result, rather timid about playing an active and visible role in the politics of their respective countries; in fact, they prefer to rely primarily on a *clientela* relationship with the bureaucracy (though, as we shall see, Italian business frequently has embarked on a more venturesome course). Both have proved extremely unwilling to negotiate with organized labor, especially at the plant level. This unwillingness stems as much from status considerations as from concern for profits.

---

[15] Gino Giugni, "L'autunno 'caldo' sindacale," *Il Mulino*, Vol. XIX, No. 207 (January–February 1970), 40–41.

In some respects, however, Italian business possesses characteristic features of its own. For one thing, there is a higher degree of concentration than in France: No French firm plays as dominant a role in the French economy as does Fiat in Italy. Then, too, Italian small business lacks the autonomy and self-assertiveness displayed by its French counterpart: The Italian small businessmen's confederation (*Confapi*) is weak and pallid by contrast with the French General Confederation of Small and Medium Enterprises, and fails to enroll more than a fraction of Italy's small entrepreneurs. Also, the so-called cult of the little man plays a far less significant part in Italian political culture, and so there is less distrust of bigness, less envy and rancor directed against the large-scale producer. Perhaps, this is the reason for a final distinction that should be drawn: Italian businessmen have dared to intervene a bit more openly in political life than do the French, although both countries are characterized by rather prudent business communities, which shrink from glad-handing public relations techniques.

The principal business pressure groups include: the rather anemic small businessmen's confederation (*Confapi*); a confederation of shopkeepers, bankers, and other commercial entrepreneurs (*Confcommercio*); and the Italian General Confederation of Industry (*Confindustria*), which represents the great majority of industrial firms and trade associations, and probably speaks for more small businessmen than does *Confapi*. To a very significant extent, *Confindustria* tends to dominate *Confcommercio* and *Confagricoltura,* and sets the tone for Italian propertied interests in their relations with organized labor and with the government.

As we have already indicated, *Confindustria*—like *Confcommercio* and *Confagricoltura*—is a *clientela* group, but it has not always been such in the years since 1945. From 1946–1955, *Confindustria* had very intimate links with the Christian Democratic party, furnishing the DC with copious campaign funds and getting a number of industrialists elected to Parliament on the DC lists. This was the period during which *Confindustria* was led by Angelo Costa, who was a close personal friend of the DC leader, Alcide De Gasperi. Then came the electoral setback of 1953 and Amintore Fanfani's rise to the position of DC secretary in 1954. The ensuing leftward shift of Italian Christian Democracy helped to bring about a shake-up in *Confindustria*. In 1956, Costa was replaced as president of *Confindustria* by the Lombard industrialist, Alighiero De Micheli. De Micheli promptly organized an electoral pressure group, *Confintesa*, for the purpose of electing Liberals, Monarchists, and Right-wing Christian Democrats to Parliament. In this mission, he enlisted the backing of *Confagricoltura* and *Confcommercio*. But *Confintesa* turned out to be a failure: In both the 1956 local elections and the 1958 general elections, candidates who ran with *Confintesa* support were, for the most part, repudiated by the voters.

In response to this electoral fiasco, *Confindustria* again changed its course. In 1961, De Micheli was replaced as president by Furio Cicogna, an ardent Catholic and a man of moderate leanings. Under Cicogna, *Confindustria* attempted to infiltrate the power structure of Christian Democracy in the vain hope of reestablishing the near-*parentela* relationship of 1946–1955. But this expedient, too, proved futile: Not only was the Christian Democratic party virtually impermeable to *Confindustria* penetration by this time, but the Christian Democratic leaders actually proceeded to move ahead with the formation of a Left-Center coalition cabinet and with the nationalization of the electric-power industry—two policies that were anathema to many Italian industrialists. *Confindustria*'s reaction was to launch a large-scale campaign of criticism against the cabinet and to give propaganda support to the Liberal party as the party most unequivocally favorable to business interests. The results of the election of 1963 were not terribly gratifying: The Liberal party doubled its percentage of the total vote, but its 7 percent hardly represented a position of strength for Italian business.

Since 1963, *Confindustria* has returned to a relatively low-profile *clientela* approach, concentrating on discreet contacts with the bureaucracy. In fact, a much more conciliatory style seems to be gaining the ascendancy lately. In April 1970, Renato Lombardi, the newly elected president of *Confindustria*, delivered an address in which he praised Italian labor unions for having helped to stimulate Italian economic progress since 1948, urged industrialists to seek to carry on a more civil dialogue with the labor unions, and promised to explore possible areas of agreement with such public enterprises as those in the IRI and ENI groups.[16] This unusually placatory overture may well be the forerunner of a more realistic outlook on the part of Italian organized business.

A number of big industrial firms do not invariably accept *Confindustria* as their spokesman on issues in which they have some special interest. These firms may have their own separate

[16] *La Stampa* (Turin), April 17, 1970.

access to the bureaucracy, their own newspapers (for example, *La Stampa* is under Fiat control), their own distinctive approach to public questions. As a result, there have been recent breaches in the formerly solid front presented by organized business. For example, during the period preceding the formation of a Left-Center cabinet, in the years between 1958 and 1962, *Confindustria* was hostile to the proposed new formula, but both Fiat and the Montecatini chemical combine were known to be favorably disposed.[17] In the last few years, to cite another instance, a number of observers have suggested that *Confindustria* is becoming more and more responsive to the wishes of small- and medium-sized firms, and is losing its grip on the large corporations.[18] If this is indeed the case, such a development would not be out of line with what is happening in some other industrial economies. But a trend of this nature would seriously endanger the prospects for the kind of rapprochement with organized labor that seemed to be foreshadowed by Lombardi's statement cited above. For small and medium-sized businessmen are apt to display the intransigence and obduracy of the weak and insecure.

It may seem rather facetious to refer to the Mafia as a business interest group. Yet, after all, the Mafia *is* engaged in a multitude of business activities—most of them, admittedly, of an illicit nature. While the Mafia is confined largely to Western Sicily and a small section of Calabria, it *does* have some suspiciously close ties with the Christian Democratic party in those areas. Clientele relationships involving mutual obligations have been established with a number of Christian Democratic politicians belonging to most or all of the party's factions.[19] Some Christian Democratic deputies are known to have received Mafia support. And quite a few Christian Democratic local leaders who rejected Mafia backing and resisted the spread of its influence, have been subjected to severe reprisals: campaign opposition, damage to their property, or, in a few grisly instances, murder. On the whole, however, the Mafia is only a marginal phenomenon in Italy.

Public corporations and agencies also act as institutional interest groups in the business field. One such group in agriculture, the Federation of Agricultural Consortiums (*Federconsorzi*), is pretty thoroughly controlled and manipulated by the Confederation of Direct Cultivators. In the business world, the two giant holding

[17] La Palombara, pp. 297–299.
[18] Giugni, 32–33.
[19] Michele Pantaleone, *Mafia e politica* (Torino: Einaudi, 1962), pp. 146–148, 157, 246–265.

companies—the Institute for Industrial Reconstruction (IRI) and the National Hydrocarburants Corporation (ENI)—have acted the part of enterprising lobbies, drumming up support for their demands in Parliament, seeking to acquire positions of power within the government parties, and trying to influence public opinion. This role has been played with particular aggressiveness and effectiveness by ENI, especially when it was under the leadership of Enrico Mattei in the years before 1962. Both IRI and ENI, but especially ENI, are said to have financed Fanfani's efforts in the late 1950s to restructure the Christian Democratic party and lead it toward a rapprochement with the Socialists. And ENI, like many a big private corporation, possesses its own mass-circulation newspaper, *Il Giorno* of Milan. During the last few years, moreover, ENI and IRI have acted on their own initiative to try to acquire controlling shares in Montedison, the chemical combine which had been formed as the result of a merger between Montecatini and Edison. According to some reports, the Italian cabinet and the Ministry of Industry and Commerce were *not* consulted in advance with regard to this novel venture.[20]

How influential is Italian business in affecting political decisions? Despite the vast sums of money at its disposal, despite the fact that most of Italy's "independent" press is under the ownership of large private corporations and often directly reflects their views, *Confindustria* and its component members have failed to transform the Liberals into a major party, to prevent the Christian Democratic party from moving toward the Left, and to block a number of major reforms, including the law removing IRI enterprises from *Confindustria* control on trade-union matters and the law nationalizing the electric-power industry. Lacking a capillary grass-roots organization to reach the masses, Italian business has done very poorly in Italian elections and in intraparty politics.

But in less spectacular ways, business has been very successful indeed. The permanent access enjoyed by *Confindustria* to the Ministry of Industry and Commerce has remained unchanged, despite all the vagaries of *Confindustria's* policies. By providing information and expertise to an overworked bureaucracy, *Confindustria* has been able to exercise much influence over the rule-application function. As any student of government and politics knows full well, to influence the execution of a policy is to influence the rule-making process itself. It is for this reason that La

[20] "The Old Capitalism Gives Way to the New," *The Economist*, Vol. 229, No. 6530 (October 19, 1968), 47; and "ENI Unsheathes Its Claws," *The Economist*, Vol. 229, No. 6530 (October 19, 1968), 91.

Palombara claims that *Confindustria*, with its strategy of position (within the bureaucracy as a trusted *clientela* group) is more effective than such mass *parentela* groups as Catholic Action, which must regenerate pressure on the bureaucracy with each new issue. For *parentela* groups usually do not have an easy rapport with the higher civil servants, and must rely on a possibly counterproductive display of electoral strength to bludgeon civil servants into compliance with their demands.[21]

CATHOLIC INTEREST GROUPS: THE CHURCH AND ITS SPONSORED ORGANIZATIONS

In Italy as in France, the Catholic church and various associations of Catholic laymen play a very active part in the process of articulating demands and exercising pressure on the policy-making structures of the political system and on the political parties. But political Catholicism in Italy is far more aggressive and all-pervasive than is the case beyond the Alps. We have already alluded to some of those special Italian features in Chapter Three: The Concordat has constitutional status and can only be altered by bilateral agreement between church and state or by a formal constitutional amendment; religion is part of the public educational curriculum; teachers at the primary and secondary levels are mostly devout Catholics; there is a greater proportion of practicing Catholics in Italy than in France; and the Catholic church has intervened very openly in Italian domestic politics in the years since World War II. None of these conditions prevail in France, where the separation between church and state remains much more significant.

Generally speaking, the French church after World War II has been more concerned with its religious mission of restoring the Catholic faith among the de-Christianized masses, whereas the Italian Catholic church has been obsessed with the communist danger and has therefore placed more emphasis on the need to build up the political power of the church and of its related lay organizations. Since the Christian Democratic party— the party most sympathetic to the church—has held a preponderance of power in the Italian government for almost a quarter century, the Italian Catholic church has enjoyed direct and privileged access to the national centers of decision making.

[21] La Palombara, pp. 390–393.

To non-Catholics, the Roman Catholic church has often seemed to be a monolithic and therefore vaguely menacing organization. Yet, even in the years before Pope John XXIII, the church was never really as united in purpose as outsiders believed it to be. There was a muted but nonetheless significant and continuing conflict between the so-called integralists, who regarded every aspect of Italian social life as the proper concern of the church, and the moderates, who wanted to set limits on Catholic intervention in the political sphere. Under Pope Pius XII (1939–1958), the integralists tended to gain the upper hand. Led by Cardinal Ottaviani and Cardinal Siri, the men of the so-called Vatican Pentagon, the church became aligned solidly on the side of socioeconomic conservatism. Throughout the 1950s, the parish priests and diocesan bishops urged the faithful to remain united in support of that party which best represented the interests of organized religion. Any rapprochement with Marxist forces was explicitly ruled out, especially in the late 1950s when the proposed opening to the Left began to emerge as a central theme in Italian politics. On the other hand, several attempts were made to pressure the Christian Democrats into admitting the extreme Right to the ranks of the government coalition.

Under John XXIII and Pope Paul VI, the church has adopted a more cautious line, more in harmony with the counsels of moderation. When it became evident, in the early 1960s, that the Holy See was no longer taking the lead in denouncing the opening to the Left, the pastoral letters and declarations of the bishops began to take on a less strident note, and many former denouncers of the Left-Center experiment lapsed into silence, with only a relatively few diehards maintaining a hostile stance.[22] Since massive Catholic intervention in the 1950s had failed to roll back the forces of communism, since the papacy was no longer making militant noises, and since the Christian Democratic party had made its commitment to the Left-Center coalition unmistakably clear, many bishops apparently concluded that continued intransigence might threaten Catholic unity. In line with this spreading realization of the need for a change of tack, the preelection statements of the Italian Conference of Bishops have become blander and blander since 1963. In 1968, the appeal for Catholic unity was expressed in much less hortatory tones than in the past, and seemed to allude to such matters as divorce and the preservation of church liberties, rather than support for the Christian

---

[22] Alfonso Prandi, *Chiesa e politica* (Bologna: Il Mulino, 1968), pp. 86–116.

Democratic party.[23] And in 1970, before the regional elections, the bishops' declaration spoke in rather vague terms of choices to be made by Catholics according to the dictates of an upright conscience.[24]

To be sure, the conflict within the church continues and the victories are not all on one side. Under Paul VI, there has been something of a partial retreat from the relaxed tolerance of Pope John XXIII. A few particularly progressive Catholic newspapers like the *Avvenire d'Italia* of Bologna have been suppressed; the progressive archbishop of Bologna, Cardinal Lercaro, has been removed; the "young Turks" of the Christian Association of Italian Workers (ACLI) have been admonished by the present head of the Italian Conference of Bishops, Cardinal Poma. But the situation has nevertheless undergone a fundamental change in the past decade. The Roman Catholic church seems to have definitely adopted a lower profile on the Italian political scene. Also, the church no longer purports to speak with a single voice, for much more autonomy seems to have been granted the bishops since the demise of Pius XII. And finally, the church's relentless hostility against communism and its allies, flaunted so openly since World War II, has been replaced by a less emotional, more pragmatic attitude. Partly responsible for this shift has been the doctrine enunciated by John XXIII in his encyclical, *Pacem in Terris*. In that document, Pope John warned that Catholics should not confuse false philosophical doctrines with certain historical or social movements based on those doctrines; for the latter are subject to change, and a modus vivendi might conceivably be reached with them without doing violence to Christian principles.[25]

Apart from the church itself, there are also a number of church-sponsored lay organizations controlled by the Catholic hierarchy, and a number of Catholic associations set up to pursue goals that are not strictly religious. (This last category of Catholic associations is not directly controlled by the church.) The most prominent church-sponsored organization is Catholic Action, with over 3 million members, many of whom are also members of the Christian Democratic party. Of course, it should be noted that two-thirds of these members are under the age of twenty-five and an unspecified but significant percentage are not even of voting

[23] Prandi, pp. 163–173.
[24] Giulio Picciotti, "Il voto dei cattolici," *Nord e Sud,* Vol. XVII, No. 126 (187) (June 1970), 29–31.
[25] Luigi Amirante, "Il Papa della speranza (rileggendo la 'Pacem in Terris')," *Il Mulino*, Vol. XII, No. 7 (July 1963), 628.

age.[26] Catholic Action has as its mission the education of its members in Catholic doctrine and the diffusion of Christian teachings among the people. The members of Catholic Action are encouraged to think of themselves as so many lay missionaries among the masses, although it is difficult to see why a church-controlled laymen's organization should succeed in reaching and convincing those "far ones" who have already turned their backs on the true faith, when the church itself has failed.[27] But if Catholic Action has largely failed in its goal of spreading Catholicism among the unbelievers, it *has* done much to socialize young devout Catholics and prepare the way for their recruitment into the ranks of Christian Democracy. In fact, in Central and Northern Italy (especially in the Veneto), "it is Catholic Action and not the Christian Democratic Party that is the main political and social organization of Italian Catholics."[28]

Catholic Action actually consists of a number of separate groups or branches: the Union of Men, the Union of Women, the Italian Catholic Action Youth (GIAC), the Italian Feminine Youth, the Federation of Italian Catholic University Students (FUCI), the Movement of University Graduates, and the Teachers' Movement. The president of Catholic Action and the presidents of the component branches are appointed by ecclesiastical authority—by a commission of bishops at the national level, by individual bishops at the diocesan level, and by parish priests at the local level. Thus, Catholic Action and its component branches are unlikely to be out of harmony with the winds that prevail in the Vatican.

Since Catholic Action was bound by the terms of the Concordat to pursue an "educational" rather than a political function, and since electoral campaigning and canvassing (unlike other pressure-group activities) are unequivocally political in nature, the leadership of Catholic Action took the initiative in 1948 in forming the Civic Committees to get out the vote for the Christian Democrats. In each parish, the Civic Committee was composed of the local leaders of Catholic Action, local ecclesiastical communities, the church-controlled Pontifical Assistance Project (POA), and the Catholic unions. In short, the Civic Committees were

---

[26] Thierry Godechot, *Le parti démocrate chrétien en Italie* (Paris: Librairie Générale de Droit et de Jurisprudence, 1964), pp. 152–154.

[27] Gianfranco Poggi, *Catholic Action in Italy: The Sociology of a Sponsored Organization* (Stanford, Calif.: Stanford University Press, 1967), pp. 220–230, 239–244.

[28] Giorgio Galli and Alfonso Prandi, *Patterns of Political Participation in Italy* (New Haven, Conn.: Yale University Press 1970), p. 175.

simply ad hoc campaign organizations supported by the various church-sponsored groups that backed Christian Democracy. They tended to be dominated by Catholic Action and to be responsive to the views of the leader of Catholic Action in the 1950s, the redoubtable Luigi Gedda.

Among the Catholic associations set up to pursue specialized nonreligious goals and not directly controlled by the church hierarchy are the Italian Association of Catholic Schoolteachers (AIMC), the Italian Feminine Center (CIF), the Christian Association of Italian Workers (ACLI), and the National Confederation of Direct Cultivators. These organizations do not require of their members the degree of religious commitment and missionary fervor that direct affiliation to Catholic Action and its component branches would entail. Nor have they been so directly subservient to the wishes of the hierarchy. As we have already seen, the Direct Cultivators have generally acted out the part of an economic pressure group within the Christian Democratic party; and ACLI has been a mainstay of the Left-wing trade-union faction within the selfsame party. In fact, in recent years, ACLI has indicated that it would no longer automatically support Christian Democratic candidates but would regard itself as free to pursue an autonomous policy.[29] What this means in terms of the next elections is by no means clear, since there is little likelihood that ACLI, with its million members, could form the rallying point for a second Catholic party.

La Palombara pointed out that Catholic Action, the Italian Confederation of Workers' Unions (CISL), the ACLI, and the Direct Cultivators all enjoy a *parentela* relationship with the Christian Democratic party.[30] That is to say, all claim the right to be consulted on the appointment of ministers and high civil servants and on the nomination of candidates for Parliament, as well as on relevant policy matters. Unlike *Confindustria*, these groups rely primarily on their power position *within* the dominant party rather than on their relationship with high civil servants in a given ministry. Also, while *Confindustria* relies primarily on its financial strength and expertise, these *parentela* groups rely primarily on their ability to deliver votes as the principal lever for assuring themselves of access to the policy makers. But as we have already suggested, this mustering of electoral pressure is a clumsy and possibly pyrrhic weapon when used against proud, easily offended

[29] Giulio Picciotti, "Le ACLI contro la DC," *Nord e Sud*, Vol. XVI, No. 115(176) (July 1969), 24–34.
[30] La Palombara, ch. 9.

higher civil servants. For this reason Catholic Action is attempting to infiltrate those interest groups which have an established *clientela* relationship with the bureaucracy and is also seeking to infiltrate the bureaucracy itself.

It is interesting to note that Catholic Action and the Civic Committees have greatly declined in power and influence since the late 1950s.[31] Whereas at one time Luigi Gedda and his cohorts were regarded as possible founders of a second Catholic party oriented to the Right, Catholic Action and the Civic Committees rapidly lost ground in the early 1960s when the papacy adopted a posture of rigidly limited intervention in the political sphere. It became evident, at this point, that the power and influence of Catholic Action and the Civic Committees depended upon the success of the integralist forces in the Catholic church. Without active church support, Luigi Gedda was just a paper tiger.

Those Catholic groups which had some specific economic or occupational interest to defend (ACLI, the Direct Cultivators) have, over the long run, been more successful in influencing the Christian Democratic party than has Catholic Action, which is primarily religious rather than social in its preoccupations. Trade unionists or farm leaders who enter the Christian Democratic parliamentary group seem to retain their identification with the economic interests for which they were elected to speak. Catholic Action leaders, on the other hand, once they have attained party or parliamentary office as Christian Democrats, seem to attribute more importance to their newly acquired role than to their preexisting role as leaders of Catholic Action.[32] In other words, economic interests seem to create a more specific and therefore binding tie between an individual and his organization than is the case with necessarily vague and diffuse religious interests.

CONCLUSIONS

In examining Italian interest groups, one observes some serious symptoms of political underdevelopment. Some interest groups—most notably, the trade unions—have been too much under the influence of political parties to do an adequate job of articulating the economic and social demands of their members. Artificial political divisions have seriously weakened the position of organized labor and, to some extent, of organized agriculture as well. And

---

[31] Galli and Prandi, pp. 180–182.
[32] Chasseriaud, pp. 234–237.

finally, some institutional interest groups, such as the Catholic church and some of the public corporations, have played a far too aggressive role in Italian politics.

However, there are signs of a more hopeful future, of an interest-group system better suited to a modern industrial society. Among these straws in the wind, there is, first and foremost, the growing movement in the Italian trade unions for a larger measure of autonomy from the political parties, and for a greater preoccupation with strictly trade-union objectives. Also there is a tendency toward less intransigence on the part of organized business, a tendency which should, in turn, spur moderating and modernizing trends in the labor movement. Finally, there is the partial withdrawal of the church from the political arena, to the extent of intervening only when religious interests are clearly at stake. And some of the Catholic organizations have begun to show a willingness to steer their own course without waiting for the latest communication from the Vatican.

All this, of course, does not foreshadow an "Americanization" of Italian politics. Rather, what appears to be developing is a pattern of pressure groups that will still have ties with political parties but will maintain a clearer separation of functions and goals. Also, pressure groups may begin recruiting and keeping their own leadership cadres, rather than relying on middle-class party activists. This possibility applies particularly to the trade unions. To the extent that they succeed in drawing their future elites from the workbench rather than the lecture hall, a healthy atmosphere of pragmatism will begin pervading what has been an unduly politicized labor movement. A more realistic labor movement may be able to acquire the economic power to build that strong democratic socialist mass movement which Italy so sorely needs. But perhaps the foundations are excessively fragile for such an elaborate structure. For the time being, suffice it to say that pressure groups are beginning to act more like pressure groups on the Italian scene, and that this trend bodes well for the future.

SEVEN
THE UNEASY BALANCE
Policy-making roles and structures

In contrast to the French Fifth Republic, where the constitutional and political domains bow to executive supremacy, the Italian political system is characterized by an uneasy and ever-shifting equilibrium between executive and legislative policy-making structures. This institutional stand-off may, in turn, be attributed partly to the Constitution, which fails to give the executive adequate tools for achieving dominance over Parliament, and partly to the party system, which fails to express a clear-cut and cohesive majority.

**THE ITALIAN EXECUTIVE:
AN ILLUSORY IMAGE OF STRENGTH**

Earlier in this book, we spoke of the absence, in the Italian political tradition, of the kind of individualist laissez-faire Radicalism typified by the French political philosopher Alain. Italian republicanism fails to echo the antiexecutive tones of French Radicalism. The almost obsessive fear of the strong leader, the potential man on horseback, that pervades the French representative tradition is missing in Italian politics. In fact, we find a greater tolerance and acceptance of the adventurous leader, not only in Italian politics, but also in Italian economic life. Enrico Mattei, the aggressive former head of the National Hydrocarbunts Corporation (ENI), had no counterpart in the French nationalized industries, or in the French private industrial sector, for that matter.

While most French cabinets during the Third and Fourth Republics were presided over by a succession of unspectacular premiers, whose names do not come readily to mind, Italian political history since 1870 seems to have been marked by a series of strong chief executives, who managed to maintain a certain ascendancy over Parliament. Agostino Depretis, Francesco Crispi, Giovanni Giolitti, each one an activist prime minister, are identified by historians as leading protagonists of a decade or more of Italian parliamentary history in the years before Fascist control. After the Liberation, the years 1946–1966 were characterized by the preponderant influence of three successive Christian Democratic leaders: Alcide De Gasperi, Amintore Fanfani, and Aldo Moro. Of course, lesser figures occasionally headed the cabinet during these periods. But there was a far more structured political situation than was the case in France in the years 1875–1940 and 1946–1958, when parliamentary politics so often appeared to be a contest among semi-anonymous bit players.

Yet, it must be pointed out that the Italian image of the strong executive is, to some degree, an illusory one. Just as Mussolini, for all his bombast, was a rather ineffectual dictator who never really succeeded in mobilizing the country for total war, men like De Gasperi, Fanfani, and Moro have been, in part, virtual prisoners of the situation they appeared to dominate. They could remain at the helm of their party organization and, on occasion, of the cabinet only by maintaining a precarious balance among the conflicting demands of the various factions and interest groups whose support they needed. The frequent price of their continued tenure of office was immobilism, although their administrations were by no means devoid of notable achievements. Thus, policy decisions would often proceed at a snail's pace, while the strong leader would emit a steady stream of ambivalent slogans and formulas, designed to placate the impatient and reassure the suspicious. Even more than in other democracies, symbolic output was a convenient substitute for policy output.

THE PRESIDENT OF THE ITALIAN REPUBLIC

While the hegemonic French president towers over his political system, the president of Italy tends to resemble, in most respects, the classic ceremonial chief of state of a parliamentary system. He exercises a number of formal executive powers: the promulgation of laws, the ratification of treaties, the making of executive appointments, the command of the armed forces. But in all these spheres, his decisions are countersigned, and in reality originated, by a member of the cabinet. Like other ceremonial chief executives, he is expected to greet visiting dignitaries, dedicate major public projects, visit calamity-stricken areas in order to comfort the populace, and pay state visits to foreign sovereigns.

Is the president of Italy nothing more than a figurehead, then, a constitutional monarch on the British model? Not exactly. True, his powers are largely ceremonial, but he has *some* functions that provide him with the means of playing a significant role in Italian politics. And even his ceremonial powers have lent themselves to a somewhat broader interpretation than would be the case for a Northern European king. For example, there is nothing to prevent a strong ambitious president from speaking out freely during a foreign state visit, or from holding a press conference and discussing current issues, or from introducing controversial material into one of his public addresses. President Gronchi, for instance, acted as if he were some kind of roving ambassador plenipotentiary during his term of office (1955–1962) and did not, as a rule, bother to clear his far-ranging and frequently embarrassing statements with the government in Rome.[1]

Among the powers of the president is the right to send messages to Parliament. The first two presidents of the Italian republic, Luigi Einaudi and Giovanni Gronchi, chose to appear personally before Parliament to deliver their messages, thus establishing a constitutional custom.[2] By addressing Parliament in person, the president can attract a great deal of public attention and can utilize the occasion to appeal to the Italian people over the heads of their elected representatives. For, unlike the British monarch, the Italian president is not bound by any requirement or expectation that he simply serve as spokesman for the cabinet. For instance, the inaugural address of President Gronchi in 1955 urged a fairer distribution of the national income, demanded that the working class be brought into the political system by seeking its support and enlisting its participation, and sharply criticized the privileged status of the big monopolies.

The president also possesses the power of suspensive veto.

---

[1] Domenico Bartoli, *Da Vittorio Emanuele a Gronchi* (Milano: Longanesi, 1961), pp. 169–176, 179–187.
[2] John Clarke Adams and Paolo Barile, *The Government of Republican Italy* (2nd ed.; Boston: Houghton Mifflin, 1966), pp. 81–82.

That is to say, he may return a bill to Parliament for reconsideration, along with a message stating his reasons for doing so. The bill may then be passed over his veto by a simple majority of those voting in each chamber. But in a multiparty, multifactional Parliament, where the passage of a bill is a slow, cumbersome, and precarious proceeding, a suspensive veto may actually spell the defeat of a strongly contested measure. Einaudi, who was not a terribly aggressive president, used the power on four occasions during his seven-year term; the activist Gronchi resorted to the veto only three times; and Antonio Segni wielded no less than seven vetoes during the scanty two years he served as president before being incapacitated by a stroke.[3] There does not seem to be any positive correlation between the use of the suspensive veto and presidential activism; and it should be added that this device has never been employed to block legislation of major political significance.

Like many other parliamentary heads of state, the president is assigned the function of appointing the prime minister and, on the latter's proposal, the members of the cabinet. And since Italy, not only has a multiparty system, but also has a faction-ridden dominant party, this function is by no means a perfunctory one. During a cabinet crisis, the president is not faced with a clearly designated course of action, as is the British monarch who simply appoints the leader of the majority party to be prime minister. First of all, the Christian Democrats usually lack a working majority in Parliament and must rely on the backing of a coalition of parties. Secondly, moreover, this dominant party normally cannot boast a single recognized leader who stands out unquestionably as a potential prime minister. The secretary of the Christian Democratic party is leader of the extraparliamentary party organization, of course; but he is regarded as only one of a sizable number of aspiring standard-bearers.

Given this relatively chaotic situation within the dominant party, and given the lack of a clear majority for any one party, the president exercises a great deal of influence during the complex negotiations that must precede the formation of a new cabinet. And at this point, an ambitious president, bent on expanding his power, may promote a candidate of his own. President Gronchi is said to have regarded Fernando Tambroni as a useful tool, a man who could be counted on to back the president's hand. It was largely as a result of Gronchi's insistence—coupled, to be sure, with the temporary absence of other viable alternatives—that

[3] Costantino Mortati, *Istituzioni di diritto pubblico*, Vol. II (Padova: CEDAM, 1967), p. 652.

Tambroni's "monocolor" (all-Christian Democratic) cabinet emerged as an abortive and nearly tragic solution to the critical deadlock of the spring of 1960. In like manner, President Gronchi would occasionally treat his formal power of appointment as more than an empty ritual, and would give strong and insistent advice to the prime minister regarding the appointment of a cabinet minister or the head of some other public agency. Such Gronchi protégés as Tambroni and Folchi relied on presidential support during most of their long careers in the cabinet.

Another weapon in the president's hands is the power of dissolution. After having heard the presidents of the two chambers, he may dissolve either the Chamber of Deputies, or the Senate, or both houses together. He may not, however, use his power of dissolution during the last six months of his seven-year term: This period is known in Italy as the "blank semester." Also, there is considerable uncertainty as to whether or not the president can dissolve Parliament without first obtaining the countersignature of the prime minister. Article 89 of the Italian Constitution baldly states that "no act of the President is valid unless countersigned by the Minister proposing it," and that acts having the force of law also need the additional countersignature of the prime minister. Does this countersignature provision apply to dissolution? The authorities differ, and precedents also fail to give a clear verdict. On the one hand, the only two instances of dissolution since 1948—the dissolution of the Senate in 1953 and again in 1958—were evidently undertaken at the request of the prime minister. On the other hand, in 1961, a number of democratic politicians openly hinted that a cabinet crisis should be avoided until the last six months of Gronchi's presidential term, when he would no longer be able to dissolve Parliament. Evidently, they feared that the president *might* try to dissolve Parliament without the consent of the prime minister, else why these exhortations not to rock the boat until the "blank semester" should begin?

But even if the requirement of ministerial countersignature *should* be binding on the president in this type of situation, an unscrupulous president could conceivably resolve a cabinet crisis by appointing one of his own supporters as prime minister and then immediately dissolving Parliament with the aid of the countersignature of the newly appointed prime minister.[4] Such an ac-

---

[4] There is some disagreement as to whether this could actually be done. See, for instance, Vezio Crisafulli, "Aspetti problematici del sistema parlamentare vigente in Italia," in *Studi in onore di Emilio Crosa*, Vol. I (Milano: Giuffré, 1960), pp. 621–623.

tion would be of dubious constitutionality; but by 1961, many Italian political leaders had developed a basic distrust of Gronchi's intentions. For the president had supported Tambroni; and under Tambroni, Italy had appeared to be tottering on the brink of a new Right-wing dictatorship.

Among the additional powers of the president are the power to nominate five senators for life and five judges out of the fifteen who sit on the Constitutional Court. Also, he has the right to refuse to authorize the presentation of government bills to Parliament or the issuance of executive decrees. On both of these scores —nonexecutive nominations and authorization—it is recognized that the president has the independent power to act. President Einaudi apparently made occasional use of his power to refuse authorization for the introduction of a government bill, and thus set a precedent. And President Gronchi won a long struggle to establish his right to make his own selection of judges for appointment to the Constitutional Court, rather than simply ratify a preemptive choice by the countersigning minister.[5]

The principal check on the president's use of his powers is the requirement of ministerial countersignature. Yet, there is considerable disagreement as to just how much of a limitation countersignature represents. For instance, the president hardly needs the countersignature of a minister when he holds a press conference or addresses some public gathering; and his messages to Parliament, while requiring countersignature, are not likely to be subjected to cabinet censorship. Also, in several types of cases countersignature is automatically forthcoming because the responsibility for action is primarily presidential—for example, in the president's suspensive veto, his nomination of life senators and Constitutional Court judges, and his appointment of a prime minister. But in the case of most of the president's formal powers— signing laws and decrees, making executive appointments, commanding the armed forces—countersignature could be withheld, for these powers are really vested in the cabinet.[6]

The other major restraint on the president's use of his powers is impeachment for high treason or for offenses against the Constitution. Impeachment may be accomplished by an absolute majority of a joint session of Parliament. In other words, there is no mechanism for removing a president on purely political grounds, no provision for a vote of no confidence. This is understandable; for, like ceremonial chief executives in other parliamentary sys-

[5] On these additional presidential powers, see Adams and Barile, pp. 78–81.
[6] Bartoli, pp. 216–222.

tems, the president serves for a fixed term of office (seven years) and is not politically responsible for his acts.

As we can see, the Italian president's location along a spectrum of ceremonial heads of state would lie somewhere between the overweening power of the president of France and the honorific impotence of some Northern European monarchs. The founding fathers in the Italian Constituent Assembly of 1946–1948 obviously did not visualize the president as a mere figurehead. But on the other hand, neither did they accept the idea that the president should be a kind of popular tribune, speaking for the nation outside of Parliament, indicating certain goals and orientations for the cabinet and the Parliament to pursue—a thesis which Gronchi was later to propound. Rather, the men of the Constituent Assembly saw the president as a mediator between the various branches of government, a guardian of the Constitution, and a holder of the balance.[7] Yet, it is very hard to confine the president to this kind of role: He is continually tempted to overstep the boundaries.

Why this temptation? Partly, we may blame the vagueness of some of the constitutional definitions of presidential powers. Then, too, the lengthy seven-year term of the president, in a political system where cabinets rarely endure for more than a year, shares some of the responsibility. Also, the fact that the president is elected, albeit indirectly, should not be overlooked. For, generally speaking, among ceremonial chiefs of state in Western democracies, only hereditary monarchs can be compelled to remain politically neutral on all issues.

On the other hand, the system by which a president is elected does not provide an adequate mandate for a Gronchi-type president. For the president is not elected by popular vote. He is elected by a so-called Electoral Assembly composed of the members of the Chamber of Deputies (630 in 1964), the members of the Senate (320 in 1964), a delegate from Val d'Aosta, and 3 delegates from each region (12 delegates in 1964, representing the 4 special regions established at that juncture). Election is by secret ballot. On the first three ballots, a two-thirds majority of the members of the Electoral Assembly is necessary to elect a president; from the fourth ballot on, an absolute majority suffices.

The secret balloting leads to a grave breakdown in party discipline, as minority factions in each party express their rancor against the party leadership by voting against their party's official candidate. This covert opposition has resulted, on several occa-

[7] Massimo Riva, "Il presidente della Repubblica in Italia: I lavori della Costituente," *Comunità*, Vol. XXI, No. 148–149 (December 1967), 13–31.

sions, in the defeat of the official nominee of the Christian Democratic party. In fact, only one of the last four presidential elections has been won by the formally designated candidate of Christian Democracy: Antonio Segni in 1962. The other three presidents—Luigi Einaudi, a Liberal economist, in 1948; Giovanni Gronchi, leader of an opposition faction in the Christian Democratic party, in 1955; and Giuseppe Saragat, leader of the Social Democratic party, in 1964—were all elected against the initial opposition of a majority of the Christian Democratic delegates. All three men needed some support from either the extreme Left or the extreme Right, or both, in order to be elected. Moreover, their elections came about only after a long, confusing, and depressing series of ballots, which did much to lower the prestige of the presidency in the eyes of public opinion. Furthermore, the partly extremist basis of their support created a certain friction between the president (who might well feel that he represents a broader and more heterogeneous constituency) and the prime minister.

This system of election, with its clandestine procedures and resulting breakdowns in party discipline, frequently turns out factional bosses capable of unpredictable adventures, rather than men of broad vistas and broker-type talents. Luigi Einaudi was a safe enough president, though strongly committed to a given economic viewpoint. Giuseppe Saragat, long-established leader of Italian Social Democracy and a man of firmly democratic outlook, was a lucky accident. However, Giovanni Gronchi was the disgruntled and frustrated leader of an opposition faction in the Christian Democratic party. And Antonio Segni, a leading spokesman of the conservative *Dorotei* faction in the Christian Democratic party, tended to view the forces of the moderate Left with signal intolerance. He is suspected by some publicists of possibly having encouraged General De Lorenzo, former head of the Italian counterintelligence agency, *Sifar*, and former commandant of the *Carabinieri* (one of Italy's most prestigious police corps) to prepare plans for a possible coup.[8]

It is because of the obvious danger of having the position of chief of state fall into the hands of a short-sighted and unscrupulous factional chieftain that some Italians have advocated the abolition of the secret ballot in presidential elections, in order that parties may do a more effective job of filtering out undesirables. But even if this problem should be resolved, a graver question will

[8] Gigi Ghirotti, "Appunti per una storia di un' estate pericolosa (I): un uomo del re e i segreti della Repubblica," *Comunità*, Vol. XXII, No. 151 (March–April 1968), 42–48.

remain: Given the prevailing uncertainty regarding the actual scope of presidential powers, can any president, however virtuous and well-meaning, be confined to the delicate mediating role envisioned by the founding fathers? Is there not an almost irresistible tendency for any Italian president to be impelled, by the length of his tenure and the political instability he confronts, to attempt to make his mark on political events? And might this tendency not lead eventually in the direction of a French-type or American-type president, with all the dangers such a development might entail?

THE PRIME MINISTER AND THE CABINET

The Italian Council of Ministers (hereafter referred to as the cabinet) and the president of the Council of Ministers (hereafter referred to as the prime minister) constitute the political wing of Italy's dual executive. While the president of Italy differs in a number of significant ways from other ceremonial heads of state in Western Europe, the prime minister and his cabinet are much more in line with the classic model of the political chief executive in a continental European parliamentary system. All the familiar earmarks are there: the selection of the prime minister by the ceremonial chief of state after a lengthy round of consultations; the appointment of a cabinet, based on the recommendations of the newly designated prime minister; and the multiparty composition of the cabinet, all of whose members are normally also members of Parliament. Nevertheless, there are certain features of the Italian cabinet that deserve special mention.

We might begin by citing the rigid and heterogeneous composition of the cabinet. While the British cabinet varies in size, and consists of only certain selected ministers, the Italian cabinet includes all the ministers, and the ministers-without-portfolio as well. Consequently, it is somewhat larger than the British cabinet and comprises at least twenty-five members (not counting the under-secretaries, who are over forty in number but who do not sit in on cabinet meetings). The obvious reason for the unwieldy size of the Italian cabinet also furnishes an explanation for its heterogeneity. Since Italy has a multiparty system, and since there are warring factions within each party, the cabinet must be so constituted as to reflect the diverse elements that temporarily support the prime minister: It must, in other words, fulfill a representative function. Not only parties, but also factions, must be placated. Failure to do so may result in the melting away of what looks on the surface like a firm majority. In fact, many cabinet crises have occurred, not as the result of a quarrel *among* the several parties represented in the cabinet, but as the outgrowth of a factional conflict *within* one of those parties.

Since the Italian cabinet is multiparty and multifactional, it can hardly be expected to perform as a united team. In other words, it ranks low with regard to solidarity and cohesion. Its members regard each other as future political opponents. Even the fact that most of the members of the Italian cabinet are Christian Democrats does not serve to avert discord. After all, a Left-wing Christian Democrat has much more in common with a Socialist than with a Right-wing Christian Democrat. And by the same token, a Right-wing Christian Democrat may feel a closer kinship with the Liberals than with his own party colleagues of more progressive leanings. Under the circumstances, it is hardly surprising that members of the Italian cabinet may fail to consult each other sufficiently, may publicly disagree with each other's policies, and may leak information about what took place at a cabinet meeting.[9]

The Italian cabinet is also ill-equipped to deal with problems in a coordinated fashion. First of all, financial policy is not entrusted to one ministry but to three: the Ministry of Finance, responsible for collecting revenues; the Ministry of the Treasury, which handles the spending of state funds and the management of the public debt; and the Ministry of the Budget and Economic Planning, which supposedly should coordinate the activities of the Finance and Treasury ministries and supervise the carrying out of the cabinet's economic objectives.[10] The system does not work as intended, however. To begin with, there is much overlapping of functions among these three financial ministries. Then, too, it is Treasury, and not Budget, which controls the State General Accounting Office and its dependent central accounting offices located in the various ministries. It is to be suggested, therefore, that while the Ministry of the Budget may have the responsibility for coordinating economic and financial policy, it is the Ministry of the Treasury that has the tools to control ministerial spending. Finally, it has long been evident that the minister of the treasury enjoys more prestige and influence than the other two financial ministers. Before Emilio Colombo became prime minister in Au-

---

[9] Examples are cited in Norman Kogan, *A Political History of Postwar Italy* (New York: Praeger, 1966), pp. 199–200.

[10] Vittorio Barbati, "Dall' Esecutivo all' Operativo," *Nord e Sud*, Vol. XVII, No. 124(185) (April 1970), 86–87, and Adams and Barile, pp. 92–94.

gust 1970, he had been minister of the treasury for a number of years and had long been regarded as the "gray eminence" behind Italian economic policy. It was Colombo who, in response to the recession of 1963–1965, suddenly released state funds for a great number of hitherto neglected projects. These funds had long before been appropriated by Parliament but their disbursement had either been delayed or temporarily diverted to other purposes by the Ministry of the Treasury.[11]

In other respects, too, the Italian cabinet falls short of the mark with regard to the coordination of policy. The Office of the Prime Minister (formally designated as the Presidency of the Council) simply houses a conglomeration of varied offices and services, such as the Central Statistical Institute and the Fund for the South. It does not, as presently constituted and staffed, provide the prime minister with the help he would need to coordinate the activities of the entire executive branch. Moreover, a bill that would provide for the reorganization and streamlining of the prime minister's Office has been stalled for many years, apparently because of lack of support, not merely in Parliament, but also and especially in the cabinet itself.[12]

The fact is that cabinet members resent and resist any attempt by the prime minister to encroach on what they regard as their autonomous spheres of influence. It is, in most cases, not the prime minister to whom they really owe their appointment: Parties and factions often stipulate the names of cabinet appointees as a precondition for supporting a given cabinet. Given the conditions surrounding their appointment, they hardly need to worry about removal from office. Shielded as they are against possible reprisals by a hapless prime minister, they operate with a high degree of independence and may ignore the prime minister's circulated memoranda with impunity. Small wonder that some constitutional scholars have compared them to feudal lords!

Since the Office of the Prime Minister is not equipped as an organ of policy coordination, less effective methods must be used to encourage some measure of cooperation among ministers. The device of the minister-without-portfolio is employed to keep certain areas of policy and certain procedural problems from falling under the control of one of the quasi-autonomous ministries. There are about six of these ministers-without-portfolio, one re-

---

[11] Ferruccio Parri, "Problemi di riforma del nostra parlamento," in Leopoldo Piccardi, Norberto Bobbio, Ferruccio Parri, *La sinistra davanti alla crisi del parlamento* (Milano: Giuffré, 1967), pp. 99–100.
[12] Mortati, Vol. I, pp. 525–526.

sponsible for relations with Parliament, one charged with supervising the Fund for the South, one assigned to the seemingly hopeless task of reforming the bureaucracy, and so on. A second technique for policy coordination is the setting up of cabinet committees. Among the most prominent of such committees are the Interministerial Committee for Credit, the Interministerial Committee for State Holdings, the Interministerial Committee on Prices, the Interministerial Committee for the Fund for the South, and the Interministerial Committee for Economic Planning. By virtue of his membership on most of these bodies, the prime minister is able to make up, to some degree, for the weakness of his office. In short, the cabinet committees *do* provide the prime minister with a means of counteracting ministerial autonomy somewhat.

The personnel of the cabinet is almost invariably made up of members of the two houses of Parliament. The ministers *do* differ from their fellow-MP's in some significant respects, however. They are generally far superior to back-benchers in culture and manners: While most senators and deputies are regarded by some observers as men of modest breeding and banal behavior, prominent leaders like Moro, Saragat, and La Malfa are erudite, mentally alert, and well-read individuals.[13] Also, as we might expect, cabinet members are classed above ordinary members of Parliament with regard to social origin. As compared to ordinary members of the Chamber of Deputies, a much higher percentage of the cumulative membership of Italian cabinets over the past twenty years has been composed of men and women of the upper middle class.[14] But progress is being made toward a greater circulation of elites. For example, such upper-class categories as large landowners, nobles, high-ranking military men, and industrialists have all but vanished from the cabinet. Many of the upper-middle-class cabinet members of the present day have middle-class or lower-middle-class parents. So, access to top decision-making posts is by no means closed off in contemporary Italy: Bright young men of relatively modest origins may conceivably make the grade, despite the formidable character of the obstacles they must overcome.

The Italian cabinet has not enjoyed a secure or stable existence. Since World War II, in fact, the average life of a cabinet has

---

[13] Marco Cesarini Sforza, *L'uomo politico* (Firenze: Vallecchi, 1963), pp. 167–169, 175–178, 200–201, 228–229.

[14] L. Lotti, "Il parlamento italiano 1909–1963, raffronto storico," in Giovanni Sartori, ed., *Il parlamento italiano 1946–1963* (Napoli: Edizioni Scientifiche Italiane, 1963), pp. 197–200; and Giovanni Sartori, "Dove va il parlamento?" in Sartori, ed., pp. 340–346. Other contributors to Sartori's volume are A. Prediери and S. Somogyi.

been slightly less than a year. And yet the Constitution contains a provision designed to safeguard the survival of the cabinet. The cabinet, which is responsible to both houses of Parliament, is not obliged to resign unless a motion of lack of confidence has been signed by at least one-tenth of the members of one of the two chambers and, three days or more after its presentation, has been adopted by a majority of those voting. It is explicitly stated that an opposing vote on a cabinet motion in one of the two chambers does not, by itself, obligate the cabinet to resign.

However, while the cabinet is not *obliged* to resign except in the case of the specific procedure outlined above, there is no way to *prevent* it from resigning voluntarily if it so desires. Most cabinet crises have not been precipitated by an explicit vote of no confidence in Parliament. Rather they have been provoked by a decision of a party parliamentary group *in* Parliament or by a decision of a party secretary or party directorate *outside* of Parliament, or by the decision of a party faction. Any one of these events may lead a prime minister to foresee the inevitable and offer the resignation of his cabinet. Thus, in 1960, Tambroni was forced to resign because two Christian Democratic factions let him know they could no longer support him. Or then again, a cabinet may resign because of an adverse vote on a cabinet bill, even if this adverse vote is the result of a defection by "snipers" (*franchi tiratori*) on a secret ballot.[15] So, in a multiparty, multifactional system, it takes more than a few constitutional provisions to ensure cabinet stability.

However, the instability of the Italian cabinet is a bit deceptive. Since the main opposition party is excluded from consideration as a possible alternative government, the only real alternative is a slight shifting of the balance of power within the prosystem majority. The Christian Democrats *must* form part of any majority coalition, in order for that coalition to have sufficient votes to survive in Parliament. The only questions, then, have been: Which allies, if any, is the Christian Democratic party to select? What factions *within* the Christian Democratic party are to get the choice cabinet posts? Since 1947, there have been relatively few cabinet formulas available: a Center coalition (Christian Democrats, Social Democrats, Republicans, and Liberals—prevalent until 1956); an all-Christian Democratic "monocolor" cabinet relying on various sources of support ranging across the entire political spectrum (employed off and on, when other solutions

---

[15] "Snipers" are members of Parliament who take advantage of a secret ballot to break party discipline and vote contrary to the instructions of their party leaders.

fail, ever since 1956); a Right-Center coalition (Christian Democrats, Liberals, Monarchists, and possibly Neo-Fascists—excluded as a possible alternative ever since the resignation of Tambroni in 1960); and the present Left-Center coalition (Christian Democrats, Socialists, Social Democrats, and Republicans—the predominant formula ever since 1962). With so few formulas to choose from, cabinet crises often bring about only marginal changes. Thus, for example, the Colombo cabinet of 1970 was remarkably similar to the Rumor cabinet that preceded it.

We have not devoted much space to the powers and functions of the Italian cabinet. This is because the Italian cabinet, being similar to cabinets in other multiparty parliamentary systems, poses no major constitutional problems. It is the cabinet that is responsible, not only for applying the rules (that is, enforcing the laws), but also for proposing a program of suggested policies and getting that program enacted by Parliament in the form of statutes. In short, the Italian cabinet plays a major role in rule making as well as rule application.

Unlike the French cabinet, the Italian cabinet has no residual or reserved powers to govern by decree in fields from which Parliament is actually excluded. Rather, it can issue decrees under two types of conditions. "Legislative decrees" may be enacted if Parliament first passes an enabling act, with a time limit attached, authorizing the cabinet to legislate on a clearly specified subject matter under well-delineated guidelines. Then, too, the cabinet may, in case of emergency, deal with the situation by means of "decree laws," which expire within sixty days of their publication unless enacted into statutory law by Parliament. The cabinet has not been compelled thus far to resort to decree laws, but has utilized the device of the legislative decree. Here, it has sometimes run afoul of the courts: On a number of occasions, the Constitutional Court has found that a legislative decree violated the terms of the parliamentary delegation of power.[16] However, one important rule-making power is not limited by the Constitution: the power of the cabinet and of individual ministries to issue "regulations" without prior authorization by Parliament. Through the use of these administrative orders, which are in practice difficult to distinguish from legislative decrees except with regard to their origin and nomenclature, the cabinet is steadily increasing its legislative power.[17]

---

[16] Paolo Barile, "Governo e parlamento," in Direzione PSI-PSDI Unificati-Sezione per la Riforma dello Stato, *Stato moderno e riforma del parlamento* (Roma: Direzione PSI-PSDI Unificati, 1967), p. 42.

[17] Adams and Barile, p. 89; and Mortati, Vol. II, pp. 665–685.

The cabinet, then, is the political executive organ (as opposed to the ceremonial presidency), and the prime minister who presides over its meetings is the constitutionally recognized head of government. Yet, the political weakness of both the prime minister and his cabinet has emerged only too clearly from the foregoing discussion. It is because of this weakness and the resulting cabinet instability that the danger of presidential encroachment arises. For the president, with his seven-year term, projects a more lasting (and hence more recognizable and reassuring) image. In this connection, it may or may not be significant that, in 1956, only 14 percent of a cross-section of the Italian people did not know the name of the president of Italy, whereas in 1959, fully 39 percent of a similar sample could not identify their prime minister.[18] When cognition is so low, are the voters likely to care who is at the helm?

THE ITALIAN PARLIAMENT

In discussing the image of the Italian Parliament, we must concentrate on two aspects of the problem: (1) the ways in which the Italian public perceives its Parliament, and (2) the views that members of Parliament entertain regarding themselves and their roles. Among the public at large, Parliament enjoys a very poor image indeed. There appears to be a fairly widespread belief in parliamentary corruption, a belief that is closely related to the prevailing view that politics itself is a dirty business. The late Piero Calamandrei, a noted legal scholar and member of the Chamber of Deputies, recounts how, during a journey by railroad, he overheard one of the men in his train compartment refer to all deputies as criminals and thieves. On being asked whether he had any proof of this charge, the man replied, " 'Who needs proof? It's enough to read the newspapers!' "[19] In fact, the press does much to nurture the prejudice of the Italian middle classes against their elected representatives. This prejudice goes back to the years of foreign domination and is simply another dimension of the low level of social trust that exists among Italians. If a man cannot trust his neighbor, how can he be expected to trust his elected representative?

---

[18] Pierpaolo Luzzatto-Fegiz, *Il volto sconosciuto dell' Italia 1956–1965* (2nd series; Milano: Giuffré, 1966), pp. 552, 867, 877.
[19] Piero Calamandrei *Scritti e discorsi politici*, Vol. I (Firenze: La Nuova Italia, 1966), pp. 322–323.

Even more intriguing, however, is the question of how the members of Parliament envision their roles; for, in democracies as in dictatorships, elite attitudes are likely to cast more light on the making of public policy than do the vague instinctive reactions of the nonparticipating masses. On this score, however, there is a dearth of helpful data. Sartori suggests that most legislators are probably so swamped with work that they have neither the time nor the patience to think in general terms about their parliamentary roles.[20] But Sartori *does* touch on role perceptions, to some degree, when he claims that legislative "outsiders" (that is, legislators who are unaware of the pressures being exerted by interest groups) are more numerous than legislative "facilitators" of interest-group demands, and than legislative "resistors," who seek to block any concessions to those demands.[21] Another study, dealing with the personality structures of Italian deputies, concludes that Right-wing deputies are more dogmatic than Left-wing deputies and that Italian professional politicians are more dogmatic than those Italian politicians who continue to depend primarily on nonpolitical careers for their livelihood.[22] Still another approach examines the abstract and ideological character of parliamentary debate in Italy, and infers from this datum that many legislators must regard Parliament as a kind of preelection forum rather than a major rule-making organ.[23] Unfortunately, these studies add up to considerably less than an adequate treatment of legislative role perceptions.

In its structure, the Italian Parliament differs in some significant ways from parliamentary bodies in most other Western European democracies. First of all, it is truly bicameral. The upper house, the Senate (with 320 members, of whom 5 are lifetime appointees), is *legally* just as powerful as the 630-member Chamber of Deputies, even though the Chamber of Deputies *does* seem to enjoy somewhat greater political prestige. To cite the most obvious earmarks of equality, a bill *must* be passed by both chambers in order to become law, and the cabinet is equally responsible to both chambers. This *legal* equality of the two chambers is

---

[20] Sartori, pp. 347–350.
[21] Giovanni Sartori, "La sociologia del parlamento," *Studi Politici*, Vol. 8 (April 1961), 151, 153–155, quoted in Joseph La Palombara, *Interest Groups in Italian Politics* (Princeton, N.J.: Princeton University Press, 1964), pp. 107–108.
[22] Gordon J. Di Renzo, *Personality, Power and Politics: A Social Psychological Analysis of the Italian Deputy and His Parliamentary System* (Notre Dame, Ind.: University of Notre Dame Press 1967), pp. 20–21, 92–117, 119–168.
[23] Giorgio Galli, *Il bipartitismo imperfetto* (Bologna: Il Mulino, 1966), pp. 299–302.

reinforced by their modes of election; the Italian Senate, like the Chamber of Deputies, is elected by popular vote and cannot, therefore, be regarded as an unrepresentative, and hence properly subordinate, chamber of revision (as had been the case with the appointed Italian Senate of pre-1922 vintage).

There are only two major differences between the electorates that vote for the two legislative chambers. First of all, there is a slight age disparity: the minimum voting age for senatorial elections is twenty-five, whereas for the election of deputies it is twenty-one. Secondly, deputies are elected from multimember circumscriptions, each consisting of several provinces and each represented in the Chamber of Deputies in proportion to its population. Senators, on the other hand, are elected from the regions. Each region is entitled to 1 senator per 200,000 population. However, no region is to have less than 6 senators, with the exception of Val d'Aosta (1 senator), Molise (2 senators), and Friuli-Venezia Giulia (3 senators). This formula results in the slight overrepresentation of several of the smaller regions. All things considered, these differences between the two electorates can hardly be said to constitute a very significant contrast. The Italian Senate, then, has every right to claim that it, too, speaks for Italian public opinion.

However, in another sense, Italian election legislation weakens bicameralism and tends to nullify the separate identity of the upper house. For as we have noted in Chapter Five, the electoral systems by which the two chambers are chosen are similar enough to insure that the two houses will not differ very sharply in their political makeup. In actual practice, both electoral systems are based on proportional representation, and consequently the political alignment and the respective strength of the various parties in the Senate tend to resemble the patterns that prevail in the Chamber of Deputies.

Yet the Constituent Assembly in 1946–1947 had taken one major precaution designed to prevent the Senate from being a carbon copy of the Chamber of Deputies. The Constitution (Article 60) provided that the Senate was to have a six-year term as compared to only five years for the Chamber of Deputies. Thus, if the two chambers did not represent significantly different electorates, they might at least be expected to represent the same electorate in different moods. But things did not work out as the founding fathers had anticipated. The Christian Democrats, facing a restive electorate and a major Communist threat, had no intention of putting up with the turmoil and uncertainty of staggered elections. At first, Article 60 was virtually nullified by dissolving the Senate at the same time as the Chamber of Deputies, as the president had a perfect right to do under Article 88. This was done in 1953 and in 1958. Finally, in 1963, the Constitution was amended to establish a five-year term for senators, thus codifying the existing practice. When two houses are as similar in composition as the Italian Chamber of Deputies and the Italian Senate, bicameralism becomes simply a method of delaying the passage of legislation, rather than giving special representation and protection to some designated minority interest.

The peculiar character of Italian bicameralism differentiates the Italian Parliament from the classic Western European parliamentary model and actually bears a certain similarity to the American pattern. But, if we consider the powers exercised by the Italian Parliament as a whole, we find that the Italian Parliament is much more in line with the Western European parliamentary systems (excluding France, which possesses a hybrid system with presidential and parliamentary features). Unlike France, the Italian Parliament is *not* limited to a list of specifically enumerated law-making powers. Rather, it can pass any law that does not violate some provision of the Constitution. Nor are its internal procedures laid out in exhaustive detail as is the case with the Constitution of the Fifth French Republic; like most Western European parliaments, it is relatively free to manage its own housekeeping functions and draw up its own rules with a minimum of external interference.

Its powers are, for the most part, conventional: the passage of laws, the delegation of rule-making power to the cabinet, the ratification of treaties, the approval of the budget, and the conduct of investigations. In addition, Parliament meets in joint session to elect the president of Italy, to impeach the president for high treason or offenses against the Constitution, to impeach cabinet members for crimes committed in the exercise of their functions, to elect one-third of the twenty-one elected members of the Superior Council of the Judiciary, to elect one-third of the members of the Constitutional Court, and to elect sixteen additional judges to serve on the Constitutional Court in the event the president is impeached.

Parliament may also amend the Constitution. Proposed amendments have to be passed twice by each chamber; and in each of the two houses, at least three months have to elapse between the first and second votes. The second vote of approval requires an absolute majority in each chamber—that is, a majority of the members rather than a mere majority of those voting. If two-thirds of the members of each chamber approve the proposed amendment on the second vote, it need not be submitted to a popular referendum. Otherwise a referendum may be demanded by one-third of the members of either house, by 500,000 voters, or by 5 regional councils; and the amendment will not become the law of the land unless it is approved by an absolute majority of those voting in the referendum.

This brief allusion to the use of the referendum to ratify constitutional amendments should be qualified somewhat by pointing out that the very few constitutional amendments adopted thus far in Italy have received a two-thirds majority on the second vote in each chamber, and that therefore there has been no occasion to resort to the referendum. There are also constitutional provisions for the use of direct legislation as a means of introducing ordinary bills or repealing ordinary laws. For one thing, a bill may be introduced, not only by the cabinet or by private members of Parliament, but also by a petition signed by 50,000 voters. And a law may be submitted to a referendum for possible repeal, on the request of 500,000 voters or 5 regional councils. But the referendum remains a dead letter. Enabling legislation to provide the legal implementation for this procedure has not, as yet, been passed. In power since 1946, the Christian Democrats have been unwilling to provide the Communists with opportunities for appealing to the people over the heads of their elected representatives. Only in 1970, with the prospective parliamentary passage of a divorce law, did the Christian Democrats begin to contemplate with some measure of urgency the need to enact the referendum provision of the Constitution.[24] For a referendum seemed to be the only hope for removing the impending divorce law from the books.

Let us now direct our attention to the organizational structure of the Italian Parliament. Despite the cultural differences that tend to widen the divergences between political systems, all legislatures have certain common roles that may be examined for purposes of comparison: a presiding officer, a network of committees, organized groups of like-minded partisans or factional collaborators. It is hard to imagine any democratic legislature that does not possess these characteristic features of a representative assembly.

The two presiding officers in the Italian Parliament are offi-

[24] John Clarke Adams *The Quest for Democratic Law: The Role of Parliament in the Legislative Process* (New York: Crowell, 1970), pp. 150–151.

cially designated as the president of the Senate and the president of the Chamber of Deputies. They are supposed to be impartial and are, in fact, prohibited from voting on bills being considered by their respective chambers. They propose the order of business for each sitting, though in the Chamber of Deputies the actual decision is made by the Conference of Presidents, consisting of the Office of the Presidency (the president of the Chamber, four vice-presidents, eight secretaries, and three questors), the presidents of the various standing committees, and the presidents of the parliamentary groups. The Conference of Presidents attempts to establish the order of business by unanimous consent. Should this unanimity be unobtainable, the Chamber decides. In practice, neither presiding officer has firm control over the order of business, given the heterogeneous nature of the assembly over which he presides.

The president of each chamber must be consulted by the president of Italy before the latter can dissolve either or both chambers, is customarily invited to talk to the president of Italy during the slow, painful process of resolving cabinet crises, and has the power to assign bills to standing committees. On this last score, his decision may be appealed, first to the junta on rules in his chamber, then to the whole house. In sending a bill to a standing committee, he has the power to decide whether that committee should report back to the whole house *in sede referente*, or should simply pass the bill itself *in sede deliberante* and send it directly to the president of Italy to be signed and promulgated. And finally, the president of each chamber appoints the members of certain select committees. Ad hoc committees of investigation are also subject to the presiding officer's power of appointment, when the chamber sees fit to create them.

While the president of each chamber is usually a widely respected figure who serves for many years and is likely to be reelected at each new term of Parliament, he is not like the virtually apolitical arbiter who presides over the British House of Commons. Like the presiding officers of the French and German lower houses, he tends usually to be a party man, and a fairly prominent one at that. Nor is the position of president of the Chamber of Deputies or president of the Senate regarded as the culmination of a man's career, as is the case with the exalted post of Speaker of the House of Commons. Rather, the Italian parliamentary presiding officer may hope to go on to become prime minister (as did Giovanni Leone, erstwhile president of the Chamber of Deputies) or actually president of Italy (as did Giovanni Gronchi, formerly president of the Chamber of Deputies, and as Amintore Fanfani, currently president of the Senate, probably hopes to do).

For such a politically prominent individual whose ambitions have not been entirely quenched, the temptation to speak out publicly against real or imagined threats to the status of Parliament is hard to resist. Thus, Cesare Merzagora, formerly president of the Senate, felt compelled in 1960 to denounce the alleged encroachments by the political parties on parliamentary prerogatives.[25] One reason for this kind of activism, apart from the political prominence and ambitions of the presiding officer, may be a kind of reaction to a frustrating role. For despite his far-flung powers, despite the prominent image the presiding officer projects, he does not exercise as much control over the conduct of business in the Italian Parliament as does the Speaker in the British House of Commons. The multiparty, multifactional situation in the Italian Parliament, and the virtual autonomy enjoyed by the standing committees and their chairmen,[26] make for the kind of complex, multilateral control over parliamentary proceedings that Americans observe when they analyze the intricacies of their own Congress.

The Italian Parliament has a number of standing committees to which bills are referred for more careful scrutiny than a plenary session could furnish. According to recent figures, there are fourteen standing committees in the Chamber of Deputies and eleven in the Senate.[27] The Italian standing committees are specialized in their fields of jurisdiction: there are committees on external affairs, justice, national defense, and so on, rather than the general-purpose standing committees (designated A, B, C, D, and E) that exist in the British House of Commons. The political parties are represented on each standing committee to a degree roughly proportional to the party strength in the chamber; that is, a party with 40 percent of the seats in the chamber should have roughly 40 percent of the seats on each committee. The members of the standing committees are chosen by their respective parliamentary groups, and each committee elects its own chairman, two vice-chairmen, and two secretaries.

Italian standing committees are fairly powerful by contrast with standing committees in Britain and France. First of all, they receive a bill right after first reading, and may subject it to drastic

[25] Kogan, p. 166.
[26] Andrea Manzella, "L'organizzazione dei lavori parlamentari in Italia," *Tempi Moderni*, Vol. XI, No. 32 (Winter 1968), 7–9.
[27] Francesco Cosentino, "Parliamentary Committees in the Italian Political System," *Journal of Constitutional and Parliamentary Studies*, Vol. I, No. 2 (1967), 5.

changes before reporting it to the floor. Furthermore, the committee chairman appears to be master of his own timetable and will expedite or slow down the progress of a bill in accordance with his own preferences: The president of his chamber seems to have relatively little influence over him. Also, the proceedings of these committees are secret: The committees do not even hold public hearings, and are therefore not subject to pressure from the press and public opinion. Finally, they have the power to pass certain bills. When the president of the chamber refers a bill to a standing committee, he decides whether the committee is to act *in sede referente* (report the bill back to the Chamber, with proposed amendments) or *in sede deliberante* (take final action on the bill: pass it and send it on to the President of the Republic, or defeat it once and for all). Thus, Italian standing committees literally act as miniature legislatures. Over three-fourths of all bills approved by the Italian Parliament are enacted through this rather unique procedure.[28]

The passage of bills by standing committees *in sede deliberante* is not as simple a process as one might think, however. To begin with, bills for the amendment of the Constitution, proposed electoral laws, delegations of legislative power, ratification of treaties, and budgetary and spending bills must all be discussed on the floor *after* being examined in committee. Also, even if a standing committee has been assigned the task of considering a bill *in sede deliberante*, that bill may be brought to the floor of the chamber on the request of the cabinet, or of one-tenth of the members of the chamber, or of one-fifth of the members of the committee. Now, the Communist party has well over one-tenth of the membership of each chamber and well over one-fifth of the membership of each standing committee. If the Communists so desired, they could make it impossible for any standing committee to pass any bill *in sede deliberante*, and could thus sabotage two-thirds of the legislative output of the Italian Parliament. But evidently, the Communists do not so desire: Even when they fulminate against the cabinet on the floor, they quietly cooperate with the majority coalition in committee. Obviously, some *quid pro quo* is involved. But it is easy to see why some observers can conclude that "Legislative work in committees is therefore a powerful factor in the integration of the parties into the parliamentary system."[29]

The Italian system of standing committees has some grave

[28] Giorgio Galli and Alfonso Prandi, *Patterns of Political Participation in Italy* (New Haven, Conn.: Yale University Press, 1970), pp. 271–272.
[29] Galli and Prandi, p. 173.

shortcomings. We have already referred to the absence of public hearings. We should also note the fact that the *in sede deliberante* procedures result in swamping the committees with a great mass of minor bills—the so-called *leggine* ("little laws")—which should ideally be dealt with by executive regulations rather than taking up valuable parliamentary time. Furthermore, the Italian standing committees lack both the prestige and the staff assistance that do so much to bolster the status of American standing committees. And all too often, committees serve as convenient quagmires for bogging down unwanted legislation. The Christian Democrats, in particular, do not need to vote against widely supported but hotly controversial reform measures on the floor: By surreptitiously holding them up in committee, they can manage to block change without risking a public confrontation.

In any multiparty Parliament, the parties organize themselves into parliamentary groups for such purposes as handling the allocation of committee assignments and maintaining cohesion and discipline among the members of the party in the legislature. Italy is no exception to this rule, and the criteria for forming parliamentary groups in the Italian Parliament are rather liberal. A parliamentary group used to consist of a minimum of twenty members. At present, however, any group of deputies or senators who represent a nationwide party (that is, a party that has run candidates in all the circumscriptions, polled over 300,000 votes, and elected at least one deputy at the circumscription level without having to rely entirely on the distribution of seats from the pool of nationally computed remainders in the National College in Rome) may form a parliamentary group, even if that group should have less than ten members. Every deputy or senator must belong to some group. For those who do not belong to a nationwide party—Independents who have seceded from some major party since the last elections, members of regional parties like the Union Valdôtaine or the Südtyroler Volkspartei—the so-called Mixed Group has been created.[30]

The parliamentary groups decide which of their members shall serve on which standing committee, and also advise the president of their chamber with regard to the appointment of investigating committees and of the various select committees. Through their respective presidents, they are represented on the Conference of Presidents, which tries to agree on the order of business for the chamber. The president of each parliamentary group is also called

---

[30] Aristide Savignano, *I gruppi parlamentari* (Napoli: Morano Editore, 1965), pp. 36–64.

in and consulted by the president of Italy during a cabinet crisis. And finally, the parliamentary groups decide what stand to take on pending legislation, and their decisions are binding on their respective members, both on the floor and in committee.

However, the parliamentary groups are not entirely free agents; for they also receive instructions from their party directorates outside of Parliament. There is, therefore, some uncertainty as to just how much independence the parliamentary group can boast. The tension between the parliamentary *group* and the extraparliamentary party executive—tension which is somewhat allayed by overlapping membership—is a phenomenon that warrants a great deal of further investigation. In at least some of the Italian parties, the parliamentary groups have claimed, and succeeded in carving out, some measure of autonomy with respect to their enforcement of the directives which they receive from the extraparliamentary party executive organs. Certainly, this would appear to be the case with the Christian Democrats.

The procedures of the Italian Parliament include certain extremely intriguing usages, which help to distinguish the Italian parliamentary system from those of other Western European countries. First, there is no effective limit on the number of private-member bills that may be introduced. As a result, the Italian Parliament has been virtually swamped by such legislative proposals, which bear a strong resemblance to minor executive orders or to private bills in the United States and Great Britain. Second, there is no conference committee to iron out differences between the Senate and Chamber of Deputies versions of a bill. Consequently, many bills trudge back and forth between the two houses until such time as contrasts have been eliminated or the bill has died of sheer exhaustion. A third point to be noted is the power of each chamber to create investigating committees. Such committees must be established, if at all, with the consent of the majority—the same majority that controls the government, and is therefore likely to be dubious about the wisdom of investigating anything at all. Opposition demands for the creation of an investigating committee to probe into a given problem have usually fallen upon deaf ears.

Perhaps the most unusual facet of Italian parliamentary procedure is the requirement, enshrined in the rules of the Chamber of Deputies, that the final vote on a bill be taken by secret ballot. This technique is not required by the Senate rules but is nonetheless frequently employed by the Senate. The obvious implications of the use of the secret ballot in place of a public roll-call include a possible breakdown of party cohesion and protective camouflage for rebellious factions. There have been occasions when recalcitrant Christian Democratic deputies (snipers) have taken advantage of the secret ballot procedure to vote against measures supported by their own party leadership. The votes against the Fanfani cabinet in late 1958 represent a case in point; the cabinet was defeated in a secret ballot on a special surtax bill.[31] Of course, when this sort of thing occurs, the cabinet can ask for a formal vote of confidence, which requires a roll-call. But sniping is an embarrassing event that indicates the existence of grave disaffection in the ranks of the majority party. It is frequently the harbinger of a cabinet crisis.

Having touched upon the image, powers, organization, and procedures of the Italian Parliament, let us address ourselves briefly to the recruitment and background of parliamentary personnel. We discussed in Chapter Two the key role played by the parties in the nomination process. This means, in effect, that the normal way to obtain a parliamentary nomination—a place on the party's slate—is to have been active in the party organization, or in some pressure group affiliated to the party, over an extended period of time. Only in Southern Italy is a party likely to seek out an apolitical notable as its candidate for Parliament; elsewhere the route of ascent is through the party or pressure-group apparatus with possibly a tour of duty in local or provincial government. For a few bright young men, moreover, a protégé relationship with some prominent party leader may provide a felicitous short-cut to Rome.

The parties also seem to hold the whip hand in the selection of cabinet members. In France, under the Fifth Republic, with a strong Gaullist majority and a lopsided concentration of power in the executive branch, the president seems to be under virtually no obligation to follow the advice of the party chiefs in nominating his cabinet.[32] This is a far cry from the Italian practice: Italian cabinets are formed after prolonged negotiations between party directorates and party parliamentary groups. But the main decisions seem to emanate from the party directorate, much to the chagrin of those Italian scholars who claim that the country is ruled by a power-mad "partitocracy" and that Parliament is being unwisely sidetracked.[33] Of course, the French executive enjoys

---

[31] Kogan, p. 137.

[32] Lowell G. Noonan, *France: The Politics of Continuity in Change* (New York: Holt, Rinehart and Winston, 1970), pp. 366–367.

[33] Giuseppe Maranini, *Storia del potere in Italia 1848–1967* (Firenze: Vallecchi, 1967), Part II, ch. 6.

greater legal powers and a more favorable party situation than does its Italian counterpart, and therefore has more freedom of action.

As for the backgrounds of Italian members of Parliament, one study provides some invaluable information about members of the Chamber of Deputies during the years 1946–1963.[34] For one thing, there were very few women among Italian deputies (less than 4 percent in 1958–1963) and their numbers are not increasing. This is hardly surprising in view of the rather subordinate position of women in Italian society in general, and in family life in particular. Then, too, there was a prevalence of university graduates in the Chamber of Deputies—over 70 percent of the total membership. As we would expect, the percentage of university graduates is much higher among deputies from the ascriptive, status-conscious South than among deputies from Northern and Central Italy. A third characteristic of Italian parliamentary personnel is the key role played by professional men. However, this role seems to be declining a bit. While lawyers and university professors together comprised about one-quarter of the Chamber of Deputies in 1958, this ratio represented a considerable decrease from 1946, when these two categories boasted over 40 percent of the membership of the Constituent Assembly.

What categories in the Chamber of Deputies have gained strength, then, between 1946 and 1958? There has been a sharp increase in the percentage of high school teachers (up from about 7 percent in 1946 to about 11.5 percent in 1958), reflecting the penetration of political Catholicism into the public schools, a result of the Concordat. There has been a significant rise in the percentage of civil servants (from about 2.5 percent to about 4 percent), reflecting the long years of Christian Democratic control of the national government and the resulting colonization of the public service with a nucleus of politically reliable Christian Democratic appointees. And there have been spectacular gains made by professional party officials (from about 12.5 percent to about 18 percent) and trade-union officials (from about 5.5 percent to about 11.5 percent). This last phenomenon may probably be explained in terms of the mass membership, cohesion, and discipline of the two giant parties, which have the funds to maintain a well-articulated grass-roots organization.

Our information about the composition of the Chamber of Deputies applies also to the Senate, but with a few intriguing variations. First, the average age of senators is higher than that of

[34] The following data about the composition of the Chamber of Deputies are drawn from Stefano Somogyi, "Costituenti e deputati 1946–1958: analisi statistica," in Sartori, ed., pp. 23–34, 50–52.

deputies, a natural consequence of the higher legally prescribed minimum age of forty for senators as compared with twenty-five for deputies. Second, there is a higher proportion of professional men (lawyers, doctors, engineers, architects) and a lower proportion of career politicians (party and trade-union officials) in the Senate than in the Chamber of Deputies. This phenomenon, too, is probably related to the age factor: the middle-aged men who enter the Senate are more likely to have established themselves in private careers. And finally, the Senate seems to contain a smaller percentage of the more prominent and active members of Parliament than its numerical relationship to the Chamber of Deputies would lead one to expect. For instance, one-third of the members of Parliament are senators, yet senators have occupied key positions in the cabinet much less than their weight in Parliament would justify: only once has a senator been prime minister since 1945, only on three occasions has a senator headed the Foreign Ministry, and both the Interior and the Defense ministries have been consistently headed by deputies.[35]

The implications of the membership fluctuations in the Chamber of Deputies are that the decline in the percentage of self-employed professionals in the Italian Parliament may foreshadow the gradual elimination of the local notable, with his personal clientele. Still another possible implication of the above data is that the party bureaucracy may be increasing its capacity to dominate the party in Parliament. Certainly, full-time party officials, who have no professional career to which they may return if they lose their parliamentary seats and are denied a salaried position within the party apparatus, are likely to be more easily regimented, more responsive to the wishes of the party directorate, than the great notables of the past. On the other hand, some of the intraparty factions are so well financed, and have access to such a dependable supply of patronage, that they may be in a position to protect their followers in Parliament from the economic and political consequences of a breach of party discipline.

LEGISLATIVE-EXECUTIVE RELATIONS

From what we have thus far observed, what may we conclude about the relationship between Parliament and the executive branch in Italy? Obviously, we do not have a clear-cut case of

[35] Alberto Spreafico, "Il Senato della Repubblica: composizione politica e stratificazione sociale," in Mattei Dogan and Orazio Maria Petracca, eds., *Partiti politici e strutture sociali in Italia* (Milano: Comunità, 1968), pp. 609–643.

executive domination, of the sort that exists in Great Britain and France. True, the president can dissolve either house of Parliament. But the glacial immobility of the Italian electorate makes dissolution a sterile and purposeless exercise, a blunted tool in the hands of the executive. It is hardly surprising, then, that the Chamber of Deputies has never been dissolved, but has always been allowed to serve out its five-year term. The party cohesion and party discipline in the Italian Parliament might be expected to strengthen the hand of the executive. But here again, the multiparty, multifactional system that prevails in Italy makes the Italian Parliament as unmanageable as the volatile French Parliament of the Fourth Republic, with its numerous corps of undisciplined, free-wheeling centrist and rightist deputies.

On the other hand, a number of structural conditions strengthen the posture of the Italian Parliament against any would-be executive domination. The absence of any limit on private-member bills; the lack of tight cabinet control over the agenda; the failure of the Italian Constitution to place the same rigid restraints on the law-making powers and internal procedures of the Italian Parliament that are to be observed in the case of the hapless Parliament of the Fifth Republic; the Italian executive's lack of constitutional authority to submit legislation to a referendum; the power of Italian standing committees to enact laws *in sede deliberante*; the provision for voting by secret ballot on the final reading of a bill; and the presence of a powerful popularly elected second chamber—each and all of these factors would appear to bolster parliamentary independence. And the multiparty, multifactional system also has the natural consequence of promoting cabinet instability. Lacking a safe majority, cabinets come and go, with an average life expectancy of less than a year, while Parliament is virtually sure to serve out its five-year term.

But to some degree, parliamentary strength is illusory. It has been suggested that the great number of minor private-member bills passed in committee *in sede deliberante* are actually welcomed by the cabinet as substitutes for executive decrees, which might run afoul of the Court of Accounts and the administrative courts.[36] Since these bodies cannot review statutes, the minor private-member bill obviates many inconveniences. Also, these bills, by taking up the time of the two chambers, make it difficult for Parliament to perform its control functions adequately. Investigating committees, when created, lack adequate powers; standing committees are not provided with the staff and research tools they

[36] Mauro Ferri, "La crisi degli organi legislativi," in Direzione **PSI-PSDI** Unificati, pp. 28–30.

need; and questions and interpellations are easily evaded by the members of the cabinet.[37]

These are, however, matters of secondary importance as compared to the principal feature of parliamentary weakness: the domination over Parliament by the parties. It is very frequently the party outside of Parliament that brings down a cabinet. This action may take the form of a resolution by a party congress, a statement by a party directorate, or simply a public or private declaration of nonsupport by the secretary of one of the parties in the cabinet coalition. And since no one party has a majority, domination by the extraparliamentary parties accentuates the fragmented character of Parliament itself. As one observer has suggested, Italy has a weak government dependent on a weak Parliament, an unstable government dependent on an inefficient Parliament.[38] And, one might be tempted to add, a party system that generates paralysis and deadlock, rather than clear-cut policy directives.

OTHER POLICY-MAKING STRUCTURES

It would be a grave error to depict the Italian policy-making process solely in terms of the president, the prime minister, the cabinet, and the Parliament. Other actors play a role, in Italy as elsewhere in Western Europe. Political parties and interest groups have an important part in the process, especially in a country like Italy where a weak executive may depend on a single pressure group or a single minor party for survival. Intellectuals, both within and outside the governmental and party structures, may stimulate progress toward innovation and reform: Note the great influence of such journals as *Il Mondo, Il Mulino, Comunità, Tempi Moderni,* and *Nord e Sud.* And a single giant firm, like Fiat or Montedison, may reach economic decisions that influence the nation's pattern of development as strongly as if they had been adopted by the cabinet itself.

But within the governmental sector, there are additional structures that should at least be mentioned in passing, because they play a significant and continuous role in the policy-making process. The individual ministries exercise a relatively high degree of autonomy from cabinet control. Each ministry is divided into a

[37] Parri, pp. 94–95.
[38] Norberto Bobbio, "Le istituzioni parlamentari ieri e oggi," in Piccardi, Bobbio, and Parri, p. 45.

number of directorates, which are in turn divided into divisions and sections. To maintain effective supervision over the civil servants in his ministry, the politician in charge cannot rely primarily on his under-secretaries, for they may be, and frequently are, political rivals who owe their positions not to him but to a party faction that insisted on their appointment. So the minister must have his own personal cabinet and his secretariat. This personal entourage is much like its counterpart in France: civil servants from other ministries and men who, while occupying no civil service post, enjoy the minister's confidence. This staff helps the minister to play a dominant role in a passive and sometimes hostile environment.

The bureaucracy itself is deeply involved in policy making. As of January 1, 1968, the Italian state had a total of 1,381,670 employees.[39] However, one should subtract from this total the members of the armed forces; the members of the judicial branch; the teachers and professors employed in the state schools and in the universities; and the industrial workers employed by state-owned firms. This operation reduces the total number of civil servants in 1968 to 515,949: 206,454 employed by the ministries and 309,495 working for various autonomous state agencies and enterprises.

The four principal classes in the civil service are: the administrative class (*carriera direttiva*), whose members are normally recruited from among university graduates; the executive class (*carriera di concetto*), whose members have generally completed upper secondary school; the clerical class (*carriera esecutiva*), composed primarily of people who have graduated from lower secondary school; and an auxiliary class (*carriera di personale ausiliario*). In addition to recruitment by direct entry from the various rungs of the educational ladder, it is possible to be promoted from one class to another within the service. A system of competitive examinations is employed in both cases. But the higher civil service is not staffed entirely on a merit basis: Certain positions, such as prefect, director general (head of a general directorate within a ministry), or member of the Council of State, may be filled by presidential decree on the advice of the cabinet. These are simply patronage appointees. Also, promotion within the same class is based partly on seniority, partly on merit; but

---

[39] Statistics in this paragraph are drawn from Istituto per la Scienza dell' Amministrazione Pubblica (ISAP) *La burocrazia periferica e locale in Italia: analisi sociologica.* Part I: Franco Demarchi, *L'ideologia del funzionaro* (Milano: Giuffré, 1969), pp. 96–98.

merit apparently can be used to inject political considerations into the promotion process. In addition to patronage appointments and promotions based partly on patronage, a large minority of civil servants are first brought into the service on a temporary basis, and then given permanent status by law without having to undergo competitive examinations at all.[40]

The administrative class is primarily concerned with policy-making decisions, within the fairly broad guidelines laid down by the minister. Thus, once again, we may further sift the ranks of the bureaucracy, and emerge with 33,561 members of the administrative class employed in the various ministries in 1968, and a few thousand more serving in the autonomous state enterprises. Approximately 40,000 Italian civil servants, then, occupy policy-making roles.[41]

The system by which higher civil servants are recruited is rather archaic by comparison with the method employed in France. Instead of having a single set of exams administered by a central personnel agency, each ministry in Italy announces its own openings and administers its own exams. Moreover, the exams tend to place maximum stress on legal training, rather than on the broad social-science background that characterizes recruits to the French higher civil service. Psychological and aptitude tests are generally not employed in the Italian recruitment process. Those who sign up for the available openings usually have to wait at least a year, and sometimes as long as two or three years, for the examination process to be completed and the positions to be filled.[42] Bright young men in a hurry are not likely to possess the patience this routine seems to require. A man must have an extremely strong yearning for security to put up with this cumbersome recruitment process.

The recruitment system tends to result in the overrepresentation of the South in the higher civil service; for, in the South, a higher percentage of university students choose to major in law than is the case in the technologically oriented North. Then, too, Southerners seem to place a higher value on security and status than on the opportunities and hazards of a career in business. Many of the Southern recruits in the higher civil service are of lower-middle-class (petty bourgeois) origin, in sharp contrast to

[40] ISAP, Part II: Paolo Ammassari, Federica Garzonio Dell' Orto, Franco Ferraresi, *Il burocrate di fronte alla burocrazia* (Milano: Giuffré, 1969), pp. 46–49. Data are taken from the chapter by Dell' Orto.
[41] ISAP, Part I: Demarchi, pp. 97–98.
[42] Domenico Bartoli, *L'Italia burocratica* (Milano: Garzanti, 1965), pp. 204–205.

the urbane upper-middle-class Parisians who throng the *Ecole Nationale d'Administration*.[43] Thus, while the French higher civil servants are from the most dynamic, economically developed part of France, the Italian higher civil servants stem largely from the most backward and tradition-bound regions of Italy.

Also, the training of the members of the *carriera direttiva* falls well short of the French model. Instead of the three-year course organized by the French *École Nationale d'Administration*, Italy offers only a three-month training course for higher civil servants: two months at the Higher School of Public Administration in Caserta and one month of training with a ministry in Rome. The Caserta school, moreover, seems to lack a stable and integrated teaching staff, so that the program offered to the trainees is little more than a series of assorted and ill-coordinated lectures presented by a faculty that includes professors, higher civil servants, Councillors of State, judges, and outside "experts." This heterogeneity is not undesirable per se, to be sure; but combined with the very brief training period, it makes for a certain degree of confusion.[44] The graduates of Caserta are hardly likely to be self-confident missionaries of the sort who emerge from the ENA in Paris. Rather, as we shall see, the Italian bureaucracy tends to be negative, cautious, and obstructive in its attitude toward public policy innovations.

In addition to the ministries, and the bureaucrats who staff them, there is yet another major source of policy making in Italy: the public corporations and the semiindependent agencies and enterprises that preside over the Italian public sector and over the extensive economic regulatory activities of the Italian government. Here we should cite such superholding companies as the Institute for Industrial Reconstruction (IRI) and the National Hydrocarburants Corporation (ENI). Both oversee a number of subsidiary holding companies, which in turn hold stock in a wide variety of enterprises. IRI enterprises include steel mills, automobile manufacturing plants, mechanical-engineering firms, shipyards, steamship lines, and banks; ENI is particularly well established in petroleum refining, natural gas production, and chemicals, to say nothing of textiles and motels. Supposedly, both IRI and ENI are under the supervision of the minister of state share holdings, who executes the general policies laid down by a permanent cabinet committee. But thus far, at any rate, the public corporations have

[43] ISAP, Part 1: Demarchi, pp. 200–213.
[44] Antonio Duva, "Burocrati a scuola," *Nord e Sud*, Vol. XVII, No. 123 (184) (March 1970), 52–57.

been able to pursue their own policies with a minimum of ministerial interference. The minister, possibly because of lack of support from his cabinet colleagues, has generally confined himself to underwriting the projects presented to him by ENI and IRI. Moreover, the nationalized electric-power industry, and its newly created public corporation ENEL, have been placed under the supervision of a different ministry, the Ministry of Industry and Commerce, thus preventing unified public control.[45]

Why do IRI and ENI and other public agencies and enterprises, such as the Fund for the South, enjoy so much autonomy? It should be pointed out that the executive is too fragmented, too torn by interparty and interfactional disputes, to exercise effective supervision. Moreover, the heads of these enterprises are often expoliticians rather than faceless technocrats, and are inclined to be more flamboyant and aggressive than their French counterparts. The most obvious example is Enrico Mattei, former head of ENI.[46] Mattei was a man of humble origins who had to leave school at the age of fifteen; he worked first as a painter and then as an errand boy in a tannery, and rapidly clawed his way up to a managerial position in that tannery. At the age of twenty-three, he gave up his managerial post for a job selling industrial equipment for a German firm. Later, he borrowed funds to set up his own chemical firm. During the Resistance, he served in the partisan movement as a leader of Christian Democratic units. In 1945, when many administrative posts were being distributed among deserving anti-Fascists, Mattei (whose managerial background stood him in good stead) accepted a seemingly unpromising post as commissioner in charge of the Italian General Petroleum Corporation (AGIP), a public enterprise which was apparently slated for liquidation. Seizing the opportunity thus provided, ignoring go-slow orders from above, cutting corners in every direction, Mattei plunged into large-scale exploration of the Po Valley. The natural-gas strike achieved by AGIP in 1946 provided Italy with a copious supply of cheap fuel and established Mattei's reputation.

After 1946, Mattei was able to obtain from Parliament exclusive oil exploration and exploitation rights in the Po Valley. ENI was created by act of Parliament in 1953 with a number of subsidiaries, including AGIP. Also, oil exploration elsewhere in

[45] On the lack of adequate ministerial control over the public corporations, see M. V. Posner and S. J. Woolf, *Italian Public Enterprise* (Cambridge, Mass.: Harvard University Press, 1967), pp. 34, 38–42, 96–99, 122–125, 128.

[46] On Mattei's career, see Dow Votaw, *The Six-Legged Dog* (Berkeley, Calif.: University of California Press, 1964); and P. H. Frankel, *Mattei: Oil and Power Politics* (New York: Praeger, 1966).

continental Italy was rendered so uninviting, from the point of view of foreign and Italian private companies, that ENI was in effect given a de facto exploration monopoly covering the entire Italian mainland. Mattei then moved to obtain oil concessions in foreign countries, established his own ENI-controlled newspaper (*Il Giorno* of Milan), gave heavy financial contributions to the Christian Democratic party, and proceeded to lobby for support within the ranks of the dominant party. In short, Mattei and ENI represented an important sector of the Italian power structure.

IRI, ENEL, the Fund for the South, and other public corporations and enterprises have been less prone to run their own show at all costs. But they, too, have been able to propose and carry through new policies, in the absence of clear and consistent directives from the executive branch. Thus, there is evidence that the minister has usually tended to support IRI's policies and programs.[47] IRI, too, has been headed by political administrators like Fascetti and later Petrilli, both of whom were former Christian Democratic politicians. Moreover, public enterprises like IRI and ENI are not included in the regular budget, and their accounts do not receive the same degree of scrutiny that is focused on the regular ministries.[48]

A key figure in economic policy making is the governor of the Bank of Italy. As advisor to the minister of the treasury and to the Interministerial Committee on Credit and Savings, he has a great deal of impact on Italian monetary and credit policy. He sits in on a number of cabinet committees and is invariably listened to with respect. While the minister of the treasury is politically responsible for the governor's policies, the governor is not really under the control of the minister, or of Parliament either, for that matter. Selected by the Administrative Council of his Bank, confirmed in office by a decree of the president of the republic, he is Italy's number one technocrat, the most credible Italian counterpart to the French *grand commis*.[49]

Some agencies affect the policy-making process through their control over parliamentary and executive actions. Under this rubric we might list, for later discussion in Chapter Nine, such bodies as the Court of Accounts, the Council of State, and the

---

[47] Posner and Woolf, pp. 39–40.

[48] Posner and Woolf, pp. 34–35; and Ernesto Rossi, *I nostri quattrini* (Bari: Laterza, 1964), pp. 453–454, 524–526, 529–531.

[49] Raimondo Craveri, *Politica e affari* (Milano: Garzanti, 1964), pp. 25–30; and Murray Edelman and R. W. Fleming, *The Politics of Wage-Price Decisions: A Four-Country Analysis* (Urbana, Ill.: University of Illinois Press, 1965), pp. 16–17.

Constitutional Court. And finally, Italy has an economic advisory parliament: the National Council of Economy and Labor (CNEL). Established in 1957, the CNEL is an eighty-member body, whose members are appointed by the president of Italy for three-year terms. Most are nominated by Italian interest groups, some by government research bodies, and some by the president himself. Most of its members are interest-group officials, some are independent experts. There has been considerable doubt as to the CNEL's status, especially since its sessions have to be private rather than public, and also in view of the fact that it cannot introduce legislation on its own but can merely forward its proposals to the Parliament or give its recommendations on pending bills if so requested by the Parliament or the cabinet. However, the CNEL's prestige has been raised substantially as a result of the fact that it *was* consulted by the cabinet during the preparation of the Italian Economic Plan in 1965, and that many of its proposed amendments were accepted by the cabinet.[50]

CONCLUSIONS

It is evident that the Italian governmental system defies description by neat formulas or pat generalizations. The relationship between policy-making structures is an ever-shifting balance of power with the omnipresent danger that one or another structure may break out of control and "do its own thing." No structure is unquestionably supreme. This is not parliamentary government after the manner of the Fourth French Republic; for the Italian cabinet has a longer life expectancy than did the French cabinet in the years 1946–1958, and Italian deputies (unlike the local potentates who wheeled and dealed in the French National Assembly before 1958) are rigidly regimented by their parties. Nor is this "cabinet government" on the British model. The Italian cabinet lacks a firm and secure majority, and a cabinet which cannot work as a united team is in no position to exercise strong leadership. Besides, the division of power between the president and the prime minister is stll relatively unsettled, and this fact, too, weakens the cabinet's standing. Nor is this party government (the "partitocracy" which Italian nostalgics view with alarm); for the parties, being themselves collections of warring factions, must often choose between immobilism and scission.

[50] Alberto Predieri, Piero Barucci, Mariangela Bartoli, and Gabriela Gioli, *Il Programma Economico 1966–1970* (Milano: Giuffré, 1967), pp. 62–63.

In such a situation, a bold and enterprising bureaucracy may often be encouraged to pioneer new policies. But as we have seen, the Italian bureaucracy is not up to this kind of mission; its social background makes for a standpat attitude toward political innovations. It is, rather, in the sector of the public corporations that the absence of coherent political guidance has stimulated venturesome experimentation. This tendency is not entirely healthy, for presumably the people's elected representatives should be calling the signals. Yet, the activities of IRI and ENI have done much to spur economic growth at a time when the cabinet and the Parliament were involved in their usual internecine feuds, and concerned more with the allocation of posts among various parties and factions than with actual policy issues.

This uneasy balance, with no one unmistakably in charge and with some of the supposedly lesser actors successfully evading the restraints imposed by the system, poses some major threats to Italian democracy. First of all, despite the desirable achievements of such agencies as IRI and ENI (and not *all* their achievements have been in the public interest), permitting public corporations and semi-independent agencies to engage in unlimited empire-building can create unforeseen new problems that can threaten Italian political stability. The possibility of oil pollution along Italy's coastlines is one illustration of where the absence of political restraints can lead. Another point is that, if parliamentary structures do not in fact make the big decisions, such structures will appear to be increasingly irrelevant in the eyes of public opinion. Then, too, the absence of a clearly designated center of supreme power tends to blur responsibility. If voters cannot hold any single individual or institution ultimately responsible for the failure of policy, they will tend to blame the system. The resulting alienation can undermine the foundations of Italian democracy. And finally, the persistence of institutionalized deadlock and the unclear allocation of legal and political authority may encourage one of the major actors (the president, perhaps) to attempt a Caesaristic breakthrough and achieve supremacy by arbitrary means.

Of course, these problems and imbalances are not peculiar to Italy: They are simply more acute and less expertly camouflaged in Italy than in most other Western democracies.

EIGHT
THE CLASH OF OUTLOOKS
The policy-making process

**IDEOLOGICAL DIFFERENCES
AS BARRIERS TO POLICY MAKING**

Earlier in this book, we spoke of the ideological differences that contribute to the cultural fragmentation of Italian society. These differences make it extremely difficult to develop a common sense of public purpose, and consequently have a disintegrating effect on the policy-making process. When men disagree sharply on what must be done in the first place, rather than differ on how a mutually accepted goal can best be reached, the chances are that basic policy decisions will be taken with agonizing slowness and uncertainty—assuming they are not postponed indefinitely.

The division between Northern and Southern Italy is one factor that contributes to the disintegration of policy making. For Northern and Southern intellectuals tend to differ very strongly on the proper solution to the so-called Southern question. Northerners have tended to view the Italian economy as an integrated unit, to stress the need to build on areas of strength (the Northwest Triangle) in planning industrial growth, to distrust large-scale public investment as a solution to the problem of depressed areas. Southern intellectuals instead have tended to view the economic backwardness of the South as a special problem caused by Northern exploitation, as well as by a lack of natural resources, and to expect that public intervention could remedy the imbalances brought about by past inequities.

This dichotomy is, of course, somewhat oversimplified: there are numerous Northern and Southern intellectuals whose views cannot be summed up under one of two contrasting headings. But the dichotomy calls attention to a major issue that is dividing the ranks of those Italians who believe in economic planning. The issue poses the following question: Should the Italian government take measures to slow down Northern economic growth as a means of closing the North-South economic gap? Closely related to this issue are such unsettled questions as whether or not the public sector should be strengthened at the expense of the private sector of the economy. For the stronger and more extensive the public sector of the economy becomes, the more effectively state enterprises can discriminate in favor of the South.

Not only is there basic disagreement on the proper objectives of economic planning, but also planning itself has been a very controversial principle in the years since World War II. In the immediate postwar period, the liberal subculture—more specifically, the conservative wing of that subculture—tended to dominate the economic policy-making process. Liberal economists like Luigi Einaudi and Epicarmo Corbino steered the policies of the economic ministries with a view to placing primary reliance on the free market, maintaining a stable currency and a balanced budget, and employing taxation and credit measures (rather than direct controls) to manipulate the economy. In pursuing this approach, Einaudi and Corbino had the support of Prime Minister De Gasperi. The prevalence of a classical liberal approach to economic policy had the result of postponing the adoption of a national economic plan until 1965, almost two decades after the first French plan had been promulgated. There was, of course, a great deal of governmental intervention of an uncoordinated nature, designed to cope with the problem of a single sector of the economy or a single section of the country. But there was no over-all national planning.

Why was the liberal delaying action in the economic sphere so successful? One obvious factor was the remarkable economic progress achieved by Italy after World War II (see Chapter One). There are a number of explanations for the rapid expansion that took place in post-World War II Italy. American economic aid was one factor, of course. Then, too, the loss of its colonial empire freed Italy from burdensome overseas commitments and must therefore be regarded as having some causal weight. Defeat in World War II and the accompanying damage inflicted on the Italian economy provided Italian entrepreneurs with a seemingly endless array of investment opportunities and of new tasks to perform. In such a situation, the introduction of new machinery and techniques was rendered more feasible. The rising expectations of Italian consumers also played a key role in economic expansion. Moreover, Hildebrand cites as factors the vigor and imagination of Italian businessmen, and the fact that they have enjoyed a significant bargaining advantage over a divided labor movement.[1]

Especially important in this growth process has been the role of government and the public sector, uncoordinated as this intervention was in the two decades following Liberation. The credit controls imposed by the government in 1947—classical capitalist remedies, which were bitterly criticized at the time—succeeded in checking inflation, stabilized the currency, stimulated exports, and laid the necessary foundations for healthy economic growth. The *Cassa per il Mezzogiorno* (Fund for the South) and the Institute for Industrial Reconstruction (IRI) have both channeled large quantities of investment funds toward the South (the IRI steel complex at Taranto is a case in point). The bold policies of the National Hydrocarburants Corporation (ENI)—policies resulting in the discovery of natural gas in the Po Valley and thus providing large stocks of relatively cheap fuel for industrial development—stimulated economic growth (see Chapter Seven). Then, the Italian government's decision to adopt a free trade policy toward foreign countries, and its later decision to join the European Economic Community, furnished the kind of competitive prodding which brings out the inventiveness needed for expansion.

Thus, reliance on the free market, somewhat corrected by public investment, achieved even more spectacular results in Italy than did the belated triumphs of the General Planning Commission in France. Italy's economic successes help to explain why national economic planning did not appear to be an urgent necessity until the 1960s. Interestingly, another factor cited by some writers is a cultural bias against planning. Many Christian Democratic voters actually belong to the liberal subculture and regard economic planning as the undesired first step toward collectivism. Then on the other hand, those who accept the Marxist subculture have tended to distrust the kind of economic planning which has

[1] George H. Hildebrand, *Growth and Structure in the Economy of Modern Italy* (Cambridge, Mass.: Harvard University Press, 1965), pp. 3–14, 381–391.

developed in the capitalist countries of Western Europe. They have insisted that such planning is destined to serve the interests of the big monopolies. This underlying distrust helps to account for the lukewarm attitude the Communist party assumed toward the concept of national economic planning in the Constituent Assembly in 1946–1947. It is hardly surprising, under the circumstances, that the Italian Constitution does not even employ the term "plan," but refers rather vaguely to "programs."

Still another factor was partly responsible for the tardy appearance of a national economic plan on the Italian scene. Italy lacked the kind of vigorous, united bureaucratic elite, with a strong administrative tradition and a willingness to seize the initiative, that existed in France. Also, Italians distrust their bureaucracy almost innately. If the people regard the civil service as corrupt and inefficient, they are not likely to deem such a faulty mechanism capable of directing the national economy. Moreover, the French administrative class of higher civil servants enjoys close ties with big business and commands its confidence. As we have seen, this has not been the case in Italy, where most higher civil servants come from the less industrialized areas of the country. Thus, Italy suffered from a lack of rapport between its administrative and industrial elites.

It has also been pointed out that, in Italy, the technocrats of the public and private sectors of the economy do not form a single cohesive bloc, as do the French technocrats.[2] Possibly one reason for this difference is the fact that so many heads of Italian public corporations are political appointees who lack prior close ties with big business. By the same token, there is a certain amount of friction in Italy between the legally trained, traditionally oriented higher civil servants in the Roman ministries and the free-wheeling technocrats of the public sector. So, with public-sector technocrats, private-sector technocrats, and higher civil servants failing to work in tandem, the auspices are hardly favorable for the kind of national economic planning—heavily dependent on voluntary cooperation and mutual trust—that exists elsewhere in Western Europe.

Thus, it was not until the early 1960s, when economic growth began to taper off, and when the persistence of certain problems became signally manifest, that pressure for national planning began to build. In 1965, a plan finally came into being. But basic disagreements persist regarding the form that planning

[2] Raimondo Craveri, *Politica e affari* (Milano: Garzanti, 1964), pp. 37–39, 65–67.

should take. The liberal economists, such as Papi and Di Fenizio, favor "indicative planning" on the French model, with the government using tax and credit inducements, persuasion, and encouragement to influence the workings of the market economy, and with the plan being simply a complex of economic projections rather than a set of firm commitments. Another group of economists, including Maramma and Saraceno, believe that the government is bound, in some measure, by the economic forecasts set forth in the plan, and consequently advocate some degree of direct government intervention to help make those forecasts come true. Lombardini refers to this approach as normative planning, whereas Di Fenizio refers to this school of thought as Social Christian. Then, there are economists of more or less socialist leanings (Fuà, Sylos-Labini) who insist that planning must entail significant changes in the socioeconomic system, profound structural reforms in the public sector of the economy and drastic checks on the activities of big business.[3]

These ideological divisions had much to do with early failures in the process of drawing up a national economic plan. On August 6, 1962, a ministerial decree established the National Committee for Economic Programming (CNPE), whose mission was to set guidelines for a national economic plan. The CNPE was to include the leaders of nine major interest groups (*Confindustria; Confagricoltura; Confcommercio;* the National Confederation of Direct Cultivators; the three main trade-union confederations—CGIL, CISL, and UIL; the Italian Banking Association —ABI; and the Italian Confederation of Plant Managers—CIDA), one "expert" from each of these groups, and a number of outside "experts" (mostly professors of economics) appointed by the minister of the budget. Ideological cleavages soon divided the CNPE, including its specialist section (composed exclusively of "experts"), and paralyzed its operations. The CNPE expired late in 1964, after finally issuing a report that had been prepared by its vice-chairman, Pasquale Saraceno, and that by no means reflected the unanimous views of the CNPE's membership. With the Italian bureaucracy unequipped to play a dominant role in the planning process, any organ composed primarily of interest-group representatives and professional "experts" was bound to dissolve into a set of squabbling factions. It is evident that the ideological foun-

---

[3] These schools of thought are discussed by Ferdinando Di Fenizio, *La programmazione economica* (Torino: UTET, 1965), pp. 333–335; and Siri Lombardini, *La programmazione: idee esperienze problemi* (Torino: Einaudi, 1967), pp. 75–88.

dations for the formulation of public purpose are rather shaky. Contrasting tendencies are far more numerous in Italy than in, say, Britain or Sweden.

THE PROCESS OF POLICY MAKING: THE INITIATION OF PROPOSALS

Let us now focus on the actual policy-making routines as they appear in the Italian system. We may begin by asking how problems are brought to the attention of the policy-makers. In other words, who or what first provides the motive force that eventually leads to the passage of a law by Parliament or the issuance of an executive decree by the cabinet? The standard stimulators of attention are, of course, the parties, the pressure groups, the higher civil servants in the ministries, and the individual senators and deputies. However, the respective roles of these actors differ from country to country. In Italy, there are some additional avenues by which matters can be brought to the attention of the government.

The Italian Parliament is one of the relatively few parliamentary bodies that does not restrict the introduction of private-member bills; in fact, the private-member bills constitute a growing majority of the total number of bills considered by the Chamber of Deputies and the Senate in a given year. This would appear to indicate an important role for the individual senator or deputy in the phase of initiating legislation. However, if we look at the bills that are actually enacted into law, we find that over three-fourth of these are *disegni di legge* (government bills) rather than *proposte di legge* (private-member bills).[4] Thus, the individual member of Parliament may introduce legislation freely; but government bills enjoy far better prospects for survival.

It is estimated that the great majority of government bills are drafted in the legislative offices of the various ministries, while only a small proportion are prepared by party research office staffs.[5] From a strictly quantitative point of view, then, the bureaucracy is a far more important source of demand input than are the political parties. But in a qualitative sense, the parties probably play a more meaningful role than would appear at first

[4] Alberto Predieri, "La produzione legislativa," in Giovanni Sartori, ed., *Il Parlamento Italiano 1946–1963* (Napoli: Edizioni Scientifiche Italiane, 1963), pp. 213–215; and Giovanni Sartori, "Dove va il Parlamento?" in Sartori, ed., p. 362.

[5] Alberto Spreafico, *L'amministrazione e il cittadino* (Milano: Comunità, 1965), p. 42.

glance. For the great bulk of both government and private-member bills consist of the so-called *leggine*[6] ("little laws," corresponding to private bills in Great Britain), with which the parties are hardly likely to concern themselves. One suspects, therefore, that the parties stimulate the introduction of a goodly share of the broader and more controversial bills of general application.

In addition to the bureaucracy, Italian pressure groups are involved in bringing problems to the attention of policy makers. There is reason to believe that pressure groups may be the most important and effective instruments for performing this task. First, both Parliament and the bureaucracy are very poorly equipped to gather and assess information: They suffer from a severe shortage of research facilities and (in the case of Parliament) staff assistance. Both depend on pressure groups for information, in many instances, and are therefore likely to respond favorably to initiatives emanating from such trusted sources of data. Second, Italian bureaucrats, by virtue of their conservative background and legalistic proclivities, seem to have a certain bias against innovation. They do not appear to have either the resources or the will to explore new solutions to old problems or to broach major controversial questions requiring public attention. In fact, when ministries choose to expand their functions into new areas of policy, they are apt to submit the problems involved to an outside expert for a preliminary opinion, rather than rely on their own staff.[7]

A third piece of evidence regarding the superior effectiveness of pressure groups in bringing problems to the attention of government requires that we look more closely at the role of parties in initiating policy proposals. As we have seen, parties do not usually bother with *leggine* but stick to the big, dramatic issues. We might question, however, whether the "big issues" are really that vital in affecting the course of policy and the welfare of the society. For instance, on such matters as monetary and fiscal policy, the parties tend to remain relatively silent because they feel that these complex questions do not interest the voters. The ministers are approached on these vital but arcane problems, not by deputies or party secretaries, but by the representatives of *Confindustria*, the heads of some giant corporations like Fiat or Pirelli, and a few higher civil servants.[8] Yet, ministerial decisions on fiscal or mone-

---

[6] Predieri, pp. 228–244.

[7] Giuseppe De Rita, "L'amministrazione centrale," in Associazione Italiana di Scienze Sociali, *Sociologi e centri di potere in Italia* (Bari: Laterza, 1962), pp. 61–68.

[8] Craveri, pp. 44–45.

tary matters can often have more far-reaching effects than the passage of a key bill. To cite another example, Sernini asserts that party representatives serving on planning organs have failed to present a broad strategy of their own, but have simply functioned as spokesmen for their home provinces or, more commonly, for some pressure group.[9] It would appear, then, that parties are allowing themselves to be relegated to a superficial or marginal role with regard to the initiation of policy proposals.

The evidence just examined also tends to illustrate a fourth point—that is, the dependence of the bureaucracy on the pressure groups for information and ideas. When we note that most government bills are prepared by the legislative offices of the various ministries, we are still not in a position to say how many of these bills, and how many of the numerous ministerial and cabinet decrees, have really been inspired by pressure groups with which the ministries have *clientela* relationships. Rossi claims, for instance, that the Interministerial Committee on Prices has no research office to analyze prices and costs, and is therefore prone simply to accept whatever figures are presented to it by the economic interest groups with which it deals. Consequently, its regulatory power over prices is exercised only to the extent of reconciling conflicting group claims, rather than prescribing a coherent pattern of price policy based on informed deliberation and independent access to information.[10]

Because of scanty means for obtaining data on relevant problems, the Italian Parliament is peculiarly dependent on the executive branch and on pressure groups for intelligence. Yet, the Parliament does have certain special tools at its disposal for obtaining information from the executive branch (the question, or interpellation) or for learning something about a major problem confronting Italian society (the parliamentary committee of inquiry). The harsh truth, however, is that these techniques leave much to be desired. Questions and interpellations can apparently be evaded by a determined minister and do not seem to constitute an effective way of holding the executive to account—not unless the ultimate sanction of the vote of no confidence is hovering in the background. Parliamentary committees of inquiry are generally established only *after* a problem has aroused public opinion, and has been taken up and thoroughly aired by the parties and pres-

[9] Michele Sernini, *La disputa sui partiti* (Padova: Marsilio Editori, 1968), pp. 97–98.
[10] Ernesto Rossi, Piero Ugolini, Leopoldo Piccardi, *La Federconsorzi* (Milano: Feltrinelli, 1963), p. xxx.

sure groups. As a rule, such committees do not blaze new trails: their reports are strictly descriptive and often reflect a lack of methodological rigor. In short, they do not normally bring a problem to the government's attention, but rather dramatize the fact that the government is aware of, and concerned about, the problem.[11]

Among the interest groups that play a conspicuous part in broaching major issues are what La Palombara refers to as "intellectual groups."[12] Groups of civic-minded intellectuals clustering around such periodicals as *Il Mondo, Il Mulino, Tempi Moderni, Il Ponte*, and *Nord e Sud*, seek to use the influence and prestige of their respective journals to sway the thinking of Italian elites. They publish articles dealing with major problems and shortcomings of Italian society, and frequently propose ways of attacking these problems. Occasionally, they sponsor conferences, attended by intellectuals and notables from all over Italy, which may well spawn well-publicized policy demands. They cultivate ties with sympathetic legislators of intellectual origin. While these groups suffer from a sense of self-righteous superiority vis-à-vis the less educated, and often regard themselves as models of virtue in a world of philistines, they have had some success in affecting policy. Above all, they are often the first to discuss novel concepts that will, within ten or twenty years, form the foundation for new policy. It was in this sense that the intellectual groups laid the groundwork for the opening to the Left, the development of national economic planning, and the nationalization of electric power.

Thus far we have spoken about private organizations and public agencies which contribute to the recognition of problems, as the first step in the decision-making process. But we should also cite certain types of individuals—apart from legislators, higher civil servants, lobbyists, and party leaders—who habitually play a role in this phase of the process. First, there are the technocrats, the industrial and financial managers, in the public and private sectors of the economy. The annual reports of the governor of the Bank of Italy are one example of technocratic input: These reports define the major economic, financial, and monetary problems of the year for the benefit of Italian decision makers. By the same token, a major pronouncement by the head of IRI or ENI,

---

[11] Franco Ferrarotti, "Il Parlamento," in Associazione Italiana di Scienze Sociali, pp. 43–55.

[12] Joseph La Palombara, *Interest Groups in Italian Politics* (Princeton, N.J.: Princeton University Press, 1964), pp. 185–193.

or of one of their subsidiaries, or by the chief executive of a major private firm, is always likely to attract attention and may well serve to stimulate action. A major investment decision by Fiat or Olivetti will have far-reaching consequences for Italian society, and may come to the government's attention as a fait accompli. Also, many decisions affecting the future of the Italian economy are now initiated by foreign technocrats, especially those employed by the European Economic Community.

Other influential individuals and groups are engaged in research in the social sciences, particularly in sociology and economics. Some research specialists are university professors; numerous professors of economics have served on government planning organs, for example. Apparently, ministries have preferred not to rely too heavily on social science academicians, who are interested primarily in pure research, but to seek out the advice of an intermediate category of research technicians or experts, who specialize in applying and synthesizing the ideas of pure scholars; often, these experts are not connected with a university.[13]

These types cannot be conveniently segregated into watertight compartments. Numerous individuals have, figuratively speaking, a foot in each of several camps. Thus, for instance, Pasquale Saraceno is a university professor, a top executive of IRI, and a perennial member of government planning organs and advisory boards. Many of the research technicians to whom we have alluded may have no ties at all with a university; others may be struggling for a foothold in the academic world.

There is apparently a rather ambivalent attitude on the part of administrators, politicians, trade-union officials, and businessmen toward the advice they receive from sociologists and—presumably—other social scientists. On the one hand, these decision makers seem to regard the advisory relationship as a useful method for gaining time against those who press for an early decision, or as a device for accumulating facts, or as a kind of pseudoscientific rationalization for policies already decided upon in advance of any research. On the other hand, there is a certain distrust of the social science expert, particularly if he gets out of line and tries to make policy recommendations. So, very often, the research findings are either purely descriptive, or are not utilized at all.

Another method of calling attention to problems is direct action by an anomic interest group. Thus, for example, in 1953,

[13] De Rita, pp. 61–66; and Renato Treves, "Introduzione," in Associazione Italiana di Scienze Sociali, pp. 10–13.

when the Pignone works in Florence were about to shut down, the workers (encouraged by Christian Democratic Mayor La Pira) occupied the plant. This dramatic move aroused the sympathy, not only of the Communists and Socialists, but also of many clergymen and lay members of Catholic Action. One result of this event was ENI acquisition of the Pignone plant. Similarly, riots and demonstrations may often call attention to some major problem that has been too long ignored. Although direct action has obvious limitations, is often unproductive, and can occasionally boomerang, it sometimes gets results. It is very unlikely, for instance, that after the 1970 riots the city of Reggio Calabria will be totally neglected by the Italian government with regard to future appropriations. For the 1970 riots were a clear warning that attention must be paid.

THE PROCESS OF POLICY MAKING: FACT FINDING AND CONSULTATION

We have already pointed out that the fact-finding facilities at the disposal of the Italian government are rather inadequate, so much so that both the legislature and the bureaucracy are inordinately reliant on interest groups for information. In the case of the Italian Parliament, the individual deputy or senator has no office, no secretary, no staff assistance of his own, unless he can afford to finance them out of his own pocket.[14] The standing committees, to be sure, have secretariats, operating under the supervision of a directorate of committees; but these secretariats are undermanned and can do little more than draw up the committee agenda (in accordance with the wishes of the chairman) and prepare legislative texts for transmission to the floor. A staff organ designed to serve the chamber as a whole is the Office of Legislative Studies; but this agency, too, is understaffed.[15]

The Italian government seems to have embarked recently on an effort to render the bureaucracy more capable of fulfilling its fact-finding responsibilities.[16] For one thing, the Budget Ministry is being greatly strengthened as an organ of policy coordination, in connection with the adoption of national economic planning.

[14] Predieri, p. 250.
[15] Ferrarotti, pp. 30, 34–39. This Office has produced a number of worthwhile comparative legal research reports in the late 1960s, however, so that Ferrarotti's pessimistic judgment may not be entirely justified.
[16] Mario D'Antonio, *Commenti al programma economico nazionale* (Bologna: Cappelli, 1968), pp. 1097–1100.

Aided by a Central Accounting Office, a Technical Scientific Council for Economic Planning, and a Planning Secretariat, it should be able to serve as a central clearing house for economic and social data of all kinds. Secondly, a new category of economic counsellors is being established in the upper echelons of the Italian bureaucracy; this should serve to remedy somewhat the legalistic bias—and the consequent resistance against the utilization of modern data-gathering techniques—that characterizes the Italian higher civil service. Finally, the new emphasis on economic planning probably will create continuing pressure to improve the research services of the Italian government and, above all, to establish better coordination among them, so that data available to one agency are also made available to other sectors of the governmental apparatus.

While the fact-finding resources of the Italian government leave much to be desired, the policy-making process amply provides for consultation of affected agencies and interests before a new policy is actually adopted. To begin with, it is a matter of common knowledge that the introduction of a government bill is preceded by exhaustive discussions within the directorates and parliamentary groups of the parties represented in the cabinet. The Council of State (an administrative advisory organ and administrative court) must also be consulted prior to the actual initiation of government legislation, and the National Council of Economy and Labor *may* be consulted if the cabinet so desires. Parliament, on the other hand, has the option of consulting, or neglecting to consult, both the National Council of Economy and Labor and the Council of State; and it appears that Parliament has invariably chosen *not* to seek the advice of the Council of State.[17] In the case of government "regulations" (executive orders), the Court of Accounts must be consulted first. This body may refuse to "register" an executive order, in which case the frustrated minister may appeal to the cabinet as a whole. If the cabinet sides with the minister, the Court of Accounts will be required to "register" the executive "regulation." But it will probably do so "with reservations." Such registrations with reservations are periodically filed with Parliament but seem to have little impact on the legislature's relationship with the executive.[18]

The committee stage in the consideration of a bill is obviously a form of obligatory consultation. In Italy, this stage imme-

[17] Predieri, pp. 251–252.
[18] John Clarke Adams and Paolo Barile, *The Government of Republican Italy* (2nd ed.; Boston: Houghton Mifflin, 1966), p. 105.

diately follows the introduction of a bill. Thus, there is at least one striking general similarity between American and Italian parliamentary processes: the great importance attached to the committee stage. However, in a number of vital respects, the Italian standing committee falls short of the American model. First of all, as we have mentioned, it lacks adequate staff services. Second, it almost invariably prefers not to hold public hearings, though there is nothing in the Constitution or in the Chamber of Deputies or Senate rules to prevent such hearings from being scheduled. So, standing committees do not serve as convenient rostrums from which affected interest groups may appeal to public opinion. Third, even if standing committees were to conduct public hearings, they have no power to require witnesses to attend and answer questions. There is, consequently, room for legitimate doubt as to just how much meaningful consultation actually takes place during the committee stage, which seems to serve primarily as a means of expediting minor legislation recommended by the ministries and as a convenient quagmire for surreptitiously burying controversial bills.

Apart from the introduction of government bills and the formal consultations therewith required, the executive branch of the Italian government regularly engages in a variegated pattern of advisory relationships with many assorted interlocutors. To begin with, most ministries have an advisory council reporting directly to the minister and including among its members persons appointed from outside the government. Then, too, an intricate network of cabinet committees are supposed to keep ministers informed of what their colleagues are doing. In a recent administrative shake-up, some of these committees have been abolished and a new Interministerial Committee for Economic Programming (CIPE) has been created. Sixteen ministers—the bulk of the cabinet—are members of this supercommittee.[19]

An even broader range of consultations is provided for under the new system of national and regional planning. The minister of the budget and economic programming is given primary responsibility for preparing the national economic plan. In the course of preparing the plan (for which the main guidelines are set by the CIPE), the minister consults the major economic interest groups: labor unions, industrialists, shopkeepers, farmers, artisans, cooperatives, and consumers. He also must take account of regional

[19] D'Antonio, pp. 1103–1105.

development schemes prepared by the Regional Committees for Economic Programming (CRPE's). In addition to these sources of information and advice, the minister consults the National Council of Economy and Labor, the Fund for the South, the National Electric Power Corporation, the National Committee for Nuclear Energy, the IRI and ENI corporations, and the largest private corporations. In order to avoid overlapping of functions and jurisdictional disputes, this greatly strengthened minister is expected to work in close cooperation with the minister of the treasury. He is also provided with several consultative committees (composed of civil servants and outside experts) to aid him in his task of policy coordination.

Members of the CRPE prior to the June 1970 election of regional councils included the presidents of provincial governing juntas; the mayors of provincial capitals and of other communes with over 30,000 population; the presidents of provincial chambers of commerce, industry, and agriculture; the representatives of the main labor confederations; representatives of the Direct Cultivators, of the main agricultural cooperatives, and of the artisans; and delegates from the Fund for the South and other state agencies. Yet, despite this elaborate representative apparatus, the CRPE's are mainly advisory bodies. The minister of the budget and the CIPE may accept, modify, or discard CRPE recommendations as they see fit.[20]

Despite this intricate machinery for consulting all affected agencies and interests—or perhaps partly *because* of this superstructure—there still seems to be faulty coordination and inadequate exchange of data in the Italian policy-making process. For example, in regard to the Fiat-Citroen merger and again in regard to the IRI-ENI attempt to take over the Montedison chemical combine, some ministries were not kept informed of what was about to take place.[21] It has also been charged that, in the case of the IRI project to build an automobile plant near Naples (the so-called *Alfa Sud* project), the pressure of local interests was allowed to override the advice of technical experts on the matter of the precise location of the new industrial complex.[22] In conclu-

[20] On the structure and role of the CRPE's, see Francesco Indovina, *Esperienze di pianificazione regionale* (Padova: Marsilio Editori, 1967).
[21] "The Old Capitalism Gives Way to the New," *The Economist*, Vol. 229, No. 6530 (October 19, 1968), 47.
[22] On the *Alfa Sud* project, see Luigi Barbato, *Politica meridionalista e localizzazione industriale: dalla Legge Pastore all' Alfa Sud* (Padova: Marsilio Editori, 1968), chs. 3–8.

sion, it is evident that in Italy's fragmented political culture, widespread consultations simply pose added hurdles for policy proposals to overcome.

THE PROCESS OF POLICY MAKING: THE FORMULATION OF ALTERNATIVES

The formulation of alternatives to the policies proposed by the government is supposed to be the function of the opposition. However, as we know, Italy has a splintered opposition, ranging from the Neo-Fascists on the extreme Right, through the Liberals on the Right-Center, to the Communists on the extreme Left. These opposition parties do not share the same goals. Obviously, then, lacking a concentrated opposition, a clear-cut set of alternatives to the programs presented by the government can never be constructed.

The principal opposition party *does* submit a number of private-member bills and amendments to government bills. Strangely enough, some Communist-sponsored legislation is actually adopted. A recent study reveals that, during the years 1958–1963, 523 bills were introduced by Communist party members of the Chamber of Deputies; and of these, 66 were adopted. Most of the bills adopted were, to be sure, of relatively minor importance. In fact, over two-thirds were adopted in standing committees acting *in sede deliberante,* where such legislation would be likely to attract a minimum of public attention.[23] It may well be that these Communist-sponsored bills represented a *quid pro quo* for a cooperative Communist posture in the standing committees of the Chamber of Deputies. In any event, the Communist party in the Italian Parliament does not appear to play a role of purely negative and sterile opposition.

In addition to presenting legislation of their own, the Communists have displayed a talent for associating themselves with reform measures that have been initiated by the more progressive segments of the majority coalition.[24] In so doing, they are able to

---

[23] Pierre Ferrari, "Le groupe parlementaire communiste et son activité à la Chambre des Députés du Parlement italien," in Pierre Ferrari and Herbert Maisl, *Les groupes communistes aux Assemblées parlementaires italiennes (1958–1963) et françaises (1962–1967)* (Paris: Presses Universitaires de France, 1969), pp. 47–53.

[24] Silvano Tosi, "Italy: Anti-System Opposition Within the System," *Government and Opposition*, Vol. 2, No. 1 (November 1966), 57–60.

capture some of the popularity that accrues to the reforms themselves and to strengthen their image as just another progressive, forward-looking party in the system. The fact that such reform measures are often long overdue, and have actually been held up by powerful conservative factions in the parties of the majority coalition, tends to discredit the parties in power and make the presence of a strong Communist party appear indispensable to many Italian voters.

However, the Communist party is not the only source of alternative solutions to Italian problems. Italian interest groups, which in many cases enjoy direct representation in Parliament (their officials are elected on some party's slate), offer many amendments to government bills and also sponsor bills of their own. Like the Communist party, they are especially effective during the committee stage, or on those occasions when the committees actually legislate *in sede deliberante*. Highly technical measures, which fail to attract the attention or interest of the general public, are the specialty of Italian lobbyists and are most likely to succeed either on their own or as modifications of government bills. But most of the successful amendments to government bills are presented by legislators belonging to the parties of the majority coalition (many of these legislators may be also acting as interest-group officials). On some occasions, in fact, the cabinet may encourage amendments to its own bill, not with a view to improving the bill, but rather with the intention of delaying its passage, watering it down, or even killing it. This form of "majority obstructionism" is used to hold up or defeat legislation that was promised in the last election campaign but was opposed by powerful conservative factions in the majority party.[25]

As we can see, there is very little structure to the formulation of alternatives in Italian politics. In place of a clear juxtaposition between the program of the government and the program of the opposition, Italy's proposed policies confront a myriad of petty modifications and corrections to the measures submitted by the cabinet. These numerous amendments, often presented by the cabinet's own nominal supporters, result in blurring public issues and in making it very difficult to assess responsibility for the success or failure of a given program. Because the cabinet, too, fails to speak in unison, its "program" may often be simply an uncoordinated aggregation of pet projects introduced by ministries that

[25] Piero Calamandrei, *Scritti e discorsi politici*, Vol. I (Firenze: La Nuova Italia, 1966), pp. 564–595.

may well be working at cross-purposes. In fact, we may sum up the opacity of the Italian decision-making routine by saying that, in the Italian Parliament, alternatives are about as clear as they are in the United States Congress.

POLICY DELIBERATION

The early phases of the policy-making process obviously include a great deal of public deliberation about proposed governmental measures. But let us clarify the picture by outlining the path followed by a bill after it has been introduced in Parliament, or by an executive order after it has been conceived and drafted by civil servants in a ministry. Then, we will attempt to touch upon certain characteristic features of the actual discussion of policy in Parliament.

A bill, as we know, may be introduced either by the cabinet or by a private member of Parliament. The two other possible modes of initiation—by an initiative petition signed by 50,000 voters, or by regional councils—have almost never been employed. If a private-member bill entails financial outlays, the Chamber of Deputies (but *not* the Senate) is required by its rules to vote on whether or not to take the bill into consideration. Such a private-member bill must contain a clear indication of how the new expenditures are to be defrayed. Apart from these requirements, there seem to be no major limitations on the introduction of private-member bills.

Once introduced, the bill is assigned immediately by the president of the chamber to one of the various permanent standing committees. He will instruct the committee either to report the bill back to the chamber *in sede referente* with its recommendations or to decide on final passage of the bill *in sede deliberante*. Whichever procedure is followed, the committee stage appears to be the key phase in the consideration of a bill, for many controversial measures never get out of committee. When the committee is ready to report the bill to the floor (assuming that the *in sede deliberante* procedure has not been utilized), the Conference of Presidents, which has the power to propose the order of business for each sitting, decides the bill's place on the legislative calendar.

On the floor of the chamber, the bill first undergoes a general discussion, culminating in a vote on a motion for approval. If the general tenor of the bill has won the approbation of the chamber, the bill is then discussed article by article; and at this stage amendments may be introduced and considered. After the articles of the bill have been approved, either intact or as amended, there is a final vote on the bill as a whole. In the Chamber of Deputies, the rules prescribe that this final vote be by secret ballot. Once the bill has overcome this last obstacle, it is then transmitted to the other chamber, where the same procedure is followed. If it emerges intact from this second ordeal, it is then sent on to the president of Italy for his signature. If it is defeated in the second chamber, it cannot become law. If, on the other hand, it is modified by the second chamber, however slightly, it must then go back to the first chamber for reconsideration. Since there is no provision for conference committees, this kind of shuttle can continue for years. There is, however, an abbreviated procedure available for bills of declared urgency.

In the case of executive orders (legislative decrees, decree laws, and regulations), numerous consultations are required by law or by administrative practice. If a cabinet measure is involved, rather than simply a minor regulation interesting only a single ministry, the measure usually has to be considered by a cabinet committee before obtaining the consent of the cabinet as a whole. Also, the Council of State must be consulted in an advisory capacity; and the Court of Accounts may refuse to register the executive order, thus setting in motion a complicated appellate procedure. Finally, of course, the president of Italy has the right to refuse to authorize the introduction of a government bill or the issuance of a cabinet decree.

However, these are the bare bones of the deliberative process, as described by the Constitution, the laws, the rules of the two chambers. We still do not know enough about what actually happens during these phases of policy deliberation. We still do not have much in the way of systematic case studies regarding the actual distribution of power within Parliament and within the cabinet. When and if such information becomes known, we may well discover what we have already discerned in the case of the United States Congress—that is, a different power structure functions for each issue.

On one point, however, our information is fairly explicit: We know a good deal about the character of debate on the floor of Parliament. Most of the speeches delivered in Parliament are ideological discussions of a rather general nature, better suited to campaign addresses than to legislative debates. Such themes as the Vietnam war, Marxism, capitalism, honesty, democracy, justice, progress, peace, and liberty take up time which might better be allotted to concrete policy matters. And this type of "debate" occurs even when Parliament is discussing the budget or some major piece of legislation.[26] In issues concerning more mundane problems, the members of Parliament seem to be interested only when a bill under consideration affects their local constituencies directly. When some major bill of national importance that contains highly technical provisions is under review, only a handful of senators or deputies are likely to be present.[27] In short, debate seems to cluster around the two extremes of the political spectrum: abstract philosophical discourses or pure pork-barrel demands. Empirical discussion oriented toward relatively broad goals seems to be all but absent from the floor of Parliament.

AUTHORITATIVE DECISIONS

An authoritative decision in Italy can take any one of a number of forms. One such decision is the statute, an act of Parliament passed by consent of both chambers. Once a statute has been passed, it is sent on to the president of Italy for promulgation into law. At this stage, the president may exercise his power of suspensive veto—that is, he may return the bill to Parliament with the request that it be reconsidered. If Parliament should pass the bill again, even by a simple majority, the president is then obliged to promulgate it. Suspensive vetoes do not occur very frequently; but when they do, they are rarely overridden by Parliament.

Voting on a bill may take the form of a rising vote (the most common procedure), a division (with ayes and nays gathering in separate parts of the chamber), a roll-call (required for votes of confidence), or a secret ballot (required for the final vote on a bill in the Chamber of Deputies, but sometimes also employed in the Senate). The secret ballot involves the casting of a white ball into a white urn and a black ball into a black urn (in the event of a favorable vote on a bill), or a black ball into a white urn and a white ball into a black urn (in the event of a negative vote). The procedure is not as "secret" as one might wish, for deputies have been known to peek over their colleagues' shoulders; but it does conceal the legislators' behavior from the voters at large.

However, as we have already observed, statutes also may be

---

[26] Giorgio Galli, *Il bipartitismo imperfetto* (Bologna: Il Mulino, 1966), pp. 299–302, 314–317.
[27] Vittorio De Caprariis, *Le garanzie della libertà* (Milano: Il Saggiatore, 1966), pp. 148–150.

enacted by parliamentary standing committees acting *in sede deliberante*. In fact, about three-fourths of all laws are thus adopted in committee without ever coming back to the floor.[28] This procedure is used mostly for bills of relatively minor importance, the *leggine*.

There are a number of reasons given for the heavy reliance on this unique method of legislation, where other parliamentary systems would simply resort to executive decrees. First of all, the executive branch often encourages the introduction of *leggine* to promote its more technical, less politically controversial projects, rather than run the risk of having an executive decree blocked temporarily by the Court of Accounts. In this instance, a private-member bill may actually be a government bill in disguise. Secondly, many members of Parliament react strongly against their increasing powerlessness with regard to major legislation. Where such legislation is involved, they are apt to be committed in advance to follow the line laid down by their respective party directorates and parliamentary groups. Legislators give vent to their sense of frustration, therefore, by introducing a plethora of minor bills with which the cabinet and the parties are less likely to interfere. Thirdly, the output of *leggine* is rendered necessary in many cases by the deplorable habit of the former Fascist regime of issuing numerous decree-laws dealing with relatively secondary administrative matters. Trivial as their subject matter often was, decree-laws could only be amended or repealed by a statute. Hence the need for *leggine*.[29]

There is an interesting point to be noted with regard to the *in sede deliberante* procedure. Not only do the Communists usually fail to exercise the legal option of forcing bills out of standing committee and onto the floor; they also, more often than not, vote for government bills in committee when this anomalous procedure is being employed. A remarkably high percentage of bills passed *in sede deliberante* are approved unanimously or receive no more than two negative votes. And this virtual unanimity occurs even at times of grave political crisis, when Communists and Christian Democrats are denouncing each other bitterly in parliamentary debates.[30] "The important fact is that, whether through deliberate choice or under the pressure of objective conditions, the behavior

[28] Giorgio Galli and Alfonso Prandi, *Patterns of Political Participation in Italy* (New Haven, Conn.: Yale University Press, 1970), p. 271.
[29] Mauro Ferri, "La crisi degli organi legislativi," in Direzione PSI-PSDI Unificati-Sezione per la Riforma dello Stato, *Stato moderno e riforma del Parlamento* (Roma: Direzione PSI-PSDI Unificati, 1967), pp. 28–30. See also Predieri, p. 219.
[30] Galli and Prandi, pp. 271–274.

of party deputies in parliamentary committees is different from that of deputies dealing with legislation on the Chamber floor."[31]

Other kinds of authoritative decisions include the legislative decrees, decree-laws, and executive regulations which we have discussed earlier in this chapter and in Chapter Seven. Such measures require the president's approval, which may be withheld. But a decision by IRI or ENI, or some other public corporation or holding company, to build a new plant or embark on some new investment policy is also an authoritative decision and one which is not subject to very effective cabinet control. For the cabinet, or the individual ministry involved, tends as a rule to accept the judgment of the public corporation after a process of review that borders on the perfunctory. And finally, it has been noted that an increasing proportion of far-reaching decisions are reached by direct confrontation between interest groups, especially between capital and labor, thus bypassing the formal policy-making structures altogether. These decisions receive enough support from government to give them an authoritative aura.[32]

STYLES IN CONFLICT RESOLUTION AND PROBLEM SOLVING

To speak of Italian political style is to indulge in a measure of oversimplification. For different categories of Italian decision makers are apt to approach problems in very different ways. One can, therefore, only refer to certain styles or patterns of behavior that are to be found in the Italian decision-making process, bearing in mind the fact that these styles are by no means universally applicable throughout the Italian political system.

Italian political style has often been described as ideological.[33] There is indeed a tendency to discuss public policy in highly abstract terms, using fairly generic slogans as a substitute for specific proposals to solve specific problems. All through the 1950s, Italian political life was paralyzed by a repetition of the slogans of the past. Edelman and Fleming state:

> Nineteenth-century monarchy or economic laissez-faire, confessional bonds, the relatively infrequent and moderate interventions

---

[31] Galli and Prandi, p. 273.

[32] Norberto Bobbio, "Le istituzioni parlamentarie ieri e oggi," in Leopoldo Piccardi, Norberto Bobbio, Ferruccio Parri, *La sinistra davanti alla crisi del parlamento* (Milano: Giuffré, 1967), pp. 31–33.

[33] Herbert J. Spiro, *Government by Constitution* (New York: Random House, 1959), pp. 199–200.

of government into the economy of the early twentieth century, or the stock slogans of the Second or Third Socialist Internationals molded the content of political debate. Inevitably, these appeals helped keep public opinion polarized rather than making a dialogue possible.[34]

Even reformist forces in Italian public life are victims of this ideological malady. For example, the *Il Mondo* group and other forces of the democratic Left *did* identify a number of policies that were sorely needed if Italy were to be transformed into a modern state, capable of facing up to its political and socioeconomic responsibilities. But some observers accuse the democratic Left of having demanded reform without exploring its content, of having failed to face up to the problem of developing the proper administrative tools to do the job.[35] Such goals as the opening to the Left, economic planning, and structural reforms often seemed to be ritualistic shibboleths rather than sets of proposed policies based on careful analyses of ends and means.

This same tendency toward generic approximation (colloquially in Italy, *pressapochismo*, or "just-about-ism") is to be found in the national economic plan itself. Much of the language used in the plan is vague and discursive, words are often employed in an imprecise way, the projections in the plan are very broad and general (for instance, the plan indicates how much is to be spent for scientific research but fails to specify how the money is to be allocated among various disciplines). In short, the Italian economic plan is much less detailed, much less carefully prepared than the French.[36]

This ideological syndrome is, in part, the result of the very significant role played by humanistic intellectuals in Italian public life. In an essentially elitist political culture, the intellectual elite uses its own secret language, a language for initiates, and is under little pressure to clarify its high-flown verbiage. Then, too, ambiguity is often essential as a means of keeping a diversified coalition together. Very often, a vague formula is an effective mechanism for postponing conflict until power relationships have become clearer. Slogans may therefore serve a very pragmatic palliative function, of glossing over unbridgeable differences until a consensus can be reached.

[34] Murray Edelman and R. W. Fleming, *The Politics of Wage-Price Decisions: A Four-Country Analysis* (Urbana, Ill.: University of Illinois Press, 1965), p. 79.
[35] Franco Rizzo, *Partiti Piano e Stato* (Roma: Edizioni Montecitorio, 1966), pp. 121–123.
[36] Alberto Predieri, "Il programma economico 1966–1970, aspetti giuridici," in Alberto Predieri, Piero Barucci, Mariangela Bartoli, Gabriela Gioli, *Il Programma Economico 1966–1970* (Milano: Giuffré, 1967), pp. 54–61.

Another characteristic feature of Italian political style has been evident in the role played by the state in regulating the economy. Public intervention in economic life in Italy has always had essentially conservative goals, reflecting the innate conservatism, the passion for stability and order, that marks the Italian bureaucracy. Pre-Fascist protectionism, Fascist corporativism, the institution of social assistance and social insurance programs, the Italian land reform with its emphasis on the family farm, the effort by IRI to preserve unprofitable plants with a view to preventing unemployment—a common strand in all these programs is an effort to protect established interests or to confront critical situations of poverty or dire need. There has been no real effort to modernize or to embark on far-reaching social innovations. There has been, rather, a concern for patching up an existing organism, while attempting to keep the organism essentially unchanged.

But if this has been the style of the Italian bureaucrats in the ministries, and probably also of the politicians who supervise them, the decision-making style of the technocratic managers in the public and private sectors of the economy has been quite different. First of all, the technocrats have tended to worship efficiency as a paramount value, and consequently to accept changes and departures from past traditions with much less reluctance than the bureaucracy expresses. Second, they have placed greater emphasis on precision, on the use of modern methods, and on approaching problems in an empirical fashion, unfettered by preconceptions. Third, technocrats tend to be bold and enterprising in their decision making. In place of the exaggerated concern for legal precedents and "buck passing" that exists in the Italian civil service, the Italian manager often follows the "*condottiere* principle": Enrico Mattei of ENI, for instance, "had been handed a fief to look after and he saw it as his task to enlarge its power and extent wherever possible—if at the expense of rivals, so much the better."[37]

The prevalence of the "*condottiere* principle" is perhaps one reason for the chronic lack of coordination in the Italian system of government. The relative independence enjoyed by IRI, ENI, and other public enterprises; the existence of separate and mutually contradictory development programs in the South; the feuds between ministries and even between sections of the same ministry; the tendency to cope with each new problem or crisis by creating a new agency or passing a new "special law" applicable to a speci-

[37] Andrew Shonfield, *Modern Capitalism: The Changing Balance of Public and Private Power* (New York: Oxford University Press, 1965), p. 185.

fied region or a specified city—these are all manifestations of a political decision-making apparatus that lacks a sense of common purpose and cannot seem to operate as a united team. Although this type of problem exists in most political systems, it happens to be especially acute in Italy.

POLICY IMPLEMENTATION AND THE ROLE OF THE BUREAUCRACY

The responsibility for carrying out the policies that have emerged from the decision-making process is shouldered by the members of the Italian bureaucracy. We have already noted (see Chapter Seven) that the recruitment and training of higher civil servants in Italy has been of such a nature as to enlist elements primarily from the more static or backward areas of the country, particularly the South. The relatively unattractive salary scales and the paucity of other inducements (contrasted to the career opportunities offered by the private industrial sector of the economy) combine with the generally low prestige of the public service to create a situation in which numerous administrative and technical jobs lack qualified applicants.[38]

To speak of the low prestige of the Italian bureaucracy is to indulge in something of an understatement. Bureaucracies are rarely popular, but the Italian public service enjoys particularly poor public relations. There is a general tendency—encouraged by the press and based partly on a heritage of exploitation of the Italian peninsula by oppressive foreign overlords—to regard the bureaucracy as being not merely inefficient, poorly organized, and arrogant toward the public it is assigned to serve, but downright dishonest as well. Very often these negative views are not even based on actual personal experience, but on hearsay. However, there are enough kernels of truth in these often ill-informed criticisms to give them some credence and to keep them in circulation.

How does the Italian bureaucracy react to its own social and regional origins and to its poor public image? The "typical" Italian bureaucrat is strongly influenced by his Southern origin and by his legal training. That is to say, his outlook is ascription-oriented rather than achievement-oriented: He is more concerned about his own status and personal security than about any major substantive

[38] Domenico Bartoli, *L'Italia burocratica* (Milano: Garzanti, 1965), pp. 199–201.

goals to be attained with the help of the position he occupies. He is resentful of the diminished power and prestige of the bureaucracy, a diminution he regards as a serious comedown from the status the Italian civil service could boast earlier in this century. Moreover, he is obsessed with the primacy of the law, and with the need to find a legal justification for every action, and is therefore very prone to cast about for reasons why some action should *not* be performed or even attempted. He is very critical of certain details of the bureaucratic subsystem in which he operates—the painful slowness of the promotion process, the skimpy salary scales, the lack of adequate equipment, the antiquated administrative structures and procedures—but he is not at all certain as to what kind of bureaucracy should replace the present system. There is present, in his attitudes and patterns of behavior, a medley of conflicting themes: A kind of instinctive attachment to outdated methods and routines appropriate to a predominantly static nineteenth-century society is combined with a growing but vague awareness of the fact that these methods and routines are no longer acceptable in a modern industrial country.[39] It is hardly surprising, then, that Italian public administration has failed to act as a stimulating force for innovation.

Thus far, the major pressures for bureaucratic reform and policy innovation have come from outside the bureaucracy: from the parties, from the press, from the intellectuals of the democratic Left. But these pressures do not add up to a clear and comprehensive program for reform. The parties, in fact, have failed to furnish the kind of vigorous and positive leadership that might conceivably have won the grudging support of the bureaucracy.[40] Instead, there has been an assortment of generic and uncoordinated proposals, accompanied by some rather extravagant criticisms of the civil service. The parties have perhaps only succeeded in generating a defensive reaction among aggrieved bureaucrats and possibly in alienating them still further from the public they are supposed to serve.

How well does the Italian bureaucracy perform the function of policy implementation? With agonizing slowness and indecision, most observers agree. Every decision is subjected to a multiplicity of controls and stipulated procedures: approval by a sub-

[39] Istituto per la Scienza dell' Amministrazione Pubblica (ISAP), *La burocrazia periferica e locale in Italia: analisi sociologica* Part I: Franco Demarchi, *L'ideologia del funzionario* (Milano: Giuffré, 1969), pp. 67–70. 74–76, 116–117, 196–198, 305–309, 319–331, 357–361.

[40] Jean Meynaud, *La tecnocrazia mito o realtà* (Bari: Laterza, 1966), pp. 28–29.

sidiary branch of the General Accounting Office, registration by the Court of Accounts, consultation with the Council of State for all contracts above a certain sum, and so on. The laws, and the internal regulations of the ministries, often specify a set number of "steps" every case must undergo, steps which would in reality be unnecessary where minor noncontroversial decisions are involved. And so, certain cases drag on for years, decades, even centuries in a few instances. For example, in 1954, the budget of the Ministry of the Treasury included a sum of 350,000 *lire* (about $600) to liquidate certain claims presented by applicants whose property had been damaged by the armed forces of the Kingdom of the Two Sicilies in 1859. Also, claims for subsidies to the victims of the great earthquake of 1908 are still being processed. Many cases up for administrative implementation are examined by as many as thirty different individuals, any one of whom may send a file back to the point of origin because of some minor irregularity or discrepancy. It is surprising that any cases at all succeed in running this kind of gauntlet. And yet, apart from a few isolated improvements in the bureaucracy, all efforts to achieve a comprehensive simplification of administrative procedures have been frustrated.[41]

Overcentralization also slows down the process of policy implementation. Not only are there a variety of central controls on the activities of local authorities, but also the national field services are virtually compelled to refer a great number of relatively minor decisions to Rome for the signature of the director general of the Ministerial Directorate (that is, bureau), or of the minister himself. A number of laws and decrees providing for the delegation of authority by the ministers and their directors general have failed to have much of an impact on bureaucratic procedures, on the refusal of the chief to trust his underlings, on the penchant of the minor officials for passing the buck to their superiors.[42] This centralizing tendency seems to have very strong roots in Italian culture, for also in Italian industry middle management does not play a very significant role.

Bureaucratic over-expansion is also the result of the overstaffing of numerous government offices, a legacy of the days when the bureaucracy functioned as a kind of work relief agency for the unemployed. While the United States Internal Revenue Service in the early 1960s employed about 60,000 civil servants to process over 100 million tax returns, the Italian taxation system needed

[41] Bartoli, pp. 153–157, 171–174, 179–185, and Spreafico, pp. 81–84.
[42] La Palombara, pp. 339–341.

about 30,000 employees to process a mere 4 million returns.[43] Efforts to introduce modern methods of evaluating efficiency are resisted vehemently. Italian bureaucrats who have attended a Ford Foundation-sponsored course in public administration at the University of Bologna or the University of California, and who try to preach modern administrative methods, have apparently been ridiculed by their colleagues and relegated to routine tasks.[44] The sluggishness of the Italian bureaucracy is best summarized in a true experience, related by an American journalist: In order to obtain a special license plate prescribed for diplomats or correspondents owning foreign-made cars, he had to make 71 telephone calls, fill out 18 documents, purchase 6 tax stamps, and visit 13 government offices over a period of four months.[45]

As we already know, political considerations may influence the recruitment and promotion of civil servants, despite the existence of a merit system. Even those who enter the civil service through competitive examinations may find that membership in the Christian Democratic party and responsiveness to the wishes of Christian Democratic members of Parliament and of pressure groups connected to the Christian Democratic party by *parentela* ties are frequently regarded as prerequisites for desirable assignments and promotions. At any rate, many civil servants are convinced that political criteria dominate the promotion process. A group such as Catholic Action is often active in interfering with bureaucratic careers, especially since it can inject itself into the appointive and promotional processes by virtue of its intimate, interlocking bonds with the Christian Democratic party. Since 1946, the Christian Democratic party and its affiliated *parentela* pressure groups have succeeded in colonizing large sectors of the public service, as well as the land reform agencies, the Fund for the South, and the public corporations, with their recommended appointees. The resulting network of vested interests tends, of course, to reinforce Christian Democratic supremacy.[46]

The intrusion of patronage considerations in the appointment and promotion of civil servants brings up the related possibility of bureaucratic corruption. Corruption can take a number of forms. For example, a citizen may slip an envelope containing cash (the notorious *bustarella* of Italian political folklore) to a public offi-

---

[43] Bartoli, pp. 174–175.
[44] La Palombara, pp. 280–281.
[45] Irving R. Levine, *Main Street, Italy* (New York: Doubleday, 1963), pp. 41–42.
[46] La Palombara, pp. 118, 306–348.

cial in an effort to expedite consideration of his case. Or, a special illicit privilege (a public contract, an import license, exemption from the draft, and so on) may be obtained through payment of a financial retainer. Or, a public official may simply appropriate public money for his own use, in the manner of Cesare Mastrella, a customs inspector who managed to embezzle vast sums out of tariff receipts and who enjoyed several years of *dolce vita* with his wife and his mistress before being unmasked. Or, political parties can, and do, use public funds—especially from public corporations whose finances are not subject to rigorous control by the state—to defray their campaign expenses. This last form of corruption is feasible only if a party actually holds government office, at the national or local level.

How important is corruption in the Italian bureaucracy? Italian public opinion seems to regard the civil service as being thoroughly permeated with rogues. A recent DOXA poll found that only 34 percent of a selected cross-section of voters believed that all or almost all state officials are honest, whereas 41 percent believed the contrary, and 25 percent expressed no opinion.[47] Of course, the public tends to exaggerate in these matters: It is typical of the uninformed and alienated to see dishonesty everywhere. But observers suggest that there is more corruption in the Italian bureaucracy than in the civil service of any other Western European democracy. Moreover, there seems to be a good deal of impressionistic evidence to bolster this surmise. Every few months, the press covers a big scandal. The peddling of influence is so common and habitual as to strike even the most casual observer. So, it is probably safe to assume that—while not as widespread and all-pervasive as the public believes—corruption plays a very important role in the Italian political system.

There are several plausible explanations for the situation just described. The low salaries of civil servants constitute an ever-present source of temptation. The rapid economic development Italy has been undergoing encourages various forms of profiteering, including illicit ones. The strong sense of family loyalty that characterizes so many traditional societies (including the Italian South) is likely to cause civil servants to help their families, at the expense of the broader community if need be. Also, the rigid legalistic controls imposed on the bureaucracy make it virtually impossible for an agency head to achieve his organizational goals without bypassing the law, cutting corners, and even violating

[47] Pierpaolo Luzzatto-Fegiz, *Il volto sconosciuto dell' Italia 1956–1965* (2nd series; Milano: Giuffré, 1966), p. 993.

explicit but senseless legal norms.[48] The case of the head of the National Committee for Nuclear Energy (CNEN), who was sentenced to ten years in jail, is often cited as an illustration of this last point.

Perhaps the main reason for corruption is a certain measure of public tolerance for the phenomenon. The Italian public apparently has a pretty vague and permissive perception of what, precisely, constitutes immoral conduct on the part of a public servant. For example, the practice of "cumulation of offices," under which a higher civil servant could hold down several full-time salaried government posts simultaneously and collect his full salary for each job, was officially tolerated for many years without any major public reaction. In a recent public opinion survey, 44 percent of a given cross-section of Italian voters expressed the view that a state official who does a favor for his friends or relatives without making any profit for himself is not dishonest. Only 36 percent expressed the contrary opinion, and 20 percent voiced no opinion at all. In short, as the director of the survey put it, the test of dishonesty seems to center on the question of whether or not money actually changes hands.

> The official grants a construction license in exchange for a bribe? He's dishonest. He grants such a license because the beneficiary is a relative, a friend, or a fellow-townsman? He's an honest man. The professor passes a student in exchange for cash? He's dishonest. He passes the son of his brother, or of someone who can help him to pass a competitive exam for a higher rank? He's an honest man.[49]

In such a climate of public opinion, the rigidly impartial civil servant, enforcing the law without fear or favor, is made to feel like an isolated crank.

We have already referred to the rigid legal and procedural controls that confine the discretion of Italian bureaucrats during the processes of decision making and policy implementation. These controls bear a major share of the blame for prolonged delays in bureaucratic output. They also help explain the remarkable degree of autonomy that has been granted to, and to some degree arrogated by, such public corporations as IRI and ENI. By releasing such agencies from the niggling restrictions imposed on the ministries, the Italian government has succeeded in encourag-

[48] Bartoli, pp. 218–219.
[49] Luzzatto-Fegiz, p. 993.

ing greater efficiency and initiative in the public sector of the economy. Of course, it has done so at the price of policy coordination, which is often absent in the Italian decision-making and policy-implementing processes.

SOME ILLUSTRATIONS OF POLICY MAKING IN ITALY

Case studies of the Italian decision-making process are few in number and tend to focus more on the content of policy output than on the process itself. Also, they usually tend to highlight one or two general points about the process rather than illuminate the broad spectrum of decision making from the broaching of the initial demand to the actual promulgation of a law. But they do have a certain illustrative utility.

One decision that has been reviewed at some length is the passage of the law establishing the Italian Constitutional Court.[50] Although the Court was provided for in the Constitution, legislation was needed to authorize its actual creation; and, after 1948, the Christian Democrats, with a safe majority in Parliament, were in no hurry to establish an organ that could limit the power of the political institutions they controlled. Therefore, it was not until March 1949 that the Italian Senate approved a bill providing for the setting up of the Constitutional Court. But this was just the beginning. It took a year for a special committee of the Chamber of Deputies to report the bill out to the floor; when the bill finally came up for consideration in the Chamber, the committee *rapporteur* unexpectedly proposed some major amendments. Some private-member amendments were also introduced by supporters of the government coalition, most of these amendments being designed to strengthen the cabinet's role in the selection of judges. It took almost another year for the Chamber to straighten out the tangle and approve an amended version of the bill. Then, of course, in the absence of any provision for a conference committee, the bill had to go back to the Senate to be reconsidered from the beginning—a process that consumed eighteen months—and then back to the Chamber again. It was not until March 1953 that the Chamber passed the Senate version in substantially unaltered form, and the Senate gave the bill its final approval. This tedious pilgrimage is a prime example of the shuttling of legislation be-

[50] Calamandrei, Vol. I, pp. 559–595.

tween the two houses. It also illustrates "majority obstructionism," for this government-sponsored bill was held up largely by amendments introduced by members of the government (Christian Democratic) majority.

The passage in 1952 of the bill providing for the establishment of the National Hydrocarburants Corporation (ENI) was a much smoother operation.[51] Although the chemical companies and their pressure group (the Italian Mineral Association) opposed the bill, their resistance was felt mostly during the period when the bill was still being drafted. Once the bill had been introduced in Parliament, opposition turned out to be minimal. As a matter of fact, only a handful of deputies took part in the debate. In short, once the effort to dissuade the cabinet from introducing the bill had failed, the opposition virtually surrendered. Thus, in this case at least, we can see that our earlier emphasis on such early stages of the decision-making process as initiation and consultation was by no means unjustified.

The bill for the creation of the National Electric Power Corporation (ENEL) to run the nationalized electric-power industry was introduced after a long and heated series of discussions in the press, on television, and in party gatherings, in contrast to the low-key controversy that preceded the creation of ENI.[52] This bill was a natural by-product of the formation of the first Left-Center coalition government in 1962, since powerful factions in the Italian Socialist party had demanded the nationalization of the electric-power industry as a sign of Christian Democratic commitment to reform. Introduced in the Chamber of Deputies in June 1962 under a special urgency procedure, the bill spent less than three weeks in committee before going to the floor. In the general discussion of the bill's provisions which took place on the floor, some internal tensions in the Christian Democratic party came to light —tensions which actually pitted two leftist factions against each other. And of course, the Communists lost no time in publicizing and underlining these strains within the ranks of the majority party. But by late November the bill was on its way to final promulgation, after having been passed by the Chamber, amended by the Senate, and reconsidered by the Chamber.

The complex internal divisions in the majority party and the willingness of the Communist party in Parliament to exploit these divisions and also to take full credit for the majority party's belated achievements are two of the lessons this case provides. It also appears that, when there is a firm majority behind a bill, the

[51] Galli and Prandi, pp. 288–291.
[52] Galli and Prandi, pp. 294–299.

procedural hurdles will not impose undue delays. But in order to get the cooperation of their Right-wing factions, the Christian Democratic leaders had to agree to a number of technical amendments, especially with regard to compensation.

Consideration of a relatively minor piece of legislation—a bill amending the Highway Code of October 27, 1958—revealed certain inadequacies in the consultation procedure.[53] Apparently, the minister of public works and the minister of transport, who jointly introduced the bill, had failed to sound out a number of affected interest groups during the bill-drafting stage. And this despite the fact that a consultative Automobile Committee was attached by law to the Ministry of Transport for the precise purpose of providing the minister with a chance to hear expert advice from the people most vitally concerned. Furthermore, the National Council of Economy and Labor had not been consulted. So, what appears like a complex consultative pattern on paper may fail to live up to expectations in actual practice.

In his study of the politics of wage-price decisions in Italy, Edelman points to the relatively low level of direct involvement of the Italian government in wage and price matters during the years (the 1950s and early 1960s) when Italy enjoyed a favorable balance of trade. Major decisions were reached by direct negotiations between management and labor, with the government exercising indirect influence through the use of credit policy. There is some evidence, however, that IRI and ENI firms, which negotiate separately with management and are no longer represented by *Confindustria*, were in a position to break the solid front of management resistance against wage increases and plant bargaining.[54] However, IRI and ENI are not always responsive to the wishes of the government.

The last illustrations involve two broad areas of policy: agriculture and the development of the South. The defects of the Italian agricultural system were only too obvious after World War II. There were simply too many people employed in agriculture, given the shortage of cultivable land and the predominantly hilly and mountainous terrain. Medium-sized properties constituted only a very small proportion of the land under cultivation: Most of Italian agricultural land was divided into overly large landed estates or into a myriad of tiny subsistence farms. The subsistence farmers of the Northern hills were falling farther and farther be-

---

[53] Silvia Tozzi, "Gruppi di interesse e processo legislativo. Le Modifiche al codice della strada del 27-10-1958," *Rassegna Italiana di Sociologia*, Vol. 9, No. 4 (October–December 1968), 705–713.

[54] Edelman and Fleming, pp. 286–288.

hind in their struggle against economic destruction. The Tuscan sharecroppers resented the tolerable but stagnant prospects offered by their system of cultivation, which rendered social mobility almost impossible. The insecure farm laborers of the Po Valley were in a state of chronic unrest. And in the South, hunger for land was provoking peasant squatters to occupy large estates. Excessive cultivation of wheat made for low per-acre yield, and reduced Italy's prospects for agricultural exports. Finally, much needed to be done in the way of irrigation, land reclamation, and other forms of government assistance to rural areas.

The Italian government, in attacking the problem of agriculture, has relied especially on the land reform program, the Fund for the South, and more recently, the Green Plan. Under the land reform laws, adopted in 1950, certain parts of Italy—the Sila Plateau in Calabria, the islands of Sicily and Sardinia, the Tuscan Maremma, the Po Delta, the Volturno and Sele valleys in Campania, large parts of Apulia and Lucania, and the Fucino Basin in Abruzzi—were designated as land reform zones. In these areas, public agencies were established with legal authority to expropriate land belonging to large estates (under a formula that granted generous exemptions to intensively cultivated estates) and—after making all necessary improvements—distribute it among peasant proprietors to be chosen by lot. The number of people benefiting from the program is estimated at around 500,000; but the reform barely scratched the surface of the problem of alleviating land hunger in the South. As things turned out, many of the farms set up on the expropriated land were too small to support a family adequately.

Authorities tend to disagree about the land reform. Some feel that it was a step forward, that it exercised pressure for a general rise in living standards, not only among the direct beneficiaries themselves, but also among the people in surrounding communities. Others tend to regard it as a costly failure that has evaded the real problem of setting up viable medium-sized farms. They point, for instance, to the fact that many peasants refused to live in the isolated homesteads built by the land reform agencies, that many recipients of land found their plots too small and had to abandon them, that many other peasants were compelled to take on supplementary jobs off the farm in order to make ends meet, and that the pressure of population on the land was actually aggravated. And La Palombara decries the failure to coordinate the work of the various land reform agencies.[55]

[55] Joseph La Palombara, *Italy: The Politics of Planning* (Syracuse, N.Y.: Syracuse University Press, 1966), pp. 27–28.

The Fund for the South and the Green Plan were both aimed at agricultural pump priming. The law setting up the Fund for the South in 1950 provided for special government investments and subsidies to create the preconditions for Southern economic growth. During the first years of its life, the Fund paid special attention to Southern agriculture: irrigation, water control, reforestation, land improvement, and grants to individual farmers. The Green Plan, enacted in 1961, provided for government investments and loans to aid practically every form of agriculture but with special emphasis on depressed areas. As La Palombara suggests, the Green Plan was not a plan at all, but "nothing more than authorized subsidies and easy credit for the agricultural sector."[56]

In the 1960s, the Italian government embarked on some regulatory measures designed to discourage *mezzadria* (sharecropping), and to stimulate sharecroppers to buy up the land they have been cultivating on low-interest forty-year loans. Other government policies sought to hasten the transition from excessive grain growing to greater reliance on meat products. And efforts have been made to push the formation of marketing cooperatives among small farmers.[57]

The Italian government has also tried to foster Southern industrial growth. The Fund for the South, a special semi-independent agency, operating under the general supervision of a minister-without-portfolio and an interministerial committee, was expected to accomplish a great deal. It was granted authority to spend 1,000 billion *lire* ($1.6 billion) in the South over a ten-year period, and additional funds were appropriated in later years. Its general mission was to promote Southern economic development.

At first, the Fund concentrated on building necessary infrastructures in the South—roads, bridges, aqueducts, public utilities of various kinds—as a necessary basis for industrialization; but since the late 1950s, it has been providing credit and partial subsidies for industrial investment. Moreover, it has begun to concentrate its efforts in some particularly promising areas referred to as "poles of development." Legislation passed in 1957 has supplemented the work of the Fund by stipulating that all firms owned or controlled by the state (including IRI and ENI firms) must concentrate 60 percent of their new investments in the South and eventually have 40 percent of their total investments there. While this legislation is obviously hard to enforce, there has been a

[56] La Palombara, *Italy* . . . , p. 142.
[57] H. Stuart Hughes, *The United States and Italy* (rev. ed.; Cambridge, Mass.: Harvard University Press, 1965), pp. 231–232.

response. The Finsider (IRI) steel works at Taranto, the ENI petrochemical works at Gela, and the *Alfa Sud* auto works to be built by the Alfa Romeo (IRI) Corporation near Naples are examples of a clear public effort. And all sorts of credit inducements are offered by various government agencies to private firms that will invest in the South.

Yet the South has continued to trail behind the rest of the country; in fact, in the 1951–1961 period, the proportion of Italian industrial workers employed in the South declined from 16 percent to 14 percent.[58] There are some industrial areas in the South—the Volturno and Sele valleys near Naples; the outskirts of Naples itself; the steel center at Taranto and the nearby industrial complexes developing around Bari and Brindisi; the oil refineries at Ragusa (Sicily) and the petrochemical works at Gela, Siracusa, and Augusta (all in Sicily); and finally the Eastern Sicilian industrial zone around Catania. But these are, for the most part, "islands" of industrialization surrounded by a backward hinterland.

What has gone wrong, then? First of all, as La Palombara suggests, patronage considerations have played a far too significant part in determining the allocation of development funds. Also, Southern communes were often too poor to take advantage of development aid and provide the services necessary to attract industry and tourism.[59] In the early infrastructure phase of the Fund's activities, investments for public works in the South actually redounded to the benefit of Northern industries, which supplied the necessary materials.[60] Then, too, private capital is scarce in the South; and Northern private investors were discouraged by the shortage of adequate services, the high cost of electric power, the low productivity of Southern unskilled labor, the expense of setting up job-training programs, and the distance from European markets.[61]

Investment in Southern industrial plants has been undertaken mostly by the publicly owned sector of Italian industry—notably IRI and ENI. But the big plants established at places like Taranto and Gela have been capital-intensive rather than labor-intensive— that is, they rely primarily on machinery that requires little labor to service it. Also, they have failed to stimulate the growth of

[58] See Calogero Muscarà, *La geografia dello sviluppo* (Milano: Comunità, 1967), p. 101.
[59] See La Palombara, *Italy* . . . , pp. 44–45.
[60] See Muscarà, p. 103.
[61] See Alberto Acquarone, *Grandi città e aree metropolitane in Italia* (Bologna: Zanichelli, 1961), pp. 304–305.

medium and small enterprises to serve as their subsidiaries and/or suppliers. So, all too often, they have become virtual "cathedrals in the desert," surrounded by squalid backwardness. As one observer puts it, describing the Naples region:

> In fact industry is isolated here, a drop in the ocean, a grain of sand, in a social order consisting of fishermen without boats and peasants without land. No bonds unite one factory with another, and there is no proletariat. Nor does unemployment unite the workers; it divides them, except when it explodes.[62]

CONCLUSIONS

After surveying the Italian policy-making process, we are left with a curious sense of dissatisfaction, very similar to the malaise that is experienced by students of American politics who have attempted to make some sense out of the intricacies of the United States Congress. For, after tracing the progress of a policy decision through all its prescribed stages, identifying the actors, and giving a few illustrations, we have not really emerged with wholly reliable conclusions as to the relative importance of the various protagonists in decision making. The process seems so loosely structured as to defy our efforts to develop any comprehensive theory of decision making or even to establish a hierarchy among the key role-players. In this respect, Italy certainly bears a startling resemblance to the United States.

On the other hand, we have pointed to some significant descriptive data, which may be of use to students of comparative government who wish to probe into some more difficult and intriguing problems at a later date. Similar as it is to our policy-making process in a number of respects, the Italian policy-making process does have certain identifiable features of its own: the ideological differences which divide the parties and hamper decision making; the ill-equipped and poorly motivated bureaucracy which lacks the capacity to take a firm lead toward a well-defined mission; the elaborate but possibly not very genuine apparatus for facilitating policy consultation; the absence of clear-cut alternatives on policy issues; the ideological political style; the utter lack of adequate coordination; and the widespread corruption in the bureaucracy.

[62] See Ottiero Ottieri, *The Men at the Gate* (Boston: Houghton Mifflin, 1962), p. 140. This is a translation of Ottieri's novel, *Donnarumma all' assalto*.

Obviously, these features are not uniquely Italian. They appear, in one form or another, in many other political systems, including the American system. What we need to know, therefore, is how Italy compares to other Western European nations, and to the United States, in regard to some or all of the characteristics we have listed. It is in this sense that area studies display a serious shortcoming. For by focusing on the virtues and vices of a single political system, they unintentionally exaggerate those virtues and vices, and thus bestow on the political system a misleading aura of uniqueness. We may call this the "ethnocentric fallacy," a fixation that causes numerous French scholars to treat the French system as if it were inherently *sui generis* and therefore not comparable to other political systems. Similarly, many Italian area specialists (both Italian and foreign) thrill with righteous indignation as they unveil the corruption and moral squalor that allegedly permeate the Italian political system. To be sure, many of the negative points they raise are all too valid. But political systems need to be examined from a comparative viewpoint if a realistic diagnosis is to be made.

Certainly, the Italian decision-making process further illustrates the cultural lag we have found in other portions of the Italian political system. A highly modernized Northern economy and an increasingly enlightened and secularized Northern society coexists with an archaic, overstaffed, overcentralized, poorly informed bureaucracy. The long decades of preindustrial rigidity that affected both the economy and the society as a whole before 1914 and even—to a considerable degree—during the Fascist period, have apparently left a legacy of cumbersome, overly deliberate formalism that still permeates Italian legislative, administrative, and judicial activity. Yet, when we stop to think about it, cultural lag also appears to be a feature of most modern political systems: Surely there is nothing terribly streamlined about the United States Senate. This phenomenon probably is more pronounced in Italy than in most other Western countries, but lacking firm evidence, we cannot be sure. What is needed, then, is a greater reliance on cross-national studies without sacrificing an indispensable familiarity with relevant national characteristics and intranational differences.

The discipline needs many more case studies of decision making; for there is good reason to believe that there is no such thing as a single accurate model of the Italian decision-making process. In all likelihood, rather, there are a number of types of decision making (types that need to be classified and related to other variables). In short, political scientists are still barely in the initial phases of investigating Italian policy making; there is little beyond sketchy description, although a few interesting ideas, that may serve as the bases for later theory construction, have begun to emerge. Actually, policy making is little understood in other political systems as well. It is an arduous but beckoning frontier for students of political science.

NINE
LEGALISM IN CRISIS
Italian courts and judges

Italian society is ideological in its political style and legalistic in its political orientations. There is a strong emphasis on formal legal concepts, on explicitly stated rules, rather than on dynamic processes and informal understandings. This emphasis can be observed, not only in the law schools and social science faculties, but also in the marketplace, among the common people, who feel more at home in a courtroom than in a voluntary association, and who are more subjects than participants.

PREVALENT CONCEPTIONS OF LAW

Like France and other continental European countries, Italy has a legal system in the civil-law tradition, which stems originally from Roman law. There are a number of basic differences between the civil-law tradition and the common-law heritage with which Americans are so familiar—differences with regard to both accepted legal concepts and formal procedures. In a sense, Italy provides a particularly useful example of a civil-law system. For the Italian legal tradition borrows from two other major approaches to the civil law: the French, with its literal and painstaking examination of legal codes, and the German, with its emphasis on the need to develop precise definitions of legal concepts.

A recent study of the Italian legal system stresses the abstractness and conceptualism of the Italian legal style.[1] Law is seen as a set of universally applicable principles, which are to be interpreted and applied with little concern for the facts of the individual case. In other words, Italian legal scholars, in approaching a given case, are far more interested in discovering the applicable provision in the legal code, and interpreting the precise meaning of that provision, than in analyzing the facts of the case itself and inquiring into their possible legal consequences. (In this connection, it should be noted that the term "fact" in Italian law books is used to refer to legal norms or legislation, not to concrete events.) Thus, while an American legal text usually comprises a discussion of court decisions, an Italian work on legal problems contains little discussion of actual cases and little direct relevance to reality, but rather a dispassionate logical analysis of the meanings and interrelations of abstract legal principles and legal terms.

In keeping with this rejection of empiricism, sociological, historical, and economic data have been virtually ignored during the past half-century by Italian legal scholars, who have seen their primary task as that of erecting a sound, coherent, internally consistent legal structure. This has been partly the result of a reaction against the dry and rather shallow positivism that dominated Italian sociology at the turn of the century. Partly, too, the impact of Hegelian idealism (with its view that the individual could best realize his potentialities and experience true freedom by serving a strong centralized state) on Italian political and philosophical thought, created an irrationalist bias against the systematic study of politics and society as empirical sciences. And finally, the study of legal history was a rather unattractive prospect in a country like Italy which, unlike England, lacked a relatively unified national legal tradition based on the gradual evolution of a single set of legal institutions. In the place of historical parallels and sociological fact finding, Italian jurists relied on a comprehensive legal code, which was supposedly the key to any and all problems that might arise. This was a relatively static conception of the law. However, since World War II, Italian legal scholars have begun to show some interest in sociological and historical research.

In addition to shunning empiricism, the Italian jurist has also traditionally rejected the Anglo-Saxon concept of a higher law by

---

[1] For an interesting and comprehensive analysis of the Italian legal tradition, see Mauro Cappelletti, John Henry Merryman, Joseph M. Perillo, *The Italian Legal System: An Introduction* (Stanford, Calif.: Stanford University Press, 1967).

which legislative and executive acts may be tested. He has tended to look for the law in acts of the legislature, in executive decrees, and in the interpretations of legal scholars, rather than in any underlying universal principles of the kind typified by the natural-law tradition. This attitude, of course, ruled out the possibility of judge-made law. Law was produced by the lawmaker—the legislature, the prince, the minister—and the judge's sole function was seen as that of finding the legal rule which had been intended by the lawmaker to apply to the case in hand. As for the interpretation of what the law really meant, this was seen as the function of the legal scholar in the universities. The judge was relegated, then, to the mechanical function of applying the law stated by others, and thus became a mere judicial bureaucrat with a minimum of discretion. It is for this reason, in all likelihood, that the principle of *stare decisis* has not been recognized in Italian law: A court decision is not regarded as necessarily binding on other courts in similar cases. If the law and the commentaries speak clearly and unerringly point the way—as they are supposed to do—why look to court decisions for guidance?

However, it should be realized that these concepts—the absence of a higher law, the purely mechanical function of the judge, the nonbinding nature of previous court decisions—represent a kind of legal folklore in Italy. And Italian judges, consciously or unconsciously, have frequently had to violate these concepts in their everyday behavior. Thus, judges have, in fact, interpreted the law on occasion, and have been influenced by the previous decisions of their colleagues. This was inevitable; for the legal codes, however comprehensive, could never cover every possible eventuality. So, Italian judicial decisions were never as automatic as one might assume from reviewing the above concepts. And recent events have further modified the situation. With the adoption of a rigid Constitution and the establishment of a Constitutional Court with powers of judicial review, the Italian republic has in effect given recognition to the concept of a higher law. Moreover, the functioning of the Constitutional Court, with its power to pass on the constitutionality of acts of Parliament, and the functioning of a supreme judicial organ, the Court of Cassation, with its power to review the legality of lower court decisions, have actually introduced the principle of *stare decisis* into the Italian legal system by the back door, as it were. In short, the gap which divides the Italian legal system from that of common-law countries has been considerably narrowed in the key area of underlying legal concepts and their practical application.

Furthermore, the Italian legal folklore is not only tacitly violated in practice; its main assumptions have come under explicit attack on the part of members of the judiciary itself. Within the last decade, there has been a significant movement among the younger, lower-court judges to question and challenge the supremacy of the Court of Cassation. And this rebellion has not been confined to the question of judicial promotions and distinctions among ranks, but has also been directed against some of the prevalent legal concepts. In short, the younger members of the judicial profession assert that a judge should be aware of the problems of the society in which he lives and should be prepared to address himself to those problems, and uphold certain moral values as well, when handing down judicial decisions.[2]

THE ORDINARY LAW COURTS

Italy has a single unified system of courts, enforcing national law. There is no separate hierarchy of provincial or regional courts, for the provinces and regions do not have exclusive powers of their own, apart from the very limited exclusive powers of the five special regions. The Italian judicial system consists of five well-defined tiers of ordinary law courts, a system of administrative courts, and a Constitutional Court.

At the lowest level of the structure of ordinary law courts are the *conciliatori*, individuals nominated by the president of each Court of Appeal, on the advice of the mayors of the communes in which they respectively reside. The *conciliatori* are unpaid and correspond, in some respects, to the Anglo-Saxon justices of the peace. Each *conciliatore* presides over his own petty tribunal with authority to settle claims of 50,000 *lire* ($80) or less, and to act as mediator, if the parties to the dispute so agree, in cases involving higher sums. They have no special qualifications (apart from being well-regarded citizens of their respective communes and being over twenty-five years of age) and serve a three-year term. The *conciliatori* might be described as comprising the honorary judiciary, as opposed to the judicial career service in the higher courts.

The lowest court in the judicial career service proper is that of the *pretore*. Italy is divided into some 900 pretorial districts (*preture*), a majority of which are too small in population to

---

[2] Ezio Moriondo, *L'ideologia della magistratura italiana* (Bari: Laterza, 1967), pp. 326–329. See also preface by Renato Treves, in Moriondo, pp. xiv–xx.

provide the resident *pretore* with a full work load, while a small minority (in the big metropolitan centers) are overburdened with cases. A number of *preture* have been abolished, but further progress in this direction encounters the dogged resistance of senators, deputies, and local politicoes who resent the loss of jobs and prestige that such abolitions must entail. The *pretore* has original jurisdiction over civil cases in which less than 750,000 *lire* ($1200) are at stake and over criminal cases involving a penalty of less than three years' imprisonment. He also hears appeals from the decisions of the *conciliatori*. Like the *conciliatore*, he runs a one-man tribunal, rather than sitting as one member of a panel of judges.

The next rung of the judicial ladder is the Tribunal, of which there are about 150 in Italy. It is estimated by some observers that one Tribunal per province would suffice to handle the case load, but political pressure has often been applied to avert the elimination of a given Tribunal or to promote the creation of a new Tribunal in some secondary urban center that seeks to compete with the provincial capital. Tribunals consist of three judges who sit collectively to hear civil and criminal cases on appeal from the *pretori*. On all other civil and criminal cases, they have original jurisdiction. The Tribunal also has a special section, the Court of Assize, which hears the more serious criminal cases. The Court of Assize provides the continental European equivalent of the jury trial where two judges sit with six laymen (designated as "popular judges"). In voting on the guilt or innocence of the defendant, all eight votes count equally, and a majority suffices to convict. But it is widely suggested that the two judges usually succeed in carrying the overawed laymen with them in whatever direction they wish to go.[3]

At the appellate level, there are twenty-three Courts of Appeal, each presiding over an entire region or over several provinces. Here, in civil suits, panels of five judges hear appeals from the Tribunals. Attached to the Courts of Appeal for the purpose of hearing criminal appeals from the assize courts are the Courts of Appeal of Assizes, where once again we have the composite eight-judge panel (two full-fledged judges and six "popular judges") deciding cases by majority vote. The Courts of Appeal and the Courts of Appeal of Assizes are notoriously overstaffed, whereas the Tribunals are understaffed and overloaded. The reason for this strange imbalance is the widespread pressure for pro-

---

[3] Gigi Ghirotti, *Il magistrato* (Firenze: Vallecchi, 1959), pp. 95–104.

motions among lower-court judges. As a result, the Tribunals could easily use several hundred additional judges to handle their burgeoning case load, whereas the Courts of Appeal (from which the five-judge panels are selected) teem with surplus jurists.[4]

The highest ordinary court is the Court of Cassation, which reviews both civil and criminal cases on appeal. Like the Courts of Appeal, it has far too many members to sit in plenary session but divides itself into a number of criminal and civil sections, consisting of seven-judge panels. Unlike the Supreme Court of the United States, it cannot review the constitutionality of legislative acts; this function is reserved for the Constitutional Court. To give some idea of the top-heavy table of organization of the appellate tribunals, we may cite some admittedly obsolete but nonetheless apropos figures from the late 1950s: 3613 judges in the *preture* and Tribunals, 1380 judges in the Courts of Appeal, 360 judges in the Court of Cassation.[5] As we can see, the Court of Cassation is a far cry from the nine-man United States Supreme Court.

How effectively do the ordinary courts administer justice? There is general agreement that the Italian judicial system is in crisis. Some of the reasons are related to the recruitment and training of judges and to the inadequate protection afforded judicial independence. These reasons will be dealt with later in this chapter, when those related topics are discussed. But there are also other underlying defects of the system which we may discuss at this point. For one thing, the courts are poorly equipped and staffed. The lack of adequate buildings, of sufficient office space, of secretarial help, and of essential equipment and supplies serve to harass the judge and slow down the progress of justice. A judge who must do his own typing or, worse still, write his own decisions in longhand, who lacks both telephone and dictaphone, and who must provide his own transportation, is going to waste his own time, and consequently the taxpayers' as well.

Another serious defect of the system of ordinary law courts is the excessive delays that result in clogging court calendars with a great backlog of pending cases. Delays may be attributed to a variety of factors. Many judges are rather leisurely in their habits, are slow to clear their dockets, and prepare overly long opinions. Lawyers often seek postponements in order to render their own schedules more convenient, or in order to wait for an expected amnesty to free their client. The use of three-judge panels below the appellate level, in the Tribunals, is a serious waste of man-

[4] Mario Cervi, *La giustizia in Italia* (Milano: Longanesi, 1967), pp. 159–162.
[5] Ghirotti, p. 167.

power. And the suggestion has been made to reduce the number of judicial levels, possibly combining the Tribunal and the Court of Appeal into one set of appellate courts, and having more cases settled by the *pretore*.[6] Also, the excessive variety of possible appeals tends to slow down the final disposition of a case. As a result of all these stumbling-blocks, civil cases are apt to last about six years if they reach the Court of Cassation level, and criminal cases almost three years.[7]

One last criticism of the ordinary court system is directed against the *istruttoria* or pretrial investigation. Although the judiciary is supposed to retain control over this procedure, the police have pretty much taken charge of questioning the suspect; and the judges have allowed themselves to be relegated to an almost purely formal role, and have not really been vigilant to prevent procedural abuses. The result has been seriously prejudicial to the defendant's cause.[8]

THE ADMINISTRATIVE COURTS

The Italian system of administrative justice differs in a number of significant ways from the corresponding French system. First of all, there have been, in Italy, two separate hierarchies of administrative courts, one headed by the Council of State and the other by the Court of Accounts. Whereas in France the decisions of the Court of Accounts are subject to review by the Council of State, in Italy the two administrative tribunals are mutually independent.

The Italian Court of Accounts is concerned with the handling of public money and tries to assess responsibility for alleged cases of financial mismanagement on the part of national and local public officials. At the local and provincial levels, this function used to be performed by the prefectoral council, consisting of the prefect of the province and two assistants. But a recent decision of the Constitutional Court has apparently divested the prefectoral council of all or most of its quasi-judicial responsibilities. Therefore, the job of acting as financial watchdog over the activities of local agencies seems to have been passed on to the Court of Accounts,[9] which also exercises other important duties, such as

[6] Giuseppe Pera, *Un mestiere difficile: il magistrato* (Bologna: Il Mulino, 1967), pp. 145–153.
[7] Cervi, p. 14.
[8] Achille Battaglia, *I giudici e la politica* (Bari: Laterza, 1962), pp. 47–55.
[9] Girolamo Caianiello, "Corte dei conti, anno 1970," *Il Mulino*, Vol. XIX, No. 208 (March–April 1970), 234.

advising Parliament as to the legality of executive decrees; auditing the expenditures of the state; and issuing periodic (but usually belated) reports to Parliament based on these audits.

A far more important administrative court is the Council of State, which not only advises the government on the legality of executive decrees and (if the government requests such advice) government bills, but also hears cases in which the legality of given decrees and regulations is challenged. Like the Court of Accounts, it functions as both an administrative staff organ and an administrative court. In its judicial capacity, it hears appeals from the lower administrative courts (the provincial administrative juntas, or GPAs), each of which consists of the prefect or his substitute, the provincial intendant of the Ministry of Finance, four other prefectoral officials, and four persons elected by, but not belonging to, the provincial council.

The Italian system of administrative courts also differs from the French in respect to the composition of its courts, the jurisdiction they may exercise, and the self-assertiveness they are wont to display. In the first place, it should be noted that Italian administrative courts at the provincial level (the GPAs) are manned, in large part, by full-time civil servants, who must regard their quasi-judicial duties as being of a secondary, supplementary nature in comparison to their administrative functions.[10] In France, on the other hand, such organs are staffed by full-time judges. The implications of this contrast for the relative independence and spirit of initiative of Italian and French administrative courts, are not hard to imagine.

Secondly, French administrative courts may hear two kinds of cases: suits by private citizens against the state, to recover damages inflicted by its servants, and suits questioning the legality of a given decree or ordinance. In Italy, on the other hand, damage suits against the state may only be introduced in the ordinary law courts; the Council of State will only consider whether or not a given decree is illegal. However, in one respect, the Italian Council of State appears to possess a somewhat broader jurisdiction than its French counterpart. It may judge not only the legality, but also the "merits" of executive acts—a power which it uses very sparingly indeed.[11]

This leads to the third and final point of comparison. In

---

[10] Brian Chapman, *The Profession of Government: The Public Service in Europe* (New York: Macmillan, 1959), pp. 200–203.

[11] John Clarke Adams and Paolo Barile, *The Government of Republican Italy* (2nd ed.; Boston: Houghton Mifflin, 1966), pp. 137–138.

exercising whatever legal powers it possesses, the Italian Council of State has been far less venturesome than the French.[12] Perhaps because it lacks the long and illustrious tradition which bolsters the French *Conseil d'État,* perhaps because it is, after all, a foreign import (brought in by Napoleon's victorious armies, and subjected to a later revision in 1831 to conform to certain French administrative styles of the time), perhaps because it has not usually had a largely impotent executive branch with which to deal (in pre-1922 Italy, the Italian executive was somewhat stronger and more stable than the French executive under the Third Republic), the Italian Council of State has failed to build up a substantial reputation for curbing administrative abuses. The fact that half the members of the Council of State and of the Court of Accounts are nominated by the executive, and thus may conceivably be patronage appointees, also contributes to the cautious posture of the Italian administrative courts.[13] Yet, the Italian system is more effective than the British in this respect—it simply falls well short of the French model.

THE CONSTITUTIONAL COURT

One of the chief innovations introduced by the Italian Constitution was the provision for a Constitutional Court. This may well have been a reaction to the ease with which the pre-1922 *Statuto* could be modified by a simple act of Parliament, with no provision for judicial review. Also, it is notable that, after World War II, those nations which had suffered most heavily from the domestic manifestations of Fascist dictatorship—those nations, in other words, which had fallen victim to native Fascist movements—were in the forefront of the tendency to adopt some form of judicial review. Germany, Italy, and Austria were cases in point. Thus, historical experience provided much of the impetus behind the formation of the Italian Constitutional Court. But it also helped to account for the actual guise that judicial review assumed. Instead of entrusting the function of judicial review to the highest ordinary court, the Court of Cassation, the framers of the Italian Constitution wanted to set up a special court to do the job. Their decision was based, in large measure, on the Italian legal tradition, with its lack of a *stare decisis* rule and its reluctance to

---

[12] Chapman, pp. 189–191, 217–219.
[13] Comments by Aldo Piras and Alfonso Bonacci in Direzione PSI–PSDI Unificati-Sezione per la Riforma dello Stato, *Stato moderno e riforma del Parlamento* (Roma: Direzione PSI-PSDI Unificati, 1967), pp. 164–165, 167.

entertain the concept of a higher law.[14] It was only reasonable to suspect that judges raised in that tradition would find it very difficult to combine their service on the highest ordinary court with the function of judicial review. To avoid philosophical schizophrenia, a new role would have to be created.

Political considerations imposed a long delay in the process of passing enabling legislation to set up the Court for which the Constitution had provided. It was not until 1956, when the Christian Democrats no longer had an absolute majority in the Chamber of Deputies, and when the minor Center parties that wanted the Court established had greatly augmented their bargaining power, that the long deadlock was finally broken and the Constitutional Court was created.

The Constitutional Court has fifteen members, five selected by the president of Italy, five elected by a three-fifths vote of a joint session of Parliament (a formula designed to assure the opposition parties of some representation), and five elected by the judges of the highest Italian courts: the Council of State, the Court of Cassation, and the Court of Accounts. The members serve for a twelve-year term, which is not immediately renewable. They thus lack that length of tenure which contributes to the independence and status of the U.S. Supreme Court. To be eligible to serve on the Constitutional Court, one must be or have been a member of one of the three highest courts, or one must be a professor of law or a lawyer of twenty years' standing. Several of those chosen by Parliament to serve on the Court have been senators or deputies with the required legal background.[15]

The Court's jurisdiction is quite extensive. It can decide on the constitutionality of national and regional laws, decide conflicts of jurisdiction between different national organs of government, and also between national and regional levels. Delegated legislation issued by the executive also falls within its purview; only relatively minor executive "regulations" do not have to pass inspection as "acts having the force of law."[16] And on this last score, some constitutional scholars are convinced that even "regulations" may be subjected to the Court's scrutiny.[17]

---

[14] John Clarke Adams, *The Quest for Democratic Law: The Role of Parliament in the Legislative Process* (New York: Crowell, 1970), p. 87.

[15] See the description of Justices Giuseppe Cappi and Gaspare Ambrosini in Nicola Tranfaglia, "La crisi della Corte costituzionale," *Comunità*, Vol. XX, No. 139–140 (November–December 1966), 22–23.

[16] Malcolm Evans, "The Italian Constitutional Court," *International and Comparative Law Quarterly*, Vol. 17, No. 3 (July 1968), 604.

[17] Costantino Mortati, *Istituzioni di diritto pubblico*, Vol. II (7th ed.; Padova: CEDAM, 1967), pp. 1045–1046.

Access to the Constitutional Court is fairly broad as compared to France (where only the president, the prime minister, or the president of either legislative chamber may bring a bill or law before the Constitutional Council), but is more restricted than in the United States. Any individual, group, or regional government may, during a trial in an ordinary or administrative court, raise the issue of constitutionality for the judge to transmit the case to the Constitutional Court *if he so desires*. Or the judge may himself, on his own initiative, choose to raise the constitutional question. In addition to this avenue of access, a region, the national government, or some regional or national government organ may raise the question of jurisdiction by claiming that some other level of government or some other government agency is invading its proper sphere of competence.

Why, then, is access to the Italian Constitutional Court more restricted than access to the U.S. Supreme Court? Because the U.S. Supreme Court can call up a case from the lower courts by issuing a writ of certiorari, whereas the Italian Constitutional Court must wait for judges below to authorize the sending up of a case. When a constitutional issue is raised in an Italian court, the judge may prevent that issue from reaching the Constitutional Court by simply issuing an interlocutory judgment to the effect that the constitutional claim is "patently unfounded."[18] There is nothing the Constitutional Court can do to bring up a case which has encountered this insurmountable barrier.

The effect of the interlocutory judgment on the status of the Italian Constitutional Court cannot be grasped unless one also bears in mind the fact that many, many judges of the ordinary courts have a feeling of deep animosity against this newly instituted organ of judicial review. Because of long-prevalent legal concepts, many Italian judges simply cannot accept the idea of a tribunal with power to hold acts of Parliament unconstitutional or—even worse from their point of view—to declare null and void large segments of the legal codes dating back to the Fascist regime or even to the pre-1922 constitutional monarchy. It is not so much an attachment to the authoritarian content of the codes which motivates them—though that is present, too—but rather a sincere horror at the prospect of seeing large unsightly gaps created in an integrated, coherent body of law. And these attitudes are particularly deep-rooted among the older, longer-established judges, the men who achieved success within the traditional legal

---

[18] Adams and Barile, pp. 132–133.

system and therefore still honor the legal folklore—that is, first and foremost, the men of the Court of Cassation.[19]

As a result of these attitudes, there has been a running feud between the Court of Cassation and the Constitutional Court. Over and over again, sections of the Court of Cassation have blocked appeals to the Constitutional Court by abusive use of the interlocutory judgment. In fact, if the Constitutional Court is able to pass judgment on occasional constitutional pleas, it is because some lower-court judge, some *pretore* perhaps, has agreed to transmit the issue of constitutionality to the Constitutional Court, thus braving the wrath of the Court of Cassation, which may have enough influence to block his promotion. Furthermore, in addition to the delaying action represented by the interlocutory judgment, the Court of Cassation has expressed its utter contempt for the Constitutional Court in a number of overt ways. For instance, it has issued decisions based on laws which had either very recently been declared null and void by the Constitutional Court or were in the process of undergoing review by that body. By so doing, the Court of Cassation gave the impression that its members did not keep up with legal developments listed in the *Official Gazette of the Italian Republic*.[20]

The Constitutional Court has issued some major decisions in the field of civil liberties, consigning to oblivion a number of provisions of the Fascist penal code which still remained in effect after the Liberation. At the same time, however, much remains to be done in this area if the civil liberties listed in the Constitution are to be protected against arbitrary invasion. Some of the Court's decisions in the area of civil liberties—such as the decision invalidating an existing law that had prohibited the movement of migrants from one commune to another without prior permission—have had far-reaching implications for Italian society. A second major achievement chalked up by the Court has been to delineate more clearly the boundaries between the respective powers and functions of the national and regional governments.

Yet, the Court has encountered grave difficulties in its efforts to act as constitutional watchdog for the Italian political system. It has had to face the indifference and occasional hostility of the executive branch, the apathy of public opinion, and the steady, unbending animosity of many judges in the system of ordinary law courts. As a result, it has gradually evolved toward a more cautious attitude, developing its own version of judicial self-restraint.

[19] Battaglia, pp. 127–130, 136–141.
[20] Tranfaglia, 22.

Ever since the resignation in 1957 of Chief Justice De Nicola—who was manifesting his displeasure with the failure of the executive branch to act promptly in complying with Court decisions—the Court has become ever more timid in standing up to the ruling powers. For instance, it has relied more and more often on the "doctrine of conditional rejection," upholding a given law by choosing that particular interpretation of the law which will be in conformity with the Constitution. But since the lower courts are not officially informed of its grounds for upholding said law, and since most lower-court judges do not keep up with the interpretations in the legal journals, there is no assurance that the lower courts will follow the rather labored interpretation adopted by the Constitutional Court.[21] By using this device of the doctrine of conditional rejection, the Constitutional Court has been able to rationalize the survival of a substantial proportion of the provisions of the Fascist penal code.

JUDICIAL INDEPENDENCE IN ITALY

Like other Western democracies, Italy accepts the principle of judicial independence. Accordingly, Italian judges enjoy security of tenure, and may not be removed or suspended from office without a regular hearing carried on before a disciplinary section of the Superior Council of the Judiciary (hereafter referred to as the CSM: *Consiglio Superiore della Magistratura*). This holds true also for transfers: No judge may be transferred without his own consent or, lacking that, without a formal decision by the CSM. However, a judge may be transferred from a criminal to a civil section of the same court, without either his own consent or a CSM decision; and this fate apparently has befallen a number of courageous *pretori*, who presumed to question the legality of certain arbitrary police procedures or to release defendants who had been arrested on frivolous grounds.[22] But at least it is not possible, in this day and age, to threaten an Italian judge with virtual exile from Rome to a remote rural post. And the CSM's disciplinary sections, staffed by judges, have thus far not abused their power to revoke tenure.

Independence can be threatened in a more subtle way, however, through the denial (or prospective denial) of a promotion. Italian judges, like their French counterparts, are *not* former law-

---

[21] Nicola Tranfaglia, "La politica della Corte costituzionale," *Comunità*, Vol. XXI, No. 141–142 (April 1967), 24–29.
[22] Battaglia, pp. 223–226.

yers with a long and successful legal career behind them. Rather, they are recruited into the judicial career service directly after their graduation from law school. After a year or so of apprenticeship, a judicial novice is provisionally assigned a *pretura*. A *pretore* usually hopes to move up in the judicial system as the years go on: from *pretura* to Tribunal, from Tribunal to Court of Appeal, from Court of Appeal to Court of Cassation. To be denied these promotions, to be condemned to vegetate as *pretore* for the rest of one's life, would entail severe economic and—above all—psychological deprivations. Therefore, control over the promotion process represents a possible wedge for the undermining of judicial independence.

Before the Republic of Italy was founded, the minister of justice controlled judicial assignments and promotions, and was therefore in a position to exercise subtle pressure on recalcitrant judges. To remedy this situation, to provide greater safeguards for judicial independence, the Constitution of the new republic provided for a Superior Council of the Judiciary (the CSM) to supervise the appointment, assignment, transfer, and promotion of Italian judges, and to preside over disciplinary proceedings. The CSM was to be chaired by the president of the republic and was to include the first president of the Court of Cassation and the general procurator of the Court of Cassation as ex officio members.

However, the constitutional provisions relating to the CSM were not immediately followed by enabling legislation. It was not until 1958 that Parliament finally enacted a law setting up the CSM. And this long-awaited legislation had serious defects which gravely disappointed those Italian scholars and publicists who had pressed for the establishment of the CSM.[23] The law provided, first of all, for the election of seven members of the CSM by a three-fifths vote of a joint session of Parliament, and the election of fourteen other members by the judges of the ordinary courts. But in the election of the fourteen representatives of the judiciary, the judicial branch was not to vote as a unit, but rather by separate colleges, with the result being to overrepresent the upper echelons of the judicial profession. Six of the fourteen elected judges were to be chosen from among members of the Court of Cassation, four from the Courts of Appeal, and only four from the Tribunals. And judicial representatives from each of these three categories were to be elected by judges of their respective categories, while *pretori* were unrepresented in the CSM and judicial probationers (*uditori*) were actually barred from voting.

[23] Giuseppe Maranini, *Giustizia in catene* (Milano: Comunità, 1964), pp. 26–28, 83–144.

Not only was the CSM to be dominated by conservative senior judges of the higher courts, but also its disciplinary section —in charge of administering sanctions against judges who had been guilty of improper conduct—was controlled by members of the Court of Cassation. The same held true for the approval of promotions: Here again, a committee of senior members initiated action, with the CSM plenum granting final approval. Moreover, CSM decisions were subject to review by the Court of Cassation and the Council of State. Finally, the CSM could only act on the initiative of the minister of justice; in this respect, the executive branch was given ultimate control over the actions of the CSM. This last provision was the only major feature of the law to be declared unconstitutional by the Constitutional Court when the law finally reached that body for review. The remaining provisions, so bitterly denounced by supporters of an independent and reinvigorated judiciary, were upheld.

The creation of the CSM has simply shifted power over promotions from the minister of justice to the senior judges of the Court of Cassation and the Courts of Appeal. Judicial independence remains threatened. For an idealistic young *pretore* who has frustrated the less legitimate pretensions of the local police and has dared to refer appeals to the Constitutional Court, must come up for promotion some day. And when he does, his record is reviewed by a board composed of appellate judges. Moreover, until recently, promotion was based mostly on a perusal of the aspirant's publications and previous decisions, a subjective process that did little to discourage the overly lengthy opinions customarily prepared by Italian judges to bolster their decisions. In addition to these criteria, subjective tests of character were applied, based on the views of the aspirants' hierarchical superiors.

These restraints, real or potential, on their independence were bitterly resented by Italy's younger judges. And so there was an increasingly widespread demand for equalizing judicial salaries, for giving trial-court judges the same status and prestige enjoyed by appellate-court judges, for applying literally the constitutional provision to the effect that "Judges differ only in diversity of function" (Article 107). As time went on, reformist elements were able to obtain control of the ANMI (National Association of Italian Magistrates), much to the chagrin of the higher-ranking members of the judiciary, many of whom seceded to form the UMI (Union of Italian Magistrates).[24] Thus, a fragmented soci-

[24] Moriondo, pp. 320–329.

ety has even produced a fragmented judiciary. Despite the victory of reformist currents in the ANMI, the more extreme demands of the younger judges are unlikely to be adopted: No professional group is likely to discard willingly the principle of a hierarchy based on experience and talent. However, in one vital respect, a major step toward the safeguarding of judicial independence has been taken. A recently adopted law has made promotion from a Tribunal to a Court of Appeal an almost automatic proceeding based mostly on seniority.[25] This shift in criteria tends to lessen the possibility that pressure and subtle intimidation will be applied against fledgling judges by their superiors in the hierarchy.

JUDICIAL RECRUITMENT AND TRAINING

As we have already noted, Italian judges embark upon a judicial career immediately upon graduation from law school. A young law school graduate may, at that point, decide to become a lawyer, in which case he will first serve an apprenticeship (the *pratica*) in the office of an attorney and then—after a year of *pratica*—take a state examination for admission to practice as a *procuratore*. Or the graduate may prefer the judicial profession, in which case he will take a state examination in Rome for probationary admission to the bench as *uditore giudiziario*. The two careers are segregated from each other from the very beginning. Lawyers do not, as a rule, shift to the judicial profession; if they did, they would have to start at the bottom of the hierarchy— hardly a promising expedient for a successful attorney. The only exception to this rule regulating entry into the judicial hierarchy is a legal provision to the effect that, under special circumstances, the CSM may call to the office of Counselor of the Court of Cassation individuals who have shown outstanding merit as professors of law or as lawyers with fifteen years of practice.

What are the implications of this separation between the bench and the bar? First of all, there is lacking that rapport, that sense of mutual fellowship and trust which unites the legal and judicial professions in countries like Great Britain, where any distinguished barrister may hope eventually to be summoned to the bench. This basic cleavage between the two professions makes it very difficult for lawyers to take the public interest into account: They are likely to approach their cases strictly from a tactical

[25] Cervi, pp. 32–33.

point of view, with little concern for the public interest, since they are unlikely ever to be called upon to exercise a public function.[26] Second, it stands to reason that Italian attorneys tend to be rather resentful about their exclusion from the prospect of a judicial career. One consequence of this frustration is apt to be a negative overreaction, in the form of an obsession with financial profits. This syndrome is partly responsible for the heavy reliance placed by Italian attorneys on a variety of dilatory procedural techniques, designed to prevent a case from reaching the point of decision, and thus designed to maximize fees.[27] Third, Italian lawyers are prone to feel a certain contempt for judges because of a difference in their professional styles: The lawyer sees himself as an individualistic entrepreneur who has made, or is making, the grade; he sees the judge as a conforming bureaucrat who has managed to stay the course by trimming his sails to the prevailing wind.[28]

Moreover, the Italian judicial novice lacks the self-confidence and sense of independence that characterize the British county court judge who has already proved himself as a successful barrister. Instead, the Italian judge enters the profession as an inexperienced apprentice, dependent on the good will of his superiors for advancement. In a number of instances, a young man's decision to embark on a judicial career is made without adequate deliberation and without a clear knowledge of other alternative possibilities. In fact, the underlying motive for the decision may be mainly economic: the great majority of new entrants into the profession seem to come from the South and from communes with less than 50,000 population—in other words, from a static environment with restricted opportunities. Given their geographic origins, Italian judges are apt to be wedded to certain archaic social conceptions, such as a tendency to view "crimes of honor" (that is, crimes provoked by a real or imagined assault on a woman's virtue) as being not entirely reprehensible. They are also likely to reject modern concepts of efficiency and to have a penchant for subtle legal distinctions.[29]

Other features of the recruitment process also contribute to the formation of a rather hidebound, conservative judiciary. The admission exams tend to be heavily theoretical in orientation, stressing such fields as civil law, penal law, and administrative law

---

[26] Gian Paolo Prandstraller, *Gli avvocati italiani* (Milano: Comunità, 1967), pp. 127–132, 206–209, 213–214.
[27] Pera, pp. 97–103.
[28] Prandstraller, pp. 206–207.
[29] Cervi, pp. 29–37.

in terms of abstract conceptual schemes rather than empirical analysis of actual cases. Such new and relevant disciplines as criminology and legal psychology are deemphasized in the examination process. The fact that the examining commission also looks into such matters as the candidate's personal morality, and into the reputation of his family as well, makes for an atmosphere of conformism surrounding the selection process.[30]

The period that elapses between the time the candidate applies for entry into the judiciary and the time he actually draws his first salary is unnecessarily long and apparently discourages many prospective applicants from areas where attractive alternatives exist.[31] The low initial salary paid to *pretori* (much less than the starting salaries paid in France or Germany to judges on the lowest rung of the hierarchical ladder) is often regarded as offering a poor inducement to prospective recruits from the more dynamic regions of Italy. But some observers stress another factor: the inadequate preparation for a judicial career offered by the law schools, combined with the absence of any special training school for prospective judges. In such a school, it is held, values could be inculcated and the judicial profession would acquire a prestige and a sense of mission it now lacks.[32]

The training system for new judges also fails to produce a self-confident, progressive judiciary. Newly appointed *uditori* spend about a year attached as interns to various judicial and legal bodies (*preture*, Tribunals, Prosecutor's Offices), working under the general supervision of a commission of senior judges. After the year is over, the *uditore* may receive his first judicial appointment, usually as a *pretore*. As a judicial novice, often confronted by experienced attorneys, trying his wings in a new and unfamiliar situation, he is likely to find his position very awkward indeed. Within the next four years, he must take a competitive exam to win the title of judicial *aggiunto*, a title that carries the privilege of functioning as a tribunal magistrate. After three more years, a district commission of senior judges decides whether or not to confer upon him the rank of tribunal magistrate and the accompanying privilege of tenure. Further examinations are needed for eventual promotion to a Court of Appeal, and later still to the Court of Cassation. And on each of these occasions, a man is being judged by his superiors in the hierarchy, who, incidentally,

---

[30] Ghirotti, pp. 37–38.
[31] Giuseppe Di Federico, *Il reclutamento dei magistrati* (Bari: Laterza, 1968), pp. 71–104.
[32] Di Federico, pp. 123–126.

have attained their professional success by a similar route of ascent. Even when the examining commissions rise above their conservative biases—as no doubt they often do—in passing on a candidate's qualifications, the suspicion that the way to get along is to go along must be fairly widespread among Italian judges at the *pretore* level.

How does the pattern of recruitment of judges and attorneys compare with recruitment patterns of other elites in the Italian political system? The same legal training is emphasized in the examinations of recruits to the higher civil service. And both judges and higher civil servants enter their respective hierarchies directly from the universities, with some exceptions in the cases of patronage appointees and honorary judges. Lateral recruitment of men who have had a successful career in law or business or the professions, is not common in the Italian bureaucratic and judicial systems. This may account for the rather bureaucratic mentality of most Italian judges in the ordinary law courts, their unwillingness to challenge bureaucratic abuses. In Parliament, there is a large but diminishing percentage of attorneys. The local notable with a law school background seems to be giving way to the professional party politician who has never practiced law. Generally speaking, Italian lawyers are less prone to enter politics than their American colleagues. Perhaps, the fact that most Italian lawyers are free-lance entrepreneurs, rather than members of a law firm with partners who can handle the practice during their absence, may help to explain this contrast.[33]

There has been no serious effort to limit the number of members in the bench and the bar, respectively. As a result, Italy has far more than its share of judges and lawyers, a larger quantity than exist in a number of European countries of comparable population. Yet, despite the fact that Italy has many more judges than Britain, for example, Italian judicial personnel is so poorly allocated among the various judicial districts, and so prodigally wasted in the multimember courts, that the British court system is far superior to the Italian in handling its responsibilities. The great proliferation of surplus lawyers in Italy makes for a grim struggle to capture a larger share of the existing pool of litigation, to create pretexts for new litigation, and to find ways of dragging out existing litigation as long as possible. Thus, there is no real correlation between the number of judges and lawyers in a given society, on the one hand, and the efficiency of judicial output in that society,

---

[33] Prandstraller, pp. 198–200.

on the other.[34] In fact, the correlation may actually be inverse, as the chief function of the system becomes, not rule adjudication, but the maintenance of its own personnel.

THE COURTS IN ITALIAN SOCIETY

As we have already noted, the Italian judiciary has occasionally had a rather thorny relationship with the executive branch of government and with the governing Christian Democratic party. As long as a judge has been willing to act as a kind of legal bureaucrat, upholding the legality of government actions, there has been no friction. But as soon as a judge begins to challenge the actions of the police, or the partisan statements of high-ranking clergymen, or (in the case of the Constitutional Court) the constitutionality of statutes, censorious statements from party leaders and ministers, and executive acts of calculated disrespect for the judge or court involved, begin to manifest themselves. It is safe to say that the majority party, and the executive branch which that party has largely controlled for the past twenty-five years, do not wholeheartedly accept the principle of a fully independent judiciary.

However, there is really only a minority of judges who are nonconformists: a number of members of the Constitutional Court; and some idealistic *pretori* and Tribunal magistrates who are ready to break a lance for constitutional liberties, putting their future careers on the line in the process. The bulk of the judiciary does not challenge or antagonize the executive branch and/or the ruling party. Yet, this conforming majority is out of tune with the prevalent current values of Italian society. Many judges are prisoners of an authoritarian past, during which they served the constitutional monarchy and the Fascist dictatorship with equal docility. Their past experience has left a residue of nostalgia for autocracy, of lack of sympathy for labor demands, of an exaggerated concern for property rights, and of distinctly rightist sympathies. How else can one explain the amazing performance staged by most Italian courts with regard to the events of 1943–1945? On the one hand, all sorts of legal loopholes were discovered to permit former members of Fascist torture gangs to go free. On the other hand, veterans of the Resistance were unrelentingly prosecuted and sen-

---

[34] According to Cervi, there are over 6000 judges in Italy, as compared to 4000 in France and 500 in Britain. See Cervi, pp. 26–37. In 1967, there were over 38,000 lawyers in Italy. See Antonino Di Giorgio, "Come riformare la giustizia," *Nord e Sud*, Vol. XVI, No. 120(181) (December 1969), 81.

tenced for offences committed against persons and property during the civil war. In their cases, moreover, the full rigor of the law was much more likely to be applied. Moreover, in obiter dicta, some judges found a way of labeling men who had fought against Mussolini's Italian Social Republic, or against the earlier Fascist regime, as traitors to their country.[35]

What sort of public image do the courts project? Accusations of venality and corruption are few and far between. It is interesting to note that the alienated Italian public does not view the judiciary as dishonest. But there is a widespread tendency to distrust the judicial process as costly, cumbersome, and unimaginative. The members of the legal profession suffer even more severely in the public eye: Many accuse them of deliberately dragging out judicial proceedings in order to pad their fees.[36] In short, there is a frightening lack of confidence in the legal and judicial systems.

CONCLUSIONS

In the early 1960s, when American social scientists were accustomed to approach comparative politics in a spirit of self-congratulatory self-delusion, it would be possible to conclude this account of the Italian judicial system by depicting it as the aberrant product of an authoritarian political tradition. Today, we recognize that the Italian judicial system contains many of the same defects that afflict judicial systems in other Western democracies. The long delays, the crowded dockets, the high costs, the antiquated procedures are not unknown in the United States.

However, there is a difference in degree. For instance, the surplus of lawyers in Italy has the effect of multiplying and prolonging litigation. There is less money available in Italy to give the judges the necessary tools to do the job properly. The Italian system is also less flexible than the American, since all courts are national courts, and all changes in the structure of the system must be approved by Parliament. In short, in a wealthier nation with a federal system, the courts—bad as they may be—are still somewhat more likely to meet the needs of the public.

There is also a more serious difference between the American and the Italian judicial systems, one that explains the crisis of the

---

[35] Battaglia, pp. 75–121, 192–195.
[36] On the public attitude toward judges and lawyers, see Maranini, pp. 13–14, and Prandstraller, pp. 202–206.

Italian legal tradition. Basic disagreement exists in Italy today over the proper function of the courts: Those who see the judge's proper role as simply one of applying the explicit provisions of the legal codes are pitted against those who want the judge to preserve the letter and spirit of the Constitution. This cleavage is reflected in the rivalry between the Court of Cassation and the Constitutional Court. By splitting the ranks of the judiciary, this issue facilitates the work of those who would sap judicial independence. Thus, the courts are put on the defensive, are dragged into political controversy, are beset by enemies on all sides. And Italian legal institutions face a crisis even more severe than the crises that are afflicting the bench and the bar in other, more prosperous Western democracies.

Recruitment and training procedures pose a series of internal threats to the independence of the judiciary. The Anglo-Saxon systems, with all their defects, tend to recruit as judges men who have already made their mark in life and who are therefore likely to have acquired a certain breadth of outlook and generosity of spirit. Instead, the Italian system, with its recruitment of direct entrants from the universities, with its hierarchy of ranks, with its concentration of power in the hands of the senior judges in the higher courts, tends to attract much the same kind of people who are dominant in the bureaucracy. Drawn from the less developed areas of the country, unsympathetic with recent economic, social, and political changes, anxious to rise in the hierarchy, and therefore eager to please the judges of the higher courts, the average Italian judge is apt to be highly conservative in outlook. Such a judiciary contains strong elements of skepticism vis-à-vis democratic institutions and cannot be entirely relied upon to support the present constitutional system.

TEN
THE LOWERED PROFILE
The country's role in world affairs

THE ITALIAN PEOPLE AND THE OUTSIDE WORLD

Some American scholars doubt the existence of a strong sense of national identity among the Italian people. One such attitude is expressed in the writings of the American political scientist, Norman Kogan:

> Italians can identify with other Italians but not with Italy. They can exult or suffer over the victories or defeats of Italian soccer teams or beauty queens engaged in international competition. But few of them would die for Italy. This indifference is perhaps even greater today than in the recent past because of the absence of an aura of legitimacy about present political institutions, and the decline of idealism since the struggle for liberation.[1]

Kogan's judgment appears to be excessively harsh. It must be borne in mind that the Italian performance in World War II, uninspiring as it was, could be attributed in large measure to the fact that the war was obviously not a just one, and that Italian

---

[1] Norman Kogan, *The Politics of Italian Foreign Policy* (New York: Praeger, 1963), p. 22.

independence was not really at stake. A far better test of the Italian sense of national identity was provided by the general all-out effort that followed the tragic debacle of Caporetto in 1917, when the Austrian armies seemed on the point of breaking through into the Po Valley. Certainly, the Resistance movement, and the hopeless struggle against overwhelming Nazi forces waged by isolated Italian garrisons in the Aegean Sea after September 8, 1943, were true tests of the Italian people's love of country. Italians are prepared to sacrifice a great deal for their country when they see the stakes as relevant; the normally apathetic masses seem to be capable of instinctive reserves of loyalty. For in the minds of most Italians, local parochialism cannot furnish a viable alternative to the present Italian national state. A return to the sovereign city-states of the Renaissance is beyond the realm of possibility.

On the other hand, the sickly jingoism that infected significant numbers of middle-class Italians in the years before 1940 has been largely dispelled, surviving only among the splinter movements of the extreme Right. Today, Italian elites seem to be concerned primarily with domestic problems, and to harbor no illusions regarding their country's ability to claim great-power status. The necessity of an alliance with the United States is widely accepted. The possibility of a neutralist stance is generally discounted. To the extent that some measure of self-assertiveness still persists, it takes the form of wistful efforts to affirm an Italian presence in various parts of the world through economic and cultural ties, or of unsolicited offers to mediate in international disputes between the great powers.

How do Italians view the world around them? Evidence from public opinion polls seems to indicate that Italians are fairly sympathetic toward the United States, prevalently diffident toward the Soviet Union, and somewhat antipathetic with regard to Britain.[2] But these attitudes are, to some degree, reflections of domestic political postures: Christian Democrats are most likely to support a close alliance with the United States and to express fear and distrust of the Soviet Union, whereas Italian Communists are likely to take precisely the opposite stance. When the United States is closely identified with some major interest group (the church or *Confindustria*), those who oppose the aspirations of that group—anticlericals in the case of the church, Left-wing Christian Democrats in the case of *Confindustria*—are likely to

[2] Kogan, pp. 22–24.

adopt an anti-American tone.[3] Moreover, these attitudes toward other countries are not immutable. In the late 1950s, the overwhelming majority of Socialist (PSI) deputies favored an Italian policy of neutrality in the cold war.[4] By 1963, the Socialist party (presumably including most of these same deputies) had accepted NATO as a permanent Italian commitment. It was evident that a change in the domestic political situation (the decision of the Socialist party to support a Left-Center cabinet) had changed what many considered to be an adamant Socialist stand against Italian alignment with the West. As a matter of fact, by 1963, Italian public opinion vis-à-vis the United States and Russia seemed less directly related to interparty distinctions: Communists were less likely to suspect the United States of seeking world domination and Christian Democrats were less suspicious of the intentions of the Soviet Union.[5]

Italian public opinion also appears to favor European integration. But the percentage favoring it is much smaller than in other major Western European countries. Moreover, less than half of those who favor European integration actually want a European federal system under a single federal government. And over one-third of the Italian electorate professes to have no information, or no opinion, on the general subject of a European federation.[6]

Indeed, the basic characteristic of Italian public opinion in the field of foreign affairs is a very low level of interest and information, well behind nations like France and Germany. In the sphere of foreign affairs, the Italian public tends to be apathetic. This apathy is itself the result of a number of factors. Of course, the restricted educational opportunities in Italy help to account for a generally passive body politic. But other causes should be cited: the low level of newspaper circulation, the inadequate and superficial coverage of foreign affairs by the mass media, and the tendency of public-opinion survey organizations like DOXA to take only an occasional and marginal interest in foreign policy issues.[7]

---

[3] Kogan, pp. 24–25; and Giovanni Bechelloni, "Opinione pubblica e politica internazionale; note su alcuni saggi d'opinione," in Istituto Affari Internazionali, *La politica estera della Repubblica italiana*, Vol. III (Milano: Comunità, 1967), pp. 979–985.

[4] Lloyd A. Free, *Six Allies and a Neutral* (New York: The Free Press, 1959), p. 175.

[5] Bechelloni, pp. 983–985.

[6] Jacques-René Rabier, *L'Information des Européens et l'integration de l'Europe* (Bruxelles: Institut d'Études Européens, Université Libre de Bruxelles, 1965), pp. 36–44, 54–55.

[7] Bechelloni, pp. 975–977.

GOALS OF ITALIAN FOREIGN POLICY: PAST AND PRESENT

During the period 1870–1945, Italy was regarded as a great power with major responsibilities in the international state system. The questions as to what role Italy should play in the European balance of power, what allies she should seek, what enemies she should prepare to oppose with her armed strength if need be, tended to divide Italian policy makers during this span of time. Some, primarily interested in the redemption of Trento and Trieste from Austrian rule, advocated an alliance with the Entente powers (Britain, France, and Russia) against the Central powers (Germany and Austria-Hungary). Others, seeking colonial expansion in the Mediterranean, saw Britain and France as the chief barriers to Italian imperial aspirations and pushed for an alliance with the Central powers. Policy makers of cautious, moderate bent—men like Cavour, Visconti Venosta, Giolitti—recognized that Italy was the weakest of the great powers, and pursued a foreign policy of limited goals, avoiding excessive commitments but trying to maintain Italian bargaining power in the European balance of power. Other Italian foreign policy makers—men like Crispi and later Mussolini—saw Italy as a potential imperial power, a third Rome that would eventually dominate North Africa and the Balkans. Both the aggressive imperialists and the moderates proved to be capable of embarking on foreign adventures for the purpose of promoting national unity, "building a nation" from the various peoples who inhabited the Italian peninsula.

The disastrous experience of two world wars, and of a Fascist interlude, has served to educate the Italian people to understand the dangers of an excessively nationalistic stand. Emerging from World War II with a shattered economy, Italian policy makers abandoned the delusions of grandeur that had bemused their predecessors. They sought a lowered profile on the international scene. A return to imperial expansion was utterly out of the question, given Italy's limited power and resources. On the other hand, the more cautious policy followed by moderates like Giolitti in the past—a policy of jockeying for an advantageous position in the balance of power—was also ruled out by altered circumstances. For the European balance of power was a thing of the past, and had been replaced by a confrontation between two superpowers, the United States and the Soviet Union. Nor did a policy of isolation or neutralism seem feasible. To go it alone, as Sweden and Switzerland had done, requires a strong, domestically financed military establishment to deter aggression. Italy, it was felt, lacked the resources to maintain such a defense force without outside assistance.[8] For these reasons, Italy was under great pressure to join one of the two power blocs in order to obtain the protection and military assistance that such an alignment would entail.

The basic options in recent Italian foreign policy were decided upon during the years 1945–1957. In 1947, by accepting the invitation to join the group of nations receiving economic aid from the United States under the Marshall Plan (European Recovery Program), Italy became a full-fledged member of the Western European economic bloc. In 1949, when the Italian Parliament, after a long and heated debate, ratified the North Atlantic Treaty, Italy in effect shouldered a firm military commitment to the Western alliance. In 1951, Italy joined the European Coal and Steel Community, a first step toward the Common Market, which was to be established by the end of the decade. In 1957, the Italian Parliament ratified the treaties providing for a European Economic Community and a European atomic energy authority. In short, by 1957, Italian foreign policy had assumed a basically Atlantic and European orientation, backing United States defense policies in NATO, while wholeheartedly supporting progress toward a united Europe.

Along with the consummation of these fundamental choices, Italy has settled, or nearly settled, some potentially troublesome frontier problems. The annexation of Trieste and of its surrounding Zone A by Italy, and of the adjacent Slavic-inhabited Zone B by Yugoslavia, has paved the way for more normal and even friendly relations between Italy and her south Slavic neighbor. Furthermore, significant cultural concessions to a hitherto neglected German-speaking minority have done much to pacify the Tyrolese population of Bolzano Province, and to smooth out relations between Italy and Austria.

Italy's close alignment with the United States and with the nations of NATO is based only in part on the fear of possible Soviet aggression. Kogan places considerable emphasis on the importance of domestic problems in influencing Italian foreign policy. It is not so much Soviet armed strength that is viewed with misgivings by Italy's ruling elites, Kogan claims, but rather the possibility of a basic change in Italy's socioeconomic structure—a change presumably engineered by Italy's powerful Communist

---

[8] On this point, see Paolo Emilio Taviani, *Saggi sulla democrazia cristiana* (Firenze: Le Monnier, 1961), pp. 138–141. Taviani is a prominent Christian Democratic political leader, who has served as minister of defense.

party.⁹ Thus, domestic considerations loom very large in influencing Italian foreign policy: before 1914, nation building; today, the maintenance of the socioeconomic status quo. Similarly, Italy's strong adhesion to the European Economic Community (EEC) and to the principle of European unification may be explained largely in domestic terms: In a broader economic and/or political community, it is hoped, Italy's surplus population could easily be absorbed into the active labor force.¹⁰

While national security, domestic social stability, and the amelioration of certain social problems appear to be the chief goals of Italian foreign policy, there are other objectives that seem to animate Italian policy makers from time to time. For one thing, there is a widespread desire to establish an Italian presence in the world, to make certain that Italy's voice is heard, and to show the flag even in areas where vital national interests are not directly involved. This natural desire for international recognition manifests itself in a variety of ways: state visits by an Italian president or prime minister to remote foreign lands (the pilgrimages of President Gronchi between 1955 and 1962 are cases in point), offers to mediate in disputes among the superpowers (even though such mediation is usually unsolicited and often downright unwelcome), invitations to hold international conferences in Italian cities, and so forth. The same concern for "cutting a fine figure" abroad helps to account for the strong public support ENI received when it embarked on expensive investments in the Middle East.

Another Italian objective seems to be of interest mainly to Left-wing Christian Democrats like the late Enrico Mattei (former head of ENI), Giorgio La Pira (formerly mayor of Florence), Amintore Fanfani (who has served as both prime minister and foreign minister), and Giovanni Gronchi (former president of Italy). Men of this political persuasion appear to envision Italy as a bridge between Europe and the underdeveloped countries of Asia and Africa. Some of them openly sympathized with President Nasser during the Suez crisis of 1956, and today tend to show some favor for the cause of the Arabs in their confrontation with Israel. As these men see it, Italy is no longer a colonial power and is therefore ideally suited for the task of regaining the confidence and good will of the underdeveloped countries of the world, whose people tend to fear and distrust the West.

⁹ Kogan, pp. 135–141.
¹⁰ Renato Giordano, *Il mercato comune e i suoi problemi* (Rome: Opere Nuove, 1958), pp. 12–14, 55–56.

Finally, there is a strong opportunistic element in Italian foreign policy, as there is in the foreign policy of any nation. This tendency may be seen in the acquiescence of the Italian government when big Italian corporations, both public and private, conclude trade agreements with the Soviet Union or with some other Communist country. It also is revealed in the alacrity with which Italy modifies her foreign policies to conform to the prevalent *Zeitgeist*.[11] During the years of the cold war, Italy seemed to be the most intransigent and fanatical of America's allies. In 1970, as it became evident that American policy toward Communist China was shifting, Italy was one of the first previously hostile nations to recognize the mainland regime. Whether the order of the day is rigid confrontation or detente, the Italian government is almost embarrassingly prompt to jump on the bandwagon.

ITALIAN DEFENSE POLICY

We have already alluded to the Italian decision to enter NATO and thus to rely on the American nuclear umbrella and on the solidarity of the other Western European nations. Entry into NATO naturally entailed some measure of Italian rearmament. So Italy once again has a military establishment, albeit of modest dimensions: about twenty divisions, a small navy, and a moderate-sized air force.

The defeat of the Italian armed forces in World War II, and the absence of any colonial war to be waged after 1945, created a situation in which the Italian armed forces acquired neither the prestige nor the grudge against the system that characterized the military in France. Military appropriations were a relatively low percentage of the national budget, if one compares Italy with other NATO countries. And most of the funds spent for military purposes seemed to go for food, salaries, and pensions, rather than new weapons and equipment.

In NATO, Italy has been denied a position in the policy-making inner circle and has therefore pressed for the equality of all NATO members. But generally speaking, the Italian government has shown remarkable docility vis-à-vis its NATO allies, and has not pioneered any striking innovations in the field of defense policy, apart from requesting NATO acceptance of the need for a special Italian naval presence in the Mediterranean, an area more

---

[11] Kogan, pp. 41–42, for a discussion of the "wave of the future" syndrome.

crucial to Italy than to some of her allies. This relatively passive and complaisant Italian role in NATO is understandable in view of Italy's limited military muscle. One example of the accommodating line adopted by Italy was the Italian decision in the late 1950s to allow the United States to install intermediate-range ballistic missiles in Northeast Italy. This decision was hardly inevitable—the North Atlantic Treaty did not require it and, in fact, Norway had refused to allow the construction of missile bases on her soil—but the Italian government acceded to the American request.[12]

In view of Italy's rather modest defense capabilities, and also in view of the absence of any Italian involvement in war since 1945, one might well assume that the Italian armed forces would not be likely to pose a threat to the stability of democratic institutions. Yet, the Sifar scandal, in which a former Italian general (De Lorenzo) was accused by a number of informants of having prepared a possible coup d'etat, indicates that the Italian army is not immune to the attractions of possible intervention in Italian politics.[13] So, although the military appears to have suffered a sharp drop in power and status under the republic, prolonged social and economic difficulties accompanied by political disorder might well provoke a military revolt. Italian observers do not rule out this possibility entirely.

THE COLONIAL HERITAGE

Before World War II, Italy had succeeded in carving out a colonial empire in North and East Africa. Part of this empire had been acquired prior to Mussolini's reign: Eritrea, Italian Somaliland, and Libya. Ethiopia had been occupied by the Fascist regime in the 1930s. These colonies had not done a great deal to augment Italian national power; but, in seizing colonial possessions, Italy was simply emulating that worldwide trend toward colonization of backward territories which both Britain and France were promoting. Thus, Italian acquisition of Eritrea, Italian Somaliland, and even Libya, in the years before 1914, aroused little real opposition, since such acts of aggression were in accordance with the

[12] Aldo Garosci, "L'Italia e il Patto atlantico," in Istituto Affari Internazionali, Vol. II, pp. 555–556.
[13] Gigi Ghirotti, "Appunti per una storia di un' estate pericolosa (I): un uomo del re e i segreti della Repubblica." Comunità, Vol. XXII, No. 151 (March–April 1968), 42–48.

colonizing spirit of the age. But the invasion of Ethiopia was a different matter, for Ethiopia was a member of the League of Nations and as such had a far stronger claim on the world's conscience.

After World War II, Italy was stripped of her colonial possessions. Libya became an independent sovereign state in 1952; Ethiopia regained its independence after a very brief and destructive colonial interlude, and was authorized by the United Nations to annex Eritrea; and Somaliland was given its independence somewhat later, in 1959, after a prolonged Italian trusteeship. The Italian government put up a stiff resistance in the United Nations against the loss of these territories, not so much because of their intrinsic value, but rather because the loss of the colonies might have a serious impact on Italian public opinion. Finally, however, Italy had to yield to the inevitable and proposed a face-saving compromise program that proved acceptable to the General Assembly. In return for a ten-year trusteeship over Somaliland, Italy renounced all her claims to her former colonies.

The loss of the colonies was actually a hidden boon for Italy. Funds that would have been squandered on the African territories were available for investment in the Italian South. Early, peaceful withdrawal from the colonies saved the Italian armed forces from the kind of inglorious and expensive rear-guard action which France and the Netherlands had had to conduct. In future years, Italian entrepreneurs, both public and private, would be welcome in Africa, Asia, and the Middle East; for they were not suspected as possible advance scouts for colonial encroachments.

MAKERS OF ITALIAN FOREIGN POLICY

In order to dramatize the complexity and lack of central direction that characterize the Italian policy-making process in the realm of foreign affairs, one Italian writer resorts to a deliberately exaggerated statement: "The first reply to be given to the question: who is it that makes foreign policy in Italy? should be the following: no one."[14]

One evident source of confusion, discussed at length by Negri, is the ambiguous role of the president of Italy.[15] His pow-

---

[14] Pietro Quaroni, "Chi è che fa la politica estera in Italia," in Istituto Affari Internazionali, Vol. III, pp. 811–813.
[15] Guglielmo Negri, *La direzione ed il controllo democratico della politica estera in Italia* (Milano: Giuffré, 1967), pp. 39–69.

ers fall considerably short of those exercised by the king of Italy under the royal prerogative in the days of the constitutional monarchy. Nevertheless, they are defined in rather vague terms in the Constitution and thus lend themselves to the broad interpretation an activist president like Gronchi chose to propound.

Some of the presidential powers are recognized as purely formal in nature. For instance, the president has the power to accredit and receive diplomatic representatives (that is, the power to nominate ambassadors and recognize foreign governments) but these powers are really exercised by the foreign minister and the cabinet, who must keep the president informed and presumably listen to—but not necessarily take—his advice. It should be noted that an effort made by President Segni, shortly before he suffered a paralytic stroke in 1964, to induce the foreign minister to withdraw certain ambassadorial nominations, was apparently unsuccessful. The prime minister backed up his foreign minister against the claims of the chief of state.[16]

The president also ratifies treaties. But since these treaties have already been approved by the cabinet, and frequently also by Parliament, the president's role is again largely a ceremonial one: He can, at the most, advise the Council of Ministers or the Parliament to reconsider the treaty, if it contains unconstitutional provisions. However, there is some perplexity about the scope of the president's power in this matter: Conceivably, some future president might simply refuse to ratify a treaty of which he disapproved. The denouement of such an eventuality is hard to predict. On the other hand, there seems to be no doubt whatsoever regarding the purely formal character of the president's power to declare war after the Parliament has deliberated: here, the president is surely bound to reflect the will of Parliament.

In some other respects, the president has a more far-reaching influence, however. He *must* be kept informed by the government about the affairs of state, and is entitled to receive all Foreign Office documents on current problems. He has the right to give advice to the foreign minister. And, of course, he is entitled to correspond with foreign statesmen, though constitutional custom has it that he should keep the foreign minister informed as to the content of such correspondence. He can also visit foreign nations in his capacity as ceremonial chief of state, but it is understood that such visits should take place with the consent of, and in consultation with, the cabinet and the foreign minister. Of course,

[16] Negri, p. 47n.

in the case of an activist president like Gronchi, it is difficult to hold the chief of state to these rules: Gronchi granted some controversial interviews to foreign newsmen, had meetings with the Soviet ambassador (meetings at which he presented his own policy recommendations), and generally discussed political issues with foreign statesmen during his formal trips to foreign nations. On one occasion, he sent a letter to President Eisenhower making a number of proposals of his own; and the general secretary at the Foreign Office felt compelled to suspend transmission of the letter to the United States. The rationale, later approved by the foreign minister, was that the proposals in the Gronchi letter were out of line with the policy of the cabinet.[17]

The main responsibility for conducting Italian foreign policy rests in the Foreign Ministry under the broad supervision of the prime minister and the cabinet. Theoretically, it is the cabinet that is collectively responsible for foreign affairs; but the cabinet lacks a secretariat, lacks advance notice or resources for the study of policy proposals. So, very frequently, the prime minister and the foreign minister originate a proposal, consult the secretaries of the parties that form part of the cabinet coalition, and only report to the cabinet when the new policy is already in the process of being carried out. If, on the other hand, there is strong disagreement between the prime minister and the foreign minister, then the cabinet will be called upon to decide between them. So collegial rule tends to break down in practice, much as it does in most cabinets, in the field of foreign affairs.

Treaties and major foreign policy initiatives are, of course, subject to parliamentary control. Treaties require parliamentary ratification, though "agreements in simplified form" do not.[18] Questions, interpellations, and the general debates on foreign affairs, as well as the hearings held by the foreign affairs committees of the two chambers, are some of the ways in which executive action can be subjected to careful and skeptical deliberation, or publicity, or both. But rigorous party discipline, which is especially pronounced in the field of foreign affairs where countervailing pressures from the constituency are rare, makes this parliamentary supervision rather ineffective.

We must not emerge from this discussion with the impression that the foreign minister, when he enjoys the backing of the prime

---

[17] Domenico Bartoli, *Da Vittorio Emanuele a Gronchi* (Milano: Longanesi, 1961), p. 177.

[18] Negri, pp. 91–94. The government, thus far, has not abused its power to stipulate such agreements.

minister, is a kind of uncontrolled czar in the field of foreign policy. True, cabinet control over his actions is often rather weak. But by the same token, he has a great deal of difficulty controlling his colleagues and other makers of foreign policy. Among his cabinet colleagues, the minister of defense, the minister of agriculture, and the minister of foreign commerce are only three examples (others might be cited as well) of ministers who regularly make decisions with serious foreign-policy implications and who do not necessarily follow the Foreign Office line. Such public corporations as IRI and ENI often make decisions affecting Italy's foreign relations, and do not always feel compelled to discuss these decisions in advance with the Foreign Ministry. Giant corporations like Fiat feel free to reach agreements with foreign corporations, without necessarily considering the impact of these agreements on Italian society. Pressure groups that have close *clientela* relationships with certain selected ministries may use those ministries to promote their own interests in the shaping of Italian trade policy: the agricultural pressure groups play an especially notorious role in this regard.[19] And finally, the foreign minister may have trouble controlling his own civil servants—when Fanfani was foreign minister he found himself warring against his subordinates and was provoked into sponsoring his own bureaucratic faction, the so-called Mau-Maus.[20] Party conflict intrudes into the most sacred precincts of the bureaucracy. In short, the policy-making process in the field of foreign affairs shows the same chronic lack of coordination and the same absence of a clear sense of direction that observers may discern in the field of domestic policy.

CONCLUSIONS

Italian observers are not happy with Italian foreign policy and the process by which it is formulated. Some of the complaints are fairly familiar ones, harking back to Chapter Eight. Thus, as we have seen, the lack of coordination, the lack of a clear sense of direction, and the interagency and intraagency feuds are also present in the field of foreign affairs. The lack of adequate information and of information-gathering techniques, the shortage of intellectuals interested in, and qualified to give, such information

---

[19] Mario Di Bartolomei, "L'agricoltura nella politica estera italiana," in Istituto Affari Internazionali, Vol. III, pp. 872–889.
[20] Piero Ottone, *Fanfani* (Milano: Longanesi, 1966), pp. 114–117.

and accompanying advice—these, too, are familiar lamentations.[21] And then, we have noted some additional sources of unhappiness vis-à-vis Italian foreign policy: the obsession with asserting an Italian presence everywhere; the urge to offer unsolicited mediation; the disruptive overtures to the uncommitted oil-producing countries.

Yet, all things considered, the field of foreign policy is one in which Italy faces no grave difficulties. The lower profile and the cutting of commitments have left Italy relatively free to face domestic problems and have reduced the above shortcomings to their proper proportions.

---

[21] See, on this point, Quaroni, pp. 808–810, 819–820. See also Enzo Forcella, "Gli intellettuali e la politica internazionale," Istituto Affari Internazionali, Vol. I, pp. 103–116.

CONCLUSION
THE IMPLICATIONS OF POLITICAL LAG

The central theme of this work has been political lag: the sharp contrast between a booming economy and a rapidly changing society, on the one hand, and a stagnating political system, on the other. Political lag is a fairly common phenomenon throughout the world; but it assumes particularly striking dimensions in Italy, because of the extraordinary changes that have been taking place in Italian society.

Our examination of the Italian economy and of Italian society offers a picture of fairly uniform progress, often of a rather spectacular variety: a high rate of economic growth, the spread of industrialization from the Northwest Triangle into adjoining regions, the migration from South to North and from rural to urban areas, the massive infusion of government money for public works and industrial projects in the South, the building of superhighways like the *Autostrada del Sole* to link the various Italian regions more closely together, and the significant improvement in Italian living standards throughout the peninsula.

In contrast, we have seen many symptoms of a lagging polity, trailing far behind a society in flux. The socialization process in Italy is discontinuous, and fails to inculcate a strong positive allegiance to the system. This seems to be particularly true of the later socializing experiences—that is, those which occur after an individual leaves school. Adolescents have been found to possess a high sense of political competence, but they become prematurely disillusioned cynics by the age of thirty. This inadequate socialization process creates a low rate of meaningful political participation among Italians, and also has its impact on the process of political recruitment, where we find the middle class clearly overrepresented. It also contributes to the low level of trust Italians feel for themselves and for their government. On this score, however, Italy's tragic recent history, marked by civil conflict, is partly to blame. So, partly for historical reasons, partly for reasons connected with the process of political socialization, partly because of persisting economic and regional cleavages, Italy has a fragmented political culture, a high proportion of alienated citizens, and relatively low levels of public information and participation. While national integration no longer seems to be a major problem, the developmental crises of legitimacy and participation—to say nothing of distribution—have yet to be overcome.

The highly centralized Italian government tends to discourage grass-roots participation, especially since the local and provincial authorities have a terribly restricted tax base. The recent creation of the regions does not really alter the basically centralized character of the system but may tend to promote greater participation by local elites and also to introduce more effective feedback into the process of economic planning. In local government, then, the overall atmosphere of crisis and insolvency is partially relieved by some modernizing trends.

Some hopeful tendencies may also be discerned with regard to interest groups, which are becoming increasingly independent of the political parties and which are consequently injecting a more pragmatic style into the bargaining process. To the extent that this occurs, cultural fragmentation may be more effectively overcome.

However, in the area of party politics, the picture is one of almost unrelieved gloom. Here we find the same old oligarchic tendencies, the same incomprehensible jargon used by party leaders, the same heavy-handed reliance on patronage and perquisites, and the same politics of personal cliques and warring intraparty factions that existed in the past. The political process is essentially stagnant. The presence of a strong Communist party on the Left prevents the formation of a credible alternative to the coalition in power and thus makes for a politics characterized by very limited turnover: the incumbents are never turned out of office but simply exchange one ministerial chair for another. The accentuated rigidity of the Italian electorate rarely allows any significant shift in the respective strengths of the various parties. Thus, elections have lost much of their meaning. After all the sound and fury of the election campaign is over, relatively few parliamentary seats have changed hands; and the old problem of building a viable cabinet coalition must once again be confronted, with the likely outcome being a cabinet that looks remarkably like its predecessor. To the untutored Italian voter, who is always ready to suspect skulduggery in high places, the party system makes the whole Italian political system look far worse than it really is.

Policy-making structures and processes are also terribly archaic. No single policy-making structure has achieved a clear position of dominance; the conflict, real or potential, between the president and the prime minister weakens the authority of the executive branch; coordination and even mutual consultation are ineffectual; cumbersome procedures hamper decision making at every turn; and a highly tradition-minded bureaucracy is unprepared to fill the vacuum left by the indecisiveness and mutual antagonism of politicians. Under the circumstances, it is not surprising that even public corporations sometimes act like sovereign political entities beholden to no one. This confused allocation of authority, combined with the not unjustified public suspicion of bureaucratic corruption and the terribly inefficient court system, reinforce that same impression of low system effectiveness aroused by the political parties.

Even the socioeconomic realm, where so much progress has been made, contains areas of severe backwardness or deterioration. The South still lags far behind the rest of the country. The rural exodus is creating depressed backwaters in the more remote regions of Northern and Central Italy. Moreover, the shoddiness of the public services is beginning to focus attention on the imbalances in the Italian economy. Can industry continue to grow in a country with an inadequate school system, insufficient provision for low-cost housing, and overburdened medical services? May not industrialization, with its accompanying pollutants, impose too heavy an ecological burden on a land that has already been violated many times over by the hands of man? Finally, shifting over to social considerations, how long can an underpaid labor force be expected to accept a painfully slow removal of long-resented deprivations in the name of a favorable balance of trade?

It would appear, then, that Italy is still in the midst of a dangerous transitional phase during which democratic attitudes and processes have not yet become firmly entrenched, during which political mechanisms suited to a bygone age appear increasingly inadequate to cope with the emerging problems of the late twentieth century. When political lag exists in a particularly acute form, as it does in Italy, system survival depends upon the nature of the problems the system must confront. Fortunately for Italy, economic expansion since World War II has lessened the pressure on the political system, and has made the relative ineffectiveness of the system more tolerable. Fortunately, too, Italy is no longer burdened by weighty foreign commitments. But if a serious depression should occur, there are grave doubts as to how successfully the system could survive it. After all, it was during the brief recession of 1963–1965 that General De Lorenzo is said to have planned the arrest and detention of hundreds of leading political figures.

On the other hand, should the system endure in its present form for another decade or two, there is reason to hope that current ameliorative tendencies will be strengthened and multiplied. The healthy pragmatism now emerging in the trade-union movement and in some segments of the business community may eventually spread to the political parties. The Communist party may be replaced by a strong party of the democratic Left or, more likely, may become part of the governing coalition, as its own internal democratizing tendencies make it more acceptable to its present opponents. The church-state issue may appear increasingly irrelevant as liberalizing tendencies within the church continue to prevail. And Southern development may progress to the point of basically transforming Southern attitudes, with a resulting modernizing impact on the bureaucracy and the judiciary, where Southern elements now prevail. Much depends, then, on whether economic prosperity continues to give Italian democracy a much-needed breathing spell. For the experience of the United States demonstrates that grossly outdated and malfunctioning political institutions can long coexist with a booming dynamic economy and a highly mobile society. It is only when the system becomes overloaded with unresolved and urgent problems, only when the consumer's shoe begins to pinch, and pinch badly, that most people become concerned about the quality of the political system under which they live.

SELECTED BIBLIOGRAPHY

Chapter One

Acquarone, Alberto. *Grandi città e aree metropolitane in Italia*. Bologna: Zanichelli, 1961.
Alberoni, Francesco, and Guido Baglioni. *L'integrazione dell' immigrato nella società industriale*. Bologna: Il Mulino, 1965.
Albrecht-Carrié, René. *Italy from Napoleon to Mussolini*. New York: Columbia University Press, 1960.
Ardigò, Achille. *Emancipazione femminile e urbanesimo*. Brescia: Morcelliana, 1964.
Barbero, Giuseppe. *La riforma agraria italiana*. Milano: Feltrinelli, 1960.
Barzanti, Sergio. *The Underdeveloped Areas within the Common Market*. Princeton, N.J.: Princeton University Press, 1965.
Bianciardi, Luciano. *La vita agra*. Milano: Rizzoli, 1962.
Carlyle, Margaret. *The Awakening of Southern Italy*. London: Oxford University Press, 1962.
Clough, Shepard B. *The Economic History of Modern Italy*. New York: Columbia University Press, 1964.
Colombo, Arturo. *Rapporto sull' università italiana*. Milano: Comunità, 1962.
Comitato di Studio dei Problemi della Scuola e dell' Università Italiana. *I laureati in Italia*. Bologna: Il Mulino, 1968.
Compagna, Francesco. *La politica della città*. Bari: Laterza, 1967.
——. *La questione meridionale*. Milano: Garzanti, 1963.
Delzell, Charles F. *Mussolini's Enemies: The Italian Anti-Fascist Resistance*. Princeton; N.J.: Princeton University Press, 1961.
De Mauro, Tullio. *Storia linguistica dell' Italia unita*. Bari: Laterza, 1963.
di Lampedusa, Giuseppe. *The Leopard*. New York: New American Library, 1961.
Fenoaltea, Giorgio. *Il popolo sovrano*. Firenze: La Nuova Italia, 1958.
Fofi, Goffredo. *L'immigrazione meridionale a Torino*. Milano: Feltrinelli, 1964.
Gallino, Luciano. *Indagini di sociologia economica*. Milano: Comunità, 1962.
Germino, Dante. *The Italian Fascist Party in Power: A Study in Totalitarian Rule*. Minneapolis: University of Minnesota Press, 1959.
Ghirotti, Gigi. *Italia mia benchè*. Milano: Comunità, 1963.
Greenfield, Kent R. *Economics and Liberalism in the Risorgimento*. Rev. ed., Baltimore: The Johns Hopkins Press, 1965.
Grew, Raymond. *A Sterner Plan for Italian Unity*. Princeton, N.J.: Princeton University Press, 1963.
Grindrod, Muriel. *Italy*. New York: Praeger, 1968.
Hildebrand, George H. *Growth and Structure in the Economy of Modern Italy*. Cambridge, Mass.: Harvard University Press, 1965.

Hughes, H. Stuart. *The United States and Italy*. Rev. ed., Cambridge, Mass.: Harvard University Press, 1965.
Kish, George. *Life in Europe: Italy*. Grand Rapids, Mich.: Fideler Company, 1964.
Kogan, Norman. *A Political History of Postwar Italy*. New York: Praeger, 1966.
Levine, Irving R. *Main Street, Italy*. New York: Doubleday, 1963.
Lutz, Vera. *Italy: A Study in Economic Development*. London: Oxford University Press, 1962.
Mammarella, Giuseppe. *Italy after Fascism*. Rev. ed., Notre Dame, Ind.: University of Notre Dame Press, 1966.
Morandi, Carlo. *I partiti politici nella storia d'Italia*. Firenze: Le Monnier, 1968.
Muscarà, Calogero. *La geografia dello sviluppo*. Milano: Comunità, 1967.
Neufeld, Maurice F. *Poor Countries and Authoritarian Rule*. Ithaca, N.Y.: New York State School of Industrial and Labor Relations, 1965.
Olschki, Leonardo. *The Genius of Italy*. Ithaca, N.Y.: Cornell University Press, 1954.
Romeo, Rosario. *Breve storia della grande industria in Italia*. 3d ed., Bologna: Cappelli, 1967.
Salvadori, Massimo. *Italy*. Englewood Cliffs, N.J.: Prentice Hall, 1965.
Schachter, Gustav. *The Italian South: Economic Development in Mediterranean Europe*. New York: Random House, 1965.
Seton-Watson, Christopher. *Italy from Liberalism to Fascism*. London: Methuen, 1967.
Smith, Denis Mack. *Italy: A Modern History*. Ann Arbor, Mich.: University of Michigan Press, 1969.
Tarrow, Sidney G. *Peasant Communism in Southern Italy*. New Haven, Conn.: Yale University Press, 1967.
Tasca, Angelo. *The Rise of Italian Fascism 1918–1922*. London: Methuen, 1938.
Thayer, John A. *Italy and the Great War*. Madison, Wis.: University of Wisconsin Press, 1964.
Whyte, A. J. *The Evolution of Modern Italy*. New York: Norton, 1965.

Chapter Two

Alberoni, Francesco, ed. *L'attivista di partito*. Bologna: Il Mulino, 1967.
———, and Guido Baglioni. *L'integrazione dell' immigrato nella società industriale*. Bologna: Il Mulino, 1965.
Albertoni, Ettore A., Ezio Antonini, and Renato Palmieri. *La generazione degli anni difficili*. Bari: Laterza, 1962.
Barnes, Samuel H. *Party Democracy: Politics in an Italian Socialist Federation*. New Haven, Conn.: Yale University Press, 1967.
Bartoli, Domenico. *Da Vittorio Emanuele a Gronchi*. Milano: Longanesi, 1961.
Cammett, John M. *Antonio Gramsci and the Origins of Italian Communism*. Stanford, Calif.: Stanford University Press, 1967.
Carrillo, Elisa A. *De Gasperi: The Long Apprenticeship*. Notre Dame, Ind.: University of Notre Dame Press, 1965.
Cesareo, Giovanni. *La condizione femminile*. Milano: Sugar Editore, 1963.

Cesarini Sforza, Marco. *L'uomo politico.* Firenze: Vallecchi, 1963.
Comitato di Studio dei Problemi della Scuola e dell' Università Italiana. *I laureati in Italia.* Bologna: Il Mulino, 1968.
De Gasperi, Maria Romana Catti. *De Gasperi, uomo solo.* Milano: Mondadori, 1964.
De Mauro, Tullio. *Storia linguistica dell' Italia unita.* Bari: Laterza, 1963.
Di Palma, Giuseppe. *Apathy and Participation: Mass Politics in Western Societies.* New York: Free Press, 1970.
Fofi, Goffredo. *L'immigrazione meridionale a Torino.* Milano: Feltrinelli, 1964.
Galli, Giorgio. *Il bipartitismo imperfetto.* Bologna: Il Mulino, 1966.
———, and Alfonso Prandi. *Patterns of Political Participation in Italy.* New Haven, Conn.: Yale University Press, 1970.
Grimaldi, Ugoberto Alfassio, and Italo Bertoni. *I giovani degli anni sessanta.* Bari: Laterza, 1964.
Kogan, Norman. *The Politics of Italian Foreign Policy.* New York: Praeger, 1963.
La Palombara, Joseph. *Interest Groups in Italian Politics.* Princeton, N.J.: Princeton University Press, 1964.
Lipset, Seymour M., and Philip G. Altbach, eds. *Students in Revolt.* Boston: Houghton Mifflin, 1969.
Lo stato democratico e i giovani. Milano: Comunità, 1968.
Luzzatto-Fegiz, Pierpaolo. *Il volto sconosciuto dell' Italia 1956–1965.* 2nd series. Milano: Giuffré, 1966.
Mannucci, Cesare. *Lo spettatore senza libertà.* Bari: Laterza, 1962.
Meynaud, Jean. *Rapporto sulla classe dirigente italiana.* Milano: Giuffré, 1966.
Ottone, Piero. *Fanfani.* Milano: Longanesi, 1966.
Paulson, Belden, and Athos Ricci. *The Searchers.* Chicago: Quadrangle, 1966.
Pieroni, Alfredo. *Chi comanda in Italia.* Milano: Longanesi, 1959.
Prandi, Alfonso. *Chiesa e politica.* Bologna: Il Mulino, 1968.
Pye, Lucian W., and Sidney Verba, eds. *Political Culture and Political Development.* Princeton, N.J.: Princeton University Press, 1965.
Rabier, Jacques-René. *L'Information des Européens et l'integration de l'Europe.* Bruxelles: Institut d'Études Européens, Université Libre de Bruxelles, 1965.
Raffaele, Joseph A. *Labor Leadership in Italy and Denmark.* Madison, Wis.: University of Wisconsin Press, 1962.
Tarrow, Sidney G. *Peasant Communism in Southern Italy.* New Haven, Conn.: Yale University Press, 1967.
Weiss, Ignazio. *Il potere di carta.* Torino: UTET, 1965.

Chapter Three

Alberoni, Francesco, ed. *L'attivista di partito.* Bologna: Il Mulino, 1967.
Almond, Gabriel A., and Sidney Verba. *The Civic Culture: Political Attitudes and Democracy in Five Nations.* Princeton, N.J.: Princeton University Press, 1963.
Banfield, Edward C. *The Moral Basis of a Backward Society.* New York: Free Press, 1967.

Barnes, Samuel H. "Leadership Style and Political Competence," in Lewis J. Edinger, ed., *Political Leadership in Industrialized Societies: Studies in Comparative Analysis.* New York: Wiley, 1967.
———. *Party Democracy: Politics in an Italian Socialist Federation.* New Haven, Conn.: Yale University Press, 1967.
Barzini, Luigi. *The Italians.* New York: Bantam, 1964.
Cavallari, Alberto. *Il Vaticano che cambia.* Milano: Mondadori, 1966.
Cesareo, Giovanni. *La condizione femminile.* Milano: Sugar Editore, 1963.
Cesarini Sforza, Marco. *L'uomo politico.* Firenze: Vallecchi, 1963.
Comitato di Studio dei Problemi della Scuola e dell' Università Italiana. *I laureati in Italia.* Bologna: Il Mulino, 1968.
Jemolo, Arturo Carlo. *Chiesa e Stato in Italia negli ultimi cento anni.* Torino: Einaudi, 1949.
Kogan, Norman. *The Politics of Italian Foreign Policy.* New York: Praeger, 1963.
La Palombara, Joseph. *Interest Groups in Italian Politics.* Princeton, N.J.: Princeton University Press, 1964.
Lewis, Norman. *The Honored Society.* New York: Putnam, 1964.
Lopreato, Joseph. *Peasants No More: Social Class and Social Change in an Underdeveloped Society.* San Francisco: Chandler, 1967.
Luzzato-Fegiz, Pierpaolo. *Il volto sconosciuto dell' Italia 1956–1965.* 2nd series. Milano: Giuffré, 1966.
Prandi, Alfonso. *Chiesa e politica.* Bologna: Il Mulino, 1968.
Pye, Lucian W., and Sidney Verba, eds. *Political Culture and Political Development.* Princeton, N.J.: Princeton University Press, 1965.
Settembrini, Domenico. *La chiesa nella politica italiana 1944–1963.* Pisa: Nistri-Lischi, 1964.
Silone, Ignazio. *Fontamara.* New York: Dell, 1961.
Tarrow, Sidney G. *Peasant Communism in Southern Italy.* New Haven, Conn.: Yale University Press, 1967.

Chapter Four

Acquarone, Alberto. *Grandi città e aree metropolitane in Italia.* Bologna: Zanichelli, 1961.
Adams, John Clarke, and Paolo Barile. *The Government of Republican Italy.* 2nd ed., Boston: Houghton Mifflin, 1966.
Allen, Kevin, and M. C. MacLennan. *Regional Problems and Policies in Italy and France.* Beverly Hills, Calif.: Sage Publications, 1970.
Banfield, Edward C. *The Moral Basis of a Backward Society.* New York: Free Press, 1967.
Ciangaretti, Vincenzo. *Le radici della libertà.* Milano-Torino: Associazione Mazziniana Italiana, 1967.
Degli Esposti, Gianluigi. *Bologna PCI.* Bologna: Il Mulino, 1966.
Evans, Robert H. *Coexistence: Communism and Its Practice in Bologna, 1945–1965.* Notre Dame, Ind.: University of Notre Dame Press, 1967.
Fried, Robert C. *The Italian Prefects: A Study in Administrative Politics.* New Haven, Conn.: Yale University Press, 1963.
Galli, Giorgio. *Il bipartitismo imperfetto.* Bologna: Il Mulino, 1966.
———, and Alfonso Prandi. *Patterns of Political Participation in Italy.* New Haven, Conn.: Yale University Press, 1970.

Istituto per la Scienza dell' Amministrazione Pubblica. *Il burocrate di fronte alla burocrazia.* Milano: Giuffré, 1969.
Kogan, Norman. *The Government of Italy.* New York: Crowell, 1962.
Maranini, Giuseppe, ed. *La Regione e il governo locale.* 3 vols. Milano: Comunità, 1965.
Musitelli, Lorenzo. *Il comune nell' ordinamento amministrativo.* Milano: Pirola, 1969.
Palazzoli, Claude. *Les Régions Italiennes: Contribution à l'étude de la decentralisation politique.* Paris: Librairie Générale de Droit et de Jurisprudence, 1966.
Pryce, Roy. *The Italian Local Elections 1956.* St. Anthony's Papers, No. 3. New York: St. Martin's, 1957.
Rotelli, Ettore. *L'avvento della Regione in Italia.* Milano: Giuffré, 1967.
Sacco, Leonardo. *Sindaci e ministri.* Milano: Comunità, 1965.
Studi in onore di Emilio Crosa. 2 vols. Milano: Giuffré, 1960.
Tarrow, Sidney G. *Peasant Communism in Southern Italy.* New Haven, Conn.: Yale University Press, 1967.
Villani, Andrea. *Le strutture amministrative locali: tendenze evolutive nel campo dell' organizzazione e della finanza.* 2 vols. Milano: Franco Angeli Editore, 1968.
Zink, Harold, Arne Wahlstrand, Feliciano Benvenuti, R. Bhasharan. *Rural Local Government in Sweden, Italy, and India.* London: Stevens and Sons, 1957.

Chapter Five

Adams, John Clarke, and Paolo Barile. *The Government of Republican Italy.* 2nd ed., Boston: Houghton Mifflin, 1966.
Alberoni, Francesco, ed. *L'attivista di partito.* Bologna: Il Mulino, 1967.
Arfé, Gaetano. *Storia del socialismo italiano 1892–1926.* Torino: Einaudi, 1965.
Barbano, Filippo. *Partiti e pubblica opinione nella campagna elettorale.* Torino: Giappichelli, 1961.
Barnes, Samuel H. *Party Democracy: Politics in an Italian Socialist Federation.* New Haven, Conn.: Yale University Press, 1967.
Bassani, Mario. *Partiti e parlamento.* Milano-Varese: Istituto Editoriale Cisalpino, 1966.
Benzoni, Alberto, and Viva Tedesco. *Il movimento socialista nel dopoguerra.* Padova: Marsilio Editori, 1968.
Bettiza, Enzo. *Quale PCI? anatomia di una crisi.* Milano: Longanesi, 1969.
Blackmer, Donald L. M. *Unity in Diversity: Italian Communism and the Communist World.* Cambridge, Mass.: The M.I.T. Press, 1968.
Braga, Giorgio. *Il comunismo fra gli italiani.* Milano: Comunità, 1956.
———. *Sociologia elettorale della Toscana.* Roma: Edizioni Cinque Lune, 1963.
Catalano, Franco. *Storia dei partiti politici italiani.* 2nd ed. Roma: ERI, 1968.
Cesarini Sforza, Marco. *L'uomo politico.* Firenze: Vallecchi, 1963.
Chasseriaud, J. P. *Le parti démocrate chrétien en Italie.* Paris: Armand Colin, 1965.

Ciani, Arnaldo. *Il Partito Liberale Italiano da Croce a Malagodi.* Napoli: Edizioni Scientifiche Italiane, 1968.
Cicchitto, Fabrizio, and Gino Rocchi, Bruno Manghi, Luigi Ruggiu, Ada Sivini Cavazzani. *La DC dopo il primo ventennio.* Padova: Marsilio Editori, 1968.
D'Amato, Luigi. *Correnti di partito e partito di correnti.* Milano: Giuffré, 1965.
―――. *Il voto di preferenza in Italia.* Milano: Giuffré, 1964.
―――. *L'equilibrio in un sistema di 'partiti di corrente'.* Roma: Edizioni di Scienze Sociali, 1966.
De Caprariis, Vittorio. *Le garanzie della libertà.* Milano: Il Saggiatore, 1966.
Degli Esposti, Gianluigi. *Bologna PCI.* Bologna: Il Mulino, 1966.
De Rosa, Gabriele. *Storia del movimento cattolico in Italia.* Vol. I: *Il Partito Popolare Italiano.* Bari: Laterza, 1966.
Di Porto, Bruno. *Il Partito Repubblicano Italiano.* Roma: Ufficio-Stampa PRI, 1963.
Dogan, Mattei, and Orazio Maria Petracca, eds. *Partiti politici e strutture sociali in Italia.* Milano: Comunità, 1968.
Duverger, Maurice. *Political Parties.* London: Methuen, 1954.
Einaudi, Mario, and François Goguel. *Christian Democracy in Italy and France.* Notre Dame, Ind.: University of Notre Dame Press, 1952.
―――, Jean-Marie Domenach, and Aldo Garosci. *Communism in Western Europe.* Ithaca, N.Y.: Cornell University Press, 1951.
Galati, Vito G. *La democrazia cristiana.* Milano: Nuova Accademia Editrice, 1962.
Galli, Giorgio. *Il bipartitismo imperfetto.* Bologna: Il Mulino, 1966.
―――, ed. *Il comportamento elettorale in Italia.* Bologna: Il Mulino, 1968.
―――. *La sinistra democristiana: storia e ideologia.* Milano: Feltrinelli, 1962.
―――, and F. Bellini. *Storia del Partito comunista italiano.* Milano: Schwarz, 1958.
―――, and Alfonso Prandi. *Patterns of Political Participation in Italy.* New Haven, Conn.: Yale University Press, 1970.
Giovannini, Alberto. *Il Partito Liberale Italiano.* Milano: Nuova Accademia Editrice, 1962.
Godechot, Thierry. *Le parti démocrate chrétien en Italie.* Paris: Librairie Générale de Droit et de Jurisprudence, 1964.
Hilton-Young, W. *The Italian Left: A Short History of Political Socialism in Italy.* London: Longmans, Green, 1949.
d'Ippolito, Federico. *L'unificazione socialista: storia e prospettive.* Bologna: Cappelli, 1968.
Istituto per la documentazione e gli studi legislativi. *Indagine sul partito politico,* Vol. I: *La regolazione legislativa.* Milano: Giuffré, 1966.
Landolfi, Antonio. *Il Partito Socialista: oggi e domani.* Milano: Edizioni Azione Comune, 1963.
La Palombara, Joseph. *Interest Groups in Italian Politics.* Princeton, N.J.: Princeton University Press, 1964.
―――, and Myron Weiner. *Political Parties and Political Development.* Princeton, N.J.: Princeton University Press, 1966.
Lipset, Seymour M., and Stein Rokkan, eds. *Party Systems and Voter Alignments: Cross-national Perspectives.* New York: Free Press, 1967.

Lombardini, Gabriele. *De Gasperi e i cattolici.* Milano: Comunità, 1962.
Maranini, Giuseppe. *Storia del potere in Italia: 1848–1967.* Firenze: Vallecchi, 1967.
Meynaud, Jean. *Les partis politiques en Italie.* Paris: Presses Universitaires de France, 1965.
Michels, Robert. *Political Parties.* New York: Free Press, 1949.
Passigli, Stefano. *Emigrazione e comportamento politico.* Bologna: Il Mulino, 1969.
Poggi, Gianfranco, ed. *L'organizzazione partitica del PCI e della DC.* Bologna: Il Mulino, 1968.
Rizzo, Franco. *Partiti Piano e Stato.* Roma: Edizioni Montecitorio, 1966.
Savignano, Aristide. *I gruppi parlamentari.* Napoli: Morano Editore, 1965.
Scoppola, Pietro. *Coscienza religiosa e democrazia nell' Italia contemporanea.* Bologna: Il Mulino, 1966.
Sernini, Michele. *La disputa sui partiti.* Padova: Marsilio Editori, 1968.
———. *Le correnti nel partito.* Milano-Varese: Istituto Editoriale Cisalpino, 1966.
Spreafico, Alberto, and Joseph La Palombara, eds. *Elezioni e comportamento politico in Italia.* Milano: Comunità, 1963.
Traverso, C. E., V. Italia, and M. Bassani. *I partiti politici: leggi e statuti.* Milano-Varese: Istituto Editoriale Cisalpino, 1966.
Webster, Richard A. *The Cross and the Fasces: Christian Democracy and Fascism in Italy.* Stanford, Calif.: Stanford University Press, 1960.

Chapter Six

Cavallari, Alberto. *Il Vaticano che cambia.* Milano: Mondadori, 1966.
Chasseriaud, J. P. *Le parti démocrate chrétien en Italie.* Paris: Armand Colin, 1965.
Cicchitto, Fabrizio, and Gino Rocchi, Bruno Manghi, Luigi Ruggiu, Ada Sivini Cavazzani. *La DC dopo il primo ventennio.* Padova: Marsilio Editori, 1968.
Dogan, Mattei, and Orazio Maria Petracca, eds. *Partiti politici e strutture sociali in Italia.* Milano: Comunità, 1968.
Falconi, Carlo. *Il pentagono vaticano.* Bari: Laterza, 1958.
Galli, Giorgio. *Il bipartitismo imperfetto.* Bologna: Il Mulino, 1966.
———, and Alfonso Prandi. *Patterns of Political Participation in Italy.* New Haven, Conn.: Yale University Press, 1970.
Godechot, Thierry. *Le parti démocrate chrétien en Italie.* Paris: Librairie Générale de Droit et de Jurisprudence, 1964.
Gruppo "Presenza," Bologna. *Crisi a "L'avvenire d'Italia."* Firenze: Cultura Editrice, 1968.
Horowitz, Daniel L. *The Italian Labor Movement.* Cambridge, Mass.: Harvard University Press, 1963.
La Palombara, Joseph. *Interest Groups in Italian Politics.* Princeton, N.J.: Princeton University Press, 1964.
———. *The Italian Labor Movement: Problems and Prospects.* Ithaca, N.Y.: Cornell University Press, 1957.
Manoukian, Agopik, ed. *La presenza sociale del PCI e della DC.* Bologna: Il Mulino, 1968.
———, and Franca. *La Chiesa dei giornali.* Bologna: Il Mulino, 1968.

Meynaud, Jean. *Rapporto sulla classe dirigente italiana*. Milano: Giuffré, 1966.

———, and Claudio Risé, *Gruppi di pressione in Italia e in Francia*. Napoli: Edizioni Scientifiche Italiane, 1963.

Neufeld, Maurice F. *Italy: School for Awakening Countries*. Ithaca, N.Y.: Cornell University Press, 1961.

Pantaleone, Michele. *Mafia e politica*. Torino: Einaudi, 1962.

Pieroni, Alfredo. *Chi comanda in Italia*. Milano: Longanesi, 1959.

Poggi, Gianfranco. *Catholic Action in Italy: The Sociology of a Sponsored Organization*. Stanford, Calif.: Stanford University Press, 1967.

Prandi, Alfonso. *Chiesa e politica*. Bologna: Il Mulino, 1968.

Raffaele, Joseph A. *Labor Leadership in Italy and Denmark*. Madison, Wis.: University of Wisconsin Press, 1962.

Rossi, Ernesto, Piero Ugolini, Leopoldo Piccardi. *La Federconsorzi*. Milano: Feltrinelli, 1963.

Chapter Seven

Adams, John Clarke. *The Quest for Democratic Law: The Role of Parliament in the Legislative Process*. New York: Crowell, 1970.

Bartoli, Domenico. *Da Vittorio Emanuele a Gronchi*. Milano: Longanesi, 1961.

———. *L'Italia burocratica*. Milano: Garzanti, 1965.

Calamandrei, Piero. *Scritti e discorsi politici*. 2 vols. Firenze: La Nuova Italia, 1966.

Cappelletti, Mauro, John Henry Merryman, Joseph M. Perillo. *The Italian Legal System: An Introduction*. Stanford, Calif.: Stanford University Press, 1967.

Cesarini Sforza, Marco. *L'uomo politico*. Firenze: Vallecchi, 1963.

Craveri, Raimondo. *Politica e affari*. Milano: Garzanti, 1964.

De Caprariis, Vittorio. *Le garanzie della libertà*. Milano: Il Saggiatore, 1966.

Dechert, Charles R. *Ente Nazionale Idrocarburi: Profile of a State Corporation*. Leiden, Netherlands: E. J. Brill, 1963.

Di Renzo, Gorden J. *Personality, Power, and Politics: A Social Psychological Analysis of the Italian Deputy and His Parliamentary System*. Notre Dame, Ind.: University of Notre Dame Press, 1967.

Direzione PSI-PSDI Unificati-Sezione per la Riforma dello Stato. *Stato moderno e riforma del parlamento*. Roma: Direzione PSI-PSDI Unificati, 1967.

Dogan, Mattei, and Orazio Maria Petracca, eds. *Partiti politici e strutture sociali in Italia*. Milano: Comunità, 1968.

Edelman, Murray, and R. W. Fleming. *The Politics of Wage-Price Decisions: A Four-Country Analysis*. Urbana, Ill.: University of Illinois Press, 1965.

Einaudi, Mario, Maurice Byé, and Ernesto Rossi. *Nationalization in France and Italy*. Ithaca, N.Y.: Cornell University Press, 1955.

Ferrara, Giovanni. *Il presidente di assemblea parlamentare*. Milano: Giuffré, 1965.

Frankel, P. H. *Mattei: Oil and Power Politics.* New York: Praeger, 1966.
Galli, Giorgio, and Alfonso Prandi. *Patterns of Political Participation in Italy.* New Haven, Conn.: Yale University Press, 1970.
Giannini, Massimo Severo. *Corso di diritto amministrativo.* 3 vols. Milano: Giuffré, 1965.
Istituto per la Scienza dell' Amministrazione Pubblica (ISAP). *La burocrazia periferica e locale in Italia: analisi sociologica.* Part I: Franco Demarchi, *L'ideologia del funzionario.* Milano: Giuffré, 1969; Part II: Paolo Ammassari, Federica Garzonio dell' Orto, Franco Ferraresi, *Il burocrate di fronte alla burocrazia.* Milano: Giuffré, 1969.
Kogan, Norman. *A Political History of Postwar Italy.* New York: Praeger, 1966.
La Palombara, Joseph. *Italy: The Politics of Planning.* Syracuse, N.Y.: Syracuse University Press, 1966.
Maranini, Giuseppe. *Il tiranno senza volto.* Milano: Bompiani, 1963.
Mortati, Costantino. *Istituzioni di diritto pubblico.* 2 vols. Padova: CEDAM, 1967.
Piccardi, Leopoldo, Norberto Bobbio, Ferruccio Parri. *La sinistra davanti alla crisi del parlamento.* Milano: Giuffré, 1967.
Posner, M. V., and S. J. Woolf. *Italian Public Enterprise.* Cambridge, Mass.: Harvard University Press, 1967.
Predieri, Alberto, Piero Barucci, and Mariangela Bartoli. *Il Programma Economico 1966–1970.* Milano: Giuffré, 1967.
Rossi, Ernesto. *I nostri quattrini.* Bari: Laterza, 1964.
Sartori, Giovanni, ed. *Il parlamento italiano 1946–1963.* Napoli: Edizioni Scientifiche Italiane, 1963.
Savignano, Aristide. *I gruppi parlamentari.* Napoli: Morano Editore, 1965.
Shonfield, Andrew. *Modern Capitalism: The Changing Balance of Public and Private Power.* New York: Oxford University Press, 1965.
Valentino, Nino. *La battaglia per il Quirinale.* Milano: Rizzoli, 1968.
———. *L'elezione di Segni.* Milano: Comunità, 1963.
Votaw, Dow. *The Six-Legged Dog.* Berkeley, Calif.: University of California Press, 1964.

Chapter Eight

Acquarone, Alberto. *Grandi città e aree metropolitane in Italia.* Bologna: Zanichelli, 1961.
Adams, John Clarke, and Paolo Barile. *The Government of Republican Italy.* 2nd ed. Boston: Houghton Mifflin, 1966.
Associazione Italiana di Scienze Sociali. *Sociologi e centri di potere in Italia.* Bari: Laterza, 1962.
Barbato, Luigi. *Politica meridionalista e localizzazione industriale: dalla Legge Pastore all' Alfa Sud.* Padova: Marsilio Editori, 1968.
Barbero, Giuseppe. *La riforma agraria italiana.* Milano: Feltrinelli, 1960.
Bartoli, Domenico. *L'Italia burocratica.* Milano: Garzanti, 1965.
Barzanti, Sergio. *The Underdeveloped Areas within the Common Market.* Princeton, N.J.: Princeton University Press, 1965.
Calamandrei, Piero. *Scritti e discorsi politici.* 2 vols. Firenze: La Nuova Italia, 1966.

Carlyle, Margaret. *The Awakening of Southern Italy.* London: Oxford University Press, 1962.
Cicchitto, Fabrizio, and Gino Rocchi, Bruno Manghi, Luigi Ruggiu, Ada Sivini Cavazzani. *La DC dopo il primo ventennio.* Padova: Marsilio Editori, 1968.
Clough, Shepard B. *The Economic History of Modern Italy.* New York: Columbia University Press, 1964.
Craveri, Raimondo. *Politica e affari.* Milano: Garzanti, 1964.
D'Antonio, Mario. *Commenti al programma economico nazionale.* Bologna: Cappelli, 1968.
Dechert, Charles R. *Ente Nazionale Idrocarburi: Profile of a State Corporation.* Leiden, Netherlands: E. J. Brill, 1963.
Di Fenizio, Ferdinando. *La programmazione economica.* Torino: UTET, 1965.
Direzione PSI-PSDI Unificati-Sezione per la Riforma dello Stato. *Stato moderno e riforma del parlamento.* Roma: Direzione PSI-PSDI Unificati, 1967.
Edelman, Murray, and R. W. Fleming. *The Politics of Wage-Price Decisions: A Four-Country Analysis.* Urbana, Ill.: University of Illinois Press, 1965.
Ferrari, Pierre, and Herbert Maisl. *Les groupes communistes aux Assemblées parlementaires italiennes (1958-1963) et françaises (1962-1967).* Paris: Presses Universitaires de France, 1969.
Forte, Francesco. *La congiuntura in Italia 1961-1965.* Torino: Einaudi, 1966.
Fuà, G., and P. Sylos-Labini. *Idee per la programmazione economica.* Bari: Laterza, 1963.
Galli, Giorgio. *Il bipartitismo imperfetto.* Bologna: Il Mulino, 1966.
―――, and Alfonso Prandi. *Patterns of Political Participation in Italy.* New Haven, Conn.: Yale University Press, 1970.
Gallino, Luciano. *Indagini di sociologia economica.* Milano: Comunità, 1962.
Germino, Dante, and Stefano Passigli. *The Government and Politics of Contemporary Italy.* New York: Harper & Row, 1968.
Giannini, Massimo Severo. *Corso di diritto amministrativo.* 3 vols. Milano: Giuffré, 1965.
Grindrod, Muriel. *Italy.* New York: Praeger, 1968.
Hildebrand, George H. *Growth and Structure in the Economy of Modern Italy.* Cambridge, Mass.: Harvard University Press, 1965.
Indovina, Francesco. *Esperienze di pianificazione regionale.* Padova: Marsilio Editori, 1967.
Istituto per la Scienza dell' Amministrazione Pubblica (ISAP). *La burocrazia periferica e locale in Italia: analisi sociologica.* Part I: Franco Demarchi, *L'ideologia del funzionario.* Milano: Giuffré, 1969; Part II: Paolo Ammassari, Federica Garzonio dell' Orto, Franco Ferraresi, *Il burocrate di fronte alla burocrazia.* Milano: Giuffré, 1969.
La Palombara, Joseph. *Interest Groups in Italian Politics.* Princeton, N.J.: Princeton University Press, 1964.
―――. *Italy: The Politics of Planning.* Syracuse, N.Y.: Syracuse University Press, 1966.
Lombardini, Siri. *La programmazione: idee esperienze problemi.* Torino: Einaudi, 1967.

Lutz, Vera. *Italy: A Study in Economic Development*. London: Oxford University Press, 1962.
Meynaud, Jean. *La tecnocrazia mito o realtà*. Bari: Laterza, 1966.
———. *Rapporto sulla classe dirigente italiana*. Milano: Giuffré, 1966.
Mortati, Costantino. *Istituzioni di diritto pubblico*. 2 vols. Padova: CEDAM, 1967.
Nelson, Lowry. *Land Reform in Italy*. Washington, D.C.: National Planning Association pamphlet, no. 97, August 1956.
Piccardi, Leopoldo, Norberto Bobbio, Ferruccio Parri. *La sinistra davanti alla crisi del parlamento*. Milano: Giuffré, 1967.
Pieroni, Alfredo. *Chi comanda in Italia*. Milano: Longanesi, 1959.
Posner, M. V., and S. J. Woolf. *Italian Public Enterprise*. Cambridge, Mass.: Harvard University Press, 1967.
Predieri, Alberto, Piero Barucci, and Mariangela Bartoli. *Il Programma Economico 1966–1970*. Milano: Giuffré, 1967.
Rossi, Ernesto. *I nostri quattrini*. Bari: Laterza, 1964.
Sartori, Giovanni, ed. *Il parlamento italiano 1946–1963*. Napoli: Edizioni Scientifiche Italiane, 1963.
Shonfield, Andrew. *Modern Capitalism: The Changing Balance of Public and Private Power*. New York: Oxford University Press, 1965.
Spreafico, Alberto. *L'amministrazione e il cittadino*. Milano: Comunità, 1965.
Votaw, Dow. *The Six-Legged Dog*. Berkeley, Calif.: University of California Press, 1964.

Chapter Nine

Adams, John Clarke. *The Quest for Democratic Law: The Role of Parliament in the Legislative Process*. New York: Crowell, 1970.
———, and Paolo Barile. *The Government of Republican Italy*. 2nd ed. Boston: Houghton Mifflin, 1966.
Bartole, Sergio. *Autonomia e indipendenza dell' ordine giudiziario*. Padova: CEDAM, 1964.
Battaglia, Achille. *I giudici e la politica*. Bari: Laterza, 1962.
Cappelletti, Mauro, John Henry Merryman, Joseph M. Perillo. *The Italian Legal System: An Introduction*. Stanford, Calif.: Stanford University Press, 1967.
Cervi, Mario. *La giustizia in Italia*. Milano: Longanesi, 1967.
Chapman, Brian. *The Profession of Government: The Public Service in Europe*. New York: Macmillan, 1959.
Di Federico, Giuseppe. *Il reclutamento dei magistrati*. Bari: Laterza, 1968.
Ghirotti, Gigi. *Il magistrato*. Firenze: Vallecchi, 1959.
Istituto per la Documentazione e gli Studi Legislativi. *Indagine sulla magistratura italiana: l'ordinamento giudiziario*. Milano: Giuffré, 1965.
Maranini, Giuseppe. *Giustizia in catene*. Milano: Comunità, 1964.
———. *Il tiranno senza volto*. Milano: Bompiani, 1963.
———, ed. *La giustizia costituzionale*. Firenze: Vallecchi, 1966.
———, ed. *Magistrati o funzionari*. Milano: Comunità, 1962.
Moriondo, Ezio. *L'ideologia della magistratura italiana*. Bari: Laterza, 1967.
Pera, Giuseppe. *Un mestiere difficile: il magistrato*. Bologna: Il Mulino, 1967.

Prandstraller, Gian Paolo. *Gli avvocati italiani*. Milano: Comunità, 1967.
Spreafico, Alberto. *L'amministrazione e il cittadino*. Milano: Comunità, 1965.

Chapter Ten

Albrecht-Carrié, René. *Italy from Napoleon to Mussolini*. New York: Columbia University Press, 1960.
Bartoli, Domenico. *Da Vittorio Emanuele a Gronchi*. Milano: Longanesi, 1961.
Dechert, Charles R. *Ente Nazionale Idrocarburi: Profile of a State Corporation*. Leiden, Netherlands: E. J. Brill, 1963.
Frankel, P. H. *Mattei: Oil and Power Politics*. New York: Praeger, 1966.
Free, Lloyd A. *Six Allies and a Neutral*. New York: Free Press, 1959.
Giordano, Renato. *Il mercato comune e i suoi problemi*. Roma: Opere Nuove, 1958.
Istituto Affari Internazionali. *La politica estera della Repubblica italiana*. 3 vols. Milano: Comunità, 1967.
Kogan, Norman. *The Politics of Italian Foreign Policy*. New York: Praeger, 1963.
Negri, Guglielmo. *La direzione ed il controllo democratico della politica estera in Italia*. Milano: Giuffré, 1967.
Rabier, Jacques-René. *L'Information des Européens et l'integration de l'Europe*. Bruxelles: Institut d'Études Européens, Université Libre de Bruxelles, 1965.
Votaw, Dow. *The Six-Legged Dog*. Berkeley, Calif.: University of California Press, 1964.
Willis, F. Roy. *Italy Chooses Europe*. New York: Oxford University Press, 1971.

INDEX

Abbate, Michele, 72
Acquarone, Alberto, 133
Action party, 134
Agriculture, 1, 38–39, 292–293
  interest groups, 206–208
Alain, 224
Alberoni, Francesco, 42
Alienation, 71–75, 100–101 116, 200
Almond, Gabriel, 54, 58, 73, 91, 95, 97, 128
Amendola, Giorgio, 71–72, 148
Andreotti, Giulio, 84, 85, 149
Anticlericalism, 21, 45, 115, 159, 185–186
Area, land, 5
Autarky, 34
Authority, images of, 103–104
Autonomy, 96–97

Badoglio, Marshal, 27
Baglioni, Guido, 42
Balbo, Cesare, 15
Banfield, Edward C., 54, 95, 103, 128

Bank of Italy, 257
Barnes, Samuel H., 79, 81, 82, 110, 130, 150
Barzini, Luigi, 93, 94, 96
Basso, Lelio, 161, 162
Berlinguer, Mario, 148
Bianciardi, Luciano, 36
Birth rate, 6
Bode, Kenneth, 97, 108
Bonomi, Paolo, 207
Bordiga, Amedeo, 157
Brigandage, 17
Bureaucracy, 3, 50, 84, 103, 216, 217, 235
  policy implementation and the, 283–289
  policy making and the, 253
  provincial, 130
Burrowes, Robert, 91
Business interest groups, 212–217

Cabinet, 3, 20, 28, 153, 170, 174, 232–238
Calamandrei, Piero, 28, 238

351

Campaigns, political, techniques used in, 196–197
Carbonari, 13
Carpi, Italy, 35
Catholic Action, 67, 79, 115, 169, 191, 204, 205, 208, 217, 219–222, 270, 286
Catholic Church, 7, 21, 168–169, 185, 191, 217–222
  Italian politics and, 113–115
  political socialization and, 67–68
Catholic interest groups, 217–222
Cattaneo, Carlo, 15
Cavour, Camillo Benso di, 14, 16, 17, 111, 323
Centers of Agricultural Action, 207
Centralization, 20–21, 117–139
Central Statistical Institute, 234
Chamber of Deputies, 84, 145, 146, 194, 195, 238–250
  See also Parliament
Change
  economic, 1–4
  political, 3
  social, 1–4
Charles Albert, King, 26
Christian Association of Italian Workers, 191, 204, 205, 210, 219, 221
Christian Democratic party, 21, 29, 30, 32, 67, 69–70, 71, 77, 78, 79, 83, 85–87, 88, 101, 105, 110, 112, 113, 114, 134–137, 141, 143, 144, 146–152, 154, 156, 157, 159, 161, 163, 164, 165, 167, 168–174, 175, 176, 177, 199, 201, 204, 205–206, 207, 208, 213, 214, 215, 216, 218–222, 231, 236, 286
  leadership, 182–185
  membership, 180–182
  voting strength, 185–194
Church and state, 21, 113–115, 168–169, 217–222
  See also Catholic Church
Cigogna, Furio, 214
City-states, 12
Civil service, 253–255, 283–289
Class conflict, 25
Class distinctions, 109–110
Climate, 8
Coal, 8
Cognition, political, 98–99
Colombo, Emilio, 233–234
Colonialism, 12
Colonies, Italian, 327–328
Communes, 117, 118–128, 132–133, 154
Communication, 10, 129–130, 192
Communist party, 3, 25, 29, 32, 60, 68, 69–71, 77, 79, 82, 89, 101, 105, 110, 112, 123, 124–125, 134–137, 141, 143, 144, 146, 147, 148, 152, 154, 155–156, 157–161, 162, 163, 166, 167, 171, 198, 209, 210, 274–275, 324–325, 336
  leadership, 182–185
  membership, 180–182
  voting strength, 185–194
Compagna, Francesco, 72
Competence, political, 99–100
Conciliatori, 301
Concordat (1929), 21, 28, 56, 113, 159, 169, 175, 217, 220, 249
Confederation of Italian Cooperatives, 191
Conflict resolution, 280–283
Congress of Vienna, 13
Constitution (1948), 25, 28–29, 49, 117, 135, 137, 159, 224, 228, 229, 236, 241, 300
  amendment of, 241
Constitutional Court, 28, 29, 41,

135, 136, 229, 258, 300, 303, 304, 306–310
  establishment of the, 289–290
Constitutional development, 26–33
Consumption, 37
Corbino, Epicarmo, 261
Corporations, public, 2, 105, 215, 255–257, 286, 288
Corruption, political, 286–288
Costa, Angelo, 213
Council, communal, 118–119
Council of Ministers, see Cabinet
Council of State, 271, 277, 285, 304, 305–306
Counter Reformation, 12
Court of Accounts, 271, 277, 279, 285, 304, 305
Court of Assize, 302
Court of Cassation, 300, 301, 303, 304, 309
Courts, 300–319
  administrative, 304–306
  ordinary law, 301–304
Courts of Appeal, 302, 304
Covelli, Alfredo, 178
Crime, 42, 123
Criminal code, 29
Crispi, Francesco, 225, 323
Croce, Benedetto, 60, 72, 111
Culture, political, 52, 92–116
  alienation and, 100–101
  definition of, 92
  violence and, 101–103

Dante Alighieri, 13
D'Azeglio, Massimo, 15
Decentralization, 20, 119
Decision making, 224–297
Decisions, authoritative, 278–280
Defense policy, 326–327
Deforestation, 8
De Gasperi, Alcide, 84–87, 114, 144, 163, 169, 170, 174–175, 176, 213, 225, 261

Degli Esposti, Gianluigi, 125
De Lorenzo, General Giovanni, 231, 327, 336
Demarchi, Franco, 132
De Martino, Francesco, 165
De Mauro, Tullio, 10
De Micheli, Alighiero, 213–214
Democracy, Italian, 49, 51, 124, 138, 198
De Nicola, Chief Justice Enrico, 310
Depretis, Agostino, 29, 31, 225
Development
  constitutional, 26–33
  economic, see Economic development
  history of, 5–51
  political, 9–33, 49
  social, 12
Dialects, 9–10, 13, 97
Di Fenizio, Ferdinando, 264
Di Palma, Giuseppe, 69
Distribution, crisis of, 49
Distrust, social, 93–96, 102, 103, 116, 166
Divine Comedy (Dante), 13
Divorce law, 115, 178
Dogan, Mattei, 46, 193
Dossetti, Giuseppe, 171
Dualism, cultural, 107–109
Duverger, Maurice, 145, 151, 176

Economic development, 1–3, 5–9, 12, 33–40
  geographic factors and, 5–8
Edelman, Murray, 280, 291
Education, 47–48, 105, 122, 128
  political socialization and, 56–61
  religious, 56, 67, 113, 173
Einaudi, Luigi, 111, 226, 227, 229, 231, 261
Eisenhower, Dwight D., 330
Elections, 129, 142, 143, 163–164, 170, 174, 175, 176, 185–196

participation in, 75–76
presidential, 230
Electoral reform, 29–30
Electoral system, 194–196
Emigration, 2, 6, 41, 42, 46–47
Environmental conditions, influence of, 5–8
Eritrea, 327, 328
Ethiopia, 327, 328
Ethnic groups, 7, 9–10, 45
European Coal and Steel Community, 324
European Economic Community, 324, 325
Evans, Robert H., 124
Executive, Italian, 224–225

Facta, Premier Luigi, 27
Factionalism, 32, 33, 147–150, 156–194
Family, political socialization and the, 53–56, 116
Fanfani, Amintore, 85–87, 106, 149, 169, 171, 174, 184, 206, 207, 213, 216, 225, 244, 325, 331
Fascetti, Aldo, 257
Fascism, 25, 27, 32, 34, 41, 49, 60, 69, 71, 72, 94, 109, 169, 176, 179, 186
Federalism, 20
Federation of Agricultural Consortiums, 187, 207, 215
Ferri, Mauro, 164
Fiat, 35, 50, 110, 213, 215, 252, 266, 269, 331
Fleming, R. W., 280
Flood control, 8
Foreign control, 12–13
Folchi, Alberto, 228
Foreign minister, 330–331
Foreign policy, 323–326
makers of, 328–331
Forlani, Arnaldo, 171
French Revolution, 13, 48

Fried, Robert C., 20, 121, 122, 131, 132
Fuà, Giorgio, 264
Fund for the South, 39, 127, 234, 235, 256, 257, 262, 273, 286, 292, 293

Galli, Giorgio, 89, 125, 140, 147, 159, 161, 172–173, 182, 190, 197
Gallino, Luciano, 43
Garibaldi, Giuseppe, 15, 16, 17, 174
Gas, natural, 8
Gedda, Luigi, 221, 222
Generational differences, 105
Gentiloni Agreement, 21
Geography, influence of, 5–8
Germino, Dante, 25
Ghibellines, 11
Gioberti, Vincenzo, 15
Giolitti, Giovanni, 30, 32, 176, 225, 323
Giovane Italia ("Young Italy"), 14
Government, 224–259
local, 117–139
unitary system of, 117–139
Gramsci, Antonio, 112, 157, 161
Greene, Thomas H., 161
Green Plan, 39, 292, 293
Grimaldi, Ugoberto A., 61, 72
Gronchi, Giovanni, 86, 87, 174, 226, 227–230, 231, 243, 325, 330
Guelphs, 11

Hennessey, Timothy M., 97, 108
Highway Code, 291
Hildebrand, George H., 262
Hindenburg, Marshal von, 27
History, developmental, 5–51
Hitler, Adolf, 27
Holy Roman Empire, 11

Housing, 45, 50
Humbert II, King, 27
Hydroelectric power, 8, 34

Identity, national, sense of, 97–98, 116, 320–321
Ideological differences, 109
  as barrier to policy making, 260–265
Illiteracy, 45
Impeachment, 229
Income, per capita, 1, 35, 37
Individualism, 96–97
Industrialization, 2, 6, 26, 33–38, 47, 81
Industry, 1, 33–38, 293–295
  interest groups, 212–217
Ingrao, Pietro, 148
Initiative, 28, 29
Institute for Industrial Reconstruction (IRI), 206, 216, 255–257, 259, 262, 273, 288, 291, 294, 331
Integration, national, 18, 21–26, 48, 49, 51, 66, 97, 98, 108
Interest groups, 201–223, 252, 264
  agricultural, 206–208
  business, 212–217
  Catholic, 217–222
  characteristics of, 201–206
  labor, 208–212
  policy-making process and, 266–270
  See also Pressure groups
Interministerial Committee for Economic Programming, 272
Iron ore, 8
Irrigation, 8
Italian Association of Catholic Teachers, 191, 221
Italian Banking Association, 264
Italian Confederation of Cooperatives and Mutual Savings Funds, 204

Italian Confederation of Plant Managers, 264
Italian Confederation of Workers' Unions, 191, 204, 205, 208, 210, 221
Italian Cooperative Confederation, 208, 210
Italian Feminine Center, 221
Italian General Confederation of Agriculture, 193, 206
Italian General Confederation of Industry, 193, 204, 206, 213–217
Italian General Confederation of Labor, 191, 192, 204, 208, 209–210
Italian Movement of Peace Partisans, 204
Italian National Society, 14, 17, 94
Italian Recreational and Cultural Association, 204
Italian Social Movement, 33
Italian Union of Labor, 192, 208, 210
Italian Union of Popular Sports, 191, 204

Jews, 7, 45
John XXIII, Pope, 114, 218, 219
Judges, 300, 302, 303, 310–317
  independence of, 310–313
  recruitment of, 313–317, 319
  training of, 315, 319
Judicial system, 298–319

Kirchheimer, Otto, 68, 197
Kogan, Norman, 108, 320, 324

Labor, 1, 9, 35, 37–38, 66
  farm, 38–40, 45
  interest groups, 208–212
  See also Unions
Lag, political, implications of, 333–336
La Malfa, Ugo, 111, 175, 235
Lampedusa, Giuseppe di, 19

INDEX

Land reform, 39, 102, 168, 292
Language, 10, 11, 13, 106
La Palombara, Joseph, 18, 54, 85, 97, 107, 115, 124, 138, 151–152, 199, 204, 216–217, 221, 268, 292, 294
La Pira, Giorgio, 325
Latifondo, 39
Law, conceptions of, 298–301
  enforcement, 123
Legal system, 298–319
Legislative-executive relations, 250–252
Legitimacy, crisis of, 18–21, 25, 29, 49
Leone, Giovanni, 243
Lercaro, Cardinal, 219
Liberal party, 69, 110, 111, 134, 141, 145, 146, 149, 151, 154, 155, 156, 157, 169, 170, 175–178, 214
  voting strength, 192–193
Libya, 327, 328
Life, way of, 1, 2, 40, 42–43
Lipset, Seymour, 29
Lipson, Leslie, 30
Living standards, 1, 2, 6, 25, 34, 37, 41, 50, 108, 110, 193
Local government, 117–139
Lombardi, Renato, 214, 215
Lombardi, Riccardo, 165, 167
Lombardini, Siri, 264
Longo, Luigi, 148
Lopreato, Joseph, 47, 93
Lutz, Vera, 38, 43

Machiavelli, Niccolò, 13
Mafia, 103, 104, 126, 215
Malagodi, Giovanni, 177, 184
Mansholt Report, 45
Mannucci, Cesare, 63, 64, 87, 106, 107, 129, 197
Maranini, Giuseppe, 153, 154
Marshall Plan, 324
Martinotti, Guido, 59
Mass media, 129
  political socialization and the, 61–66
Mastrella, Cesare, 287
Mattei, Enrico, 206, 216, 224, 256, 282, 325
Matteotti, Matteo, 71–72
Matteucci, Nicola, 104, 106
Mazzini, Giuseppe, 13, 15, 16, 111, 174
Meda, Filippo, 168, 171
Merzagora, Cesare, 244
Michels, Robert, 22
Migration, *see* Emigration; Population, migration of
Minghetti, Marco, 20
Minorities, 7, 45
Monarchist party, 33, 71, 112, 114, 141, 142, 145, 146, 147, 149, 156, 157, 170, 177, 178–179, 195
  voting strength, 188
Moro, Aldo, 106, 149, 161, 163, 169, 171, 225, 235
Mosca, Gaetano, 22
Motion pictures, 98
  political socialization and, 61, 62, 65–66
Mountains, 7–8
Murri, Romolo, 112, 168, 171
Mussolini, Benito, 18, 25, 27, 32, 157, 169, 179, 225, 323

Napoleon, 13
Nasser, Gamal Abdel, 325
National Association of Agricultural Cooperatives, 208
National Association of Cooperatives, 208
National Association of Italian Magistrates, 312
National Association of Italian Partisans, 191, 204
National Committee for Economic Programming, 264
National Committee for Nuclear Energy, 273, 288

National Confederation of Direct Cultivators, 187, 191, 206, 207, 215, 221, 222, 264
National Council of Economy and Labor, 258, 271, 273, 291
National Democratic Union, 32
National Electric Power Corporation, 273
  creation of, 290
National Hydrocarburants Corporation (ENI), 216, 255–257, 259, 262, 273, 288, 291, 294, 331
  establishment of the, 290
National identity, sense of, 97–98, 116, 320–321
National League of Cooperatives and Mutual Aid Societies, 191, 210
National Peasants' Alliance, 191, 204, 207
Nationalism, 12–13
Natural resources, 8, 33
Negri, Guglielmo, 328
Nenni, Pietro, 161, 163, 167, 183
Neo-Fascists, 110, 112, 114, 141, 143, 148, 156, 157, 170, 177, 179–180
  voting strength, 188, 192
Newspapers, 129
  political socialization and, 61
Non expedit policy, 21, 168
North Atlantic Treaty Organization, 322, 324, 326–327
Northwest Industrial Triangle, 1, 6, 26, 37, 42, 43, 46, 47, 50, 51, 98, 109, 128, 188, 189, 194

Oil, 8
Olivetti, 110, 269
Ottaviani, Cardinal, 218

Pacem in Terris, 219
Papal States, 11, 14, 15, 186
Parliament, 3, 20, 28, 30, 33, 45, 153, 170, 174, 194, 203, 224, 238–252
  policy-making process and, 265–280
Participation, political, 18, 30, 49, 50, 66, 75–84, 104, 105, 139
Party system, 48, 140–200, 224
  emergence of, 26–33
  leadership, 182–185
  membership composition, 180–182
  organization structure, 151–156
  participation and, 75–84
  political socialization and, 68–71
  recruitment and, 84–90
  voting strength, 185–194
Passigli, Stefano, 193
Patronage, 3, 77, 115, 126–128, 147, 254, 286–287, 294
Paul VI, Pope, 115, 218, 219
Paulson, Belden, 125
Peasants, 16–17, 22, 40, 41, 46, 68
Peer group, political socialization and, 55
Petrarca, Francesco, 13
Pius XII, Pope, 114, 218, 219
Plebiscites, 19
Police, 122–123
Policy implementation, 283–289
Policy making, 224–297, 335
  deliberation and, 276–278
  ideological differences and, 260–265
  illustrations of, 289–295
  institutions and, 224–259
  process of, 265–276
Political development, 9–18, 49
Political lag, implications of, 333–336

Political parties, *see* Party system; names of parties
Politics, 2, 3, 52–91
 intraparty, 147–150
 link between local and national, 128–130
 local, 117–139
 religion and, 113–115, 168–169, 173, 185, 191
Poma, Cardinal, 219
Popular party, 21, 31, 32, 69, 87, 113, 134, 144, 146, 168–169, 170, 171
Population, 5
 density of, 5–6
 growth of, 5
 migration of, 2, 6, 38, 40–45, 49–50
Pragmatism, 106
Prefects, 118, 121–122, 130–131
President, 225–232, 238, 328–330
Press, 129–130
 Catholic, 192
 party, 192–193
 political socialization and the, 61–63
Pressure groups, 201–223, 286, 331
 political socialization and, 68
 policy-making process and, 266–270
 See also Interest groups
Pretore, 301–302
Prime minister, 232–238
Problem solving, 280–283
Production, problems of, 9
Provinces, 117, 118, 130–132, 154
Provincialism, 97

Qualunquists, 156

Radical party, 31
Radio, 98, 108, 129, 190
 political socialization and, 61, 63
Reale, Oronzo, 175
Recruitment, political, 84–90, 151, 182–185
Referendum, 28, 29, 242
Regional Committees for Economic Programming, 273
Regions, 117, 134–138, 139, 154
Religion, 7, 45
 politics and, 113–115, 168–169, 173, 185, 191
Representation, system of, 29, 194–195
Republican party, 32, 111, 134, 141, 142, 145, 147, 154, 156, 157, 161, 163, 170, 174–175, 177, 178, 195
Resources, natural, 8, 33
Ricci, Athos, 125
Rights, basic, 28
Risorgimento, 13–18, 22–25, 48, 94
Roman Empire, 10–11
Rossi, Ernesto, 267

Salandra, Antonio, 26, 176
Salvadori, Massimo, 9
Saraceno, Pasquale, 264, 269
Saragat, Giuseppe, 163, 166, 183, 231, 235
Sartori, Giovanni, 30, 140, 143, 145, 197, 239
Savoy, House of, 14, 27, 179
Scelba, Mario, 85, 171
Secret societies, 13–14, 18
Segni, Antonio, 227, 231, 329
Senate, 84, 195, 238–250
 See also Parliament
Senators, election of, 195
Sernini, Michele, 77, 172, 199, 267
Sforza, Marco Cesarini, 88, 89
Shell Italiana Corporation, 88
Sicily, 7, 8, 15, 16, 109, 126
Silone, Ignazio, 100

Silverman, Sydel, 127
Siri, Cardinal, 218
Size of Italy, 5
Social fragmentation, 109
Social mobility, 45–48
Social services, 37, 38
Social stratification, 45–48
Socialist parties, 30, 31, 32, 33, 70, 77, 79, 81, 82, 105, 112, 130, 136, 137, 141, 142, 144–152, 154, 155, 156, 157, 158, 161–168, 170, 171, 180–182, 322
   leadership, 182, 184
   membership in, 180–181
   voting strength, 185–194
Socialization, political, 3, 52–75, 116, 334
   Catholic Church and, 67–68
   definition of, 52
   education and, 56–61
   family and, 53–56
   mass media and, 61–66
   peer group and, 55
   political events and experiences and, 71–75
   political parties and, 68–71
   pressure groups and, 68
   workplace and, 66–67
Society, integration of, 2
Somaliland, Italian, 327, 328
Sorel, Georges, 60
Standing committees, 244–246, 279
Statera, Gianni, 58
Statutes, 278
Statuto, 26–28
Steel production, 34, 35
Student unrest, 58–60, 200
Sturzo, Don Luigi, 21, 31, 112, 114, 168, 169, 171
Subcultures, political, 109–113
   regional, 107–109
Südtyroler Volkspartei (SVP), 45, 246
Suffrage, 29–31, 142
Sullo, Fiorentino, 149, 173

Superior Council of the Judiciary, 310–312
Sylos-Labini, Paolo, 264

Tambroni, Fernando, 227–229, 236, 237
Tanassi, Mario, 164
Tarrow, Sidney G., 107, 150, 155, 181
Taviani, Paolo Emilio, 149
Taxes, 73–74, 120
Technology, 38
Television, 98, 108, 110, 129, 190, 196, 197
   political socialization and, 61, 63–66
Togliatti, Palmiro, 112, 158, 159, 161, 183, 209
Toniolo, Giuseppe, 112
Totalitarianism, 25, 94
Trasformismo, practice of, 31
Tribunals, 302, 303, 304
Trust, social, 93–96
Turati, Filippo, 112

Unemployment, 41, 209
Unification, national, 9–26, 97
Union of Italian Magistrates, 312
Union of Italian Women, 191, 204
Union Valdôtaine party, 45, 246
Unions, 66–67, 80, 191, 192, 208–212, 223, 264
Uomo Qualunque party, 100
Urbanization, 2, 6, 26, 40–45, 47, 81

Vecchietti, Tullio, 161
Venosta, Visconti, 323
Verba, Sidney, 54, 58, 73, 91, 95, 97, 128
Vetoes, suspensive, 278
Victor Emmanuel II, 14, 15, 16

Victor Emmanuel III, 26–27
Violence, political, 101–103
Vizzini, Calogero, 104

Wages, 37, 38
Weiner, Myron, 18, 124
Women, Italian, 80, 105
Workplace, political socialization and the, 66–67

World affairs, Italy and, 320–332
World War I, 22, 24
World War II, 25, 34, 72, 73, 320

Youth, Italian, 105, 116

Zangrandi, Ruggero, 61